Shojo Beat

Fushigi Yûgi
Genbu Kaiden

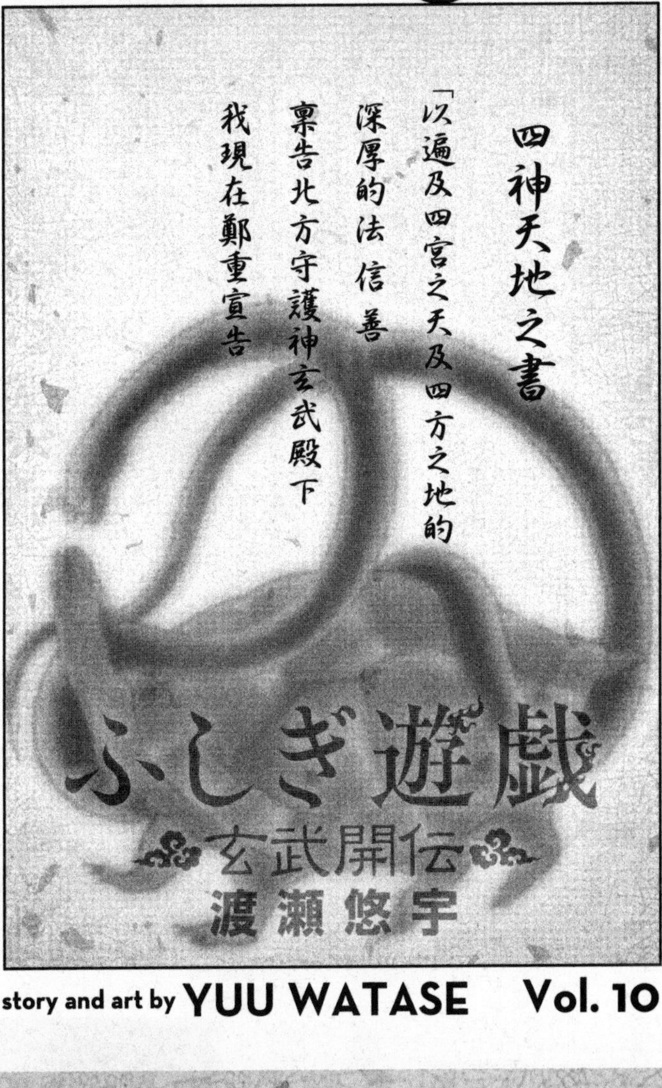
四神天地之書
「以遍及四宮之天及四方之地的
深厚的法 信 善
稟告北方守護神玄武殿下
我現在鄭重宣告
ふしぎ遊戯
玄武開伝
渡瀬悠宇

story and art by YUU WATASE

Vol. 10

CONTENTS

**TRANSLATION OF "THE UNIVERSE OF
THE FOUR GODS"**

I summon all the great forces of justice, faith and good
will from the four corners of heaven and the four
quarters of the earth to call on you, the divine Genbu.

Cast of Characters

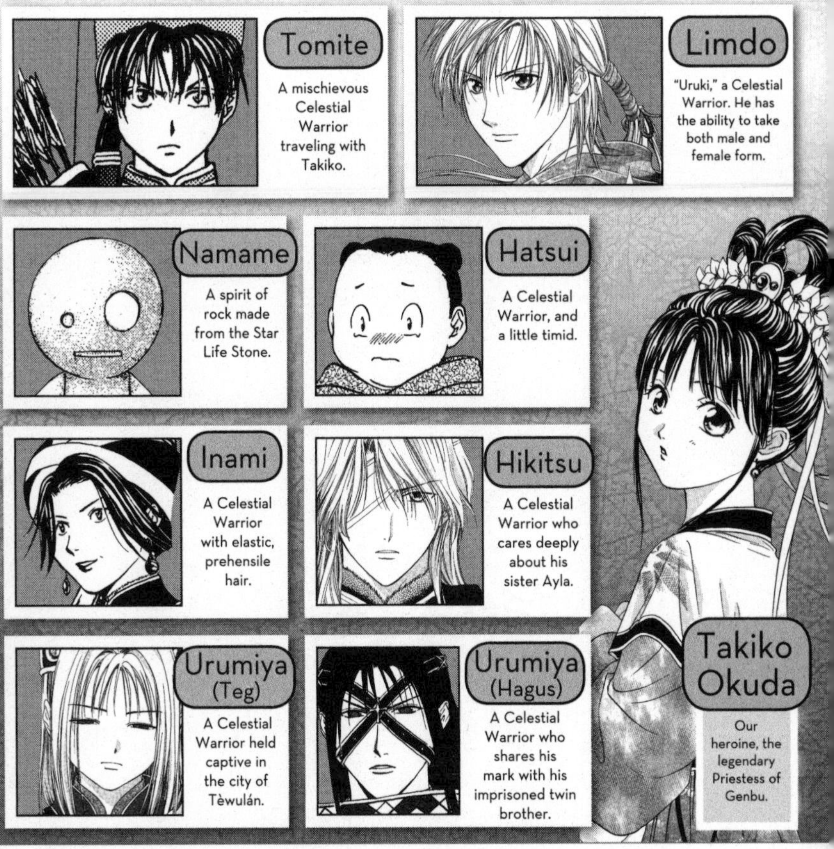
Tomite
A mischievous Celestial Warrior traveling with Takiko.
Limdo
"Uruki," a Celestial Warrior. He has the ability to take both male and female form.
Namame
A spirit of rock made from the Star Life Stone.
Hatsui
A Celestial Warrior, and a little timid.
Inami
A Celestial Warrior with elastic, prehensile hair.
Hikitsu
A Celestial Warrior who cares deeply about his sister Ayla.
Urumiya (Teg)
A Celestial Warrior held captive in the city of Tèwulán.
Urumiya (Hagus)
A Celestial Warrior who shares his mark with his imprisoned twin brother.
Takiko Okuda
Our heroine, the legendary Priestess of Genbu.

The Story Thus Far

The year is 1923. Takiko is drawn into the pages of *The Universe of the Four Gods*, a book her father has translated from Chinese. There, she is told that she is the legendary Priestess of Genbu, destined to save the country of Bêi-jîa. She must find the seven Celestial Warriors who will help her on her quest.

Takiko now knows that, to complete her quest, she will have to sacrifice her own life. Tragically, she is already dying of tuberculosis, a secret she keeps hidden from the Celestial Warriors. Determined to save the Universe of the Four Gods while she still has time, Takiko reunites with Uruki, the Celestial Warrior she loves, while dark forces gather around them...

FUSHIGI YÛGI: GENBU KAIDEN

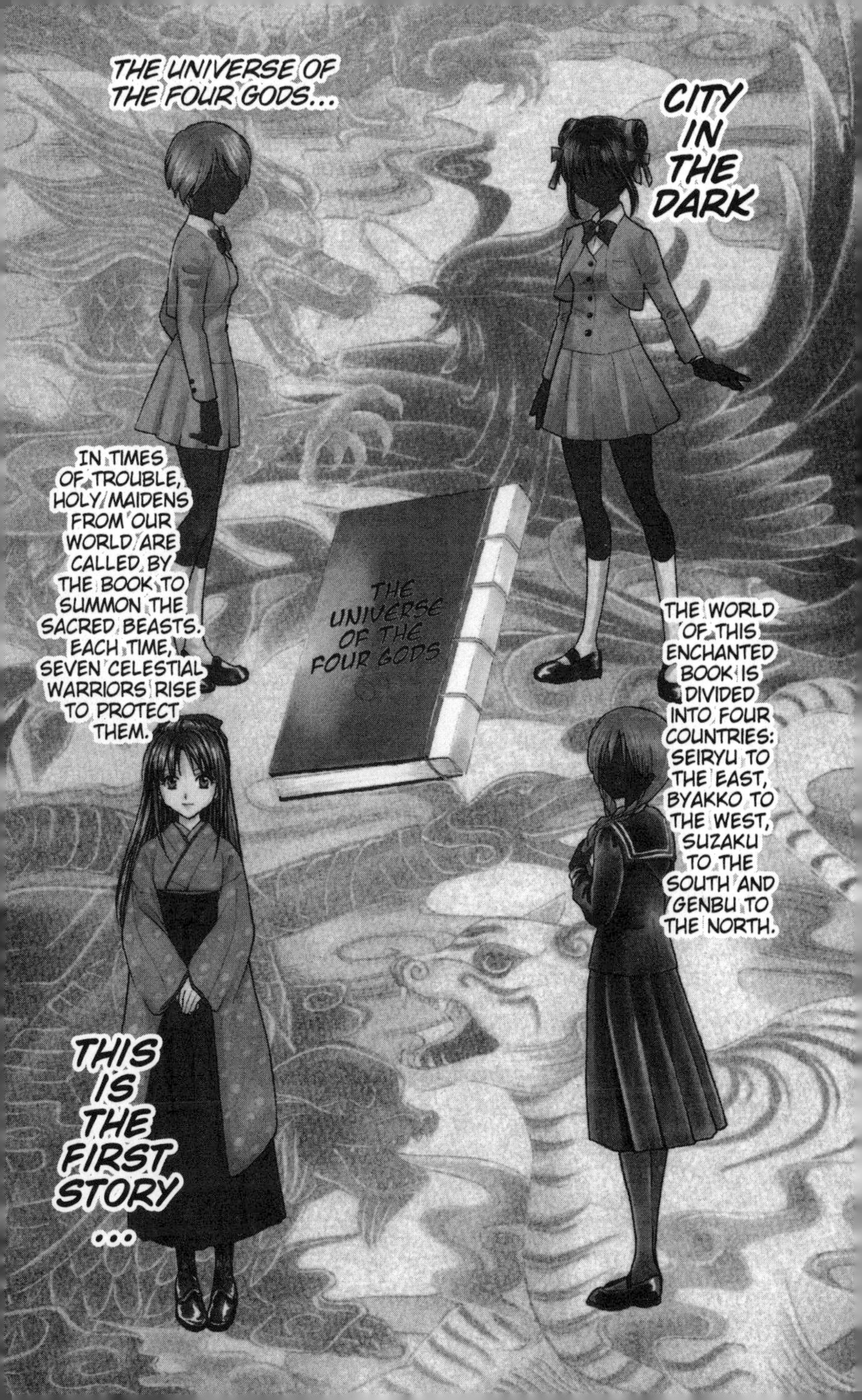

CITY IN THE DARK
THE UNIVERSE OF THE FOUR GODS...
THE WORLD OF THIS ENCHANTED BOOK IS DIVIDED INTO FOUR COUNTRIES: SEIRYU TO THE EAST, BYAKKO TO THE WEST, SUZAKU TO THE SOUTH AND GENBU TO THE NORTH.
THE UNIVERSE OF THE FOUR GODS
IN TIMES OF TROUBLE, HOLY MAIDENS FROM OUR WORLD ARE CALLED BY THE BOOK TO SUMMON THE SACRED BEASTS. EACH TIME, SEVEN CELESTIAL WARRIORS RISE TO PROTECT THEM.
THIS IS THE FIRST STORY...

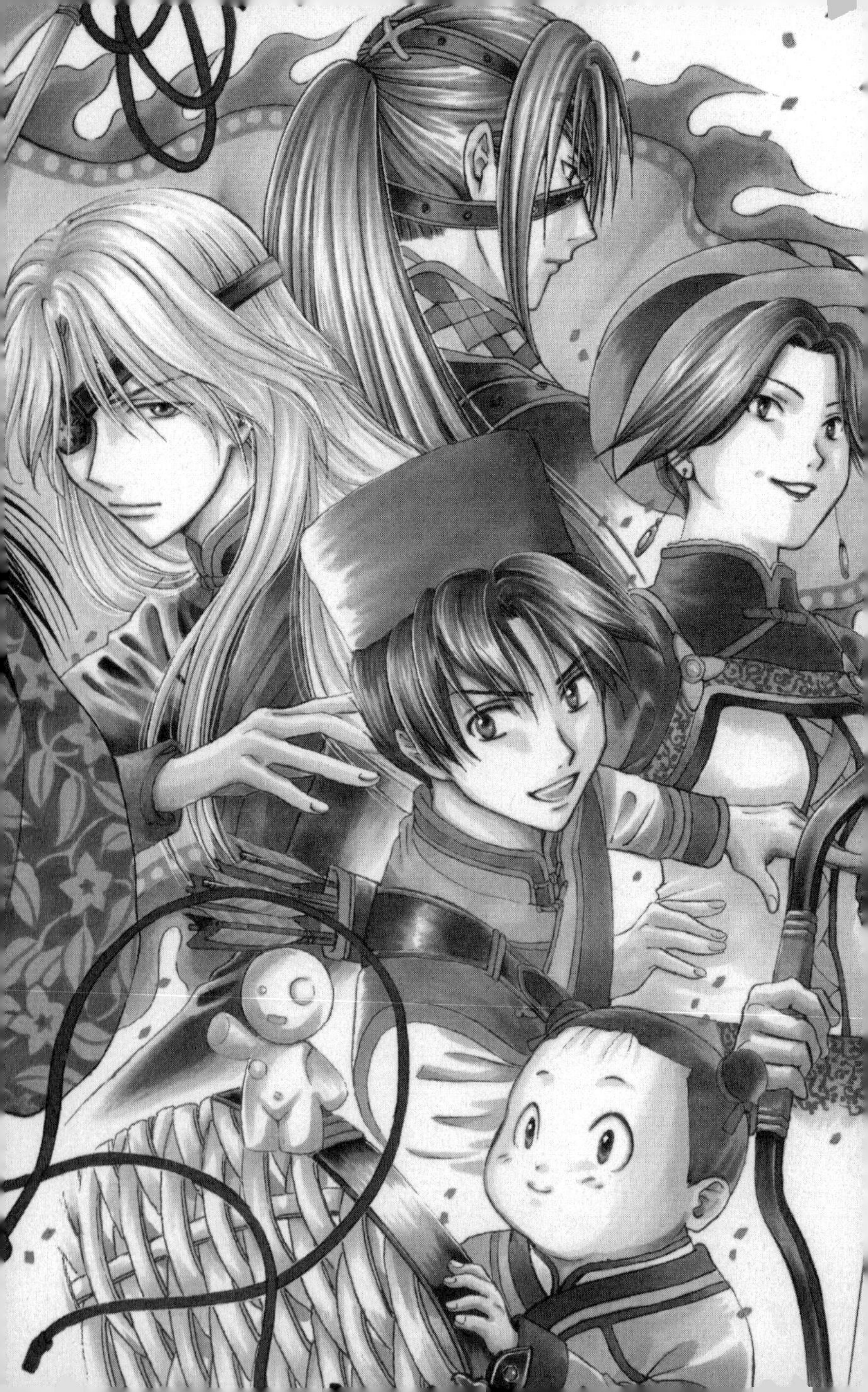

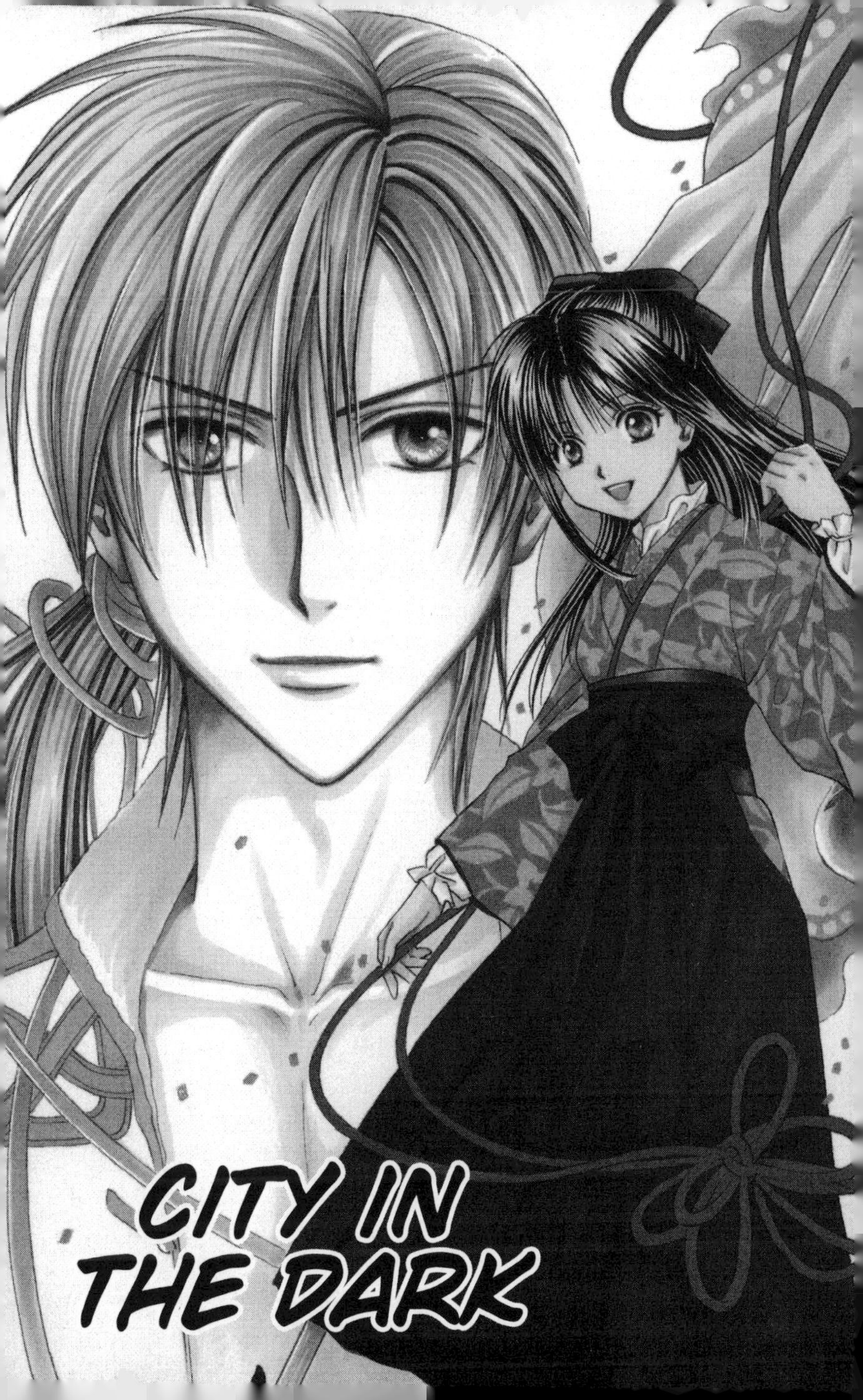
CITY IN
THE DARK

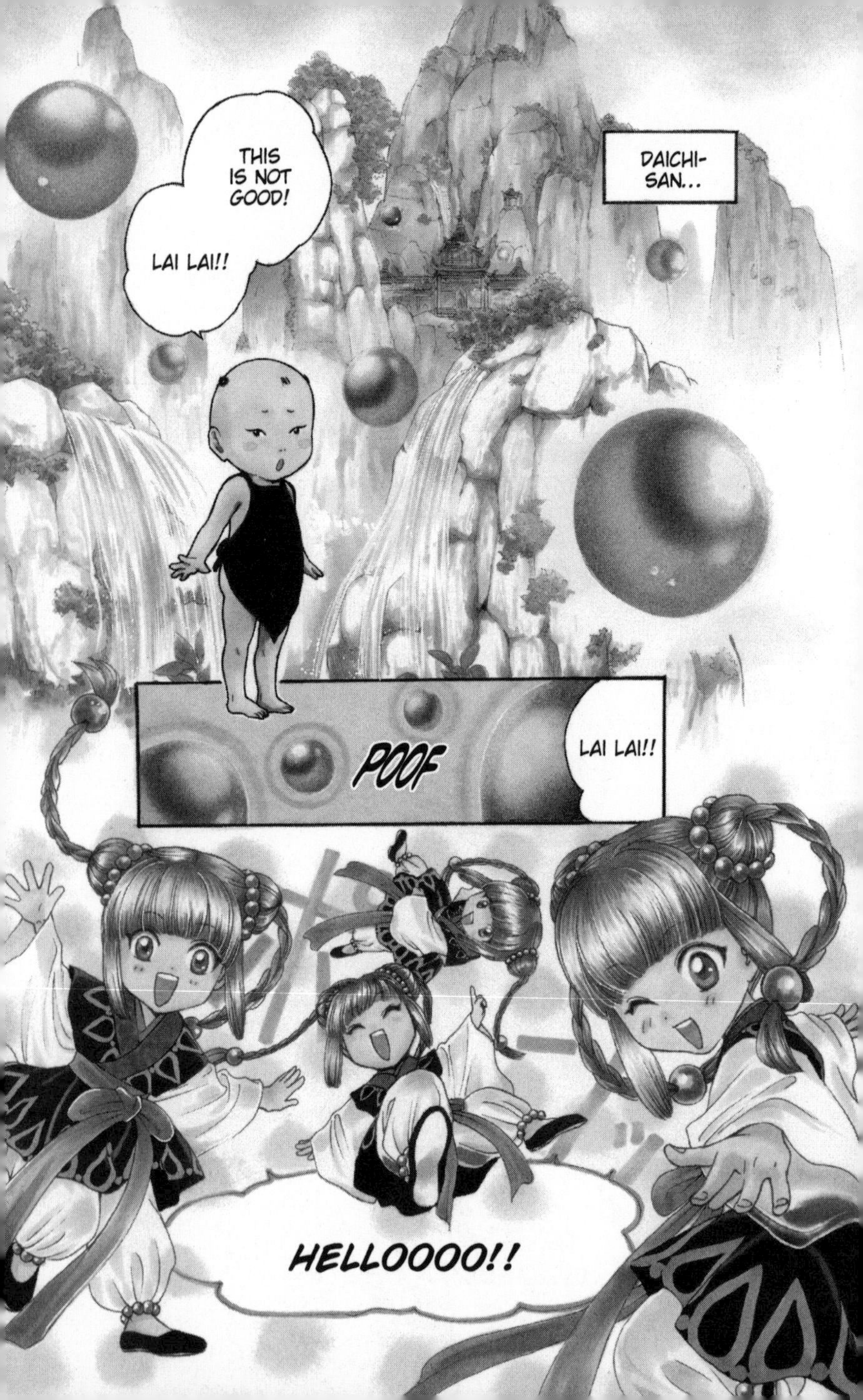
DAICHI-SAN...
THIS IS NOT GOOD!
LAI LAI!!
LAI LAI!!
POOF
HELLOOOO!!

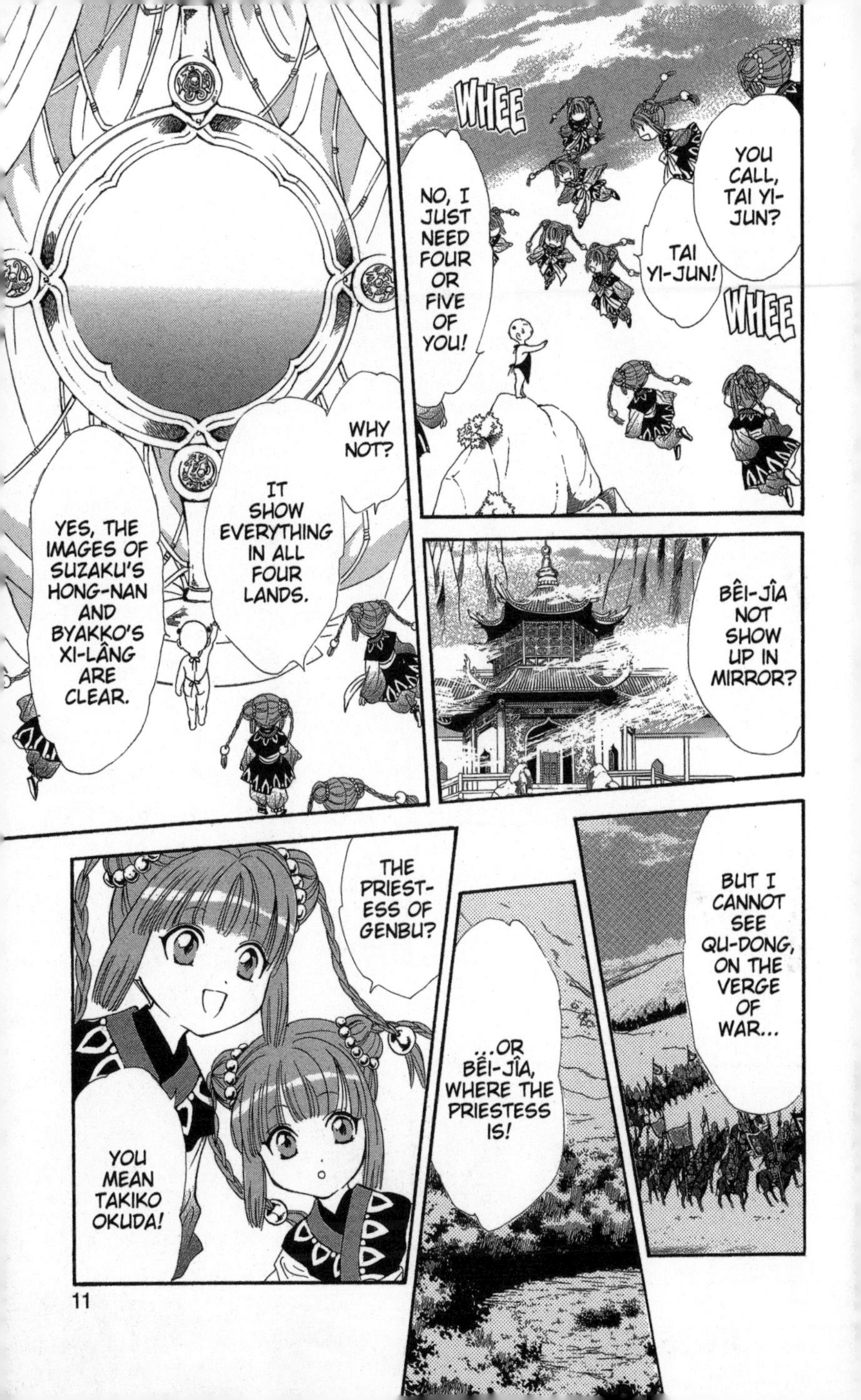
YOU CALL, TAI YI-JUN?
TAI YI-JUN!
WHEE
NO, I JUST NEED FOUR OR FIVE OF YOU!
WHEE
BÊI-JÎA NOT SHOW UP IN MIRROR?
WHY NOT?
IT SHOW EVERYTHING IN ALL FOUR LANDS.
YES, THE IMAGES OF SUZAKU'S HONG-NAN AND BYAKKO'S XI-LÂNG ARE CLEAR.
BUT I CANNOT SEE QU-DONG, ON THE VERGE OF WAR...
...OR BÊI-JÎA, WHERE THE PRIESTESS IS!
THE PRIESTESS OF GENBU?
YOU MEAN TAKIKO OKUDA!

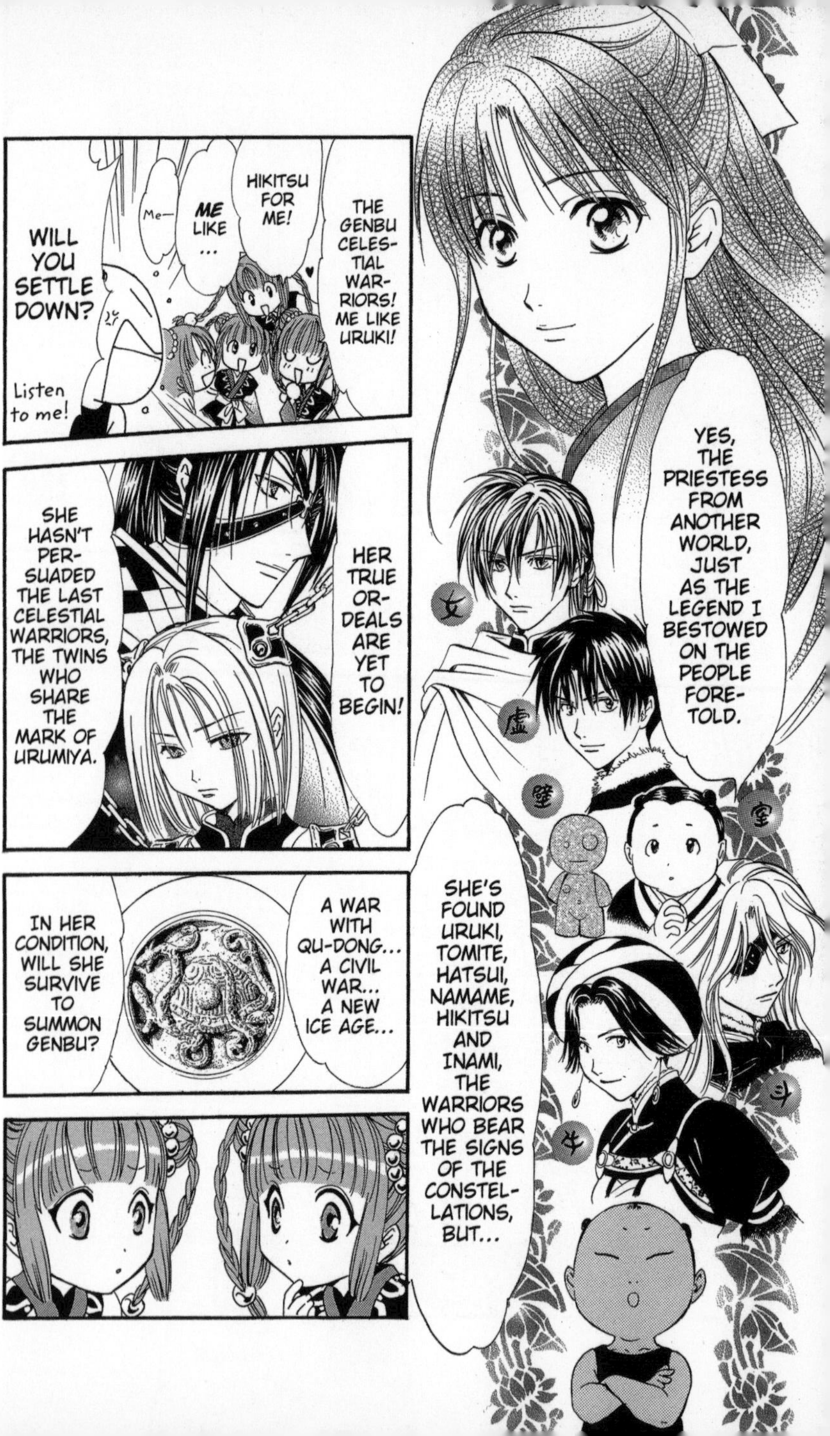
YES, THE PRIESTESS FROM ANOTHER WORLD, JUST AS THE LEGEND I BESTOWED ON THE PEOPLE FORETOLD.
SHE'S FOUND URUKI, TOMITE, HATSUI, NAMAME, HIKITSU AND INAMI, THE WARRIORS WHO BEAR THE SIGNS OF THE CONSTELLATIONS, BUT...
THE GENBU CELESTIAL WARRIORS! ME LIKE URUKI!
HIKITSU FOR ME!
ME LIKE...
Me—
WILL YOU SETTLE DOWN?
Listen to me!
HER TRUE ORDEALS ARE YET TO BEGIN!
SHE HASN'T PERSUADED THE LAST CELESTIAL WARRIORS, THE TWINS WHO SHARE THE MARK OF URUMIYA.
A WAR WITH QU-DONG... A CIVIL WAR... A NEW ICE AGE...
IN HER CONDITION, WILL SHE SURVIVE TO SUMMON GENBU?

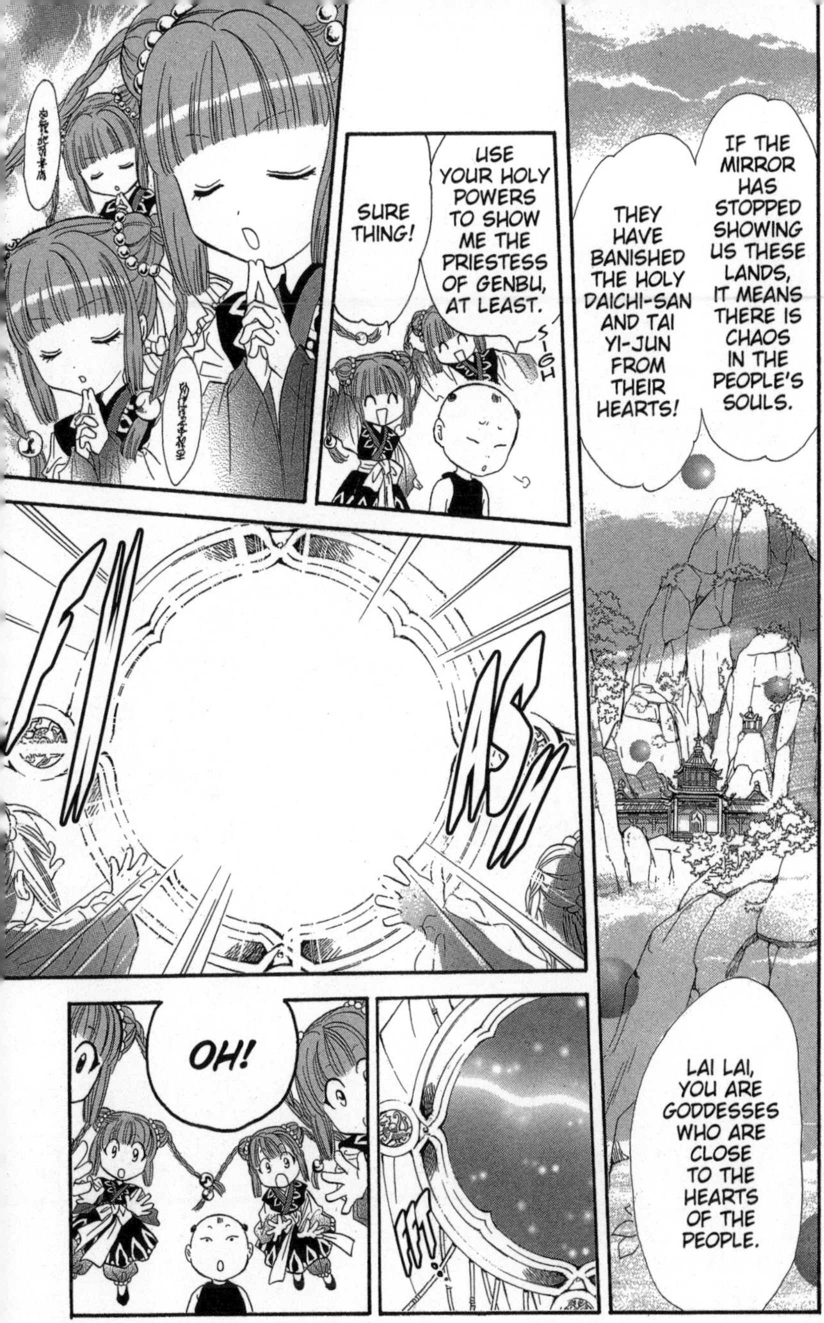
IF THE MIRROR HAS STOPPED SHOWING US THESE LANDS, IT MEANS THERE IS CHAOS IN THE PEOPLE'S SOULS.
THEY HAVE BANISHED THE HOLY DAICHI-SAN AND TAI YI-JUN FROM THEIR HEARTS!
LAI LAI, YOU ARE GODDESSES WHO ARE CLOSE TO THE HEARTS OF THE PEOPLE.
USE YOUR HOLY POWERS TO SHOW ME THE PRIESTESS OF GENBU, AT LEAST.
SURE THING!
SIGH
FLASH
OH!

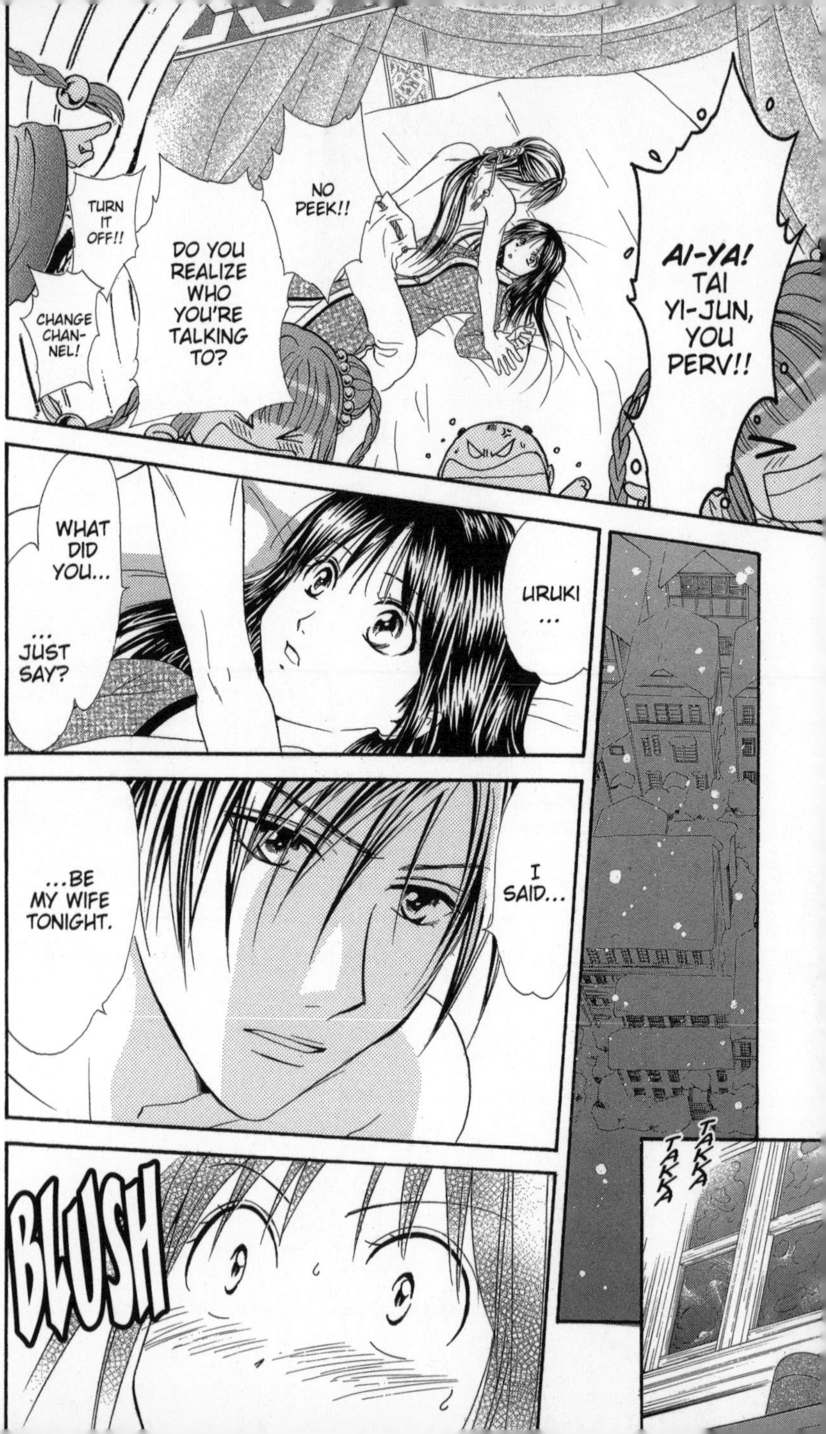
AI-YA! TAI YI-JUN, YOU PERV!!
NO PEEK!!
DO YOU REALIZE WHO YOU'RE TALKING TO?
TURN IT OFF!!
CHANGE CHAN-NEL!
URUKI ...
WHAT DID YOU...
... JUST SAY?
I SAID...
...BE MY WIFE TONIGHT.
TAKA TAKA
BLUSH

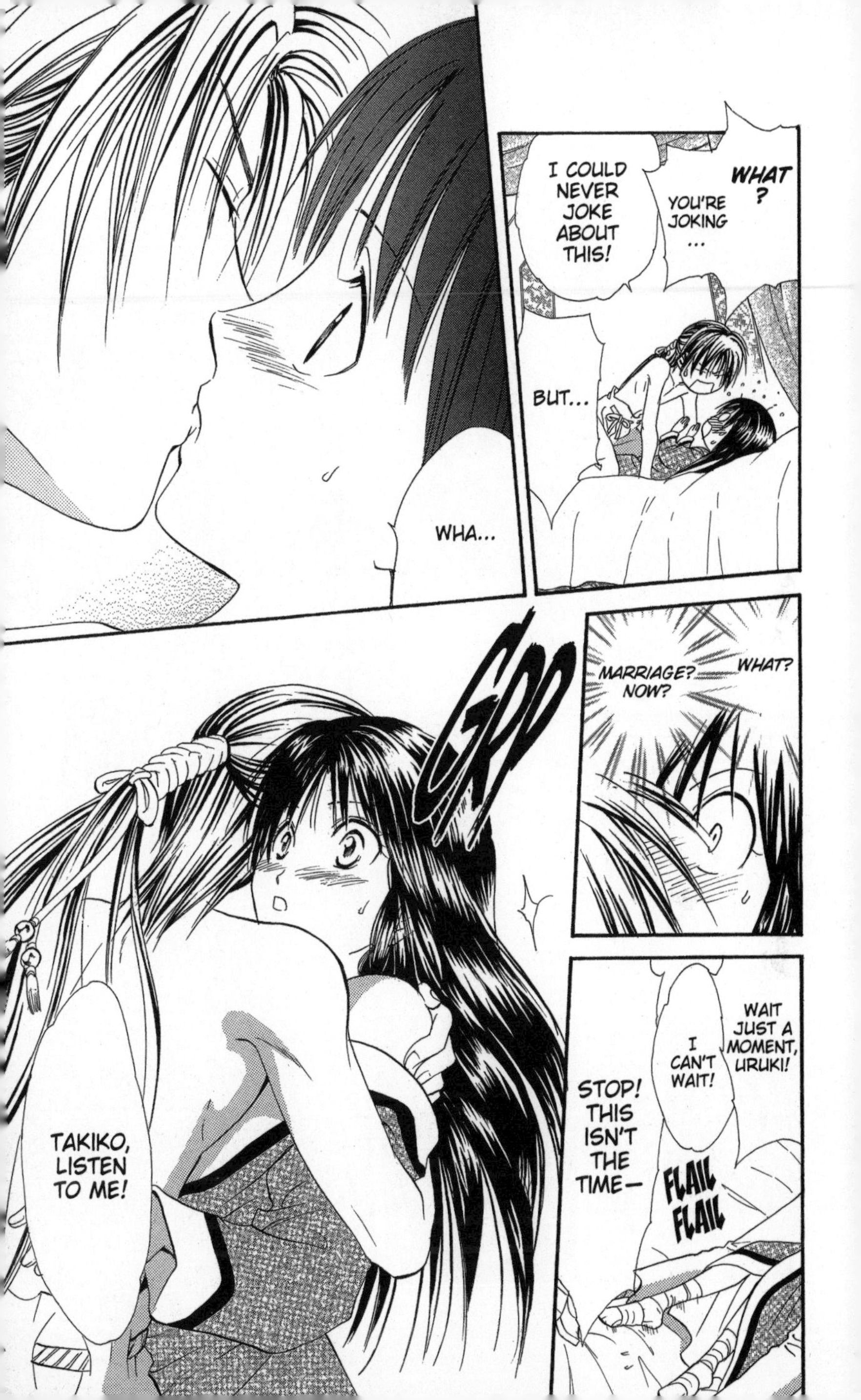
WHAT?
YOU'RE JOKING...
I COULD NEVER JOKE ABOUT THIS!
BUT...
WHA...
WHAT?
MARRIAGE? NOW?
WAIT JUST A MOMENT, URUKI!
I CAN'T WAIT!
STOP! THIS ISN'T THE TIME—
FLAIL FLAIL
TAKIKO, LISTEN TO ME!

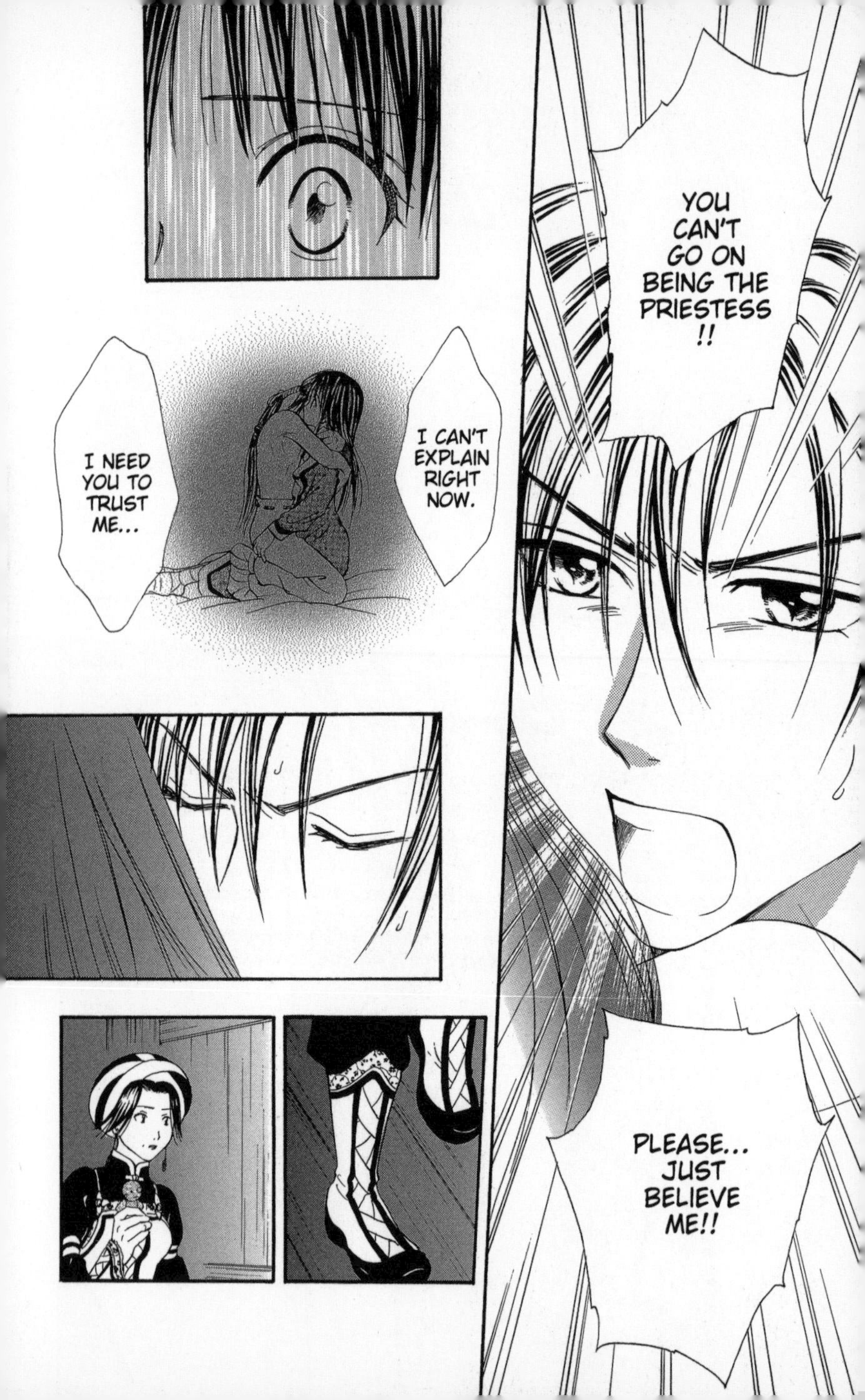
YOU CAN'T GO ON BEING THE PRIESTESS!!
PLEASE... JUST BELIEVE ME!!
I CAN'T EXPLAIN RIGHT NOW.
I NEED YOU TO TRUST ME...

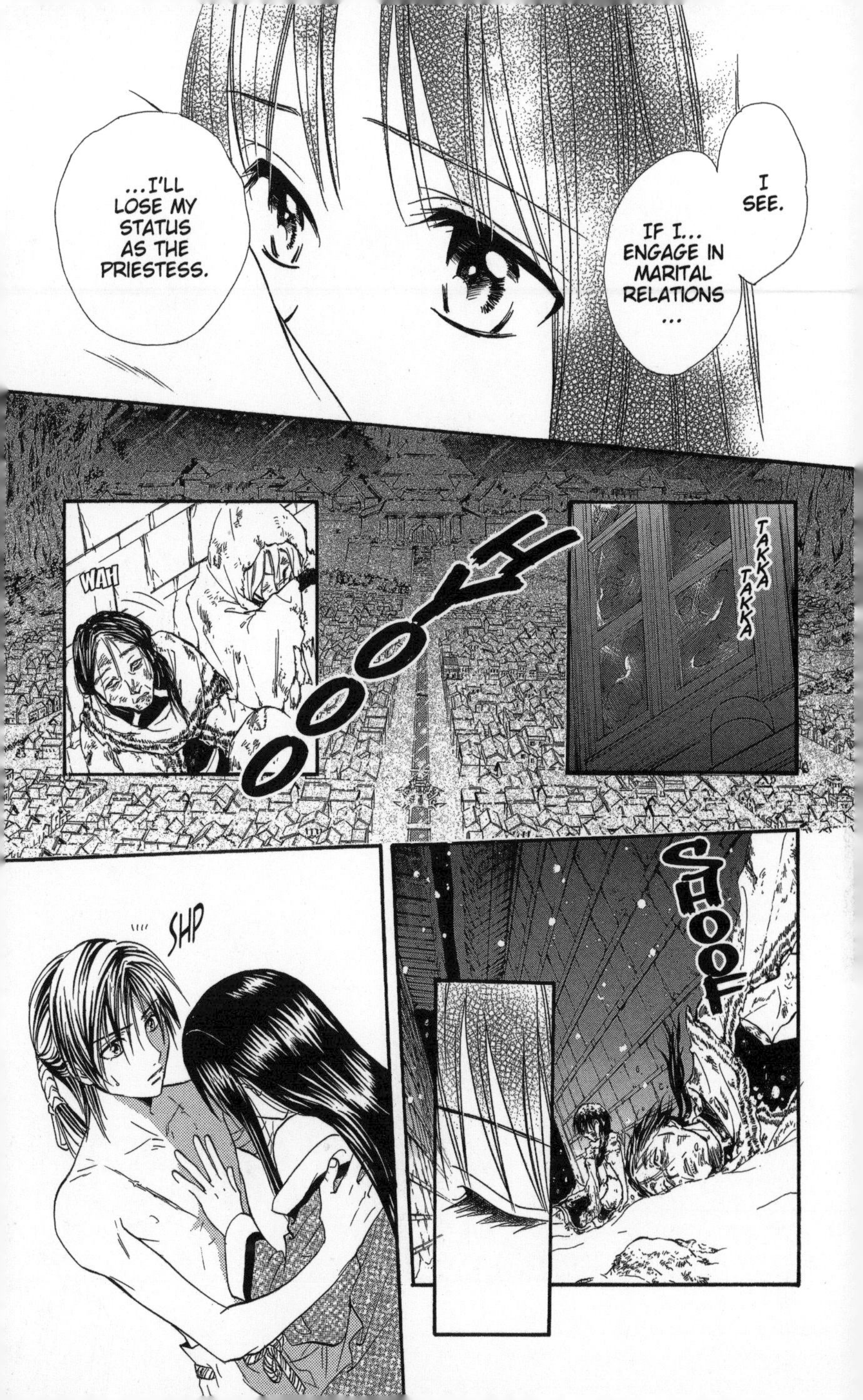
I SEE.
IF I... ENGAGE IN MARITAL RELATIONS ...
...I'LL LOSE MY STATUS AS THE PRIESTESS.
TAKKA TAKKA
HYOOOOO
WAH
SHOOF
SHP

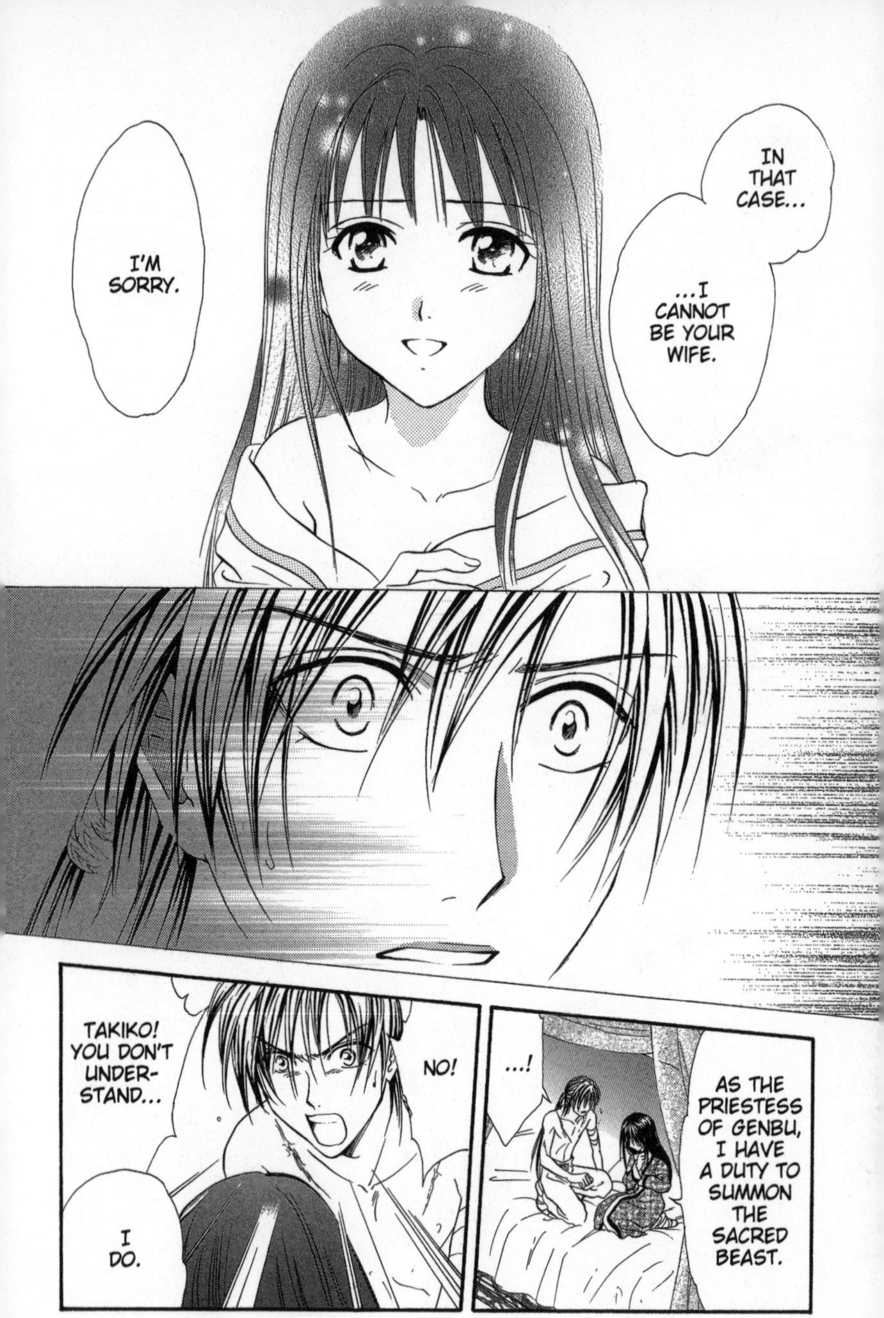
IN THAT CASE...
...I CANNOT BE YOUR WIFE.
I'M SORRY.
AS THE PRIESTESS OF GENBU, I HAVE A DUTY TO SUMMON THE SACRED BEAST.
...!
NO!
TAKIKO! YOU DON'T UNDER-STAND...
I DO.

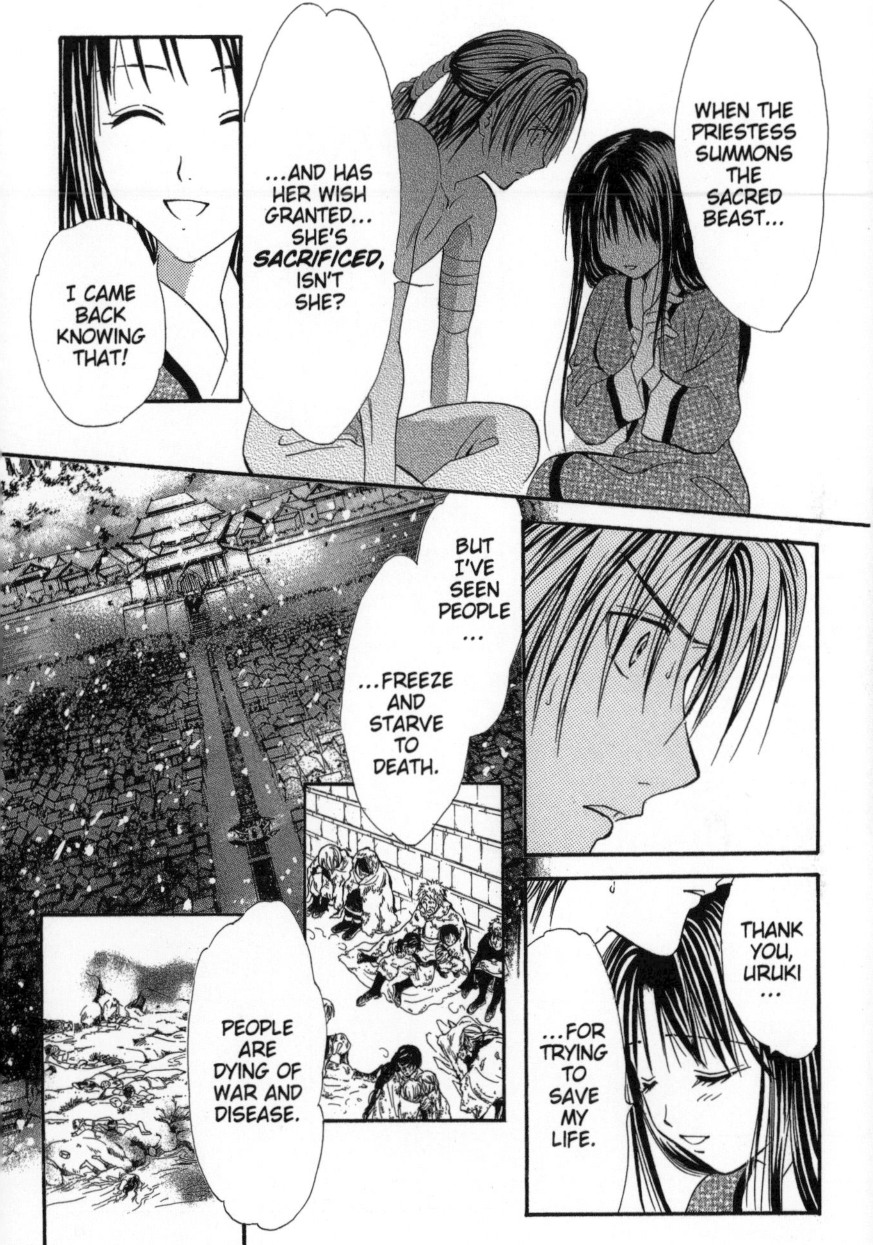
WHEN THE PRIESTESS SUMMONS THE SACRED BEAST...
...AND HAS HER WISH GRANTED... SHE'S *SACRIFICED,* ISN'T SHE?
I CAME BACK KNOWING THAT!
BUT I'VE SEEN PEOPLE...
...FREEZE AND STARVE TO DEATH.
PEOPLE ARE DYING OF WAR AND DISEASE.
THANK YOU, URUKI...
...FOR TRYING TO SAVE MY LIFE.

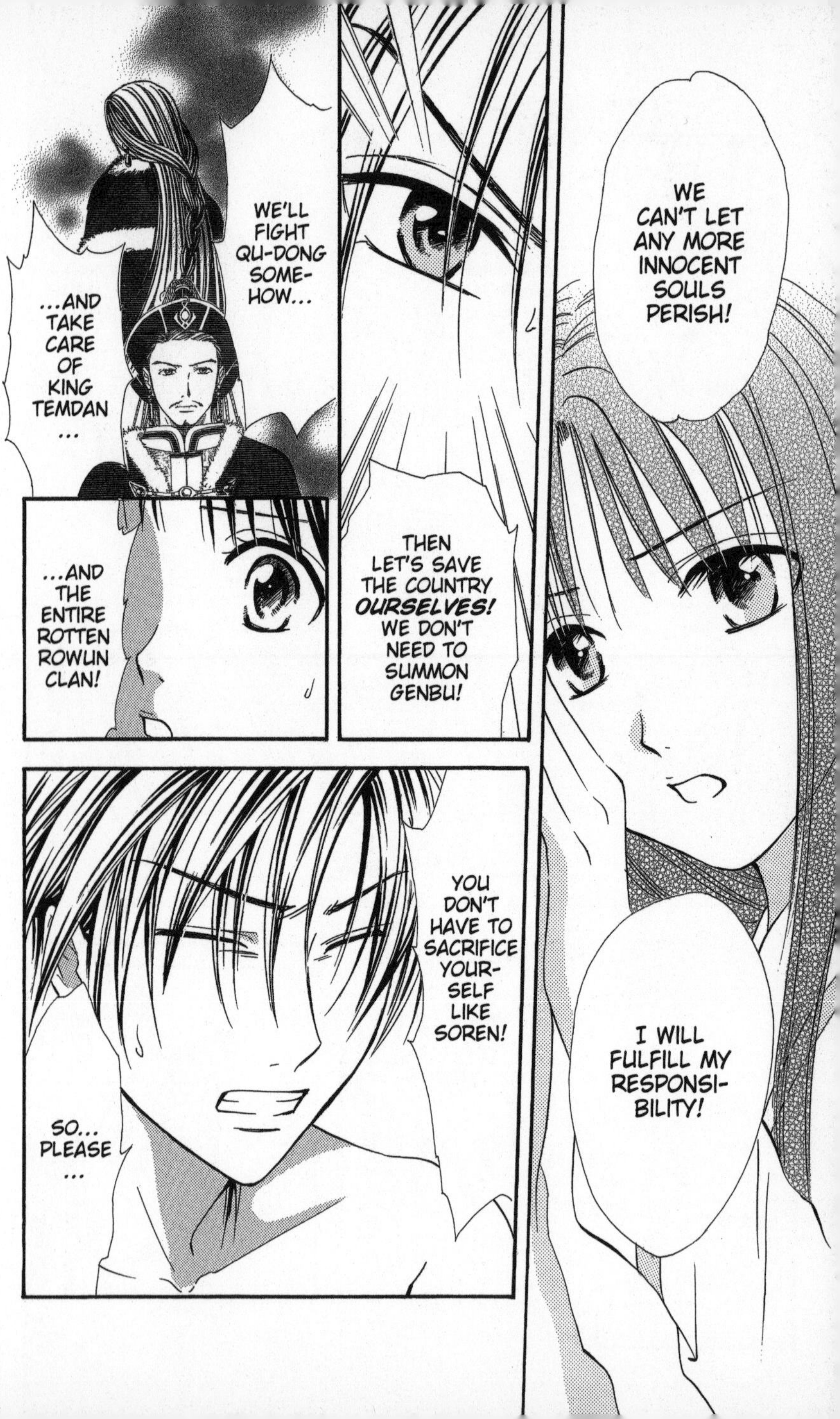
WE'LL FIGHT QU-DONG SOME-HOW...
...AND TAKE CARE OF KING TEMDAN ...
...AND THE ENTIRE ROTTEN ROWUN CLAN!
THEN LET'S SAVE THE COUNTRY ***OURSELVES!*** WE DON'T NEED TO SUMMON GENBU!
YOU DON'T HAVE TO SACRIFICE YOUR-SELF LIKE SOREN!
SO... PLEASE ...
WE CAN'T LET ANY MORE INNOCENT SOULS PERISH!
I WILL FULFILL MY RESPONSI-BILITY!

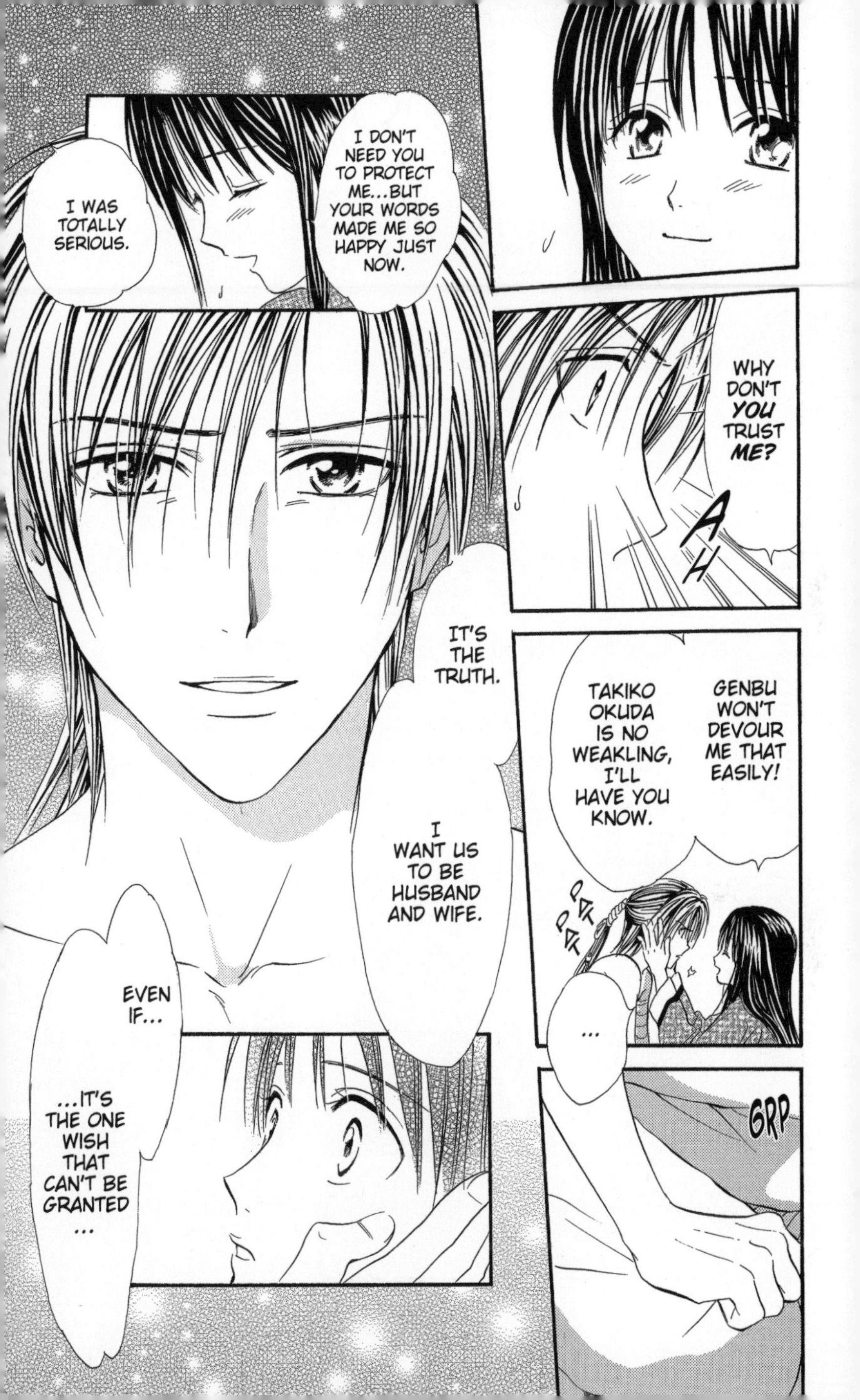
WHY DON'T YOU TRUST ME?
AH
GENBU WON'T DEVOUR ME THAT EASILY!
TAKIKO OKUDA IS NO WEAKLING, I'LL HAVE YOU KNOW.
...
GRP
I DON'T NEED YOU TO PROTECT ME...BUT YOUR WORDS MADE ME SO HAPPY JUST NOW.
I WAS TOTALLY SERIOUS.
IT'S THE TRUTH.
I WANT US TO BE HUSBAND AND WIFE.
EVEN IF...
...IT'S THE ONE WISH THAT CAN'T BE GRANTED...

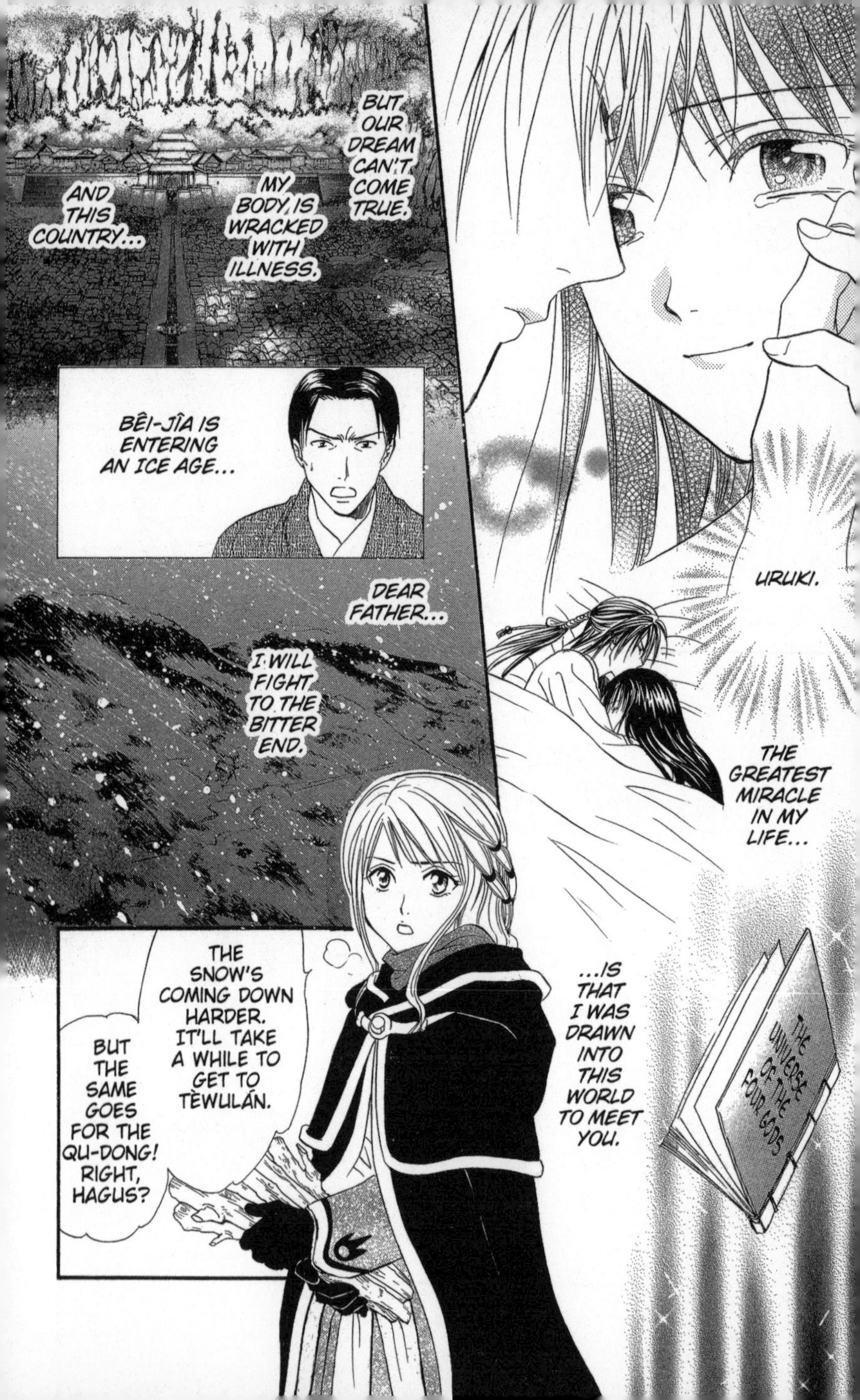
URUKI.
THE GREATEST MIRACLE IN MY LIFE...
...IS THAT I WAS DRAWN INTO THIS WORLD TO MEET YOU.
THE UNIVERSE OF THE FOUR GODS
BUT OUR DREAM CAN'T COME TRUE.
MY BODY IS WRACKED WITH ILLNESS.
AND THIS COUNTRY...
BÊI-JÎA IS ENTERING AN ICE AGE...
DEAR FATHER...
I WILL FIGHT TO THE BITTER END.
THE SNOW'S COMING DOWN HARDER. IT'LL TAKE A WHILE TO GET TO TÈWULÁN.
BUT THE SAME GOES FOR THE QU-DONG! RIGHT, HAGUS?

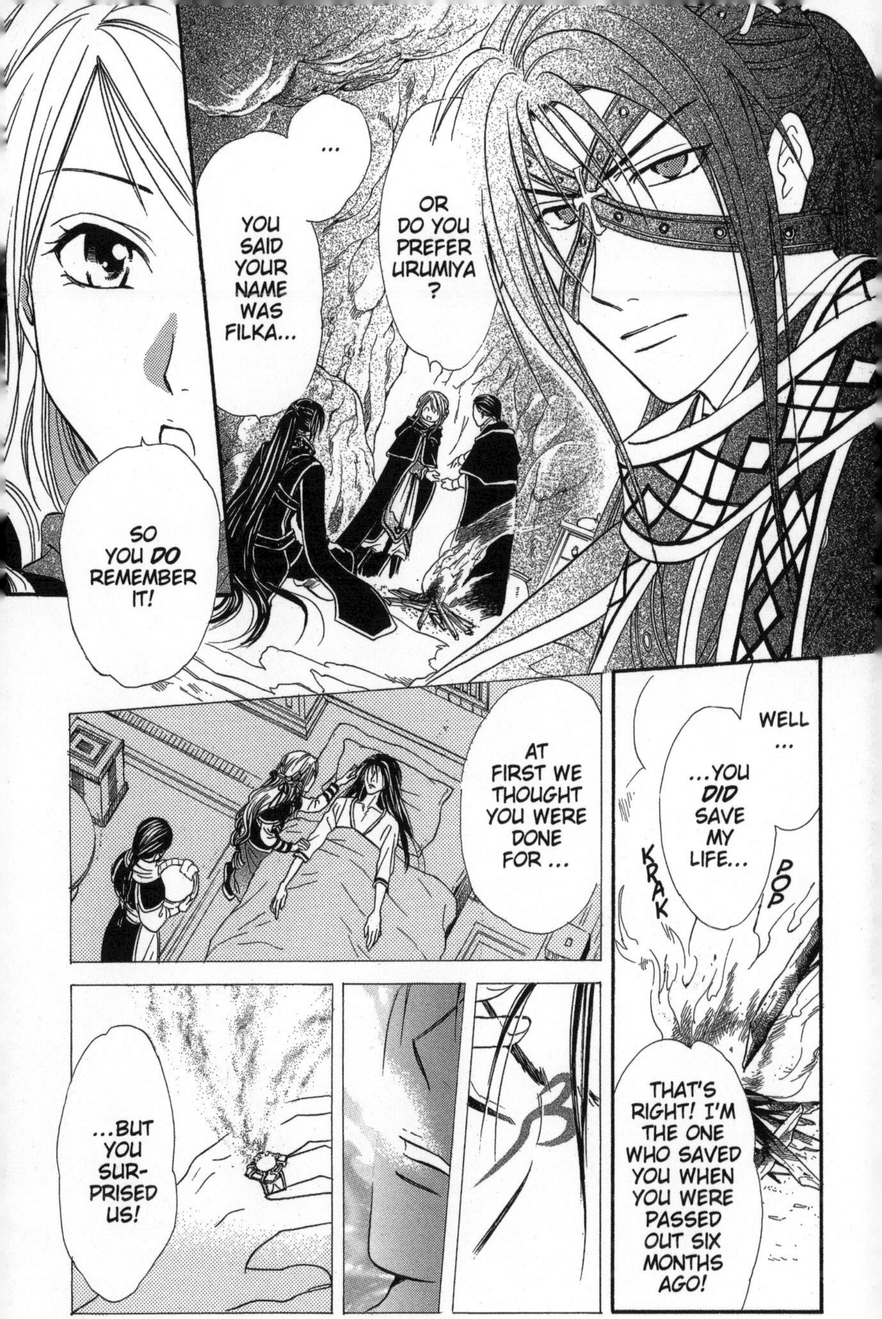
...
YOU SAID YOUR NAME WAS FILKA...
OR DO YOU PREFER URUMIYA?
SO YOU *DO* REMEMBER IT!
WELL ...
...YOU *DID* SAVE MY LIFE...
KRAK
POP
THAT'S RIGHT! I'M THE ONE WHO SAVED YOU WHEN YOU WERE PASSED OUT SIX MONTHS AGO!
AT FIRST WE THOUGHT YOU WERE DONE FOR ...
...BUT YOU SUR-PRISED US!

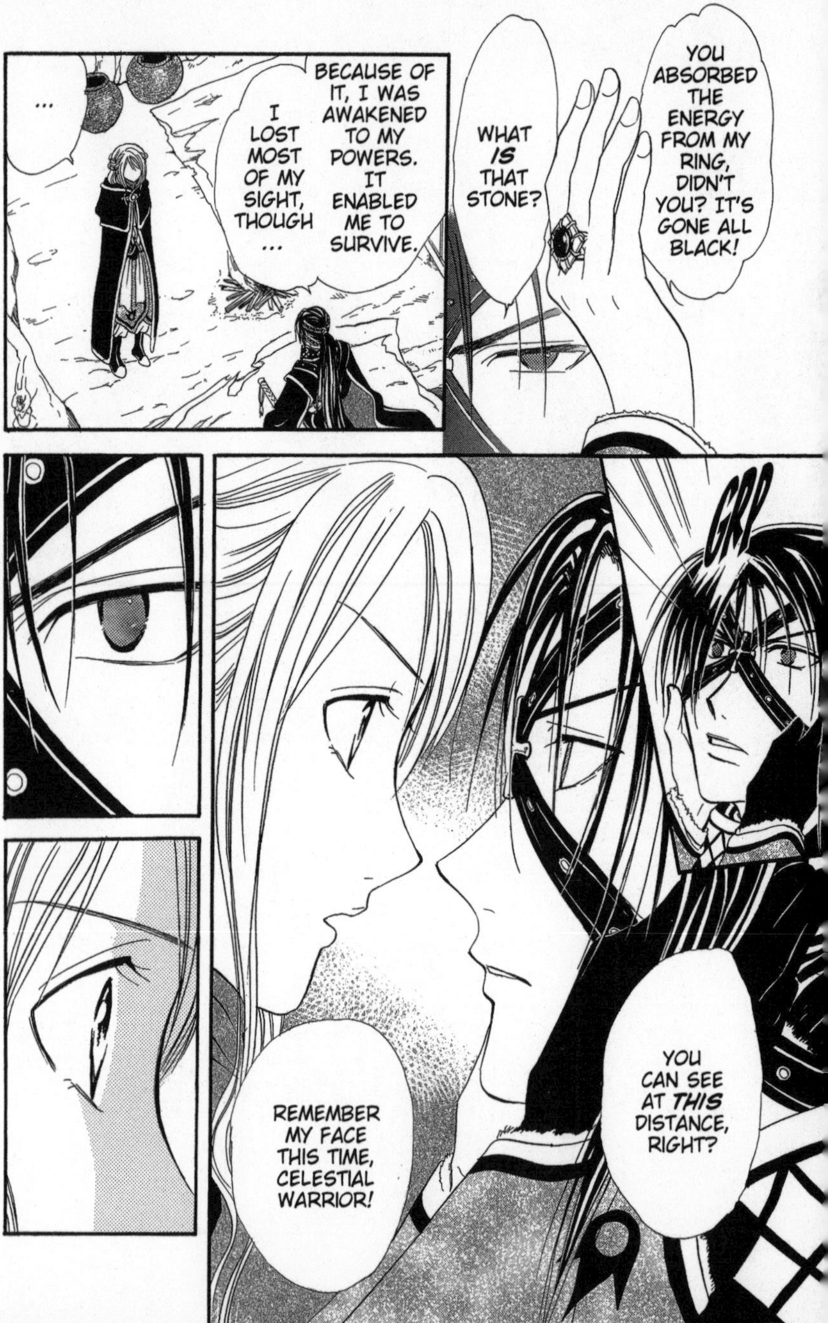
YOU ABSORBED THE ENERGY FROM MY RING, DIDN'T YOU? IT'S GONE ALL BLACK!
WHAT *IS* THAT STONE?
BECAUSE OF IT, I WAS AWAKENED TO MY POWERS. IT ENABLED ME TO SURVIVE.
I LOST MOST OF MY SIGHT, THOUGH ...
...
GRP
YOU CAN SEE AT *THIS* DISTANCE, RIGHT?
REMEMBER MY FACE THIS TIME, CELESTIAL WARRIOR!

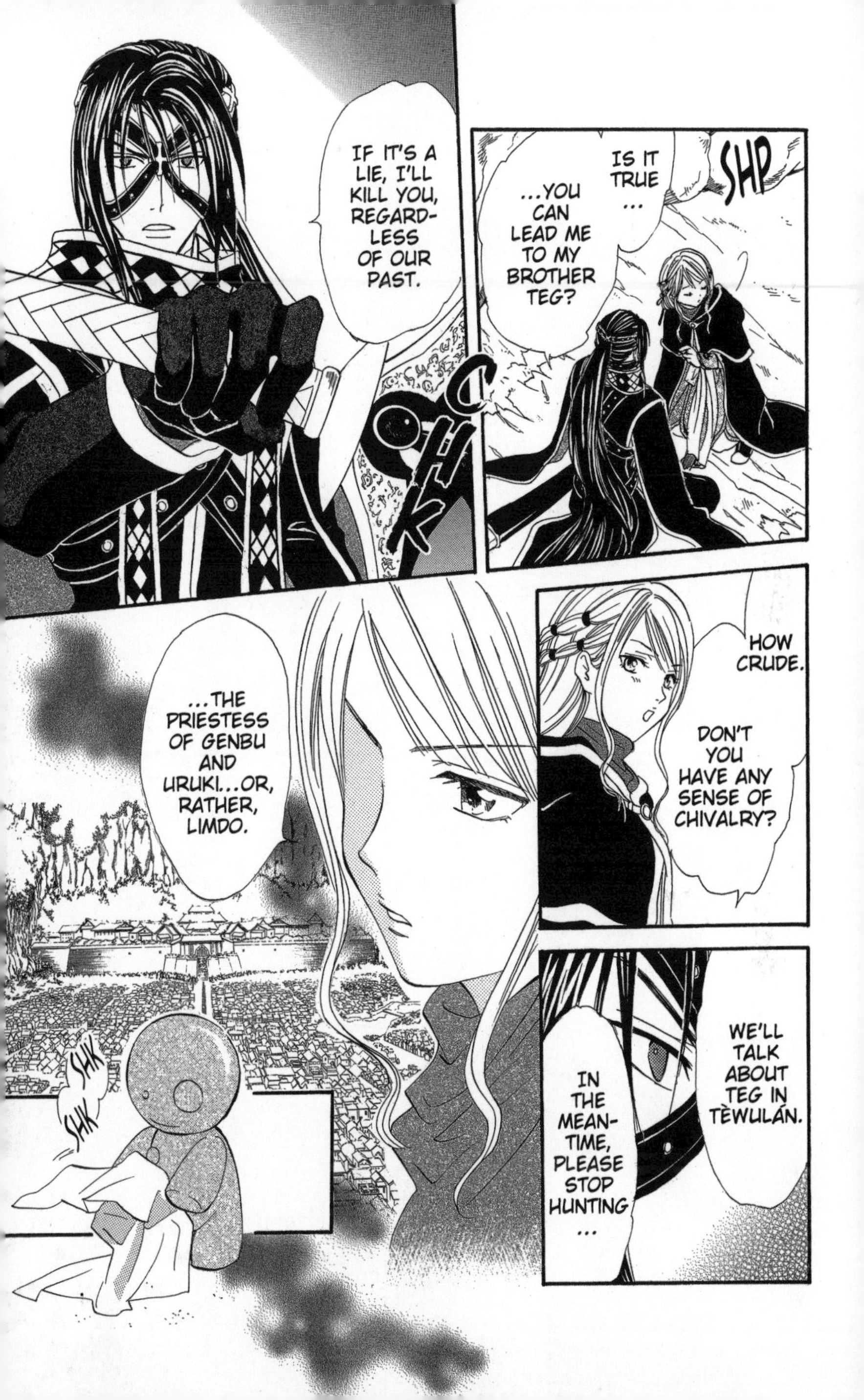
SHP
IS IT TRUE ...
...YOU CAN LEAD ME TO MY BROTHER TEG?
IF IT'S A LIE, I'LL KILL YOU, REGARDLESS OF OUR PAST.
CHK
HOW CRUDE.
DON'T YOU HAVE ANY SENSE OF CHIVALRY?
WE'LL TALK ABOUT TEG IN TÈWULÁN.
IN THE MEANTIME, PLEASE STOP HUNTING ...
...THE PRIESTESS OF GENBU AND URUKI...OR, RATHER, LIMDO.
SHK
SHK

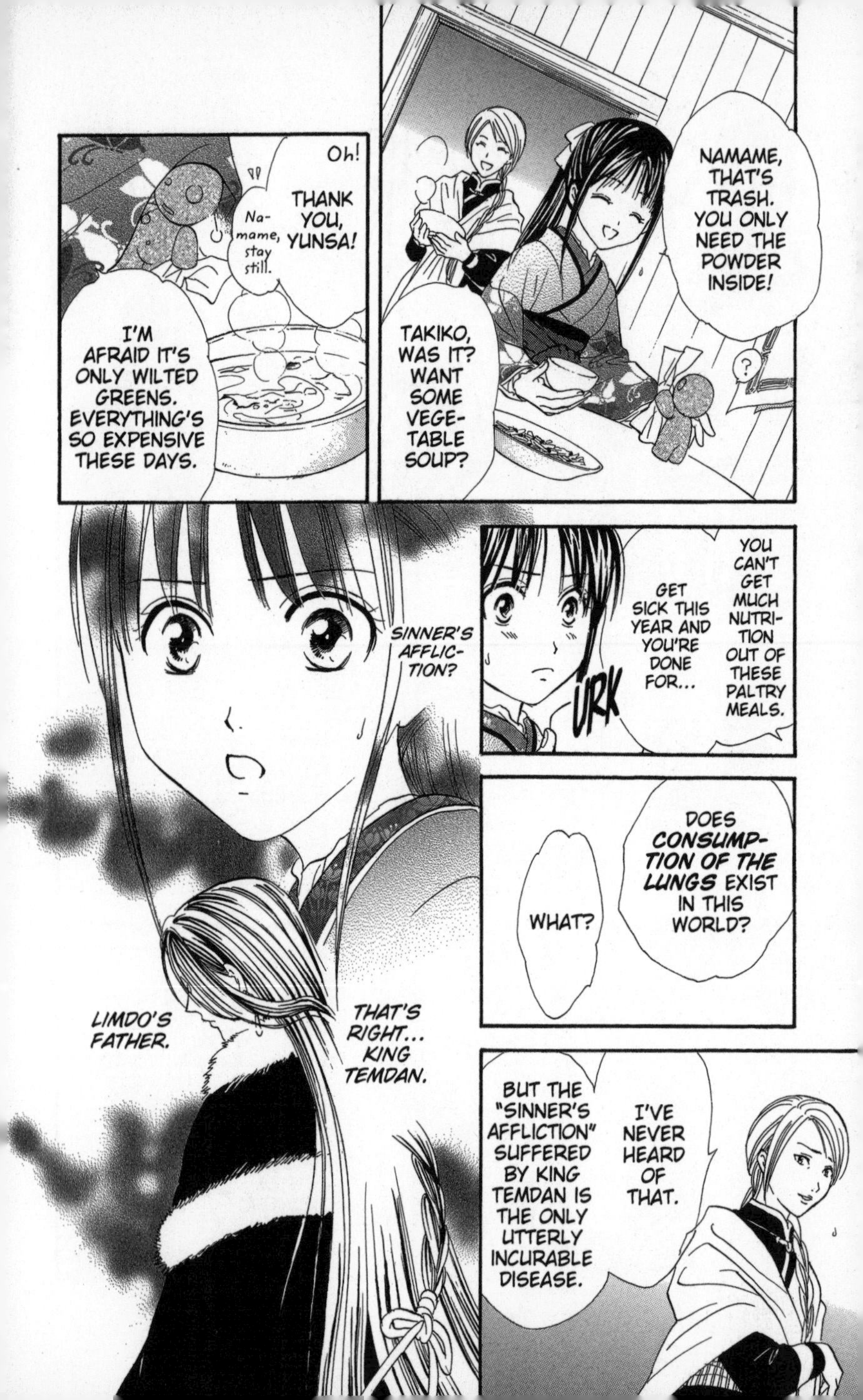
NAMAME, THAT'S TRASH. YOU ONLY NEED THE POWDER INSIDE!
?
TAKIKO, WAS IT? WANT SOME VEGE-TABLE SOUP?
Oh!
THANK YOU, YUNSA!
Na-mame, stay still.
I'M AFRAID IT'S ONLY WILTED GREENS. EVERYTHING'S SO EXPENSIVE THESE DAYS.
YOU CAN'T GET MUCH NUTRI-TION OUT OF THESE PALTRY MEALS.
GET SICK THIS YEAR AND YOU'RE DONE FOR...
URK
DOES CONSUMP-TION OF THE LUNGS EXIST IN THIS WORLD?
WHAT?
I'VE NEVER HEARD OF THAT.
BUT THE "SINNER'S AFFLICTION" SUFFERED BY KING TEMDAN IS THE ONLY UTTERLY INCURABLE DISEASE.
SINNER'S AFFLIC-TION?
THAT'S RIGHT... KING TEMDAN.
LIMDO'S FATHER.

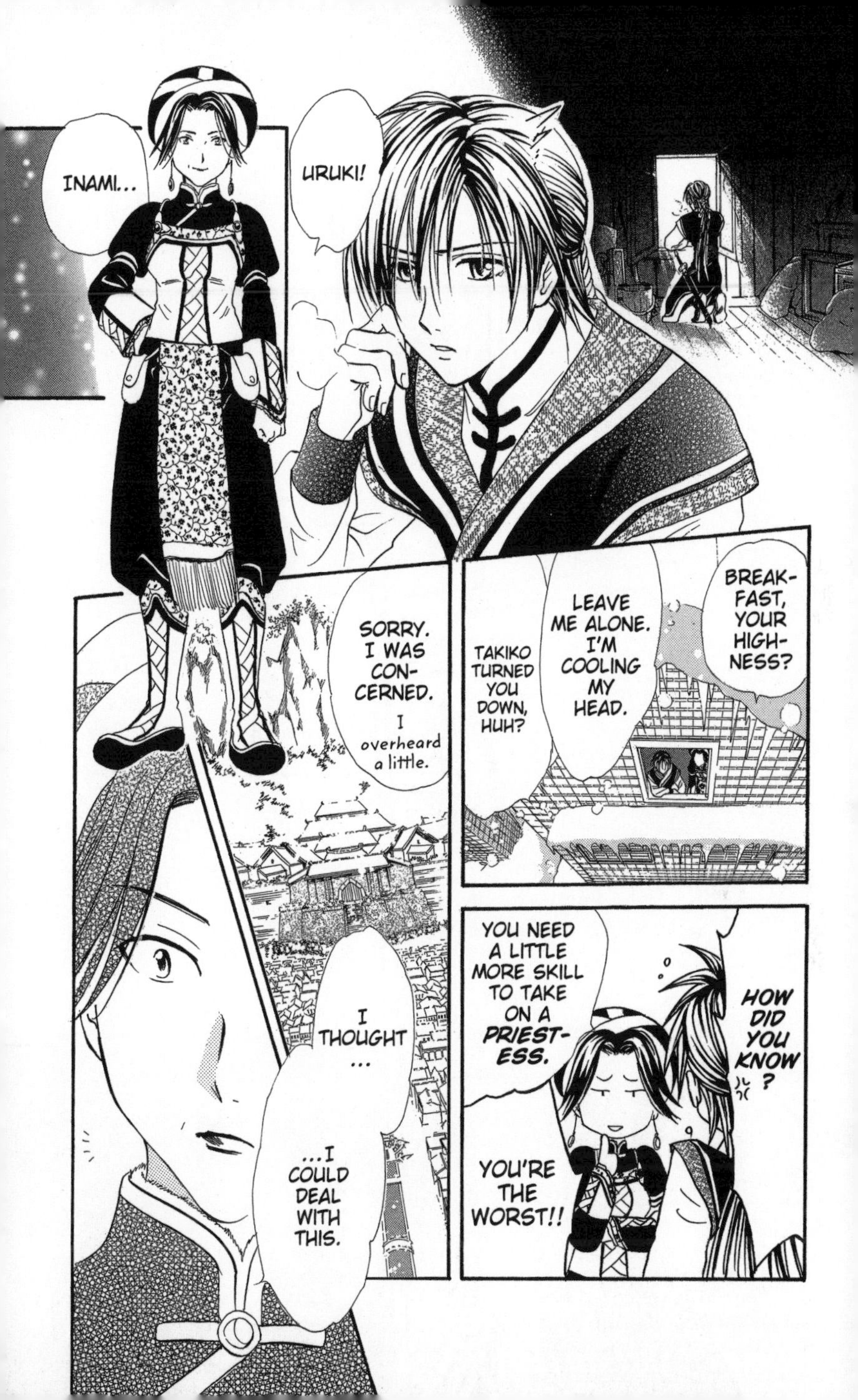
URUKI!
INAMI...
BREAK-FAST, YOUR HIGH-NESS?
LEAVE ME ALONE. I'M COOLING MY HEAD.
TAKIKO TURNED YOU DOWN, HUH?
YOU NEED A LITTLE MORE SKILL TO TAKE ON A PRIEST-ESS.
HOW DID YOU KNOW?
YOU'RE THE WORST!!
SORRY. I WAS CON-CERNED.
I overheard a little.
I THOUGHT...
...I COULD DEAL WITH THIS.

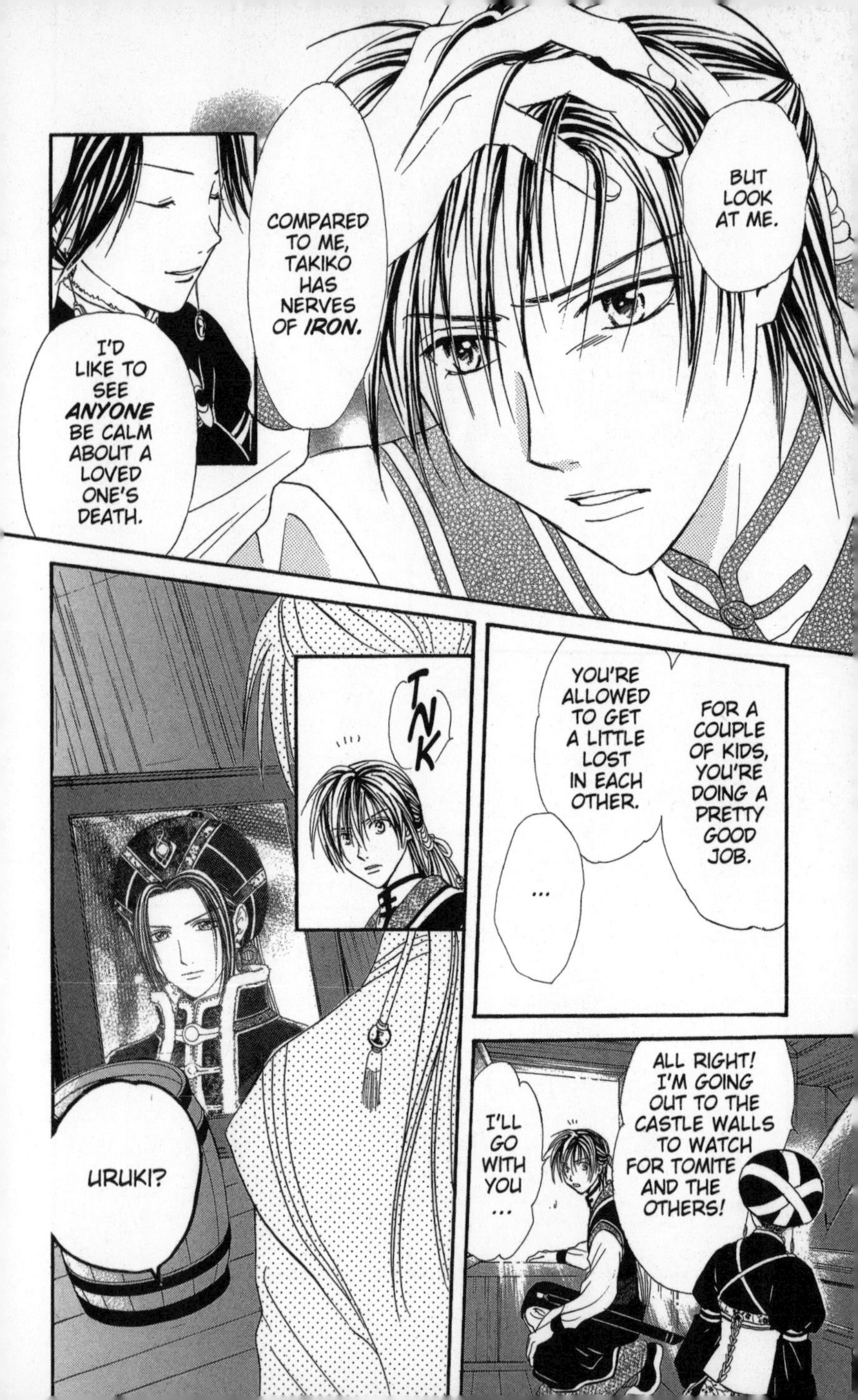
BUT LOOK AT ME.
COMPARED TO ME, TAKIKO HAS NERVES OF ***IRON.***
I'D LIKE TO SEE ***ANYONE*** BE CALM ABOUT A LOVED ONE'S DEATH.
FOR A COUPLE OF KIDS, YOU'RE DOING A PRETTY GOOD JOB.
YOU'RE ALLOWED TO GET A LITTLE LOST IN EACH OTHER.
...
ALL RIGHT! I'M GOING OUT TO THE CASTLE WALLS TO WATCH FOR TOMITE AND THE OTHERS!
I'LL GO WITH YOU ...
TNK
URUKI?

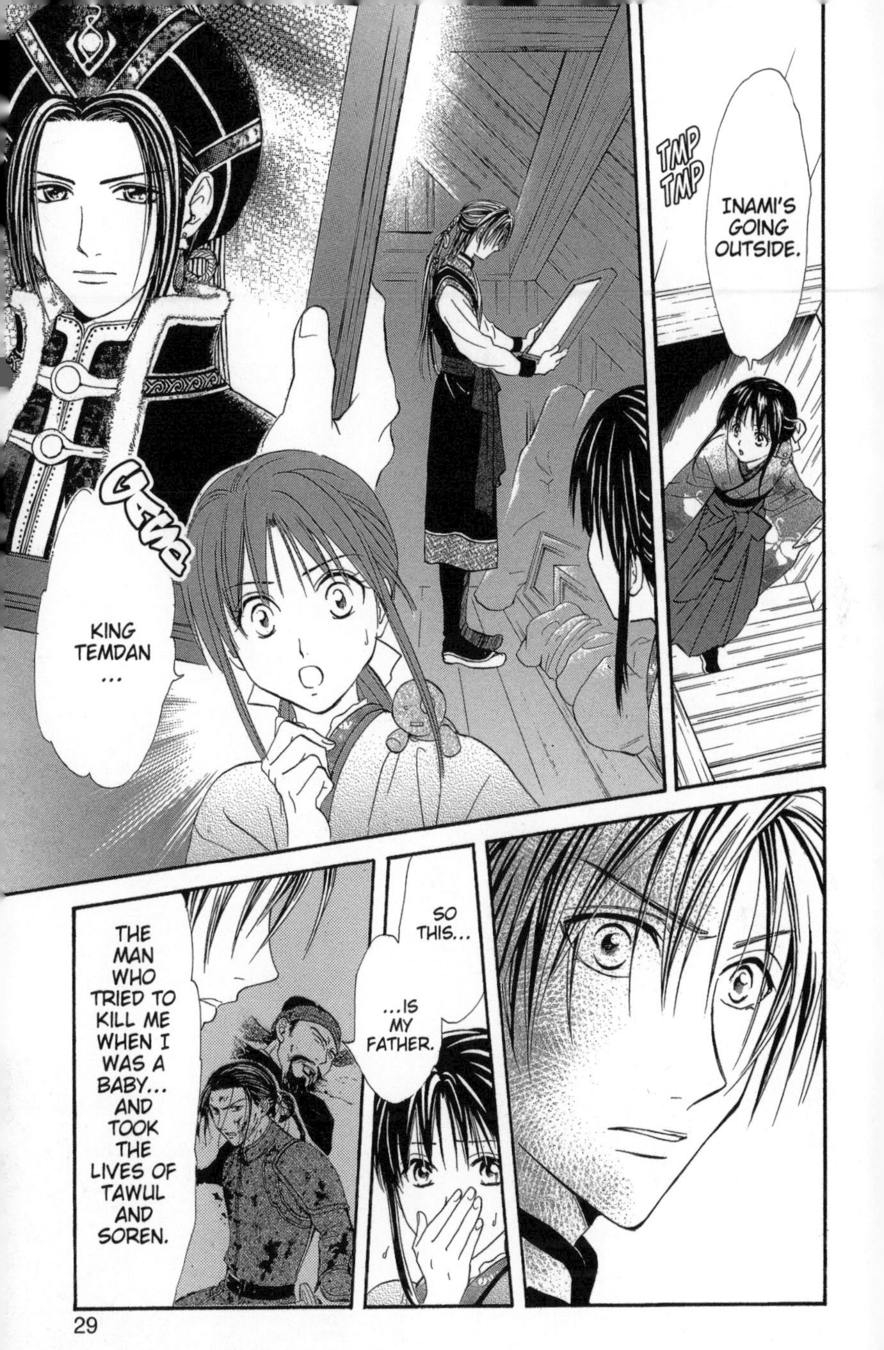
TMP TMP
INAMI'S GOING OUTSIDE.
GASP
KING TEMDAN ...
SO THIS...
...IS MY FATHER.
THE MAN WHO TRIED TO KILL ME WHEN I WAS A BABY... AND TOOK THE LIVES OF TAWUL AND SOREN.

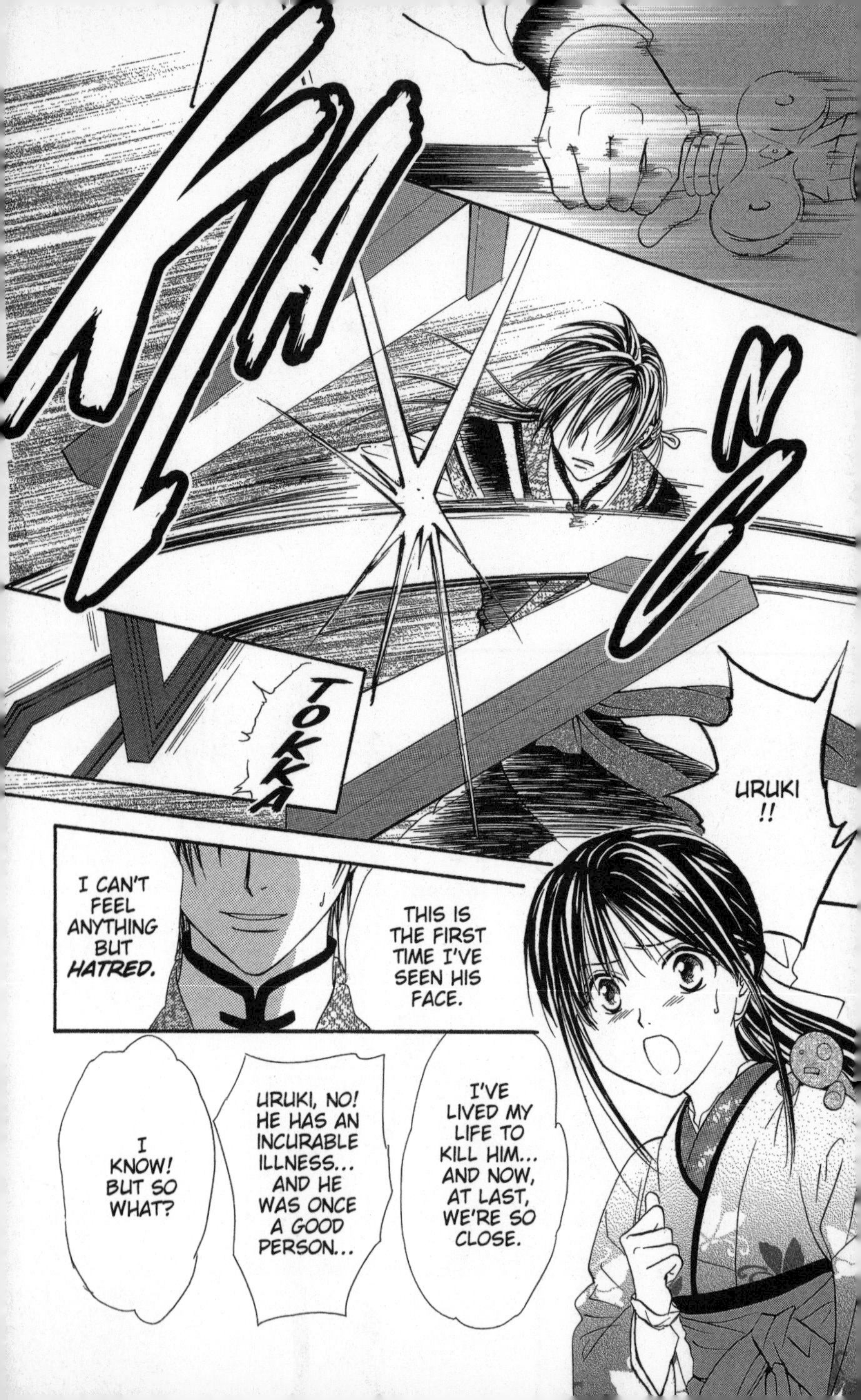
TOKKA
URUKI !!
THIS IS THE FIRST TIME I'VE SEEN HIS FACE.
I CAN'T FEEL ANYTHING BUT *HATRED.*
I'VE LIVED MY LIFE TO KILL HIM... AND NOW, AT LAST, WE'RE SO CLOSE.
URUKI, NO! HE HAS AN INCURABLE ILLNESS... AND HE WAS ONCE A GOOD PERSON...
I KNOW! BUT SO WHAT?

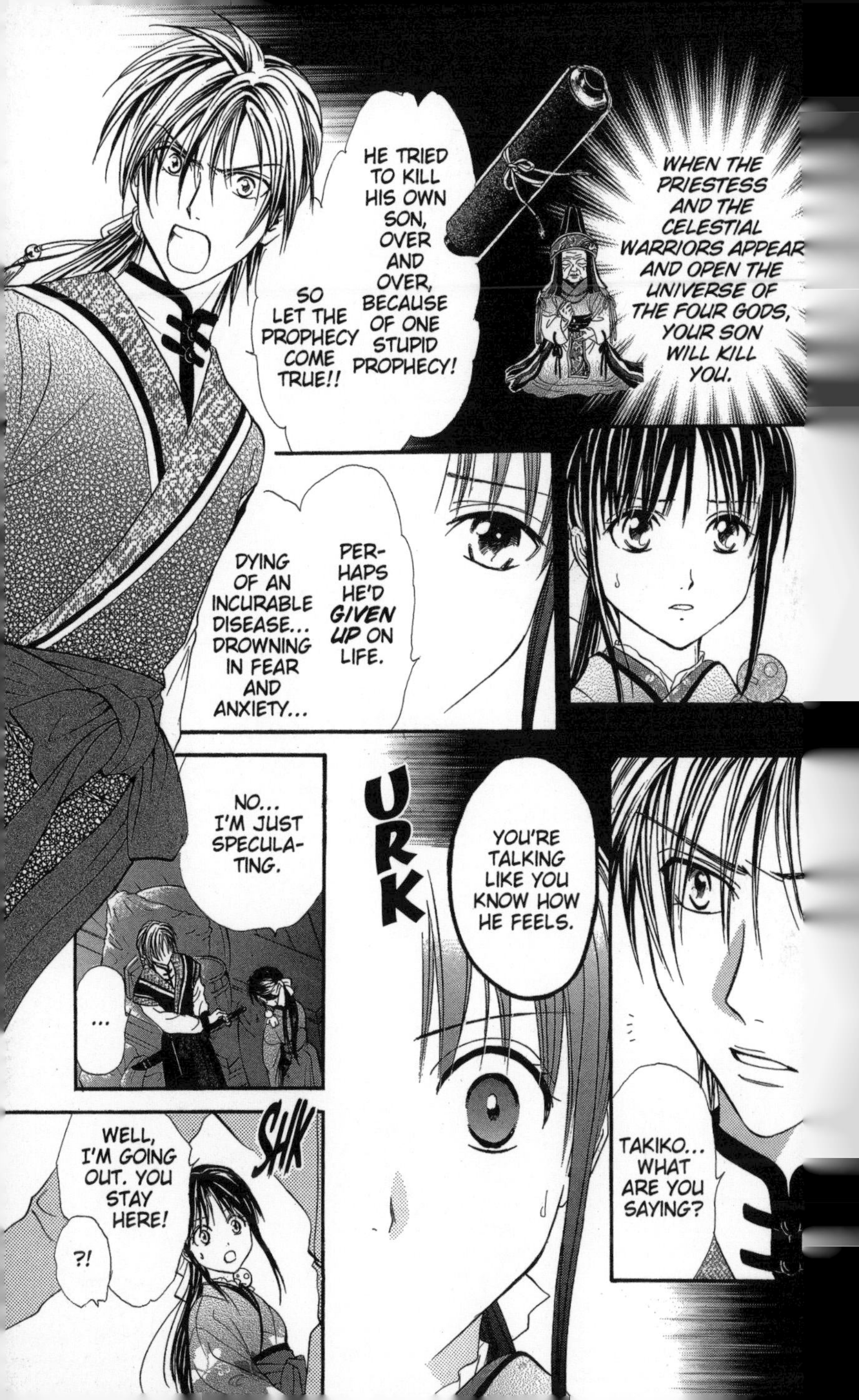
WHEN THE PRIESTESS AND THE CELESTIAL WARRIORS APPEAR AND OPEN THE UNIVERSE OF THE FOUR GODS, YOUR SON WILL KILL YOU.
HE TRIED TO KILL HIS OWN SON, OVER AND OVER, BECAUSE OF ONE STUPID PROPHECY!
SO LET THE PROPHECY COME TRUE!!
PER-HAPS HE'D *GIVEN UP* ON LIFE.
DYING OF AN INCURABLE DISEASE... DROWNING IN FEAR AND ANXIETY...
TAKIKO... WHAT ARE YOU SAYING?
YOU'RE TALKING LIKE YOU KNOW HOW HE FEELS.
URK
NO... I'M JUST SPECULA-TING.
...
SHK
WELL, I'M GOING OUT. YOU STAY HERE!
?!

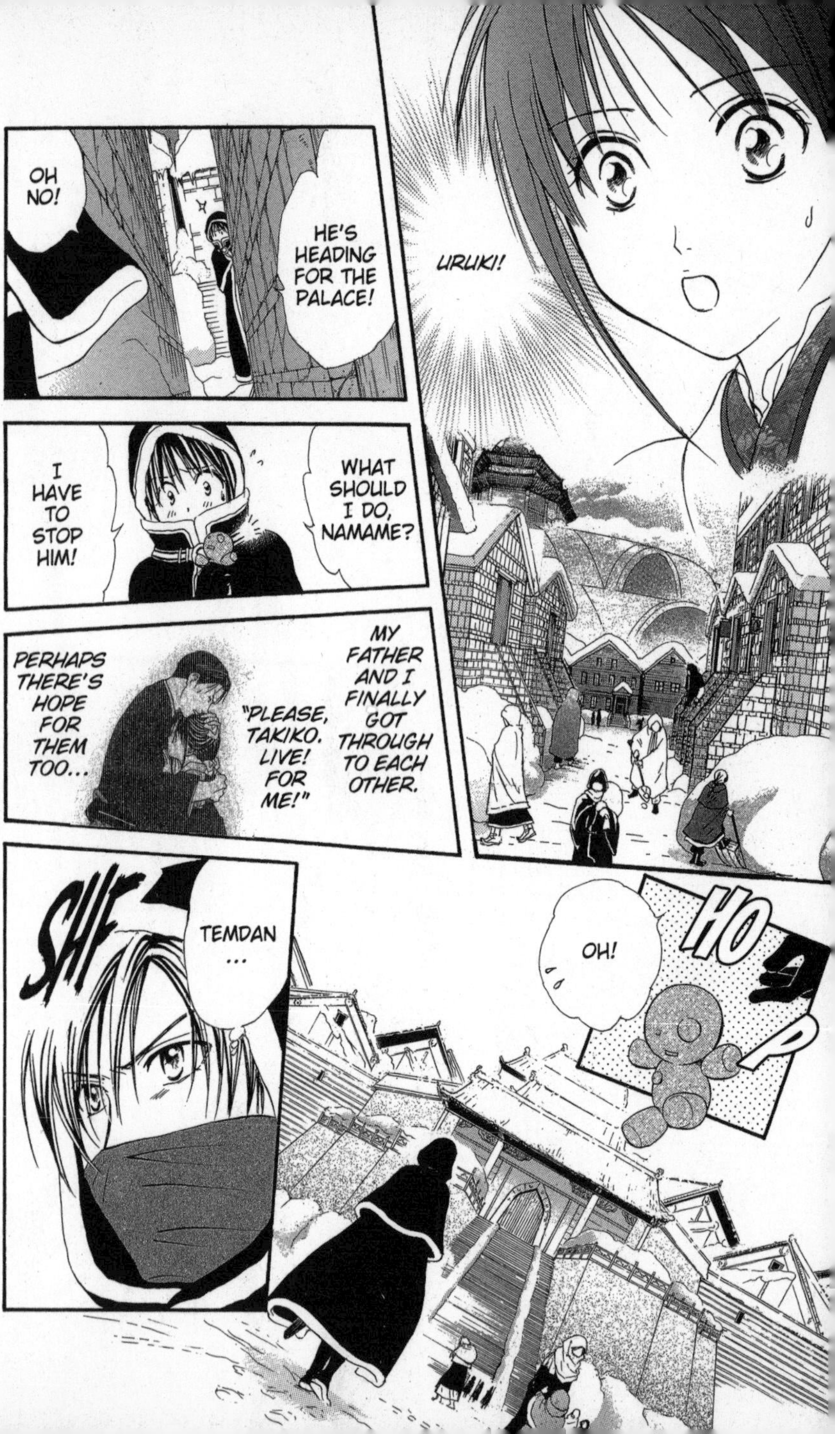
URUKI!
HE'S HEADING FOR THE PALACE!
OH NO!
WHAT SHOULD I DO, NAMAME?
I HAVE TO STOP HIM!
MY FATHER AND I FINALLY GOT THROUGH TO EACH OTHER.
"PLEASE, TAKIKO. LIVE! FOR ME!"
PERHAPS THERE'S HOPE FOR THEM TOO...
HOP
OH!
SHF
TEMDAN ...

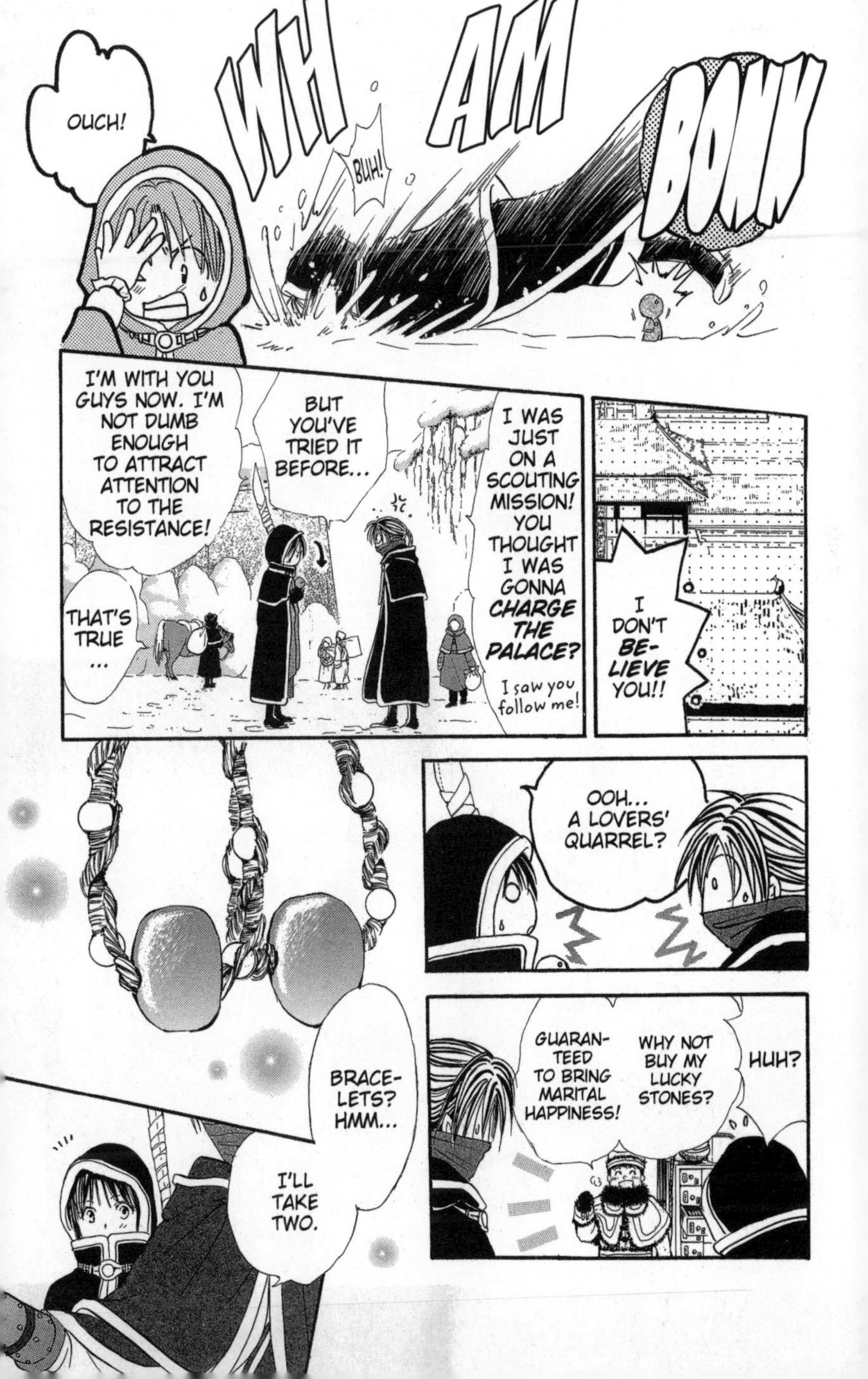

WHAM
BONK
BUH!
OUCH!
I DON'T BE-LIEVE YOU!!
I WAS JUST ON A SCOUTING MISSION! YOU THOUGHT I WAS GONNA **CHARGE THE PALACE?**
I saw you follow me!
BUT YOU'VE TRIED IT BEFORE...
I'M WITH YOU GUYS NOW. I'M NOT DUMB ENOUGH TO ATTRACT ATTENTION TO THE RESISTANCE!
THAT'S TRUE...
OOH... A LOVERS' QUARREL?
HUH?
WHY NOT BUY MY LUCKY STONES?
GUARAN-TEED TO BRING MARITAL HAPPINESS!
BRACE-LETS? HMM...
I'LL TAKE TWO.

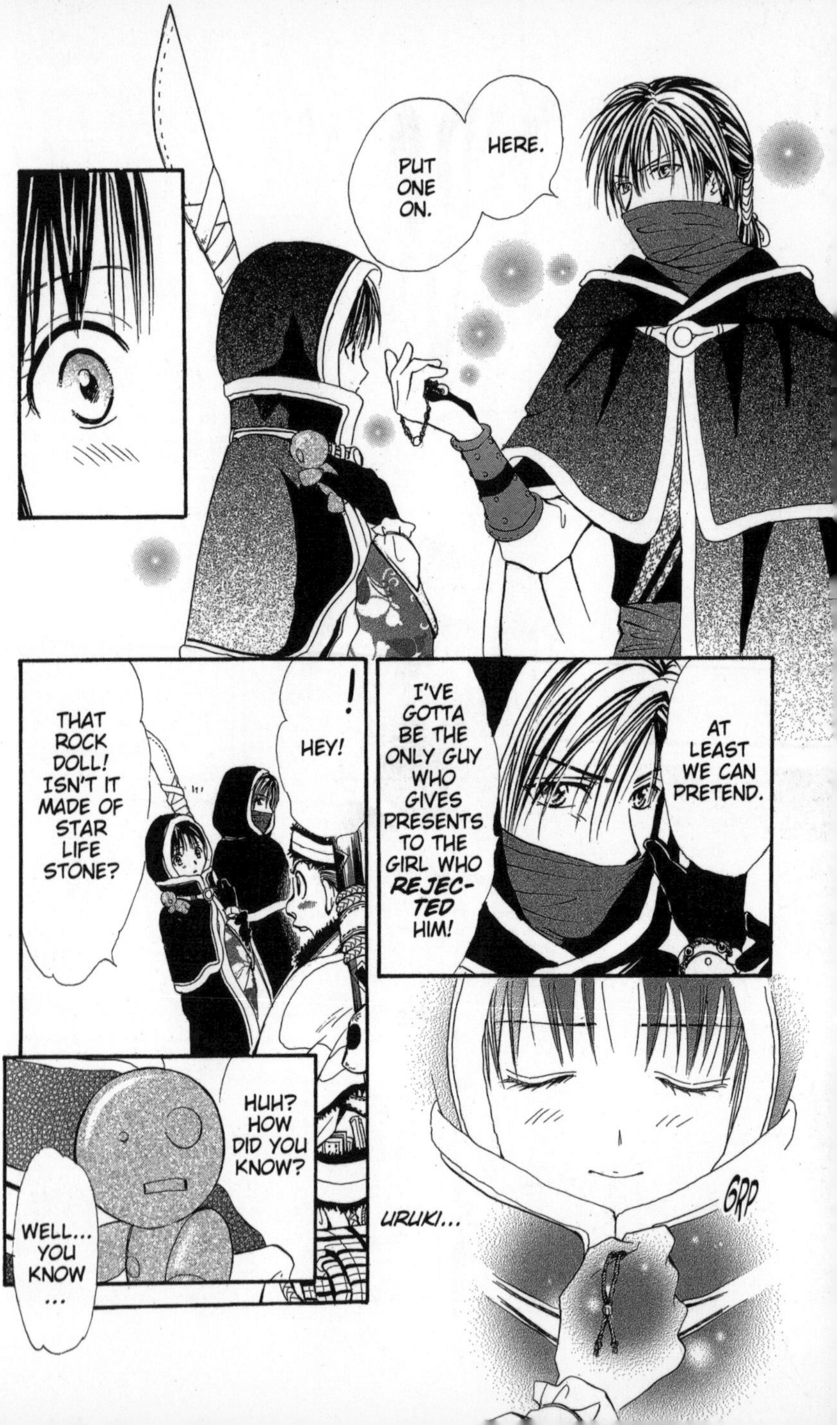
HERE.
PUT ONE ON.
AT LEAST WE CAN PRETEND.
I'VE GOTTA BE THE ONLY GUY WHO GIVES PRESENTS TO THE GIRL WHO *REJECTED* HIM!
!
HEY!
THAT ROCK DOLL! ISN'T IT MADE OF STAR LIFE STONE?
GRP
URUKI...
HUH? HOW DID YOU KNOW?
WELL... YOU KNOW ...

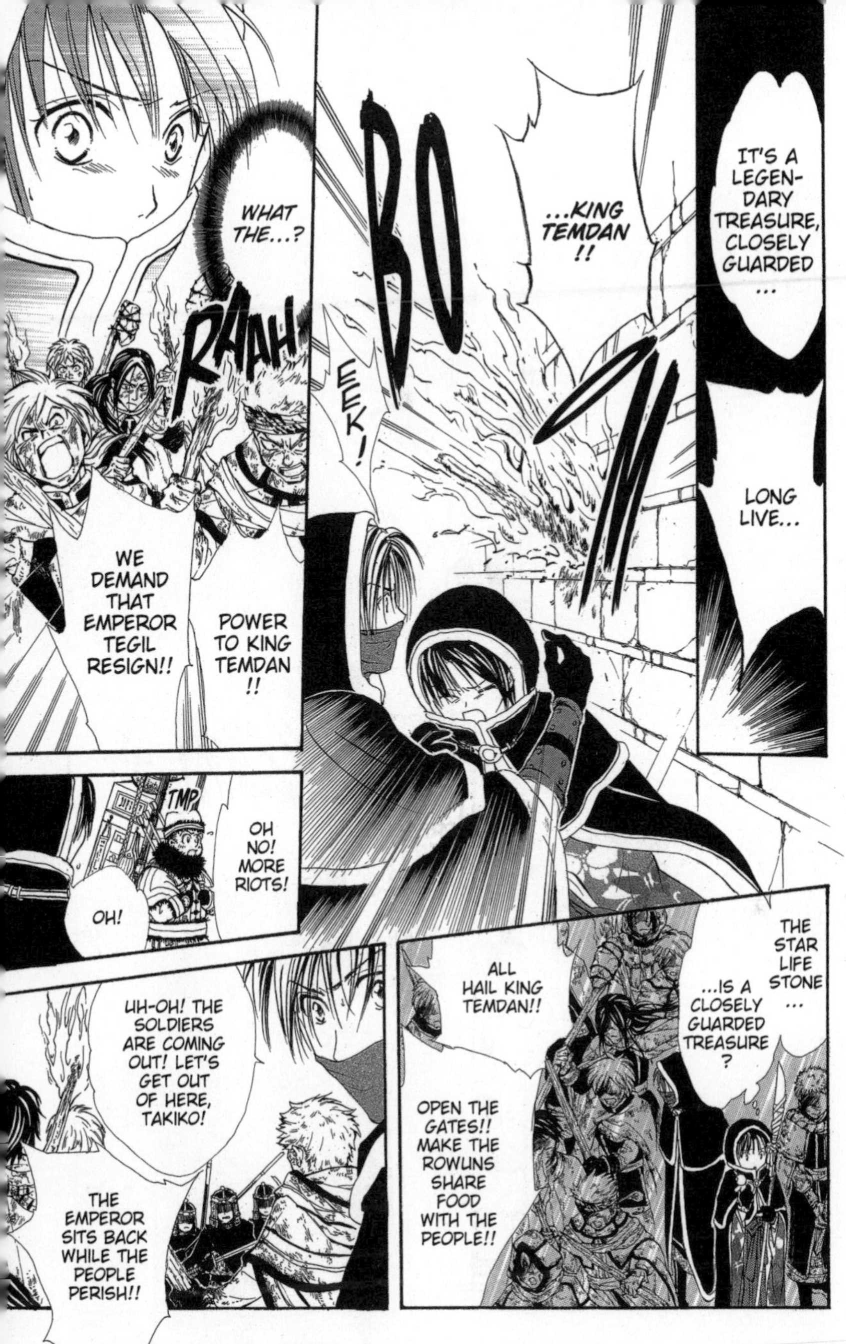
IT'S A LEGENDARY TREASURE, CLOSELY GUARDED...
LONG LIVE...
...KING TEMDAN!!
BOOM
EEK!
WHAT THE...?
RAAH
POWER TO KING TEMDAN!!
WE DEMAND THAT EMPEROR TEGIL RESIGN!!
TMP
OH NO! MORE RIOTS!
OH!
THE STAR LIFE STONE...
...IS A CLOSELY GUARDED TREASURE?
ALL HAIL KING TEMDAN!!
OPEN THE GATES!! MAKE THE ROWUNS SHARE FOOD WITH THE PEOPLE!!
UH-OH! THE SOLDIERS ARE COMING OUT! LET'S GET OUT OF HERE, TAKIKO!
THE EMPEROR SITS BACK WHILE THE PEOPLE PERISH!!

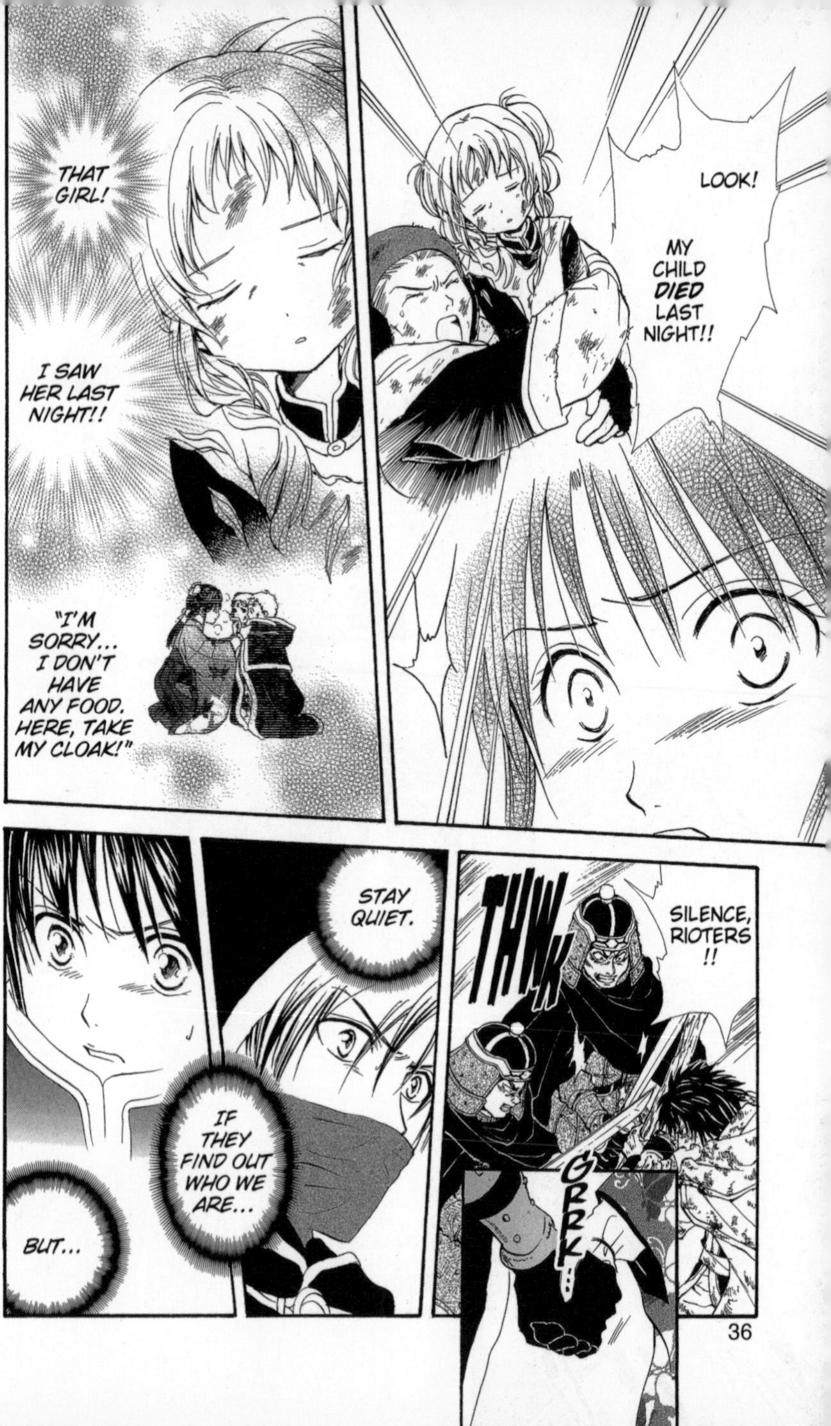
LOOK!
MY CHILD DIED LAST NIGHT!!
THAT GIRL!
I SAW HER LAST NIGHT!!
"I'M SORRY... I DON'T HAVE ANY FOOD. HERE, TAKE MY CLOAK!"
THNK
SILENCE, RIOTERS!!
GRRK...
STAY QUIET.
IF THEY FIND OUT WHO WE ARE...
BUT...

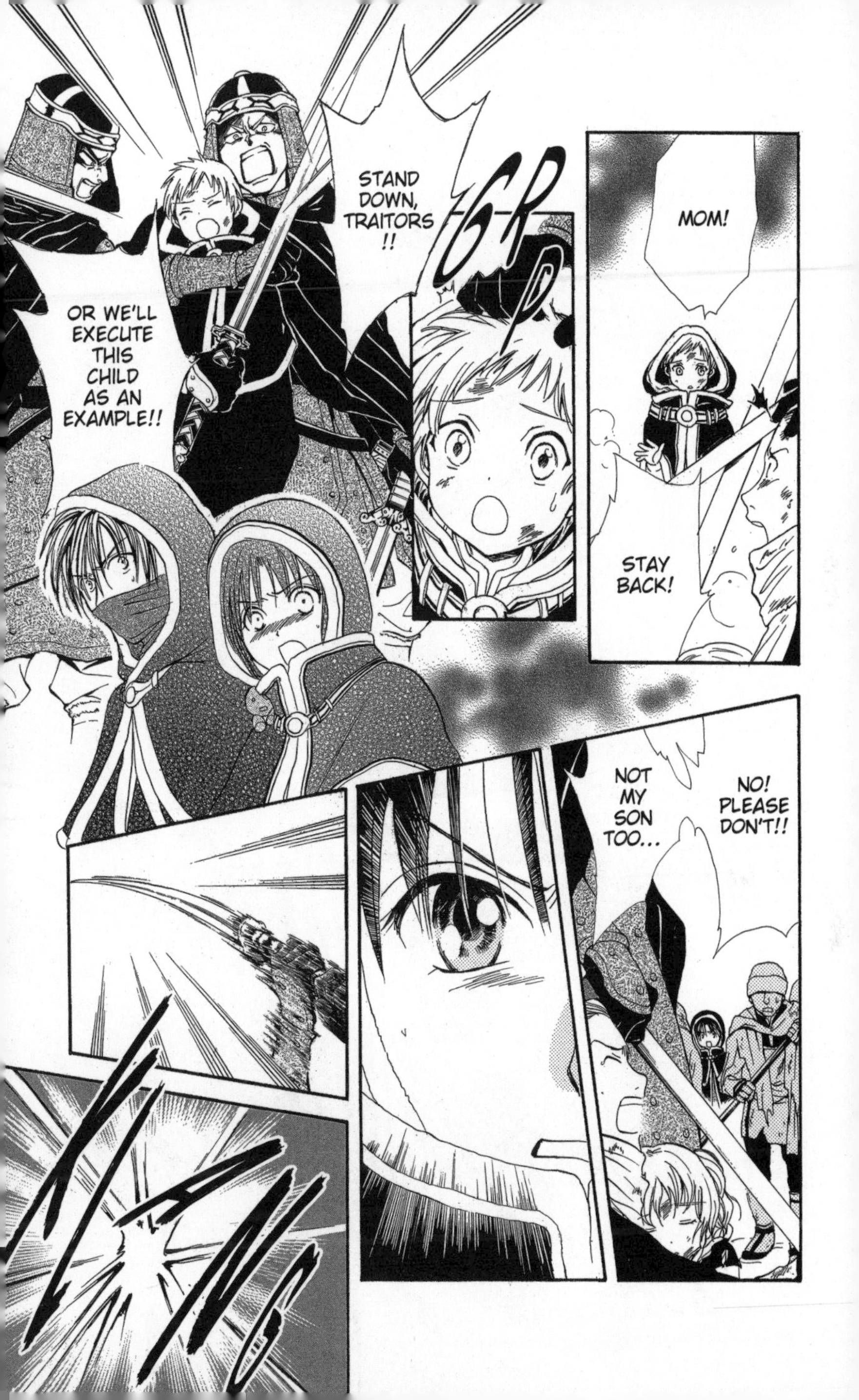
MOM!
STAY BACK!
STAND DOWN, TRAITORS!!
OR WE'LL EXECUTE THIS CHILD AS AN EXAMPLE!!
NO! PLEASE DON'T!!
NOT MY SON TOO...

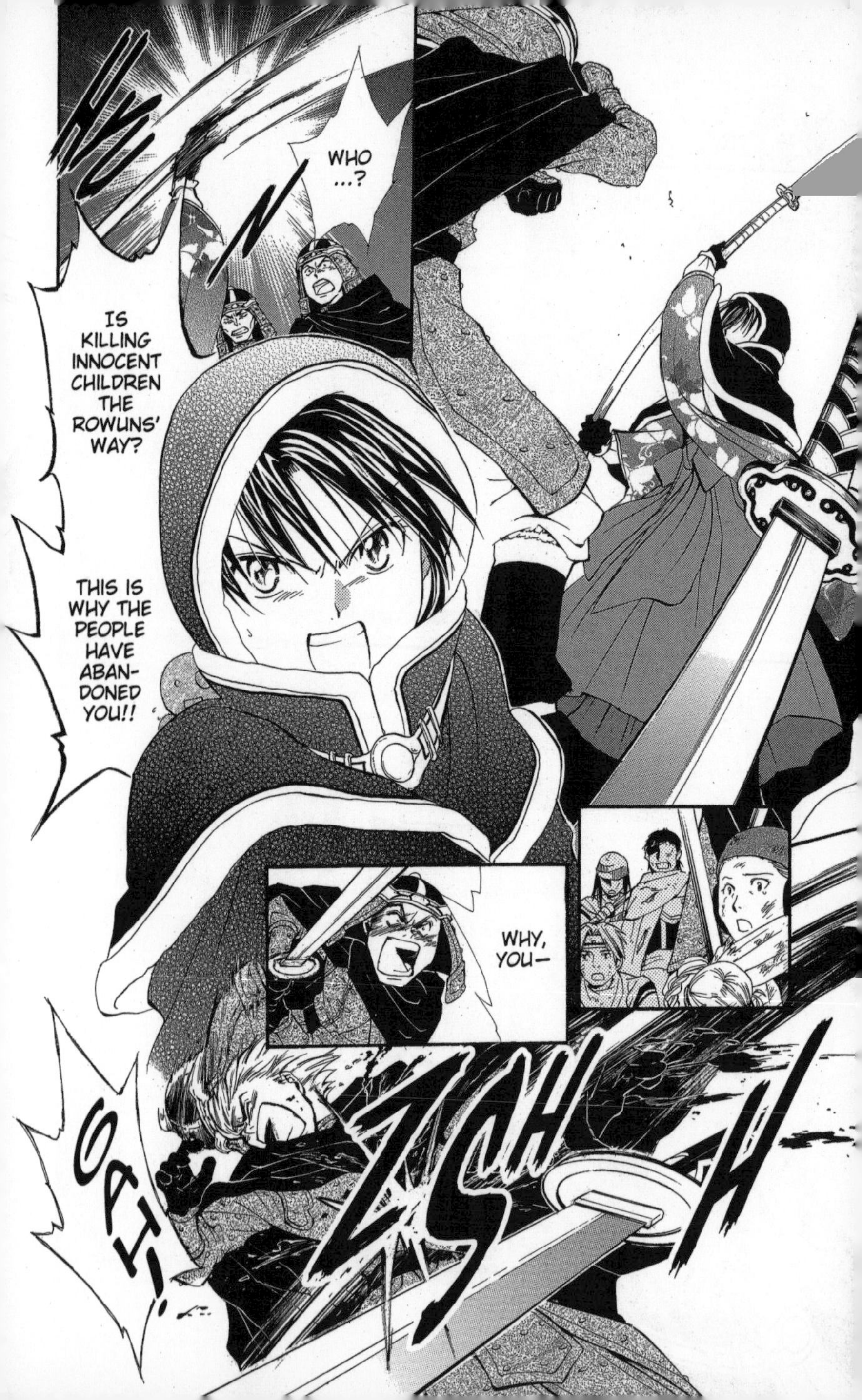
HYUN
WHO ...?
IS KILLING INNOCENT CHILDREN THE ROWUNS' WAY?
THIS IS WHY THE PEOPLE HAVE ABAN-DONED YOU!!
WHY, YOU—
ZSHH
GAH!

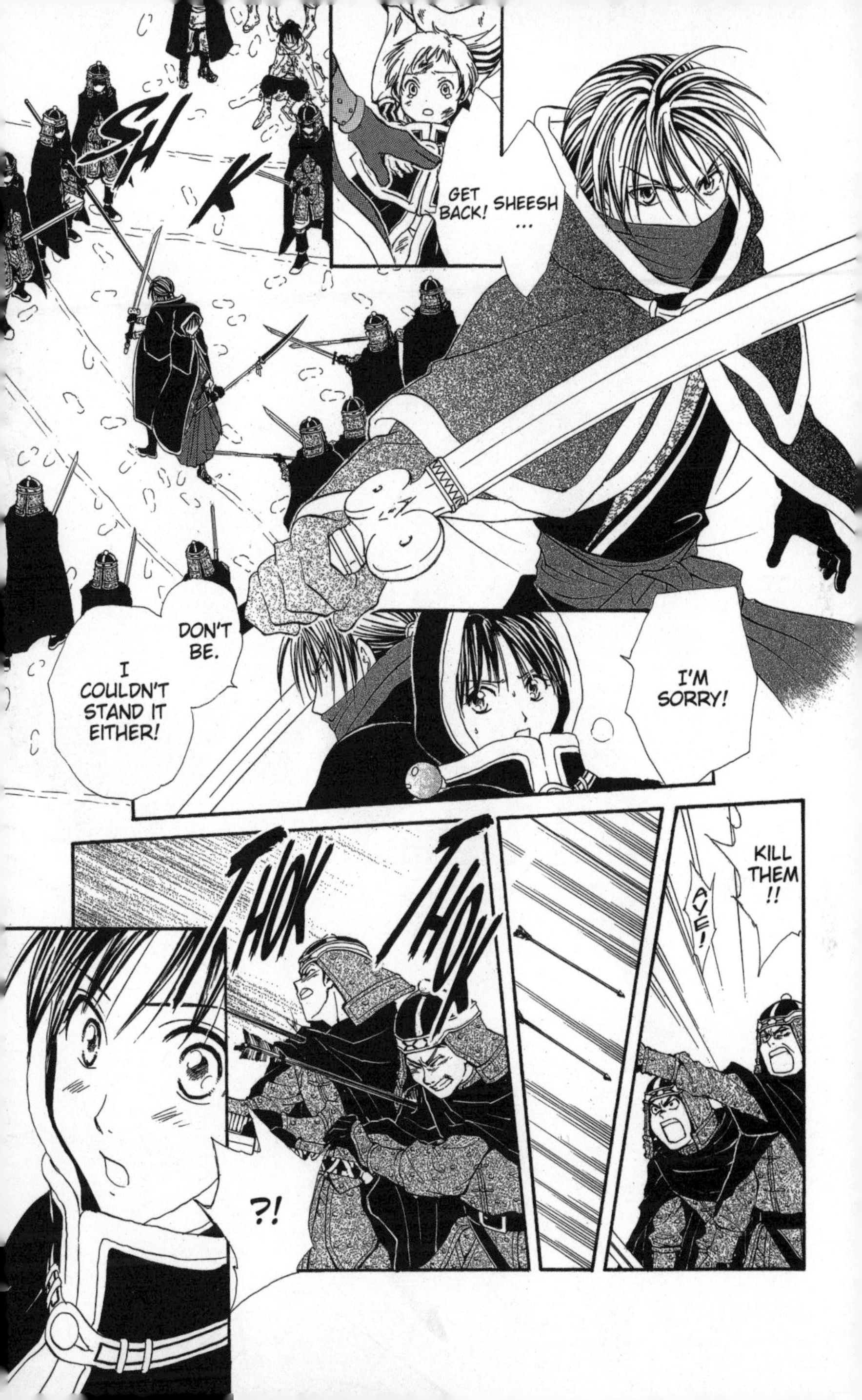
SHEESH
...
GET BACK!
SHK
I'M SORRY!
DON'T BE.
I COULDN'T STAND IT EITHER!
KILL THEM!!
AYE!
THOK
THOK
?!

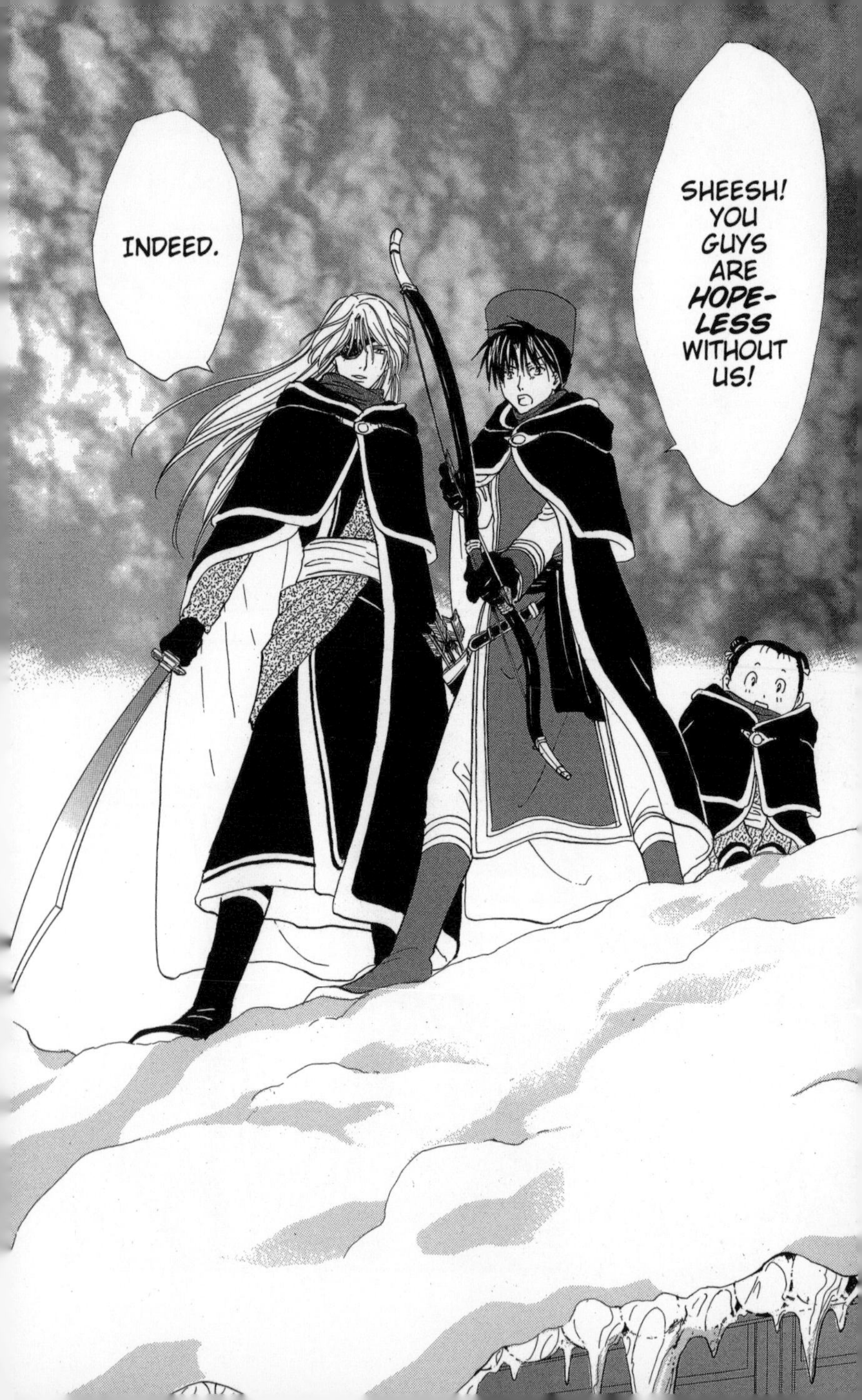
SHEESH! YOU GUYS ARE HOPE-LESS WITHOUT US!
INDEED.

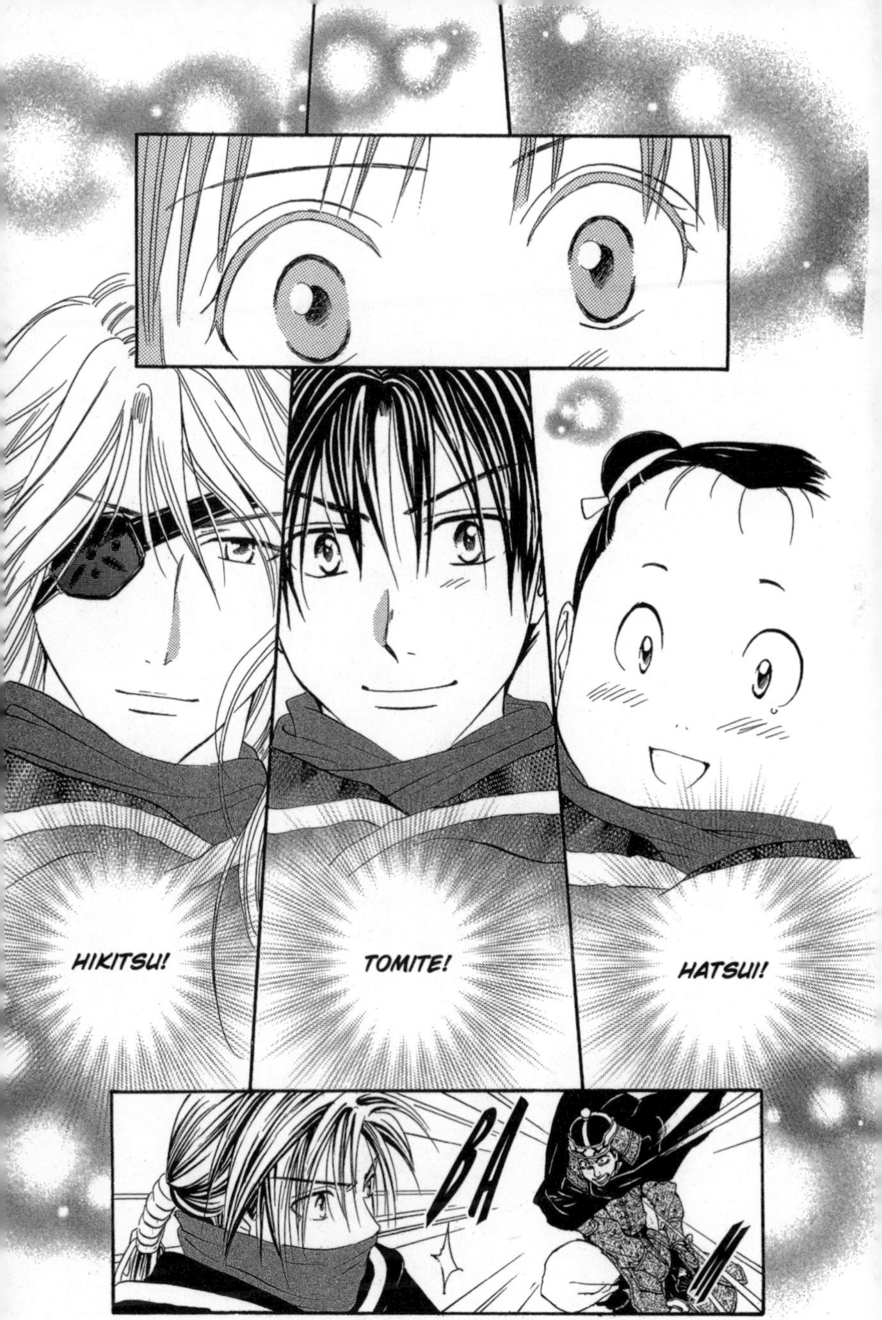
HATSUI!
TOMITE!
HIKITSU!
BA

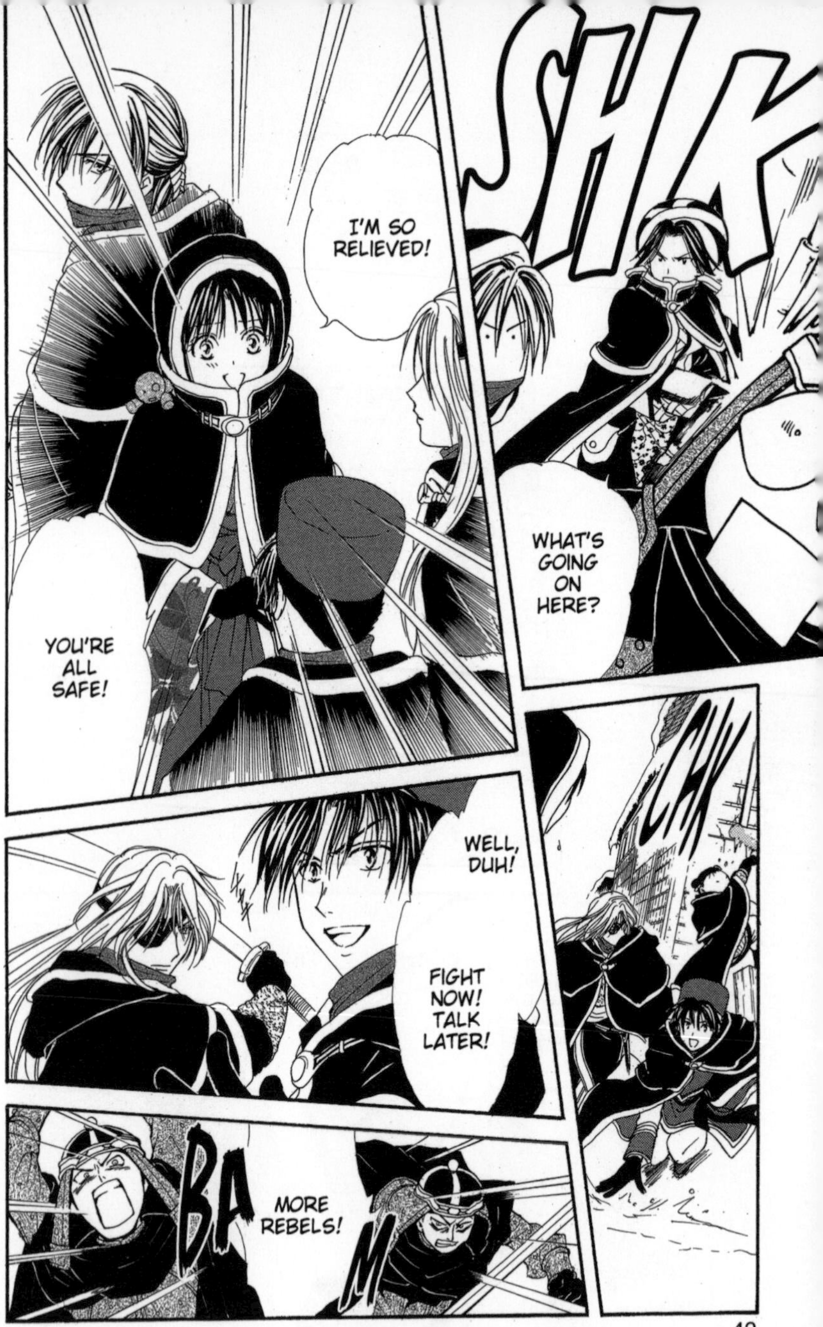
SHK
WHAT'S GOING ON HERE?
I'M SO RELIEVED!
YOU'RE ALL SAFE!
CHK
WELL, DUH!
FIGHT NOW! TALK LATER!
BAM
MORE REBELS!

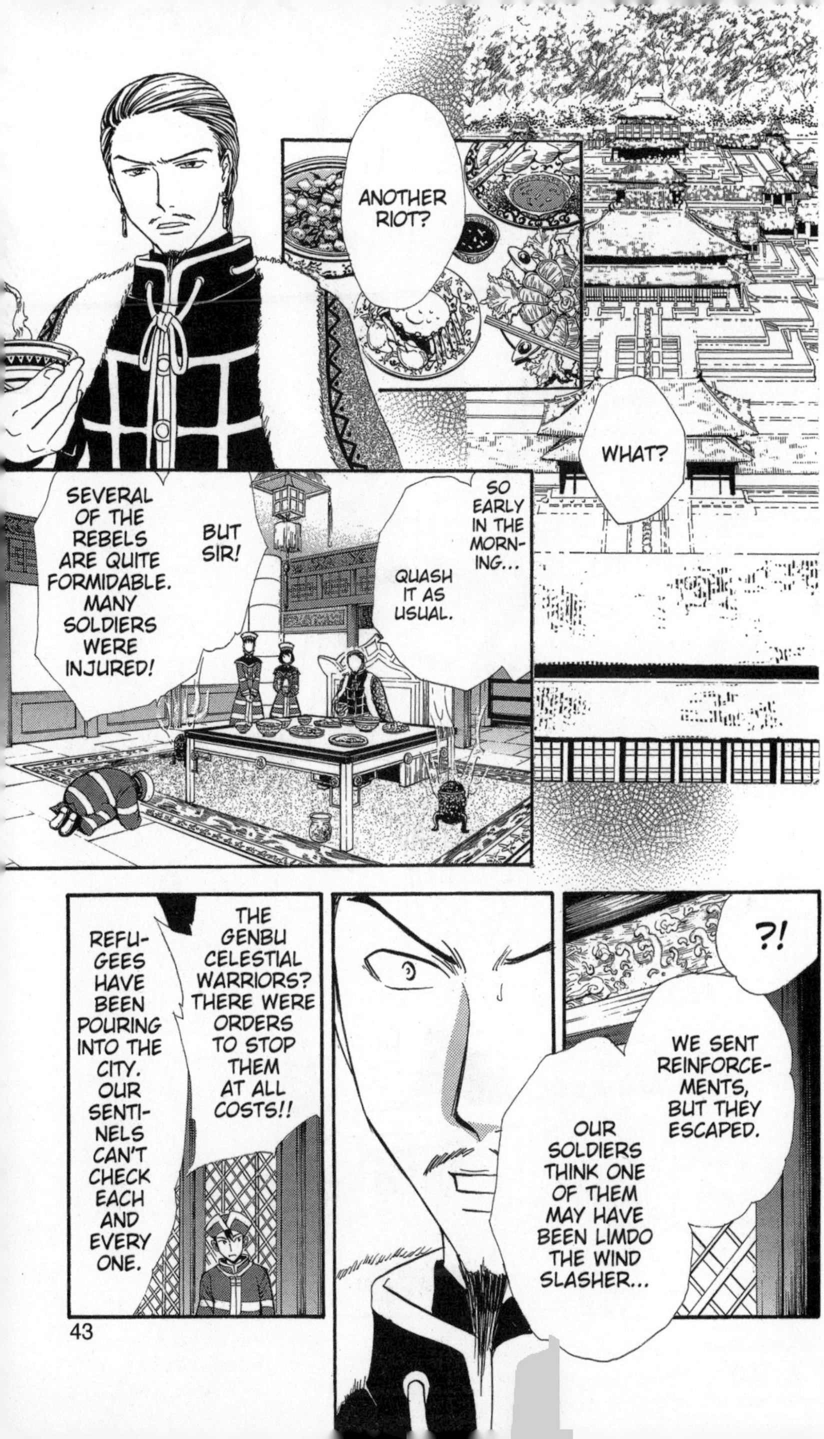
WHAT?
ANOTHER RIOT?
SO EARLY IN THE MORNING...
QUASH IT AS USUAL.
BUT SIR!
SEVERAL OF THE REBELS ARE QUITE FORMIDABLE. MANY SOLDIERS WERE INJURED!
?!
WE SENT REINFORCEMENTS, BUT THEY ESCAPED.
OUR SOLDIERS THINK ONE OF THEM MAY HAVE BEEN LIMDO THE WIND SLASHER...
THE GENBU CELESTIAL WARRIORS? THERE WERE ORDERS TO STOP THEM AT ALL COSTS!!
REFUGEES HAVE BEEN POURING INTO THE CITY. OUR SENTINELS CAN'T CHECK EACH AND EVERY ONE.

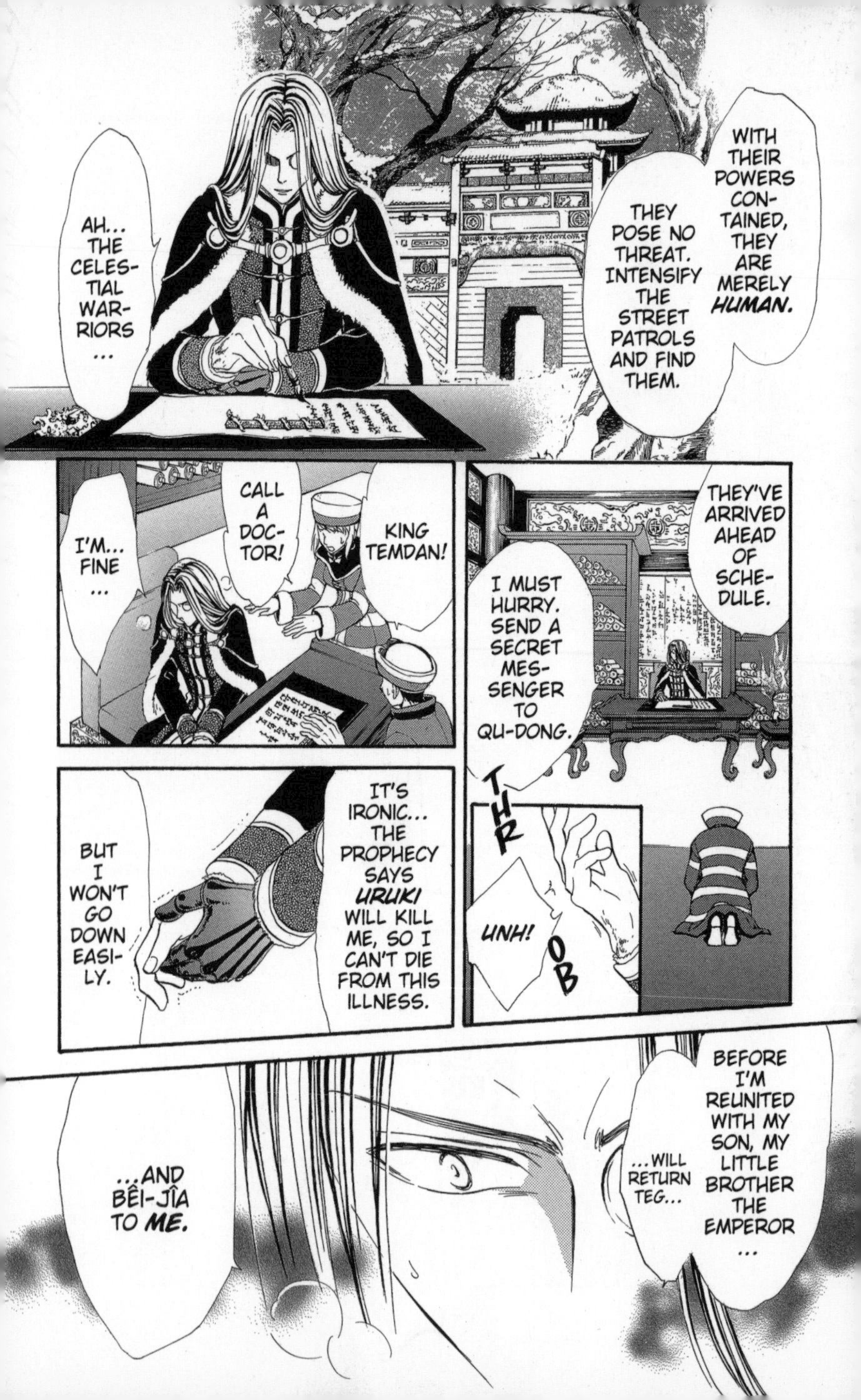

WITH THEIR POWERS CON-TAINED, THEY ARE MERELY *HUMAN.*
THEY POSE NO THREAT. INTENSIFY THE STREET PATROLS AND FIND THEM.
AH... THE CELES-TIAL WAR-RIORS...
THEY'VE ARRIVED AHEAD OF SCHE-DULE.
I MUST HURRY. SEND A SECRET MES-SENGER TO QU-DONG.
KING TEMDAN!
CALL A DOC-TOR!
I'M... FINE...
THROB
UNH!
IT'S IRONIC... THE PROPHECY SAYS *URUKI* WILL KILL ME, SO I CAN'T DIE FROM THIS ILLNESS.
BUT I WON'T GO DOWN EASI-LY.
BEFORE I'M REUNITED WITH MY SON, MY LITTLE BROTHER THE EMPEROR...
...WILL RETURN TEG...
...AND BÊI-JÎA TO *ME.*

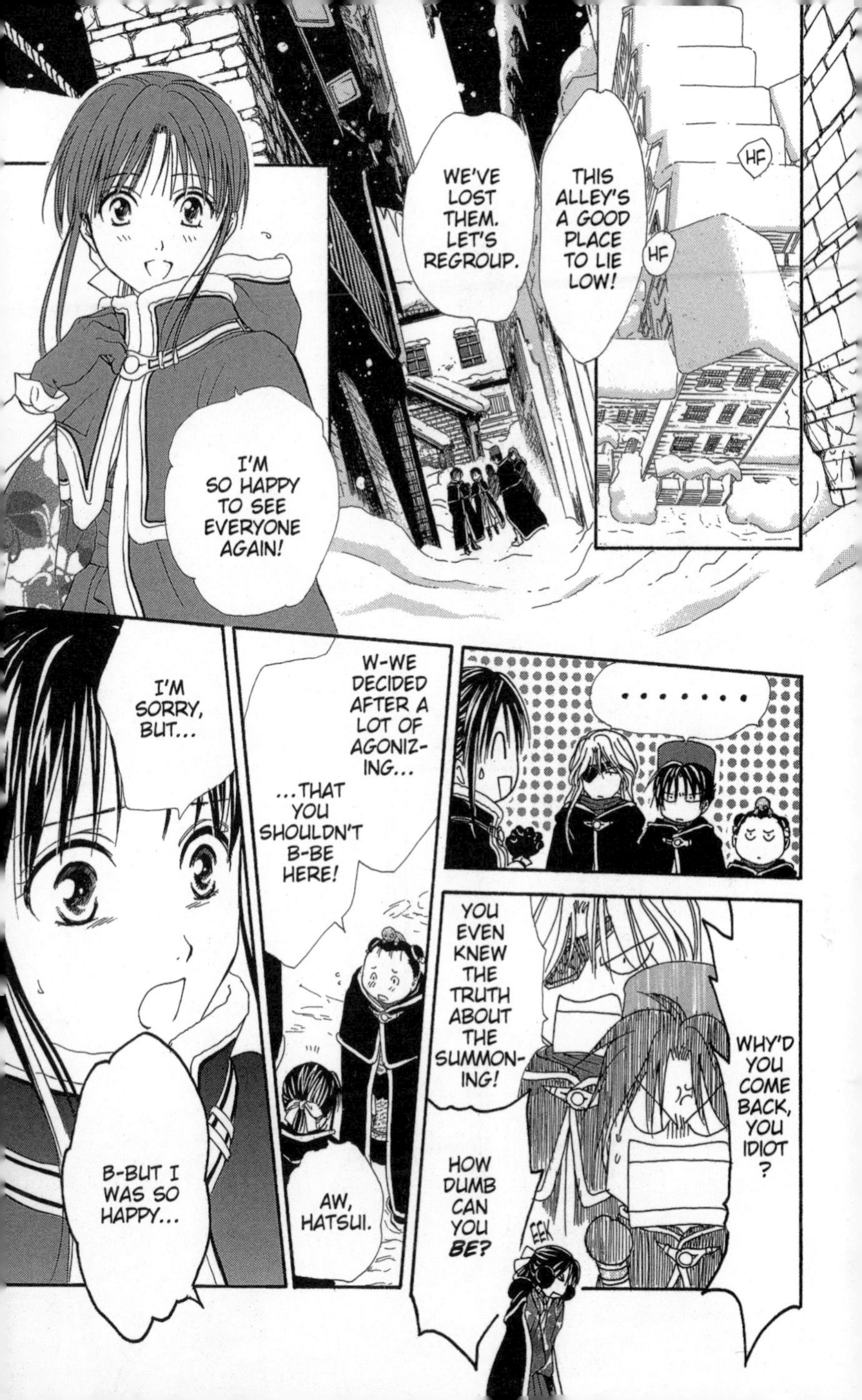

HF
HF
THIS ALLEY'S A GOOD PLACE TO LIE LOW!
WE'VE LOST THEM. LET'S REGROUP.
I'M SO HAPPY TO SEE EVERYONE AGAIN!
....
WHY'D YOU COME BACK, YOU IDIOT?
YOU EVEN KNEW THE TRUTH ABOUT THE SUMMON-ING!
HOW DUMB CAN YOU *BE?*
EEK
W-WE DECIDED AFTER A LOT OF AGONIZ-ING...
...THAT YOU SHOULDN'T B-BE HERE!
AW, HATSUI.
I'M SORRY, BUT...
B-BUT I WAS SO HAPPY...

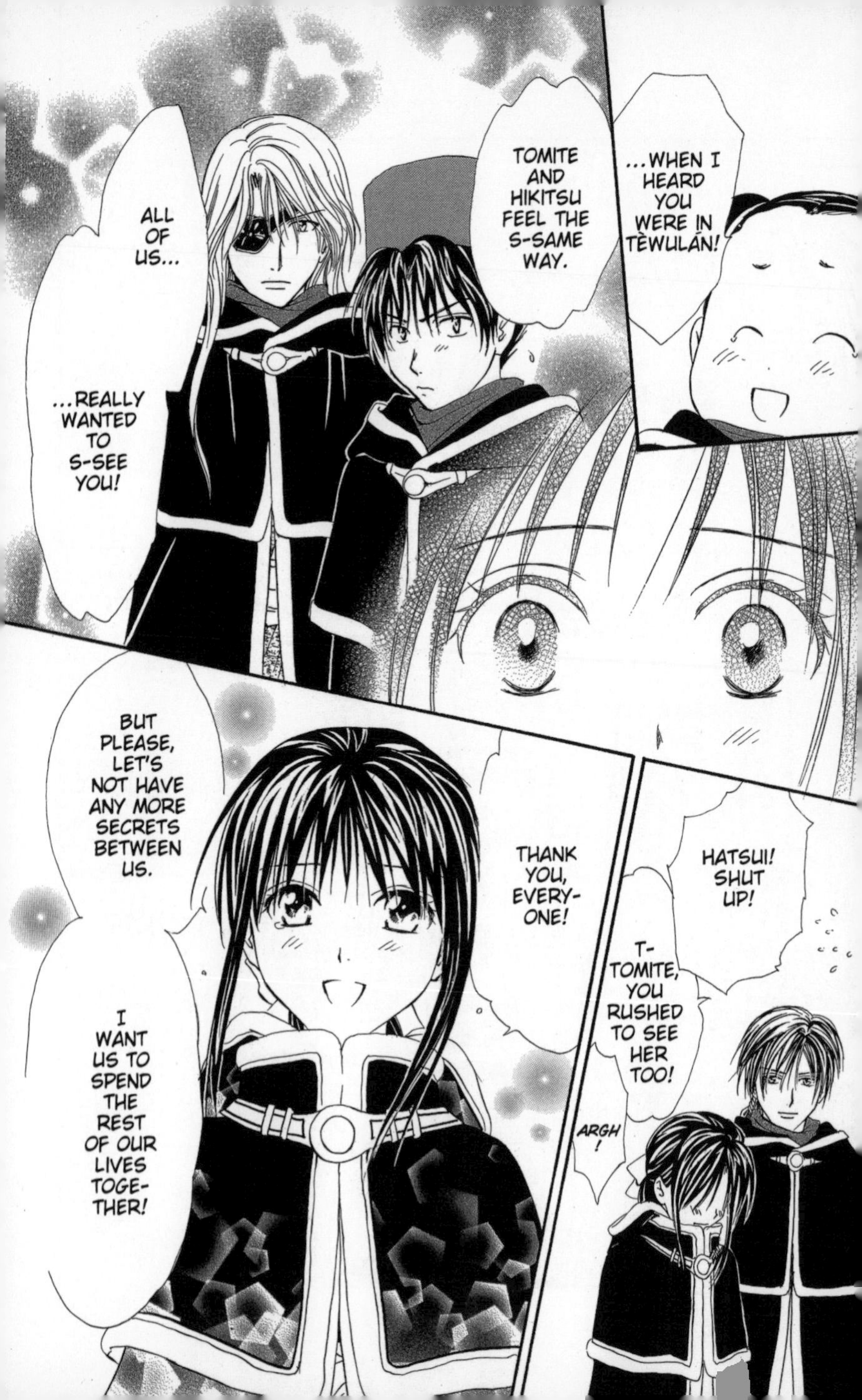
...WHEN I HEARD YOU WERE IN TÈWULÁN!
TOMITE AND HIKITSU FEEL THE S-SAME WAY.
ALL OF US...
...REALLY WANTED TO S-SEE YOU!
HATSUI! SHUT UP!
T-TOMITE, YOU RUSHED TO SEE HER TOO!
ARGH!
THANK YOU, EVERYONE!
BUT PLEASE, LET'S NOT HAVE ANY MORE SECRETS BETWEEN US.
I WANT US TO SPEND THE REST OF OUR LIVES TOGETHER!

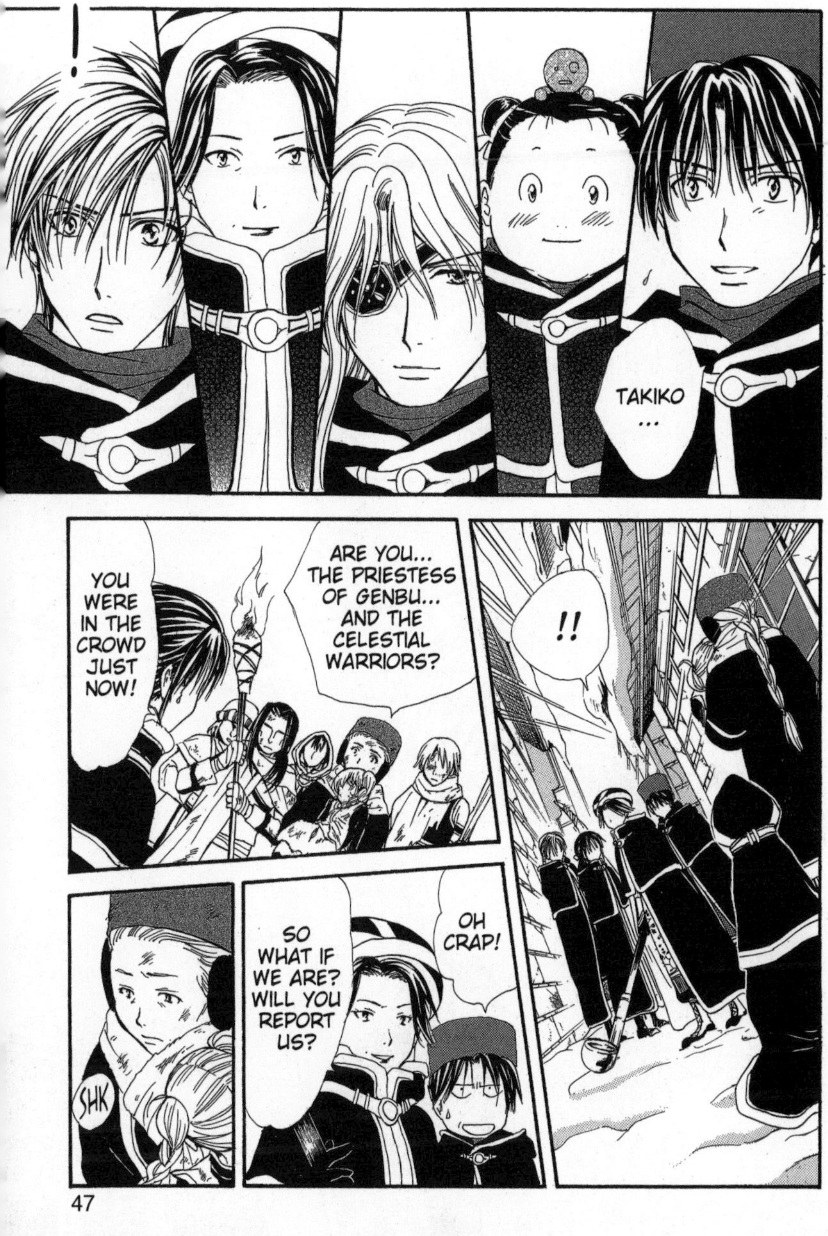
TAKIKO ...
!
!!
ARE YOU... THE PRIESTESS OF GENBU... AND THE CELESTIAL WARRIORS?
YOU WERE IN THE CROWD JUST NOW!
OH CRAP!
SO WHAT IF WE ARE? WILL YOU REPORT US?
SHK

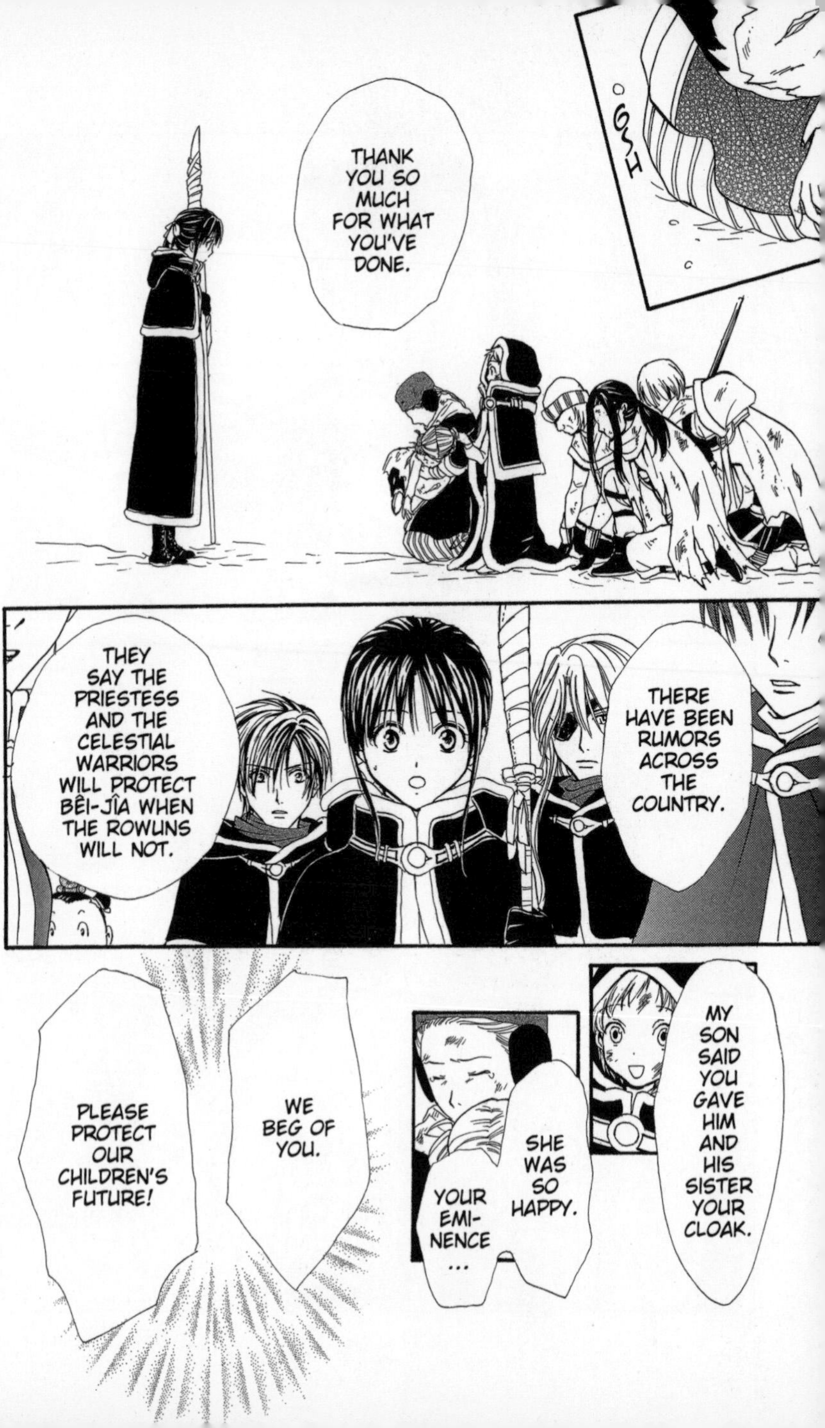
THANK YOU SO MUCH FOR WHAT YOU'VE DONE.
THERE HAVE BEEN RUMORS ACROSS THE COUNTRY.
THEY SAY THE PRIESTESS AND THE CELESTIAL WARRIORS WILL PROTECT BÊI-JÎA WHEN THE ROWUNS WILL NOT.
MY SON SAID YOU GAVE HIM AND HIS SISTER YOUR CLOAK.
SHE WAS SO HAPPY.
YOUR EMI-NENCE...
WE BEG OF YOU.
PLEASE PROTECT OUR CHILDREN'S FUTURE!

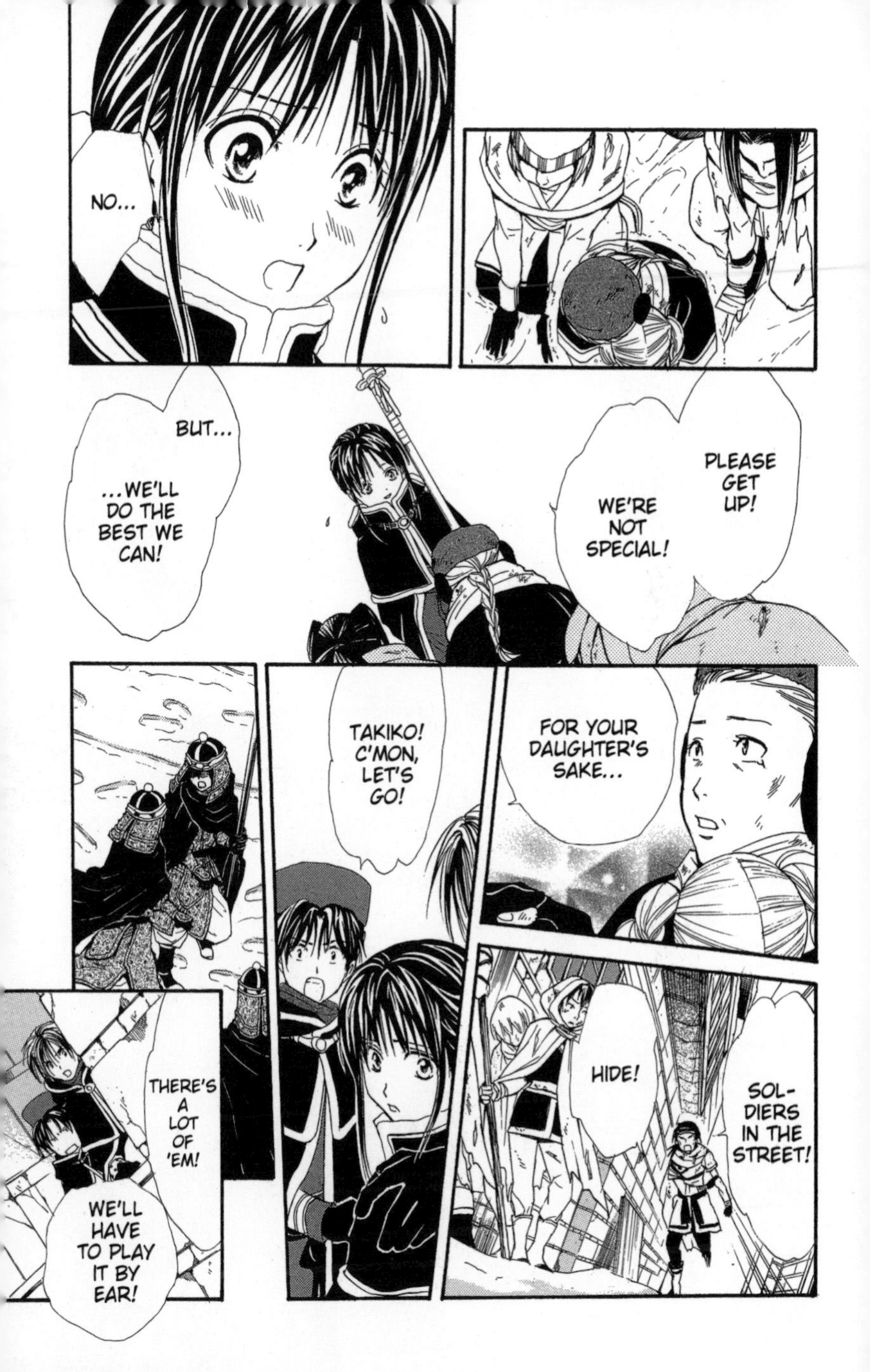
NO...
PLEASE GET UP!
WE'RE NOT SPECIAL!
BUT...
...WE'LL DO THE BEST WE CAN!
FOR YOUR DAUGHTER'S SAKE...
TAKIKO! C'MON, LET'S GO!
SOL-DIERS IN THE STREET!
HIDE!
THERE'S A LOT OF 'EM!
WE'LL HAVE TO PLAY IT BY EAR!

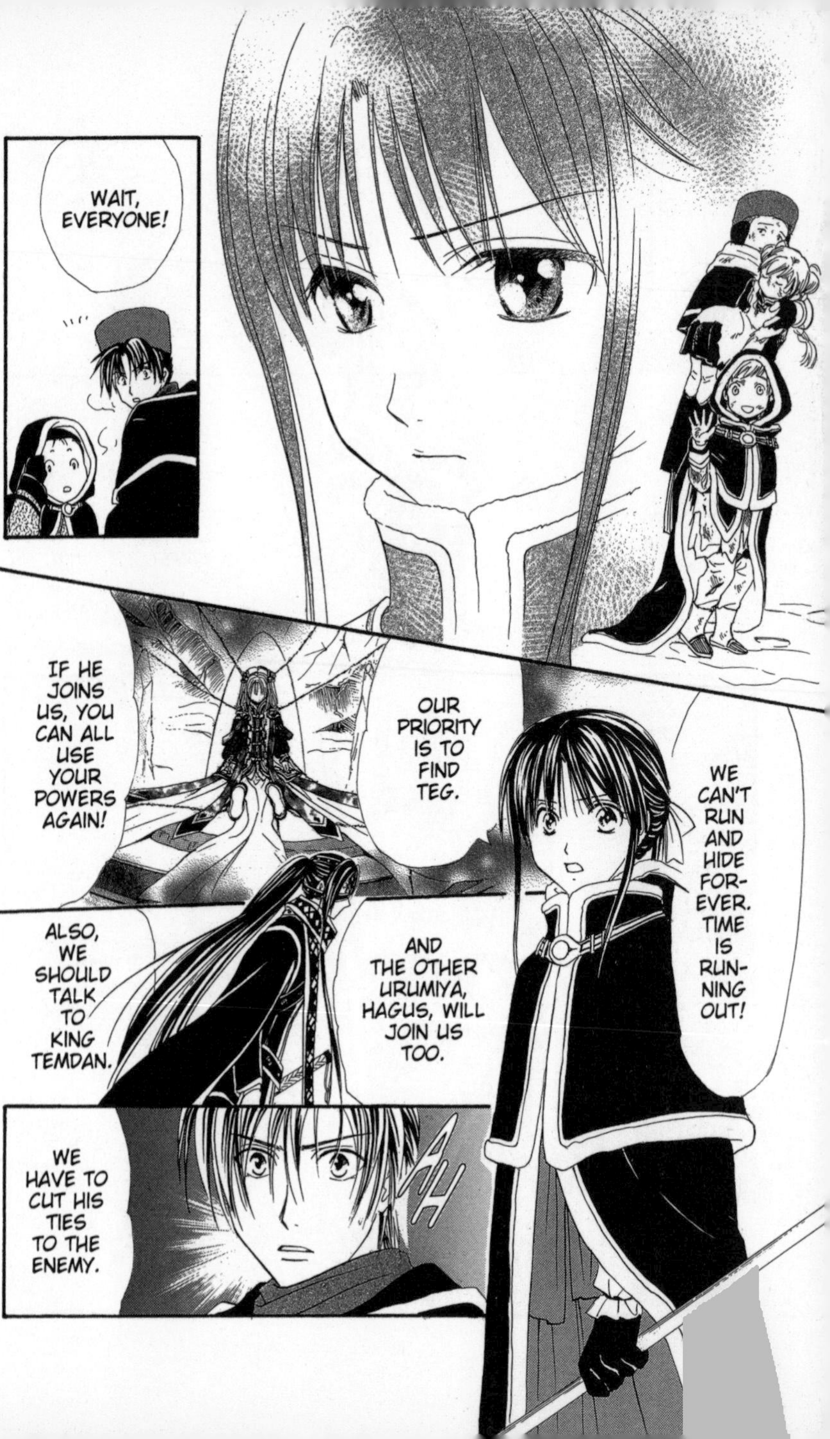
WAIT, EVERYONE!
WE CAN'T RUN AND HIDE FOR-EVER. TIME IS RUN-NING OUT!
OUR PRIORITY IS TO FIND TEG.
IF HE JOINS US, YOU CAN ALL USE YOUR POWERS AGAIN!
AND THE OTHER URUMIYA, HAGUS, WILL JOIN US TOO.
ALSO, WE SHOULD TALK TO KING TEMDAN.
AH
WE HAVE TO CUT HIS TIES TO THE ENEMY.

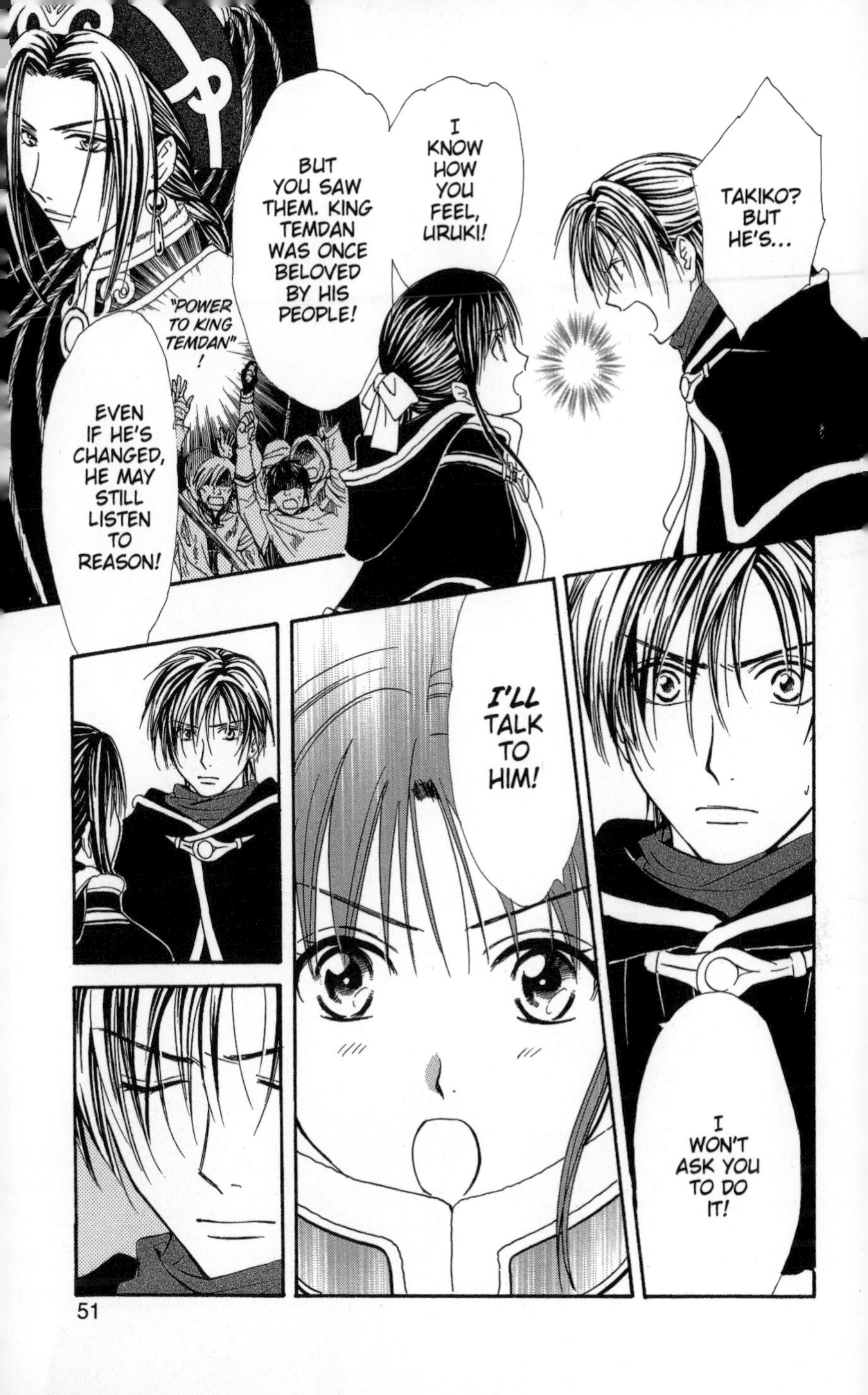
TAKIKO? BUT HE'S...
I KNOW HOW YOU FEEL, URUKI!
BUT YOU SAW THEM. KING TEMDAN WAS ONCE BELOVED BY HIS PEOPLE!
"POWER TO KING TEMDAN"!
EVEN IF HE'S CHANGED, HE MAY STILL LISTEN TO REASON!
I WON'T ASK YOU TO DO IT!
I'LL TALK TO HIM!

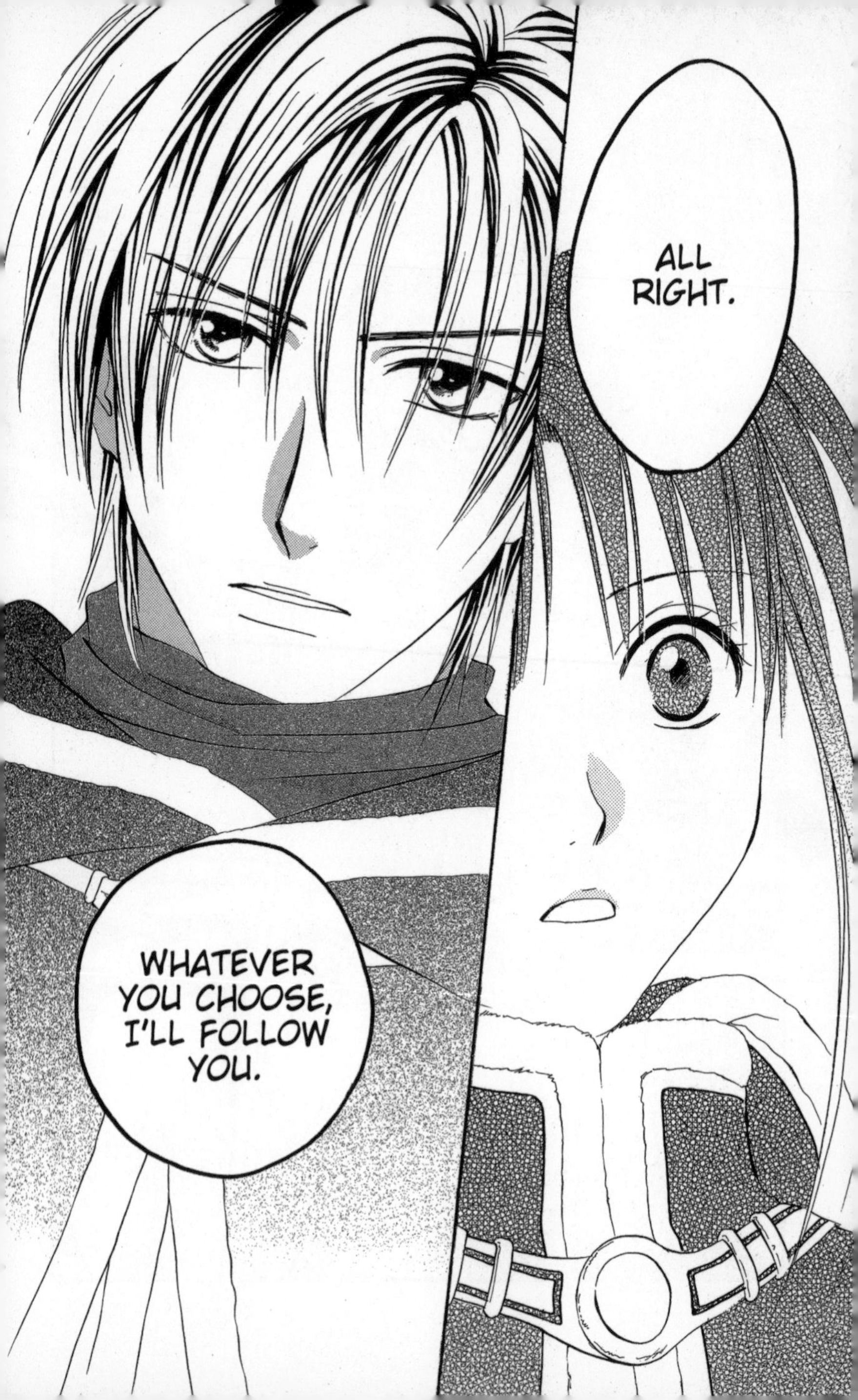
ALL RIGHT.
WHATEVER YOU CHOOSE, I'LL FOLLOW YOU.

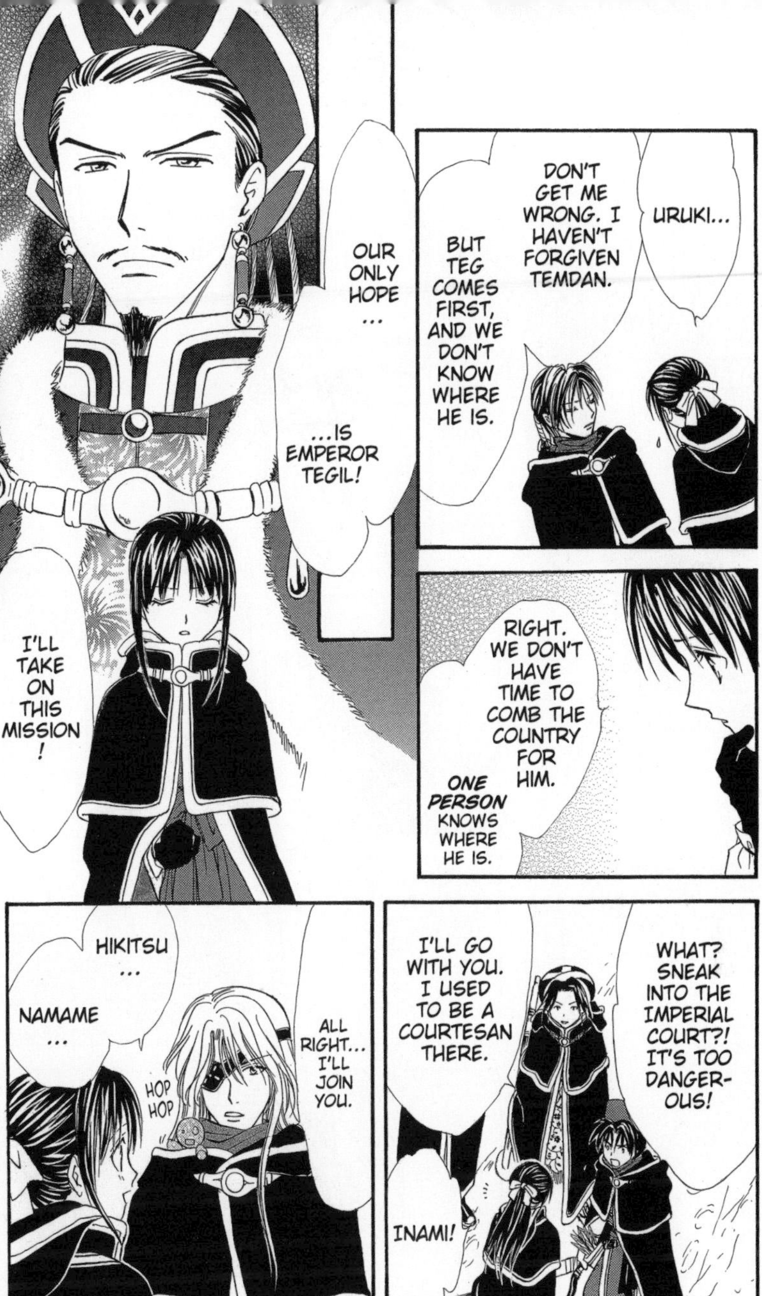
URUKI...
DON'T GET ME WRONG. I HAVEN'T FORGIVEN TEMDAN.
BUT TEG COMES FIRST, AND WE DON'T KNOW WHERE HE IS.
RIGHT. WE DON'T HAVE TIME TO COMB THE COUNTRY FOR HIM.
ONE PERSON KNOWS WHERE HE IS.
OUR ONLY HOPE...
...IS EMPEROR TEGIL!
I'LL TAKE ON THIS MISSION!
WHAT? SNEAK INTO THE IMPERIAL COURT?! IT'S TOO DANGEROUS!
I'LL GO WITH YOU. I USED TO BE A COURTESAN THERE.
INAMI!
ALL RIGHT... I'LL JOIN YOU.
HIKITSU...
NAMAME...
HOP HOP

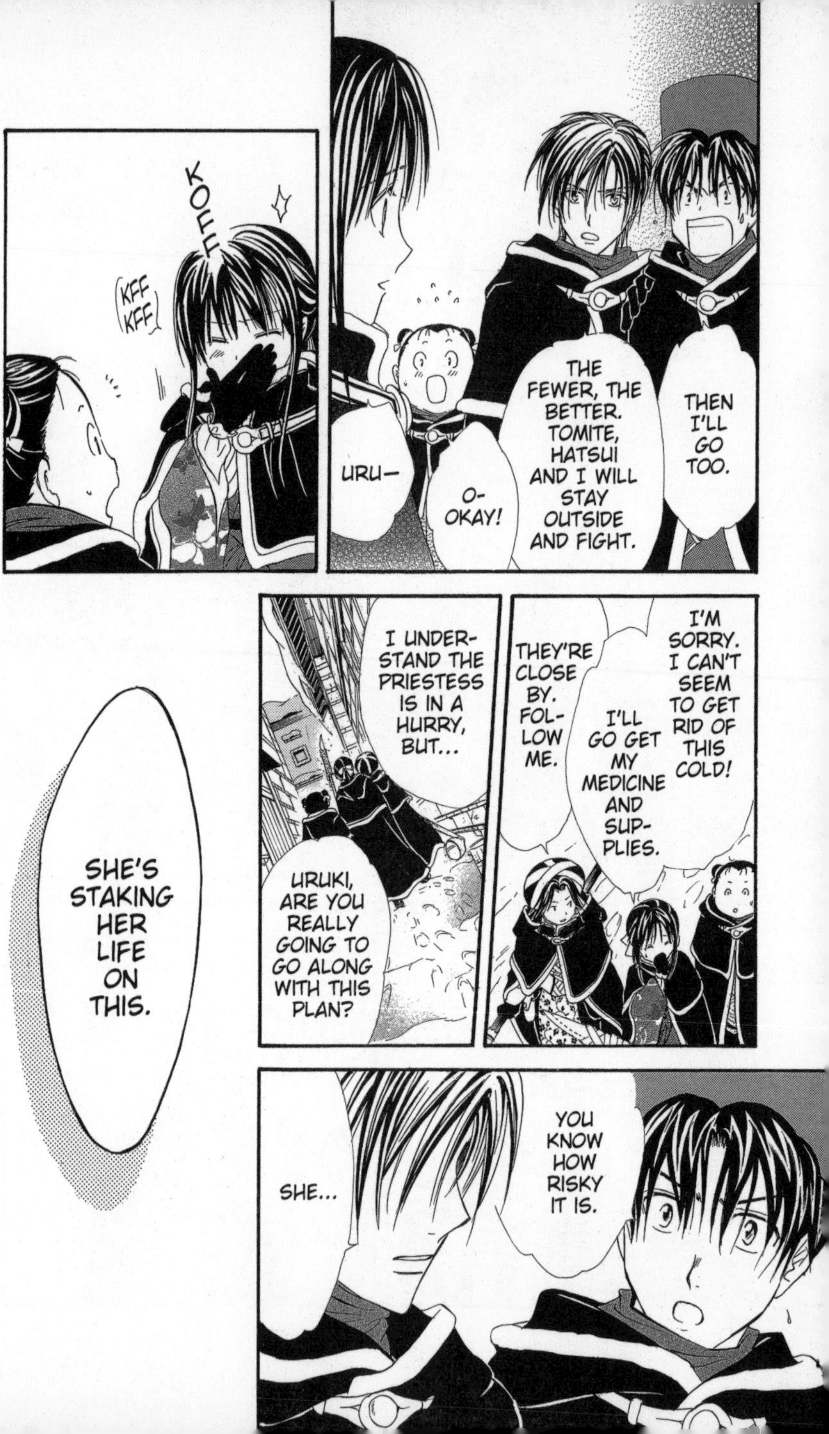
THEN I'LL GO TOO.
THE FEWER, THE BETTER. TOMITE, HATSUI AND I WILL STAY OUTSIDE AND FIGHT.
O-OKAY!
URU—
KOFF
KFF KFF
I'M SORRY. I CAN'T SEEM TO GET RID OF THIS COLD!
I'LL GO GET MY MEDICINE AND SUPPLIES.
THEY'RE CLOSE BY. FOL-LOW ME.
I UNDER-STAND THE PRIESTESS IS IN A HURRY, BUT...
URUKI, ARE YOU REALLY GOING TO GO ALONG WITH THIS PLAN?
YOU KNOW HOW RISKY IT IS.
SHE...
SHE'S STAKING HER LIFE ON THIS.

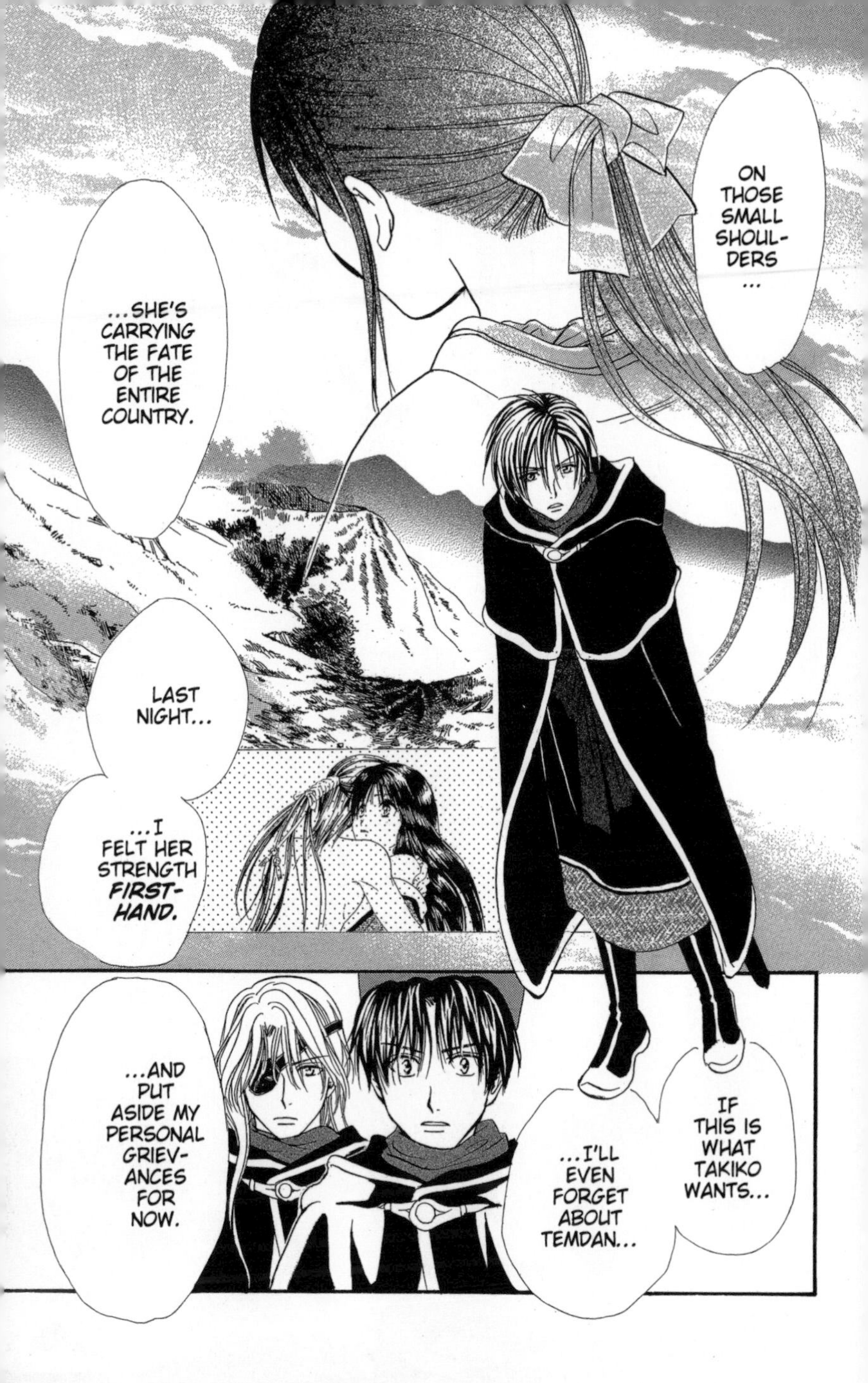
ON THOSE SMALL SHOULDERS...
...SHE'S CARRYING THE FATE OF THE ENTIRE COUNTRY.
LAST NIGHT...
...I FELT HER STRENGTH *FIRST-HAND.*
IF THIS IS WHAT TAKIKO WANTS...
...I'LL EVEN FORGET ABOUT TEMDAN...
...AND PUT ASIDE MY PERSONAL GRIEVANCES FOR NOW.

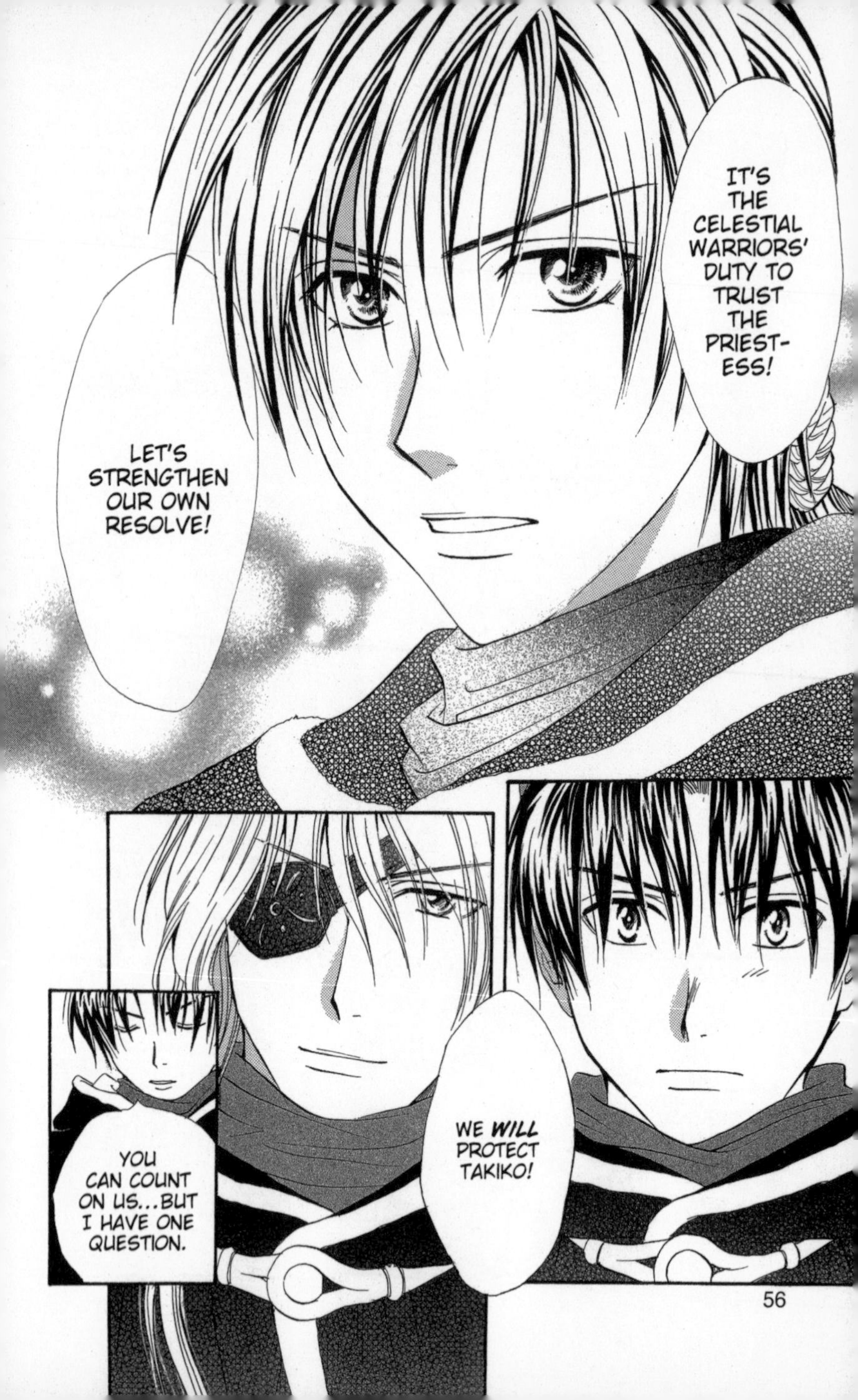
IT'S THE CELESTIAL WARRIORS' DUTY TO TRUST THE PRIEST-ESS!
LET'S STRENGTHEN OUR OWN RESOLVE!
WE *WILL* PROTECT TAKIKO!
YOU CAN COUNT ON US...BUT I HAVE ONE QUESTION.

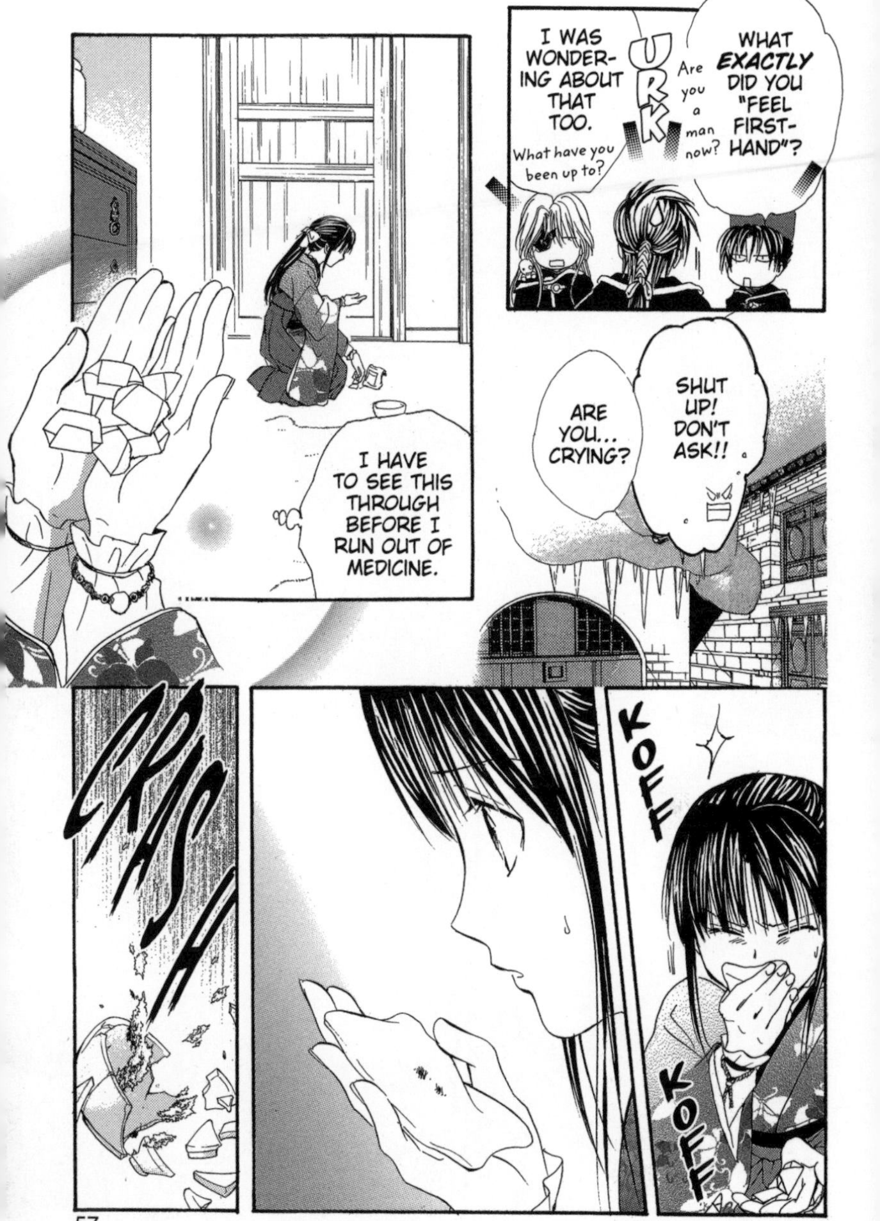
WHAT EXACTLY DID YOU "FEEL FIRST-HAND"?
Are you a man now?
URK
I WAS WONDER-ING ABOUT THAT TOO.
What have you been up to?
SHUT UP! DON'T ASK!!
ARE YOU... CRYING?
I HAVE TO SEE THIS THROUGH BEFORE I RUN OUT OF MEDICINE.
KOFF
KOFF
CRASH

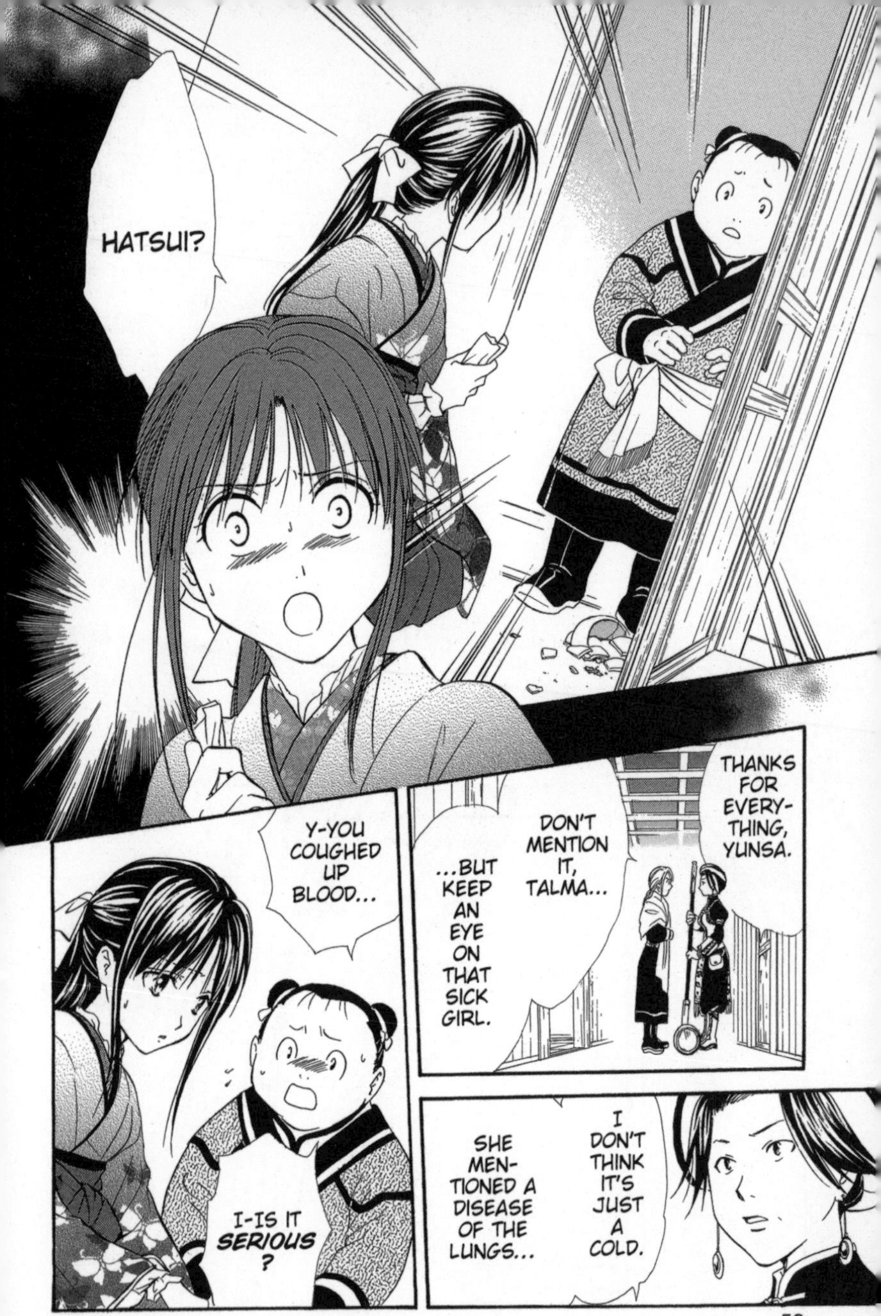
HATSUI?
THANKS FOR EVERY-THING, YUNSA.
DON'T MENTION IT, TALMA...
...BUT KEEP AN EYE ON THAT SICK GIRL.
I DON'T THINK IT'S JUST A COLD.
SHE MEN-TIONED A DISEASE OF THE LUNGS...
Y-YOU COUGHED UP BLOOD...
I-IS IT ***SERIOUS***?

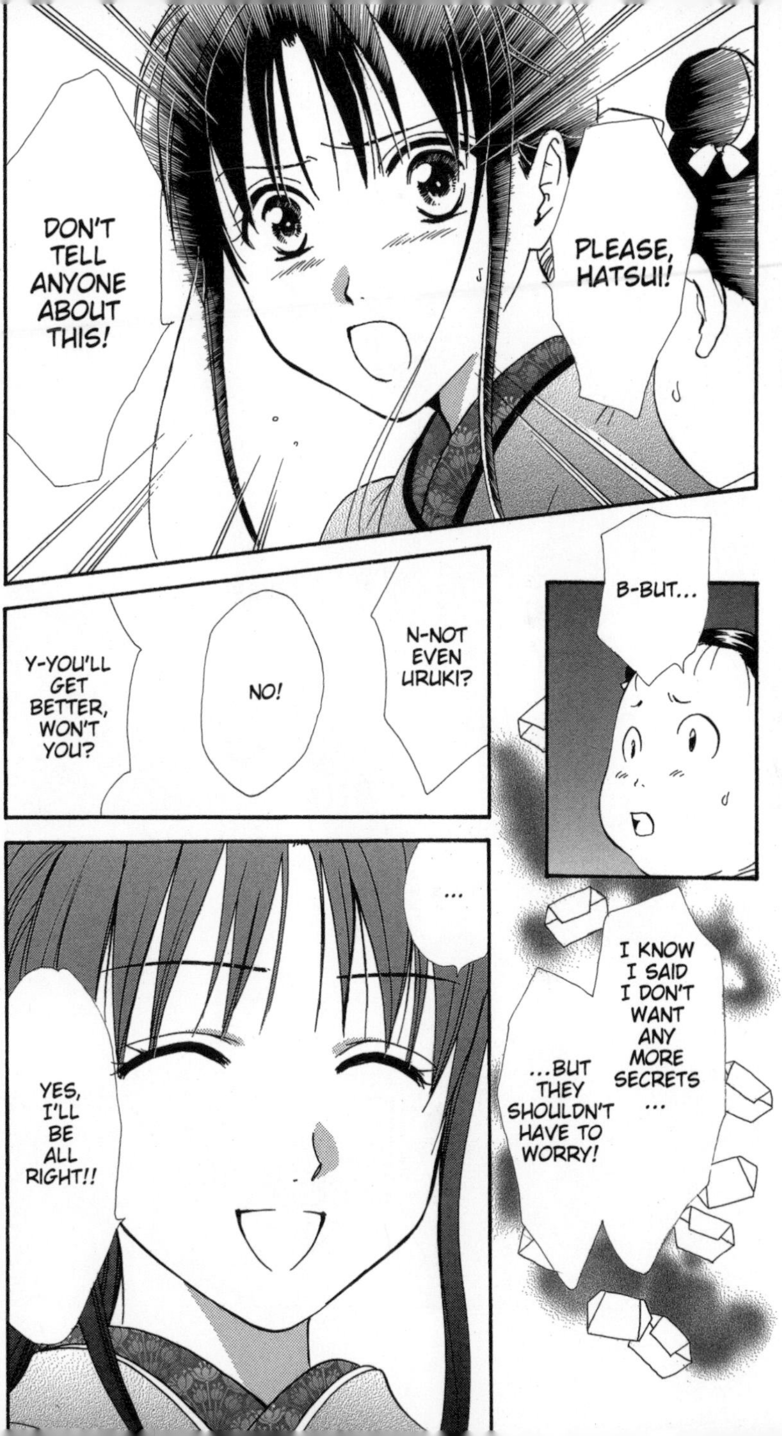
PLEASE, HATSUI!
DON'T TELL ANYONE ABOUT THIS!
B-BUT...
N-NOT EVEN URUKI?
NO!
Y-YOU'LL GET BETTER, WON'T YOU?
...
I KNOW I SAID I DON'T WANT ANY MORE SECRETS...
...BUT THEY SHOULDN'T HAVE TO WORRY!
YES, I'LL BE ALL RIGHT!!

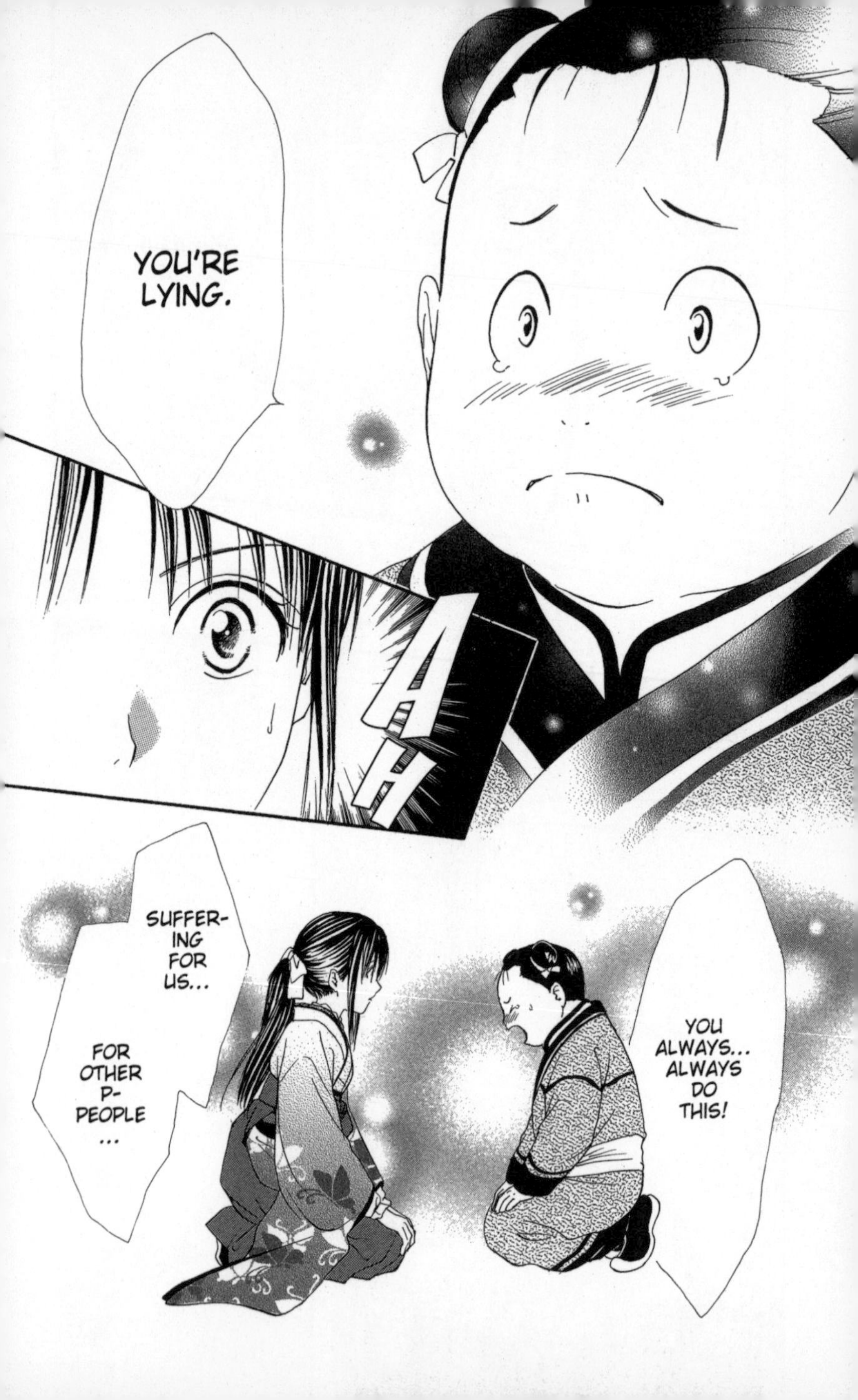
YOU'RE LYING.
AH
YOU ALWAYS... ALWAYS DO THIS!
SUFFER-ING FOR US...
FOR OTHER P-PEOPLE...

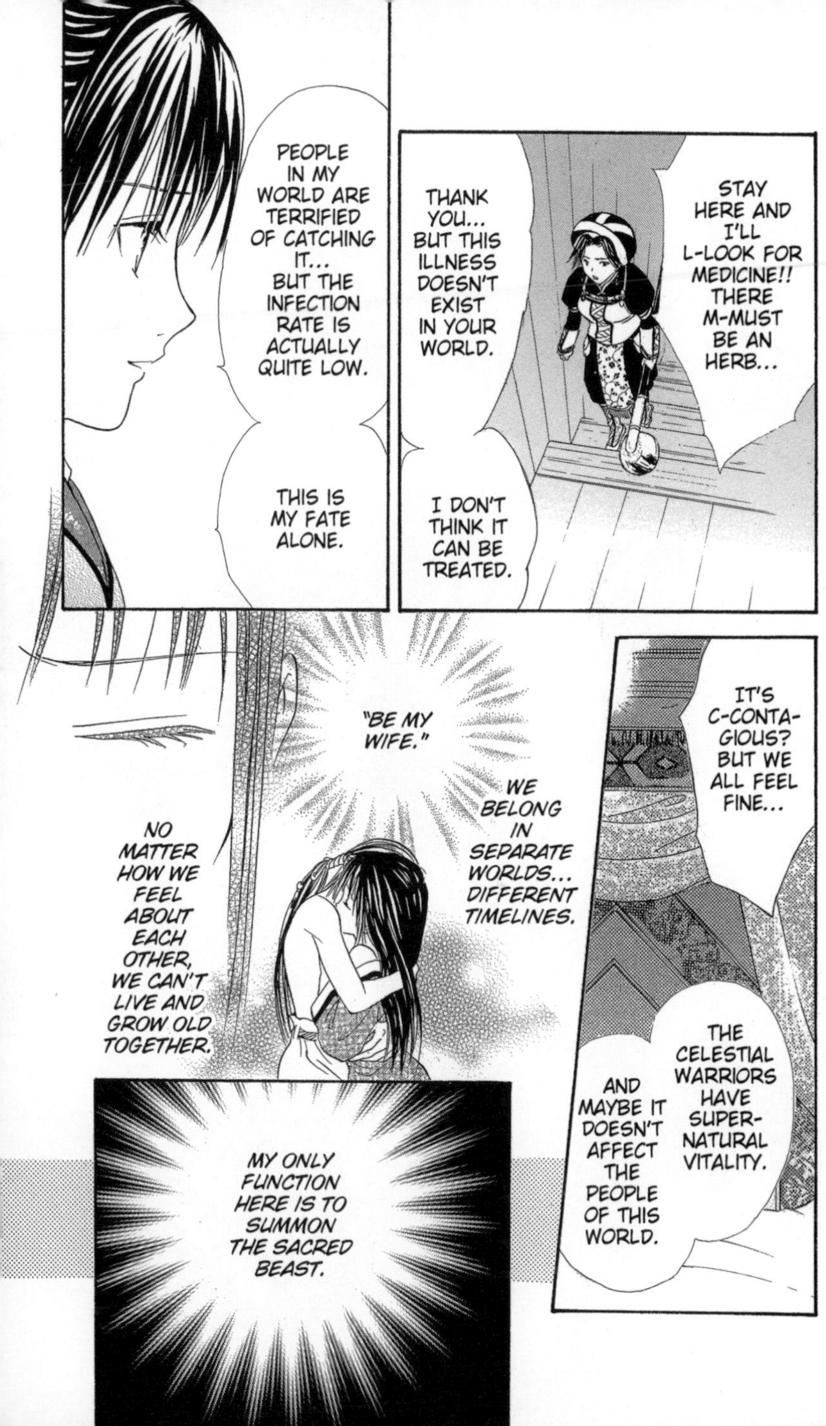
STAY HERE AND I'LL L-LOOK FOR MEDICINE!! THERE M-MUST BE AN HERB...
THANK YOU... BUT THIS ILLNESS DOESN'T EXIST IN YOUR WORLD.
I DON'T THINK IT CAN BE TREATED.
PEOPLE IN MY WORLD ARE TERRIFIED OF CATCHING IT... BUT THE INFECTION RATE IS ACTUALLY QUITE LOW.
THIS IS MY FATE ALONE.
IT'S C-CONTAGIOUS? BUT WE ALL FEEL FINE...
THE CELESTIAL WARRIORS HAVE SUPER-NATURAL VITALITY.
AND MAYBE IT DOESN'T AFFECT THE PEOPLE OF THIS WORLD.
"BE MY WIFE."
WE BELONG IN SEPARATE WORLDS... DIFFERENT TIMELINES.
NO MATTER HOW WE FEEL ABOUT EACH OTHER, WE CAN'T LIVE AND GROW OLD TOGETHER.
MY ONLY FUNCTION HERE IS TO SUMMON THE SACRED BEAST.

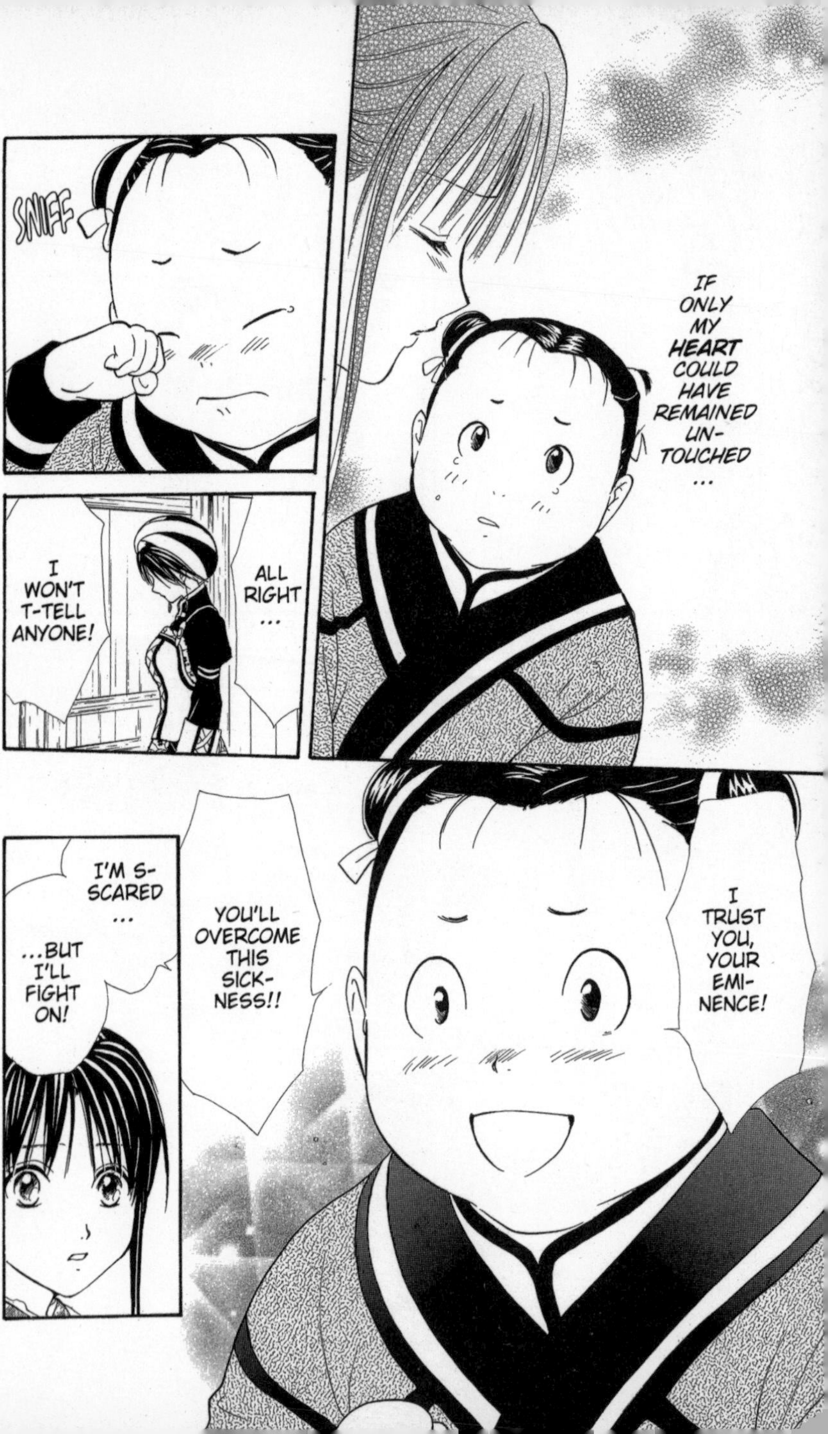
IF ONLY MY HEART COULD HAVE REMAINED UN-TOUCHED...
SNIFF
ALL RIGHT...
I WON'T T-TELL ANYONE!
I TRUST YOU, YOUR EMI-NENCE!
YOU'LL OVERCOME THIS SICK-NESS!!
I'M S-SCARED...
...BUT I'LL FIGHT ON!

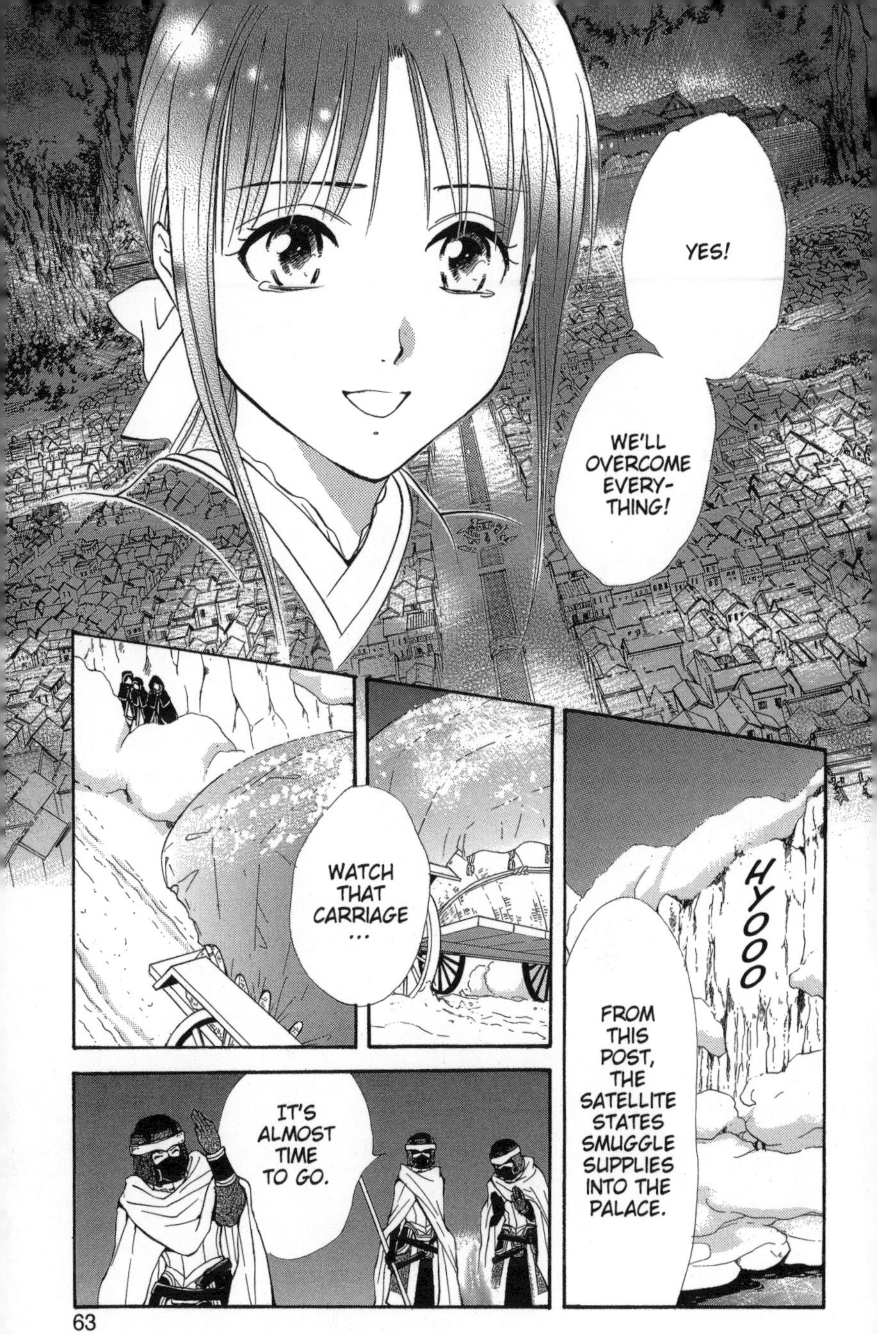
YES!
WE'LL OVERCOME EVERY-THING!
HYOOOO
FROM THIS POST, THE SATELLITE STATES SMUGGLE SUPPLIES INTO THE PALACE.
WATCH THAT CARRIAGE ...
IT'S ALMOST TIME TO GO.

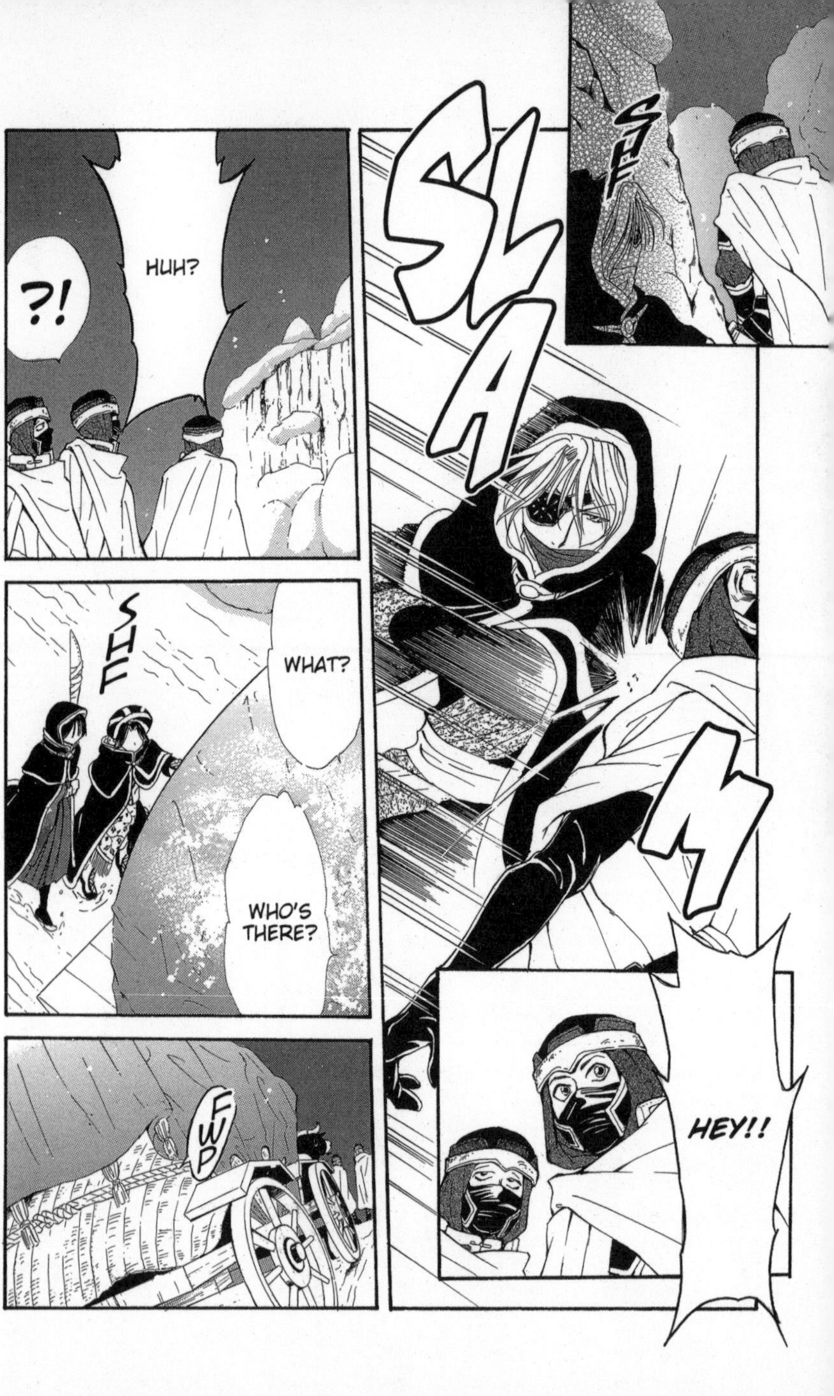
SHF
SLAM
HEY!!
HUH?
?!
SHF
WHAT?
WHO'S THERE?
FWP

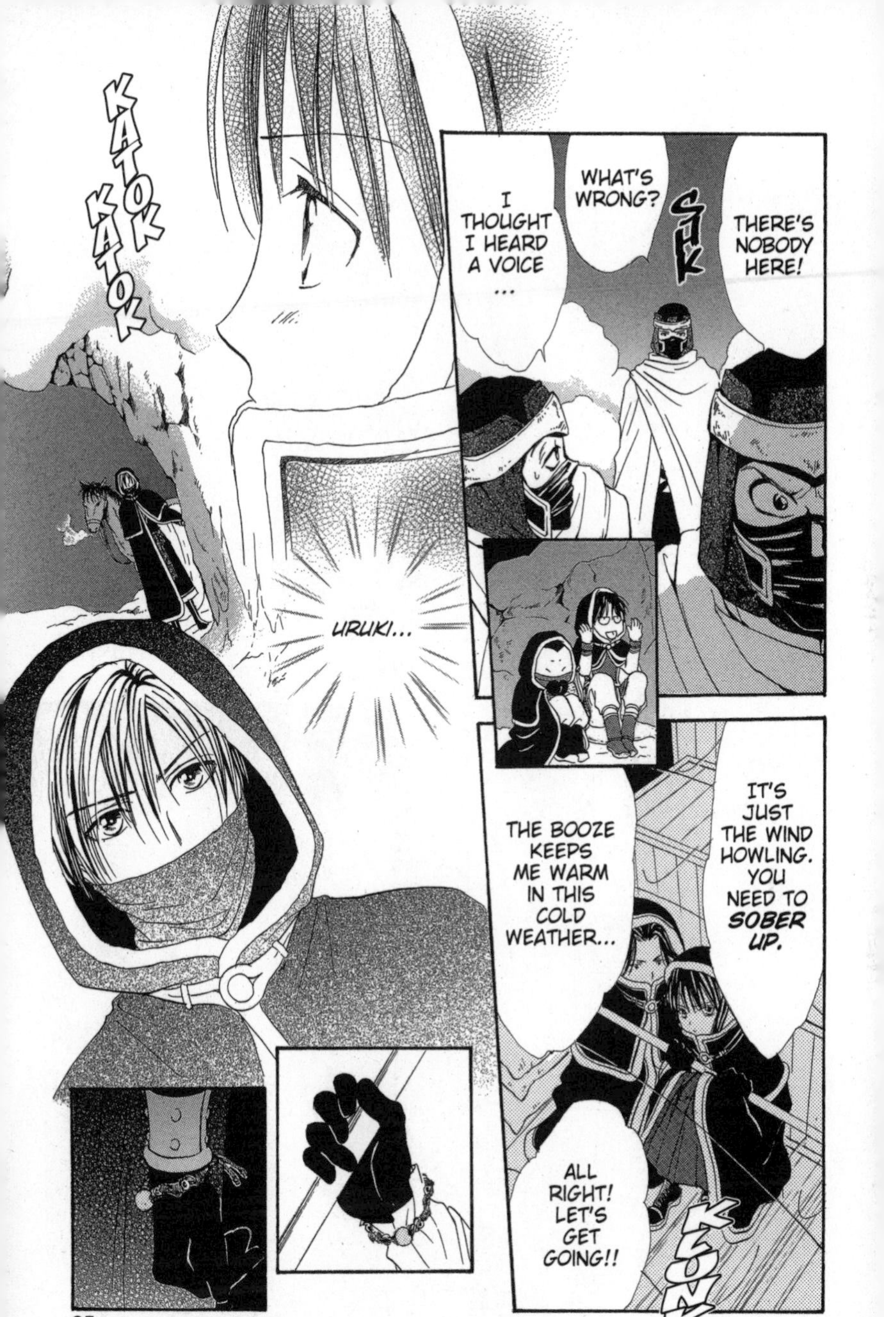
THERE'S NOBODY HERE!
SHK
WHAT'S WRONG?
I THOUGHT I HEARD A VOICE ...
IT'S JUST THE WIND HOWLING. YOU NEED TO **SOBER UP.**
THE BOOZE KEEPS ME WARM IN THIS COLD WEATHER...
KLONK
ALL RIGHT! LET'S GET GOING!!
KATOK KATOK
URUKI...

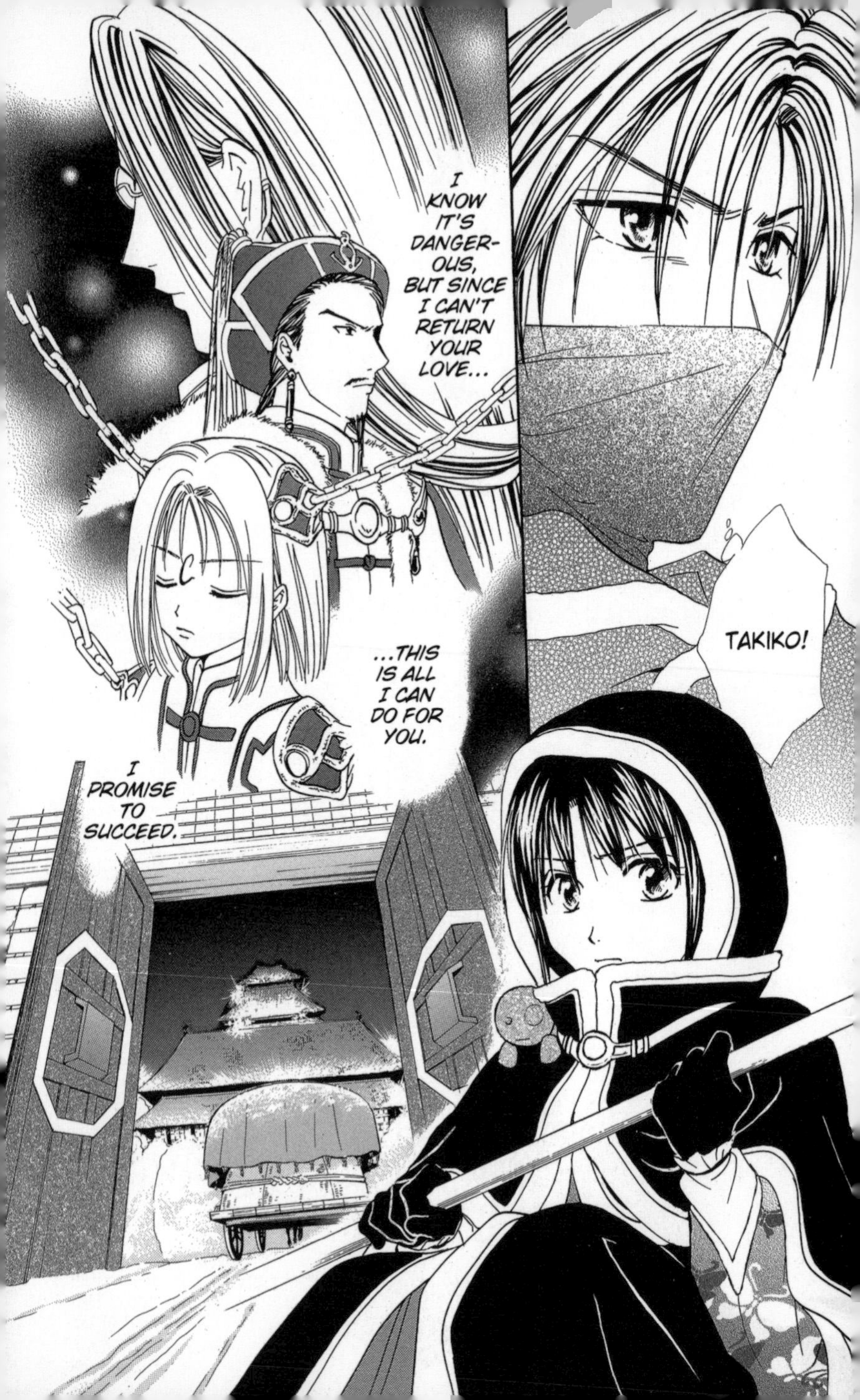
TAKIKO!
I KNOW IT'S DANGER-OUS, BUT SINCE I CAN'T RETURN YOUR LOVE...
...THIS IS ALL I CAN DO FOR YOU.
I PROMISE TO SUCCEED.

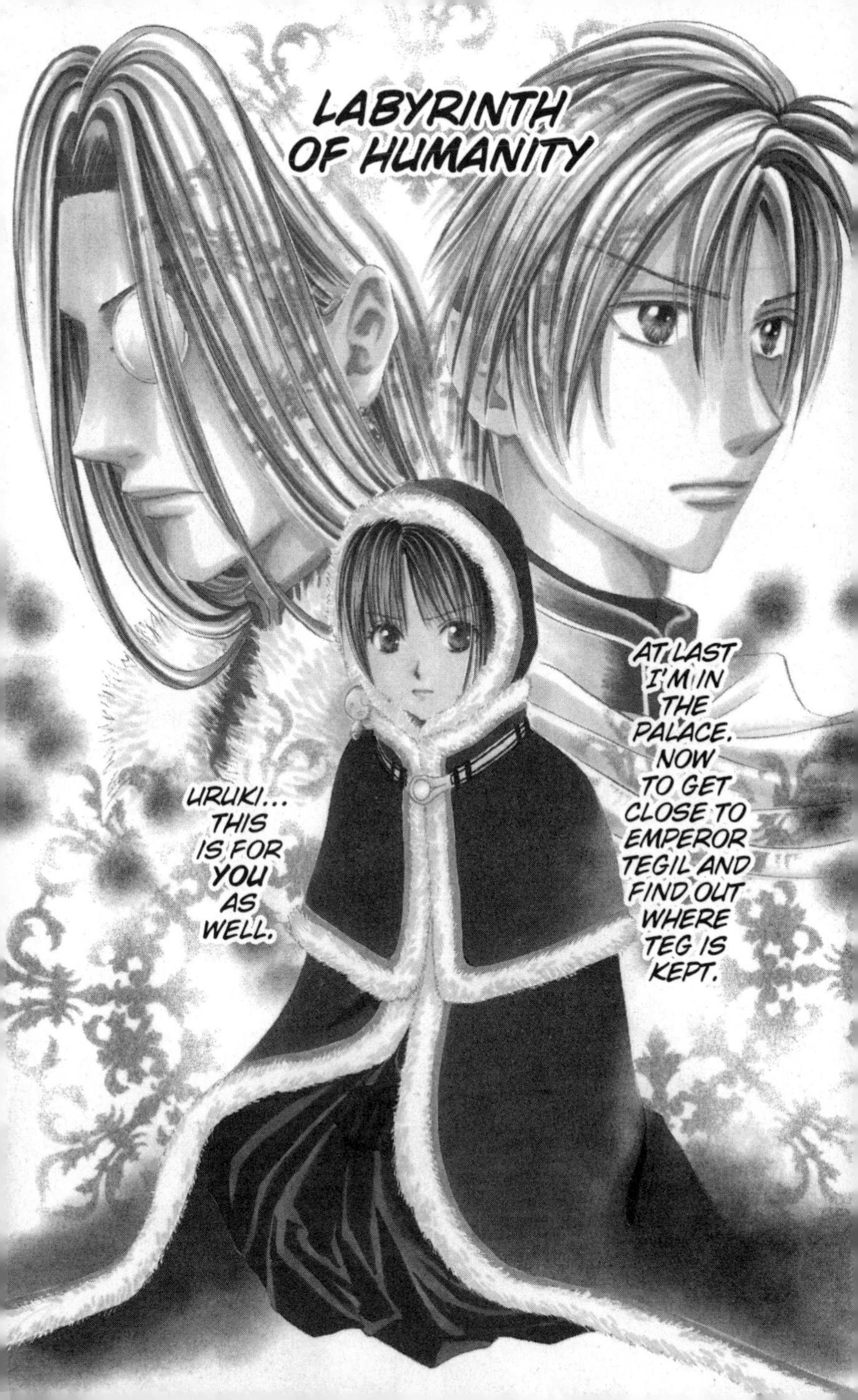
LABYRINTH OF HUMANITY
AT LAST I'M IN THE PALACE. NOW TO GET CLOSE TO EMPEROR TEGIL AND FIND OUT WHERE TEG IS KEPT.
URUKI... THIS IS FOR YOU AS WELL.

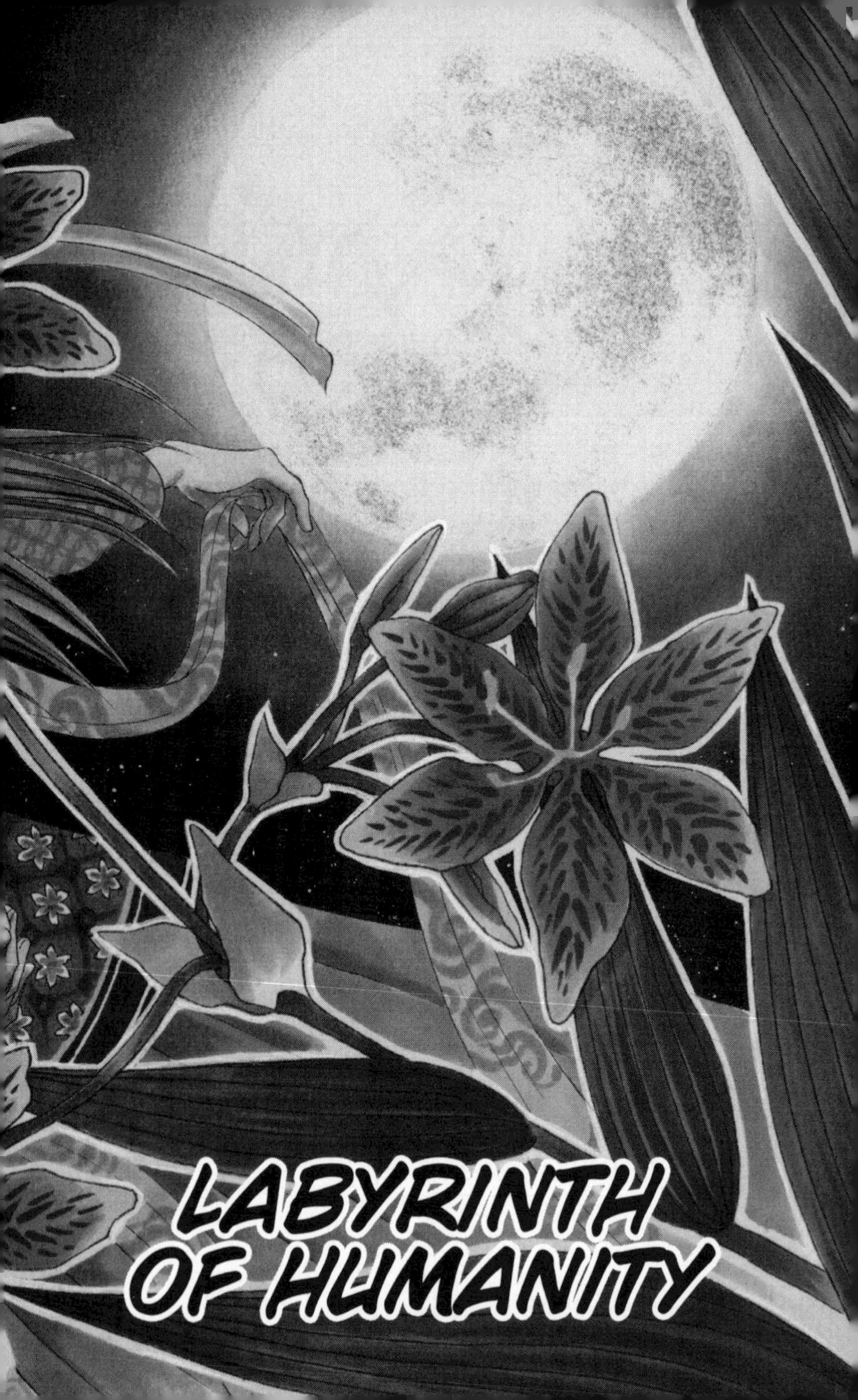
LABYRINTH OF HUMANITY

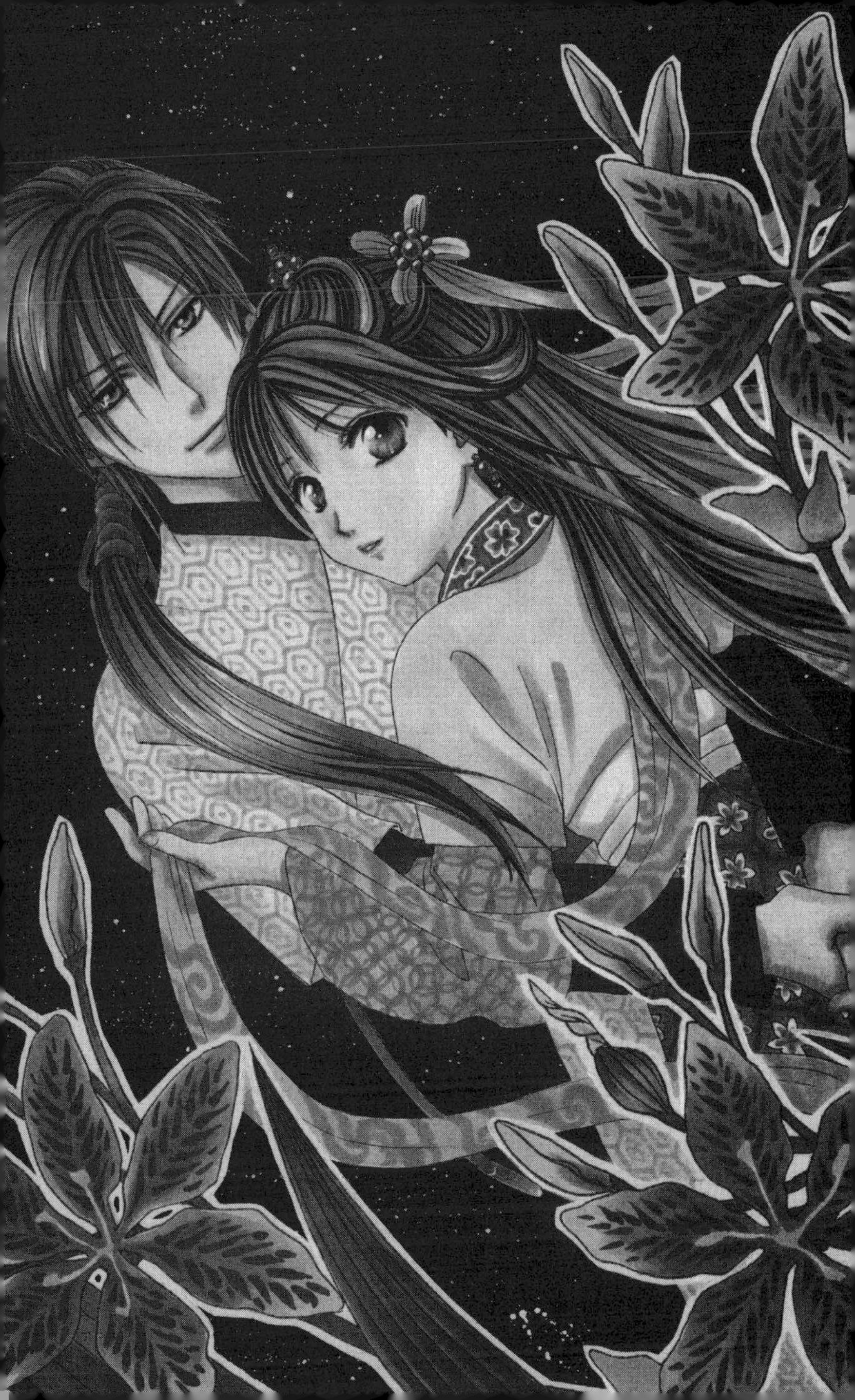

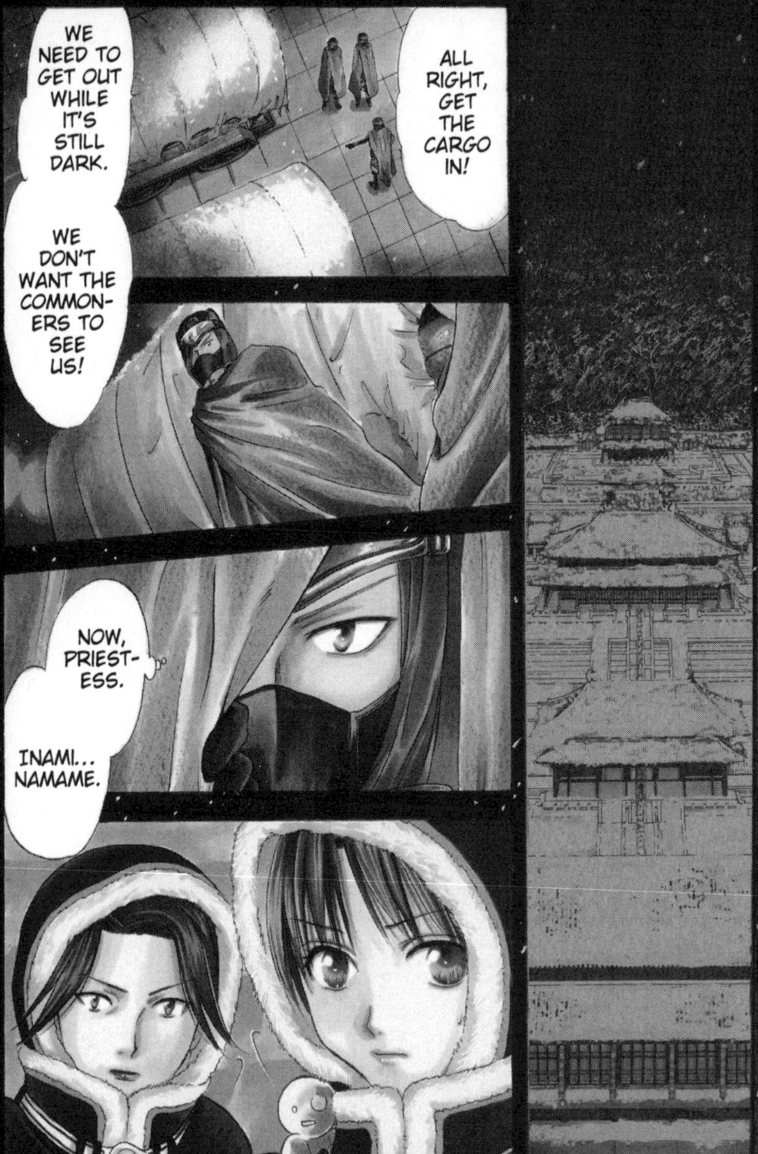
ALL RIGHT, GET THE CARGO IN!
WE NEED TO GET OUT WHILE IT'S STILL DARK.
WE DON'T WANT THE COMMONERS TO SEE US!
NOW, PRIESTESS.
INAMI... NAMAME.

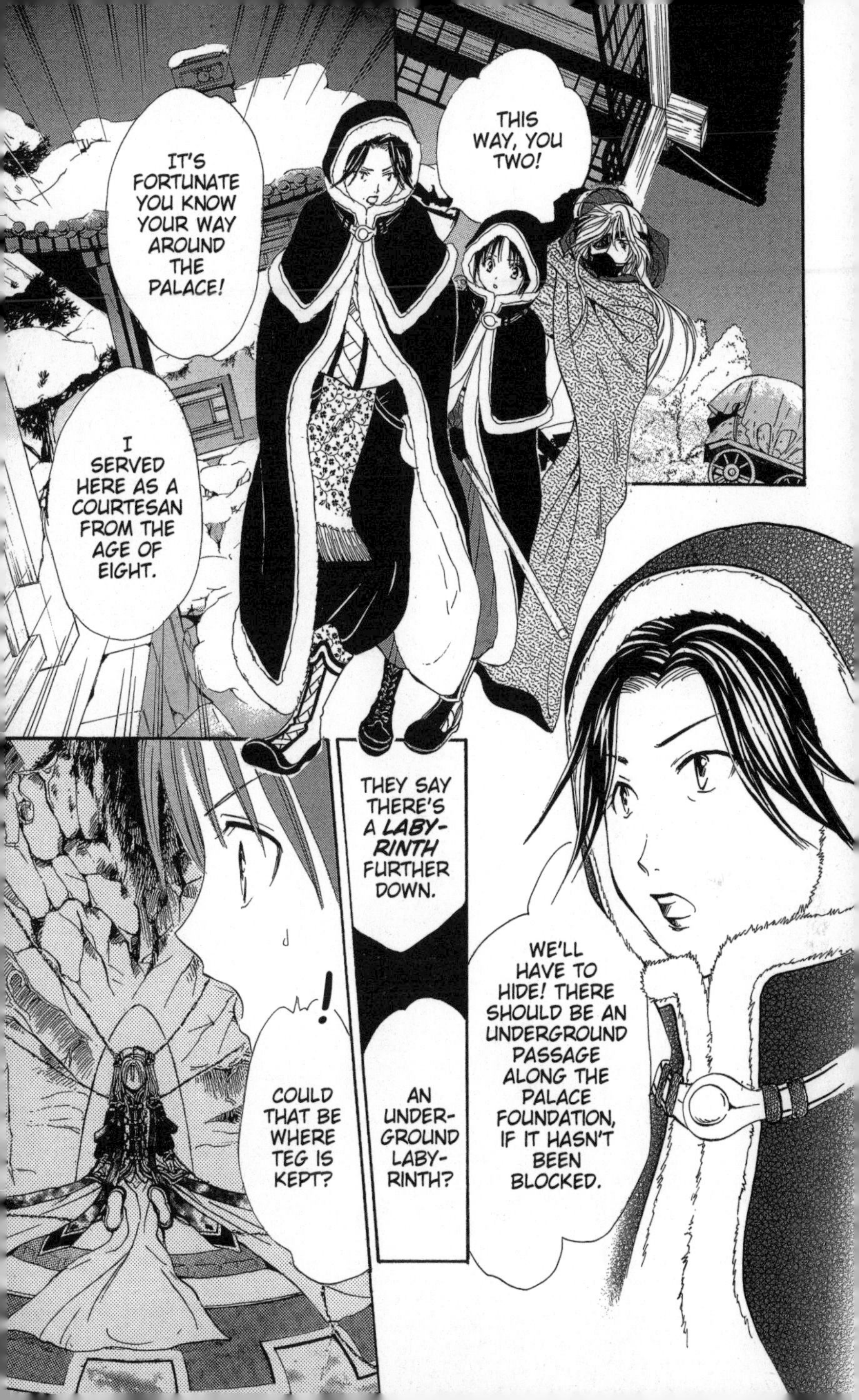
THIS WAY, YOU TWO!
IT'S FORTUNATE YOU KNOW YOUR WAY AROUND THE PALACE!
I SERVED HERE AS A COURTESAN FROM THE AGE OF EIGHT.
WE'LL HAVE TO HIDE! THERE SHOULD BE AN UNDERGROUND PASSAGE ALONG THE PALACE FOUNDATION, IF IT HASN'T BEEN BLOCKED.
THEY SAY THERE'S A *LABY-RINTH* FURTHER DOWN.
AN UNDER-GROUND LABY-RINTH?
!
COULD THAT BE WHERE TEG IS KEPT?

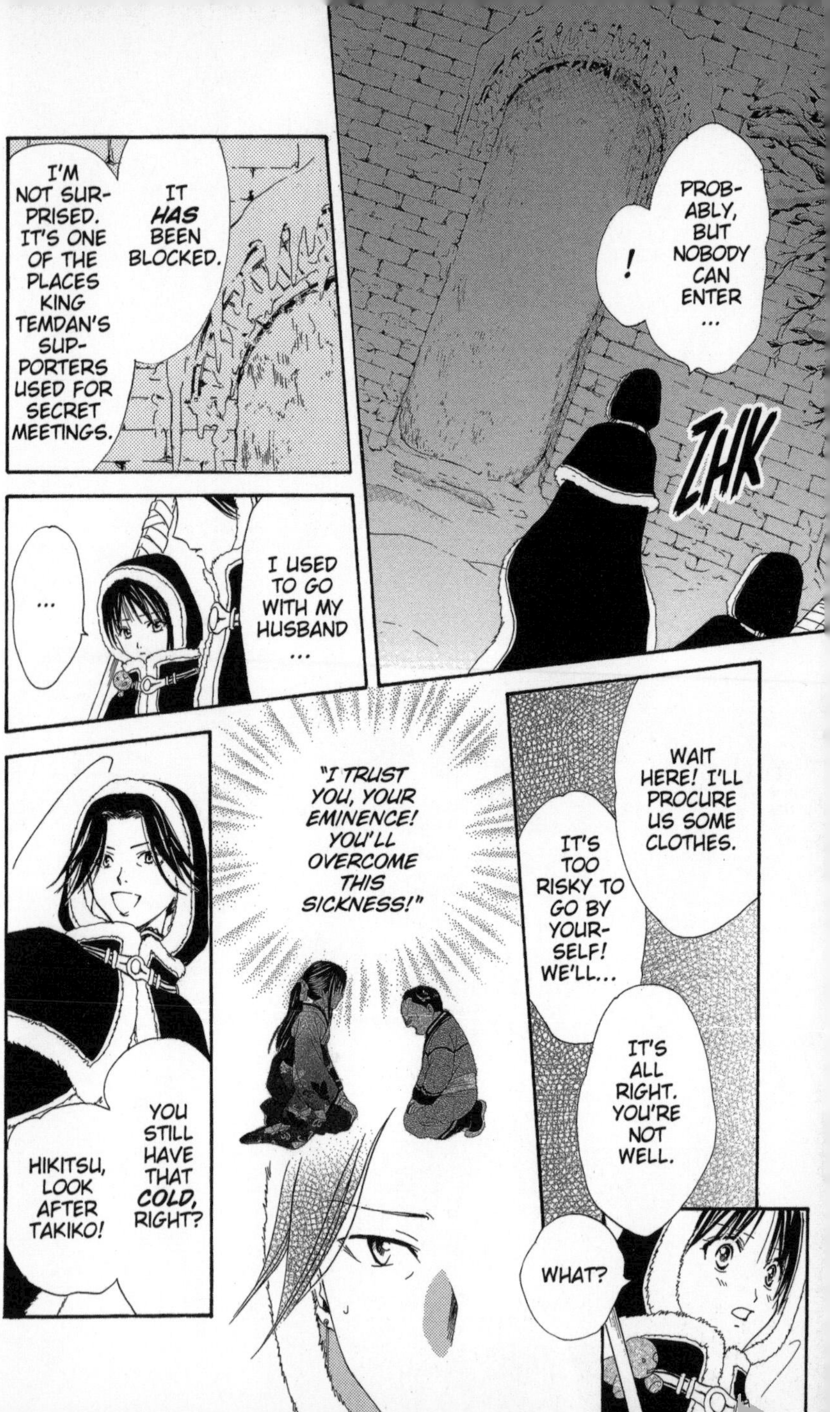
PROBABLY, BUT NOBODY CAN ENTER...
!
ZHK
IT *HAS* BEEN BLOCKED.
I'M NOT SURPRISED. IT'S ONE OF THE PLACES KING TEMDAN'S SUPPORTERS USED FOR SECRET MEETINGS.
I USED TO GO WITH MY HUSBAND...
...
WAIT HERE! I'LL PROCURE US SOME CLOTHES.
IT'S TOO RISKY TO GO BY YOURSELF! WE'LL...
IT'S ALL RIGHT. YOU'RE NOT WELL.
WHAT?
"I TRUST YOU, YOUR EMINENCE! YOU'LL OVERCOME THIS SICKNESS!"
YOU STILL HAVE THAT *COLD*, RIGHT?
HIKITSU, LOOK AFTER TAKIKO!

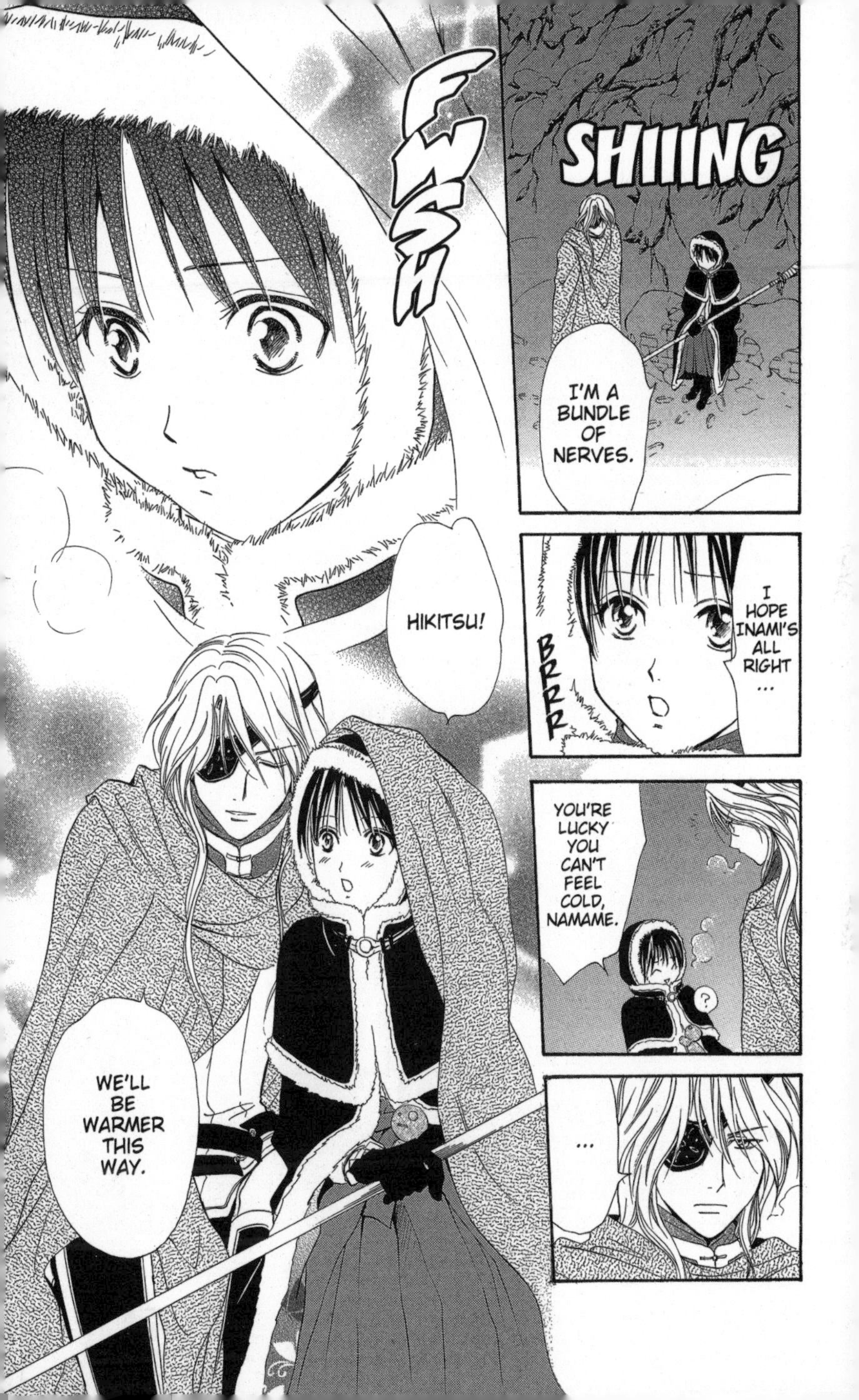
SHIIING
I'M A BUNDLE OF NERVES.
I HOPE INAMI'S ALL RIGHT...
BRRR
YOU'RE LUCKY YOU CAN'T FEEL COLD, NAMAME.
?
...
FWSH
HIKITSU!
WE'LL BE WARMER THIS WAY.

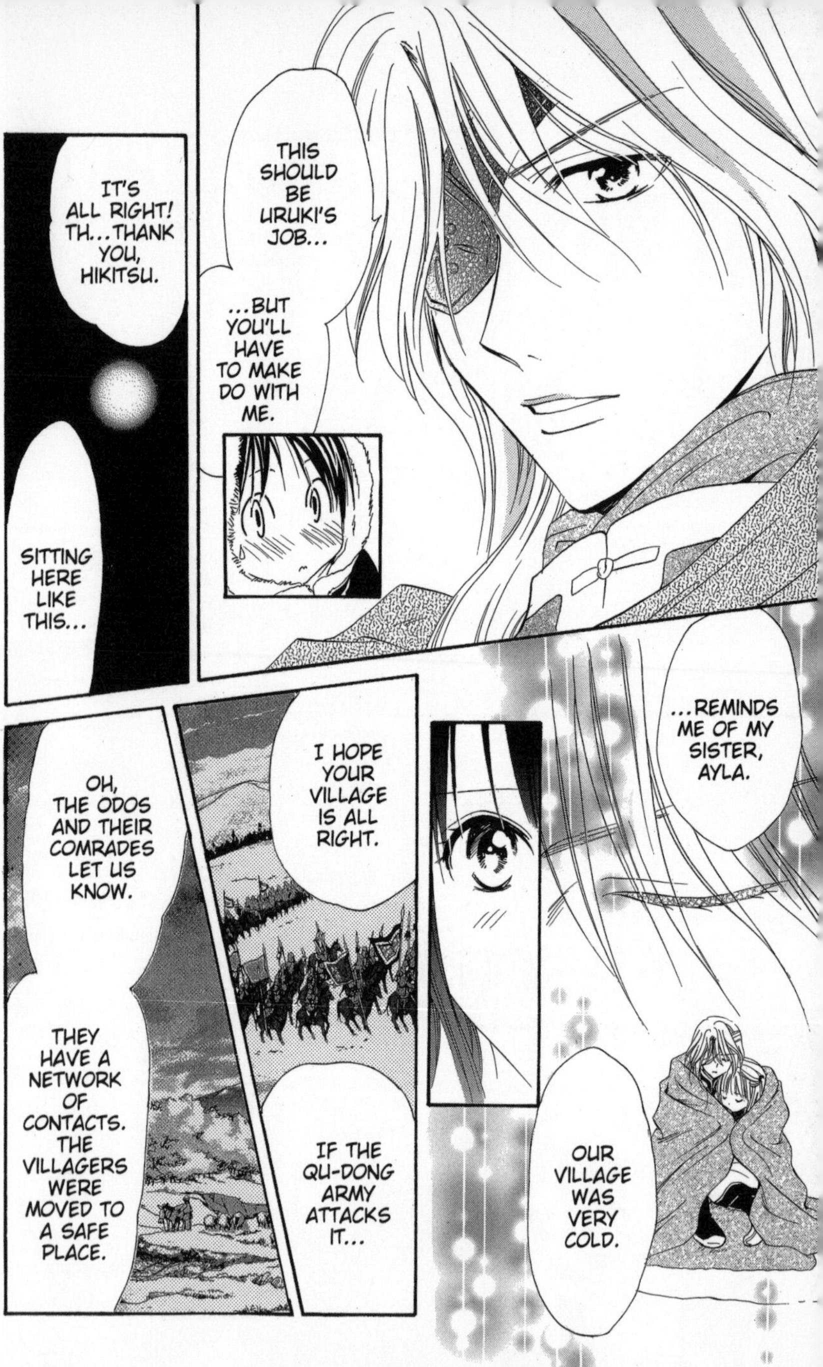
THIS SHOULD BE URUKI'S JOB...
...BUT YOU'LL HAVE TO MAKE DO WITH ME.
IT'S ALL RIGHT! TH...THANK YOU, HIKITSU.
SITTING HERE LIKE THIS...
...REMINDS ME OF MY SISTER, AYLA.
OUR VILLAGE WAS VERY COLD.
I HOPE YOUR VILLAGE IS ALL RIGHT.
IF THE QU-DONG ARMY ATTACKS IT...
OH, THE ODOS AND THEIR COMRADES LET US KNOW.
THEY HAVE A NETWORK OF CONTACTS. THE VILLAGERS WERE MOVED TO A SAFE PLACE.

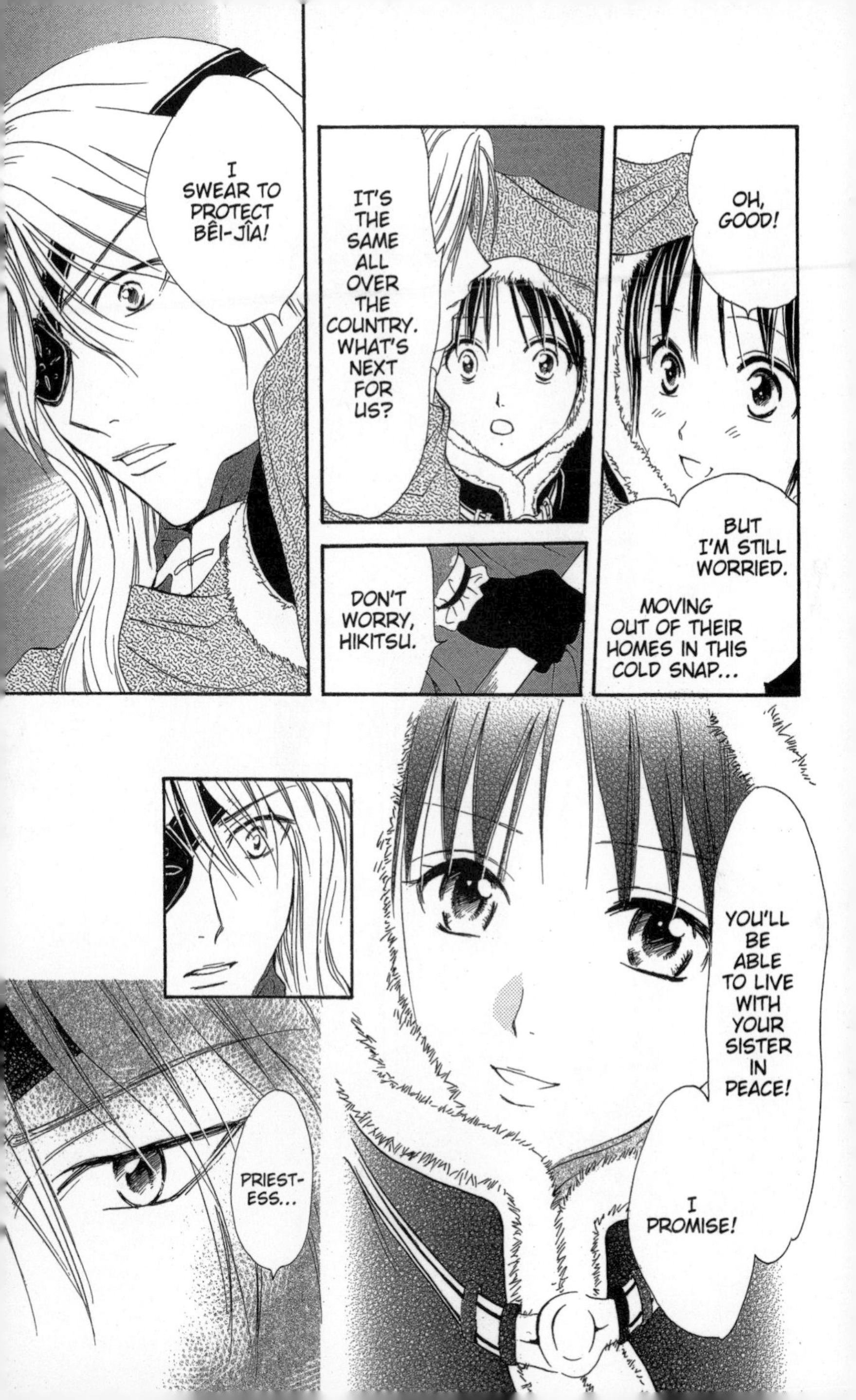
OH, GOOD!
BUT I'M STILL WORRIED.
MOVING OUT OF THEIR HOMES IN THIS COLD SNAP...
IT'S THE SAME ALL OVER THE COUNTRY. WHAT'S NEXT FOR US?
DON'T WORRY, HIKITSU.
I SWEAR TO PROTECT BÊI-JÎA!
YOU'LL BE ABLE TO LIVE WITH YOUR SISTER IN PEACE!
I PROMISE!
PRIEST-ESS...

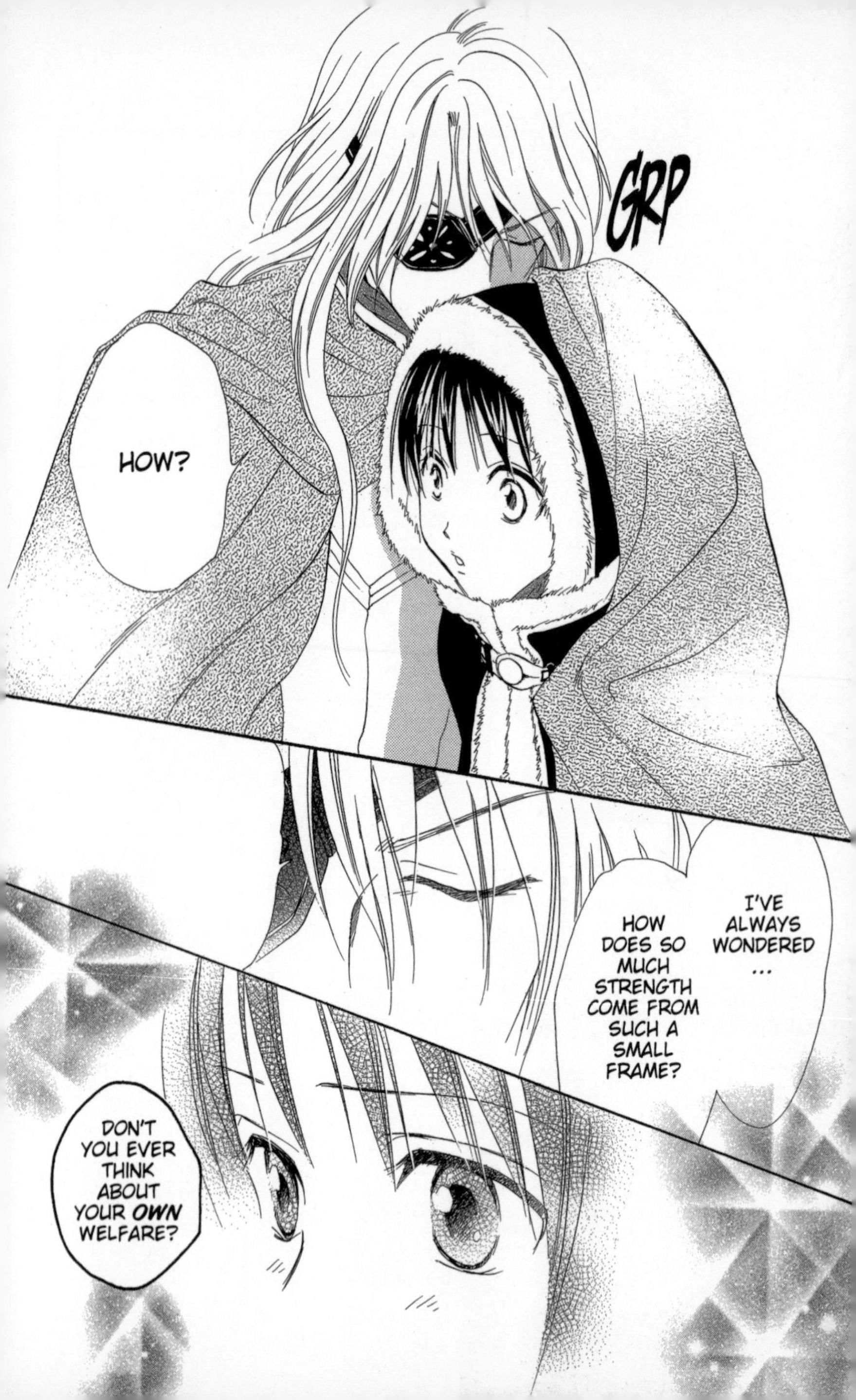
GRP
HOW?
I'VE ALWAYS WONDERED...
HOW DOES SO MUCH STRENGTH COME FROM SUCH A SMALL FRAME?
DON'T YOU EVER THINK ABOUT YOUR *OWN* WELFARE?

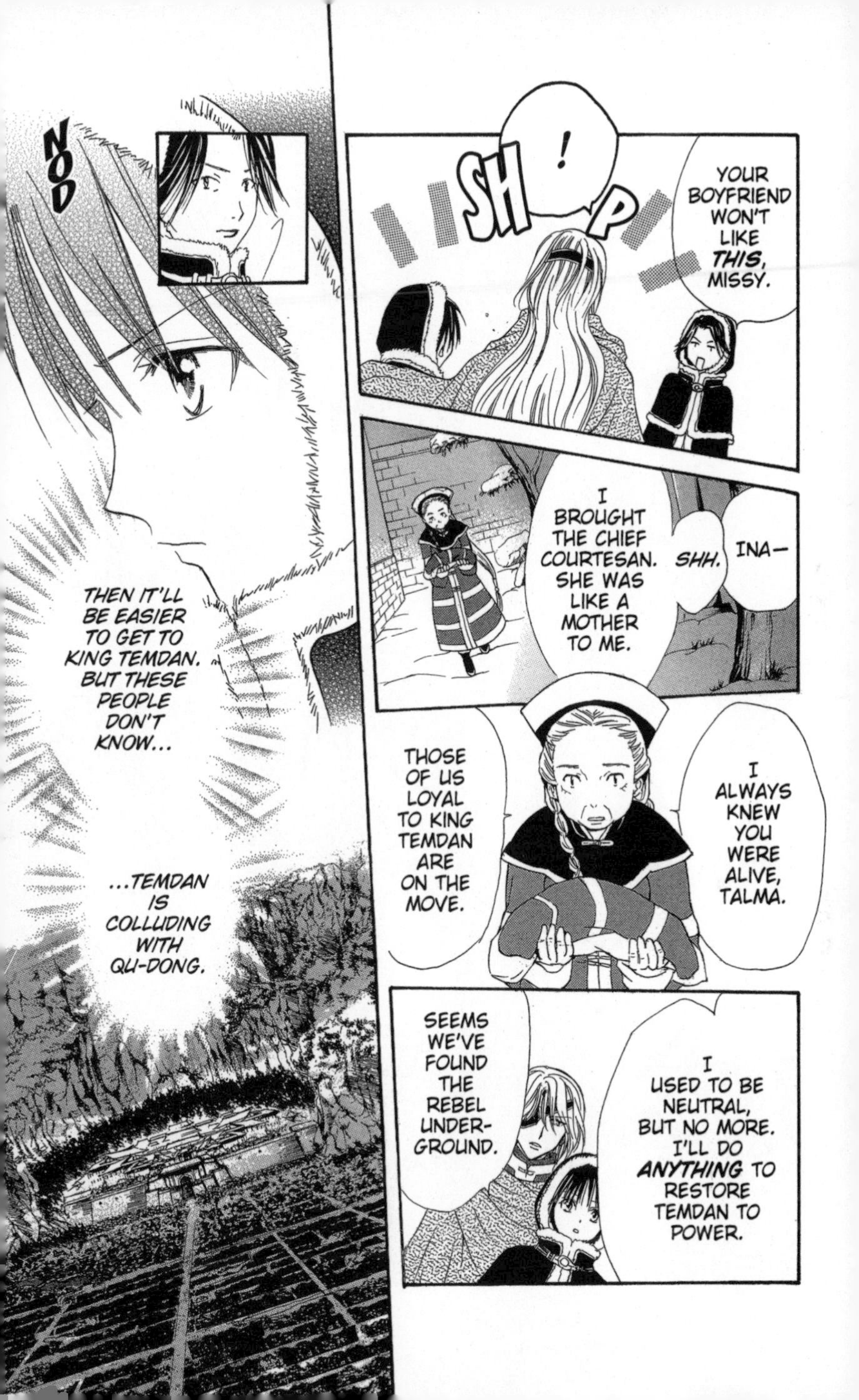
YOUR BOYFRIEND WON'T LIKE THIS, MISSY.
!
SHP
INA—
SHH.
I BROUGHT THE CHIEF COURTESAN. SHE WAS LIKE A MOTHER TO ME.
I ALWAYS KNEW YOU WERE ALIVE, TALMA.
THOSE OF US LOYAL TO KING TEMDAN ARE ON THE MOVE.
I USED TO BE NEUTRAL, BUT NO MORE. I'LL DO ANYTHING TO RESTORE TEMDAN TO POWER.
SEEMS WE'VE FOUND THE REBEL UNDER-GROUND.
NOD
THEN IT'LL BE EASIER TO GET TO KING TEMDAN. BUT THESE PEOPLE DON'T KNOW...
...TEMDAN IS COLLUDING WITH QU-DONG.

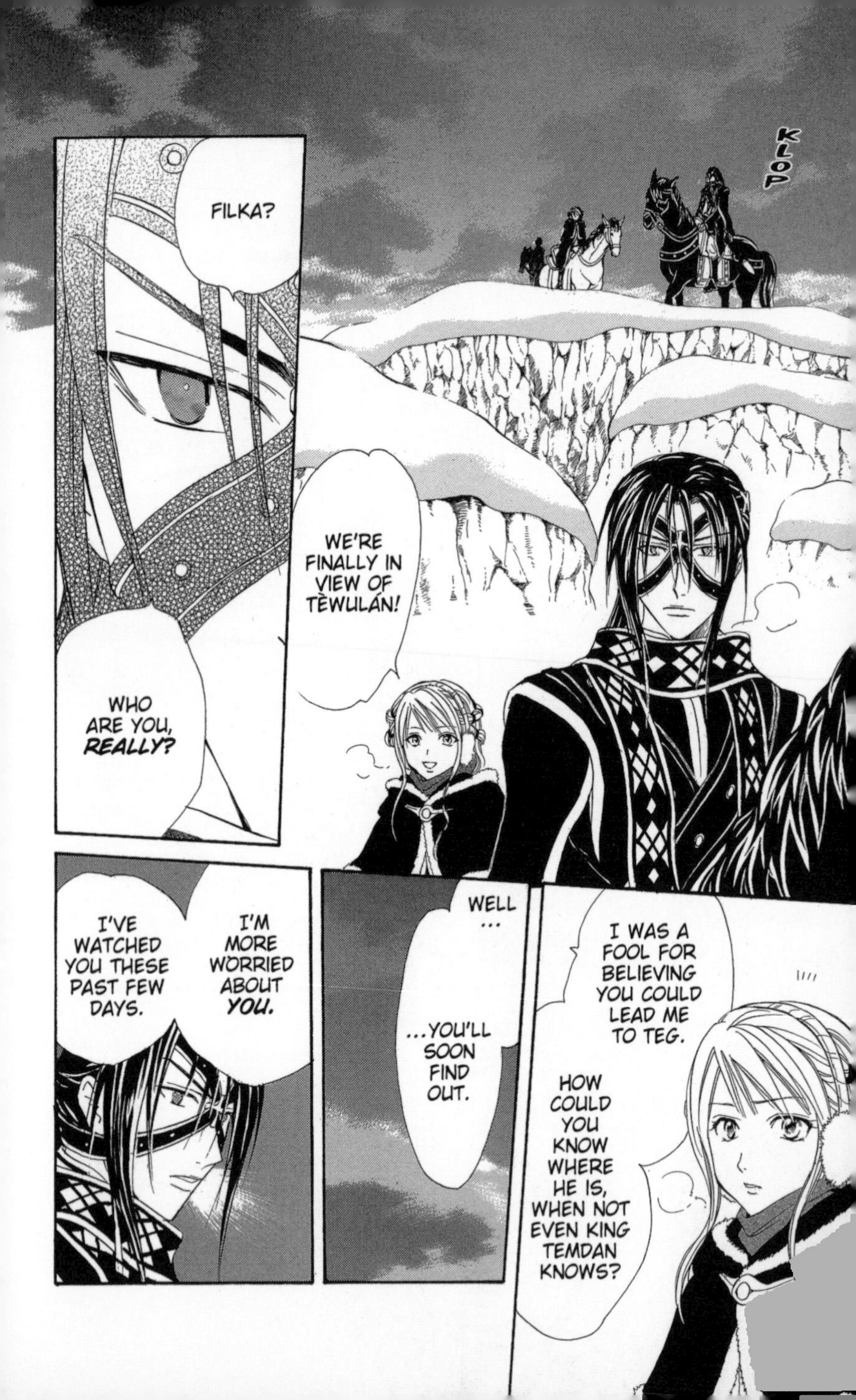
KLOP
WE'RE FINALLY IN VIEW OF TÈWULÁN!
FILKA?
WHO ARE YOU, *REALLY?*
I WAS A FOOL FOR BELIEVING YOU COULD LEAD ME TO TEG.
HOW COULD YOU KNOW WHERE HE IS, WHEN NOT EVEN KING TEMDAN KNOWS?
WELL ...
...YOU'LL SOON FIND OUT.
I'M MORE WORRIED ABOUT *YOU.*
I'VE WATCHED YOU THESE PAST FEW DAYS.

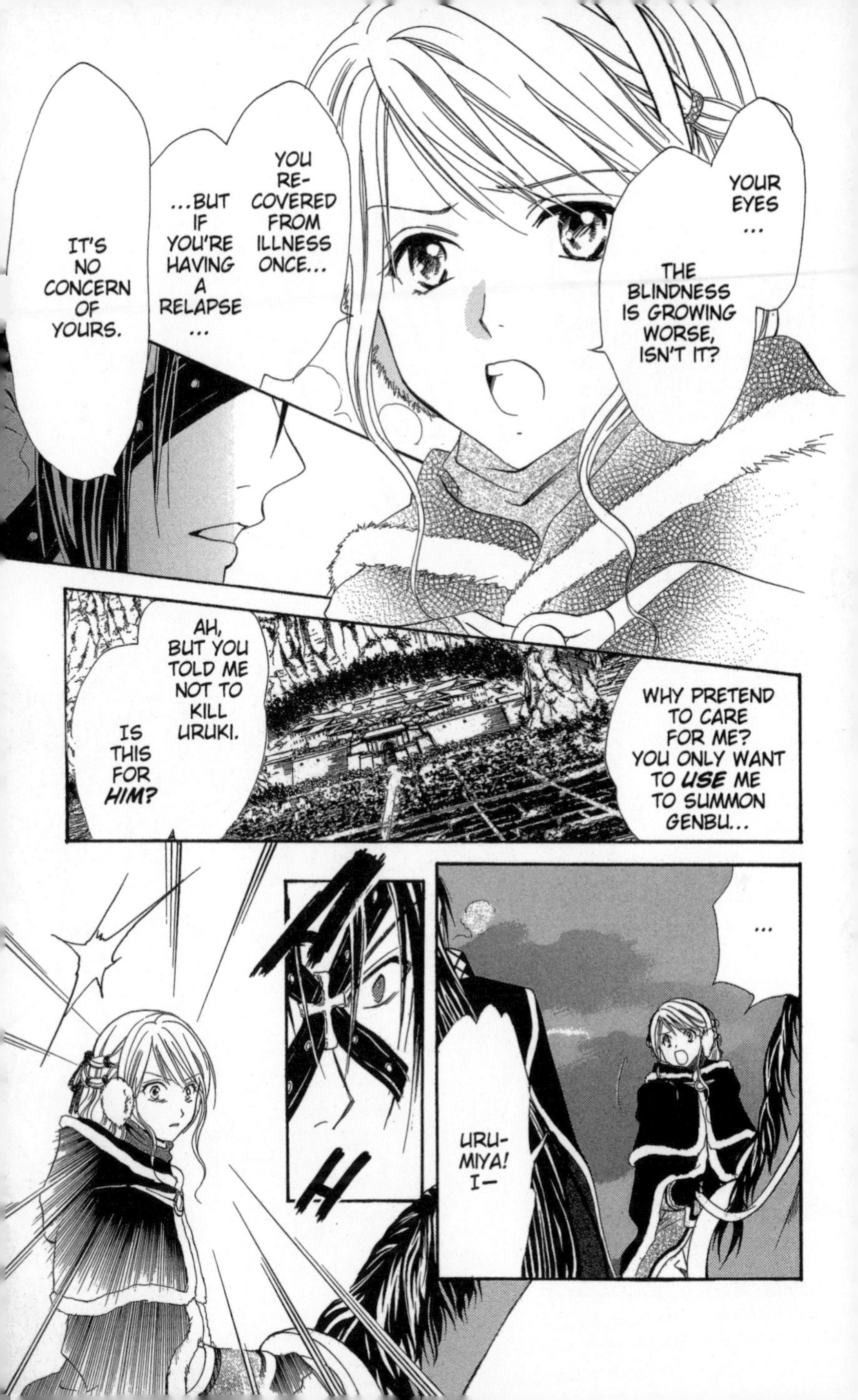
YOUR EYES... THE BLINDNESS IS GROWING WORSE, ISN'T IT?
YOU RE-COVERED FROM ILLNESS ONCE...
...BUT IF YOU'RE HAVING A RELAPSE...
IT'S NO CONCERN OF YOURS.
WHY PRETEND TO CARE FOR ME? YOU ONLY WANT TO *USE* ME TO SUMMON GENBU...
AH, BUT YOU TOLD ME NOT TO KILL URUKI.
IS THIS FOR *HIM*?
...
URU-MIYA! I—

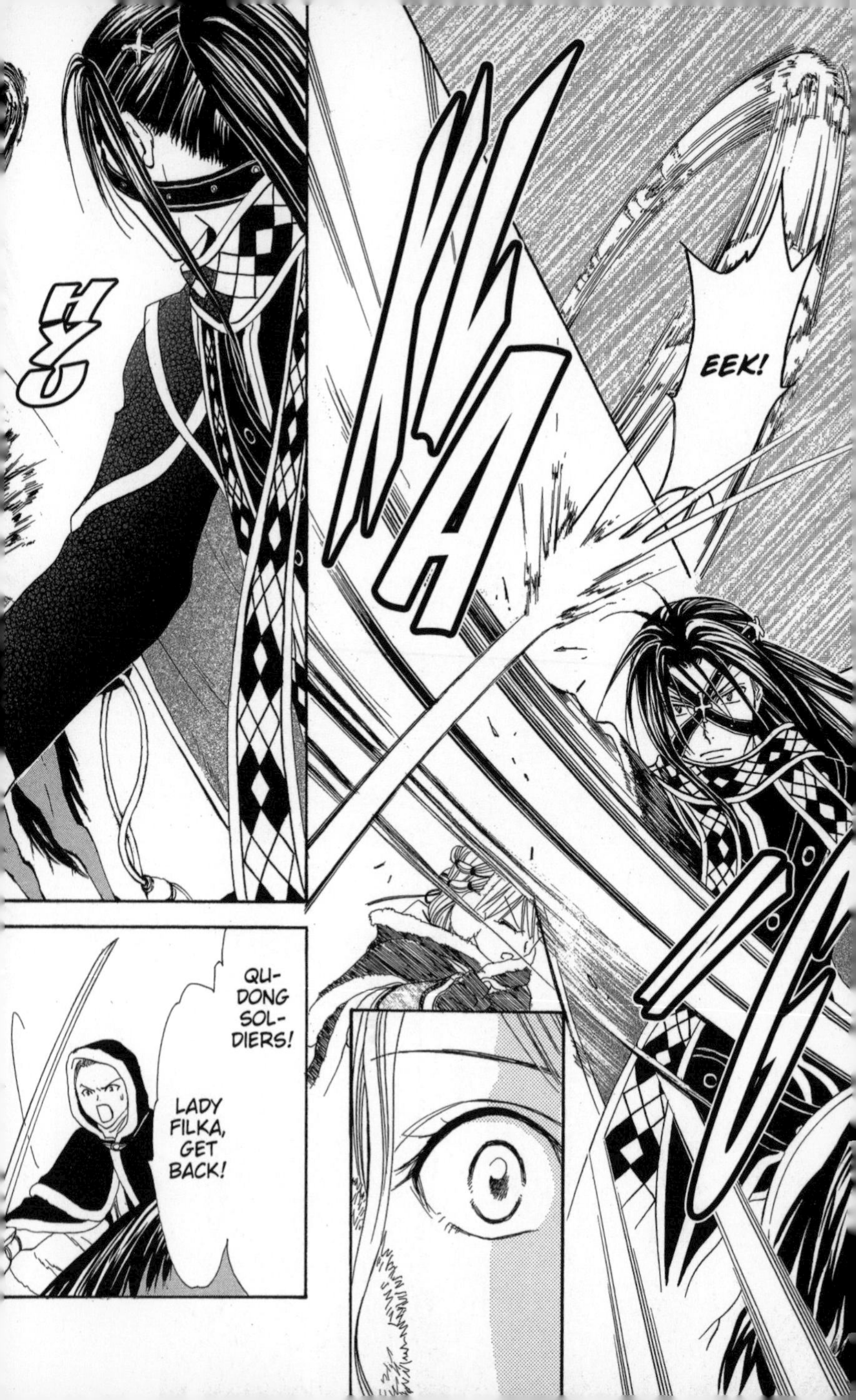
EEK!
QU-DONG SOL-DIERS!
LADY FILKA, GET BACK!

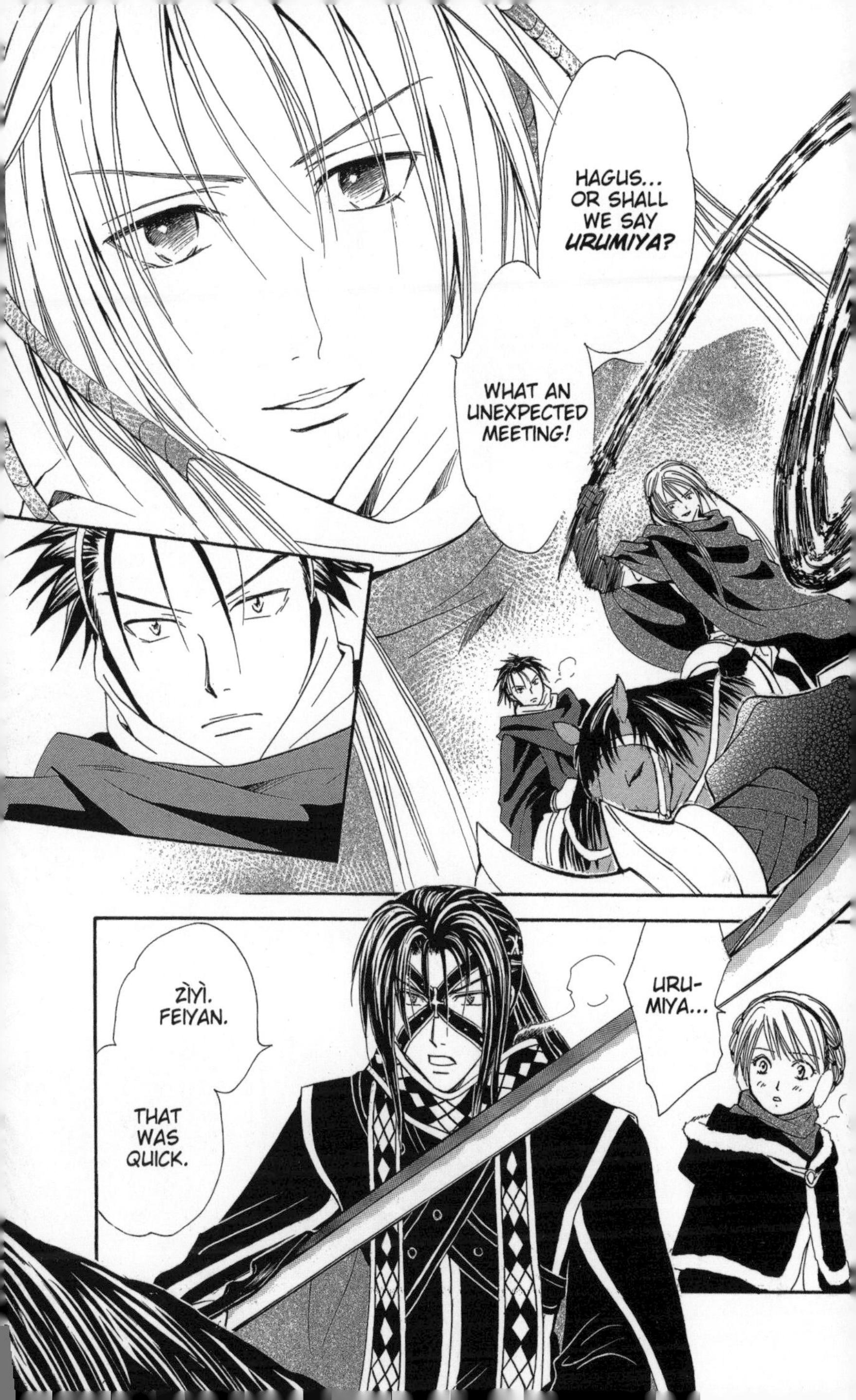
HAGUS... OR SHALL WE SAY *URUMIYA?*
WHAT AN UNEXPECTED MEETING!
URU-MIYA...
ZǏYÌ. FEIYAN.
THAT WAS QUICK.

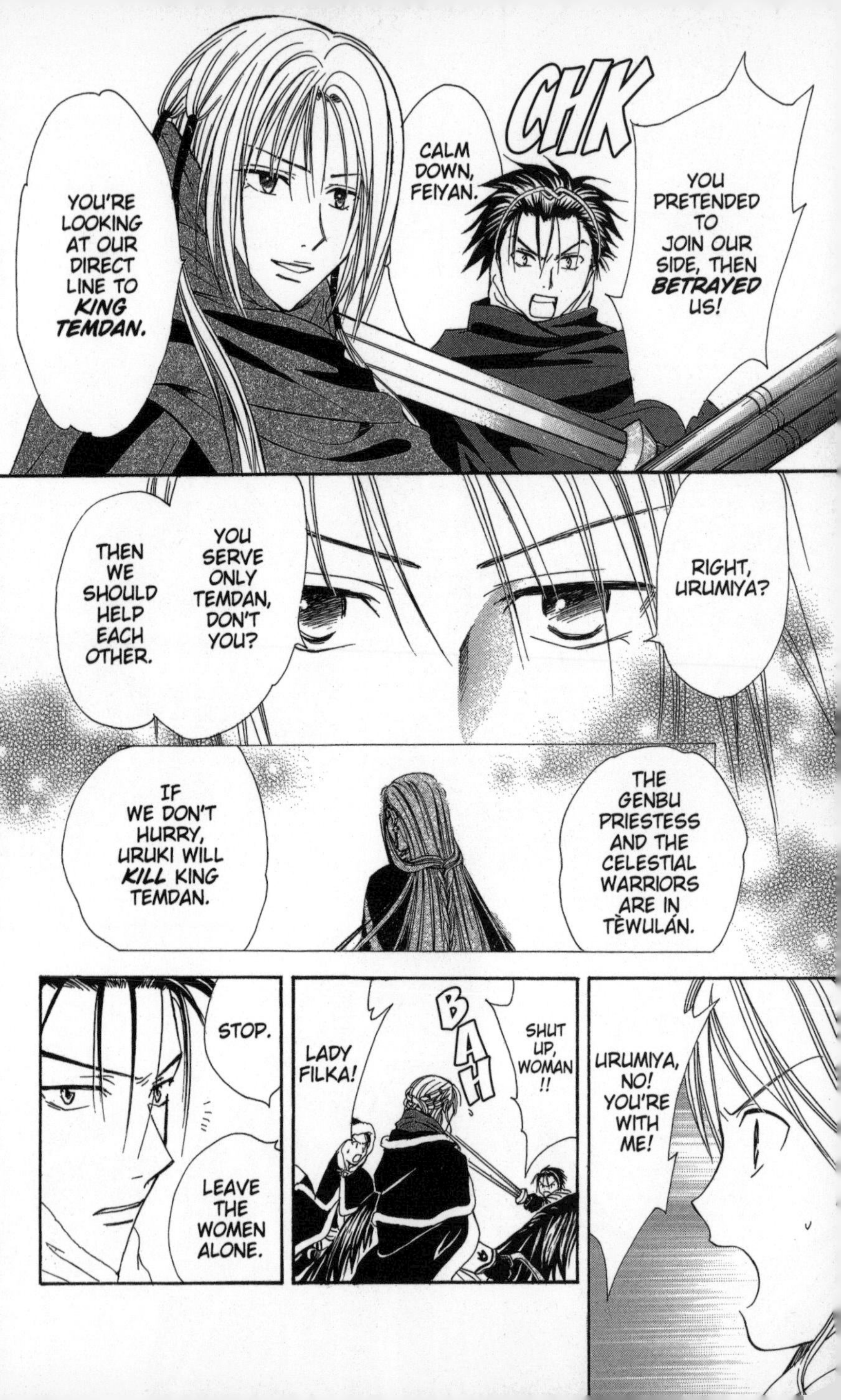
YOU PRETENDED TO JOIN OUR SIDE, THEN *BETRAYED* US!
CHK
CALM DOWN, FEIYAN.
YOU'RE LOOKING AT OUR DIRECT LINE TO *KING TEMDAN.*
RIGHT, URUMIYA?
YOU SERVE ONLY TEMDAN, DON'T YOU?
THEN WE SHOULD HELP EACH OTHER.
THE GENBU PRIESTESS AND THE CELESTIAL WARRIORS ARE IN TÈWULÁN.
IF WE DON'T HURRY, URUKI WILL *KILL* KING TEMDAN.
URUMIYA, NO! YOU'RE WITH ME!
SHUT UP, WOMAN!!
BAH
LADY FILKA!
STOP.
LEAVE THE WOMEN ALONE.

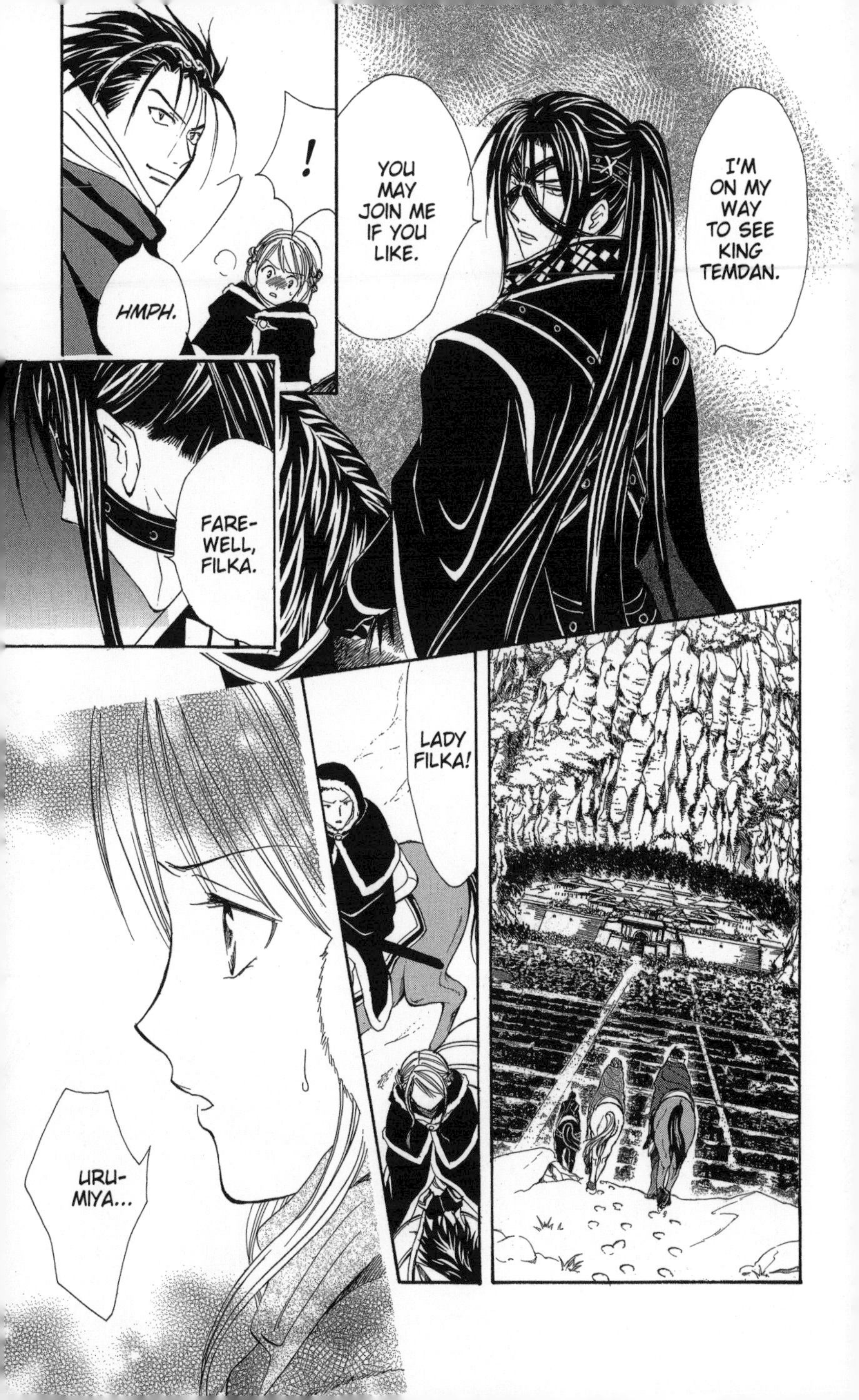
I'M ON MY WAY TO SEE KING TEMDAN.
YOU MAY JOIN ME IF YOU LIKE.
!
HMPH.
FARE-WELL, FILKA.
LADY FILKA!
URU-MIYA...

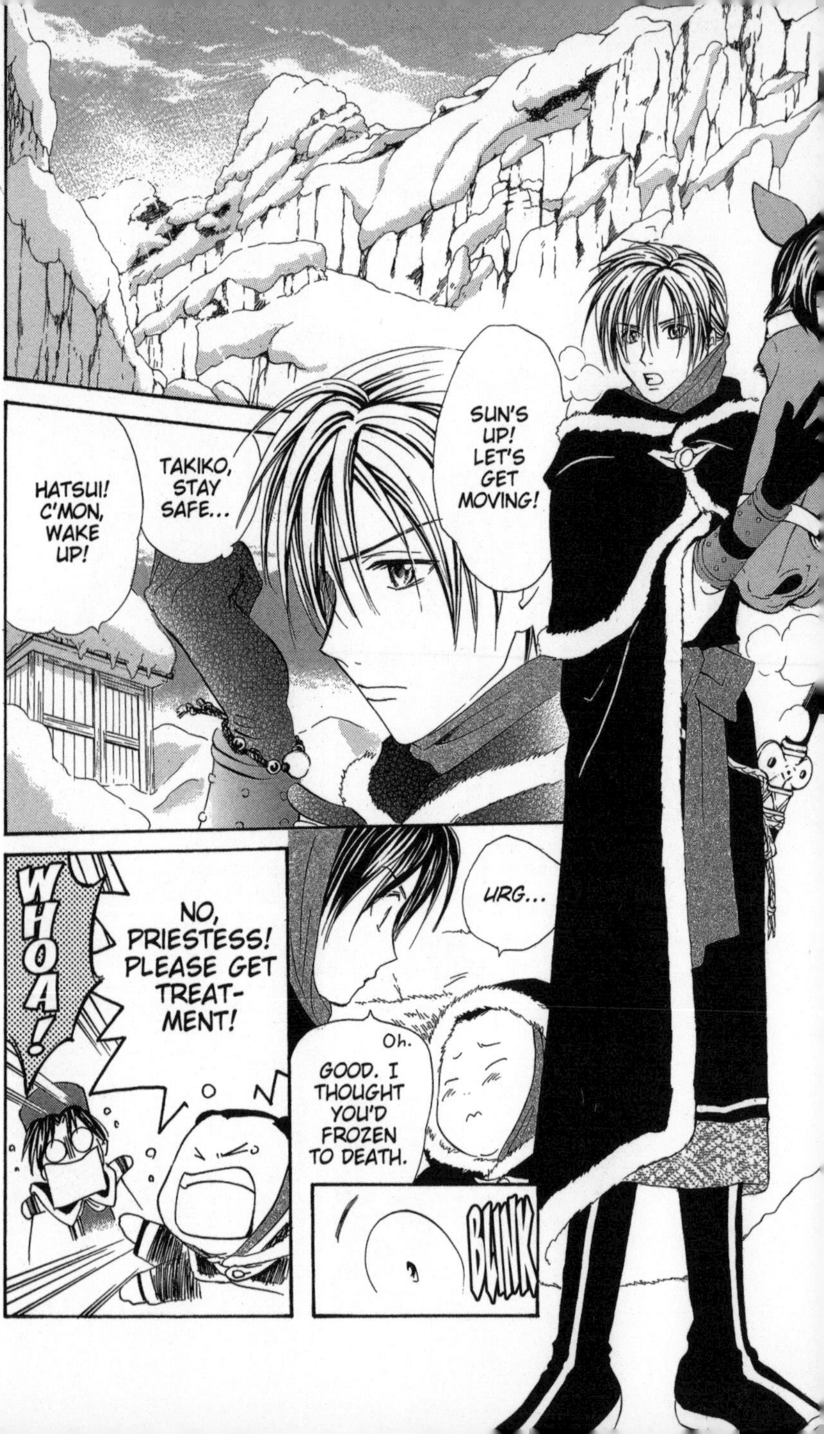
SUN'S UP! LET'S GET MOVING!
TAKIKO, STAY SAFE...
HATSUI! C'MON, WAKE UP!
URG...
Oh.
GOOD. I THOUGHT YOU'D FROZEN TO DEATH.
BLINK
NO, PRIESTESS! PLEASE GET TREAT-MENT!
WHOA!

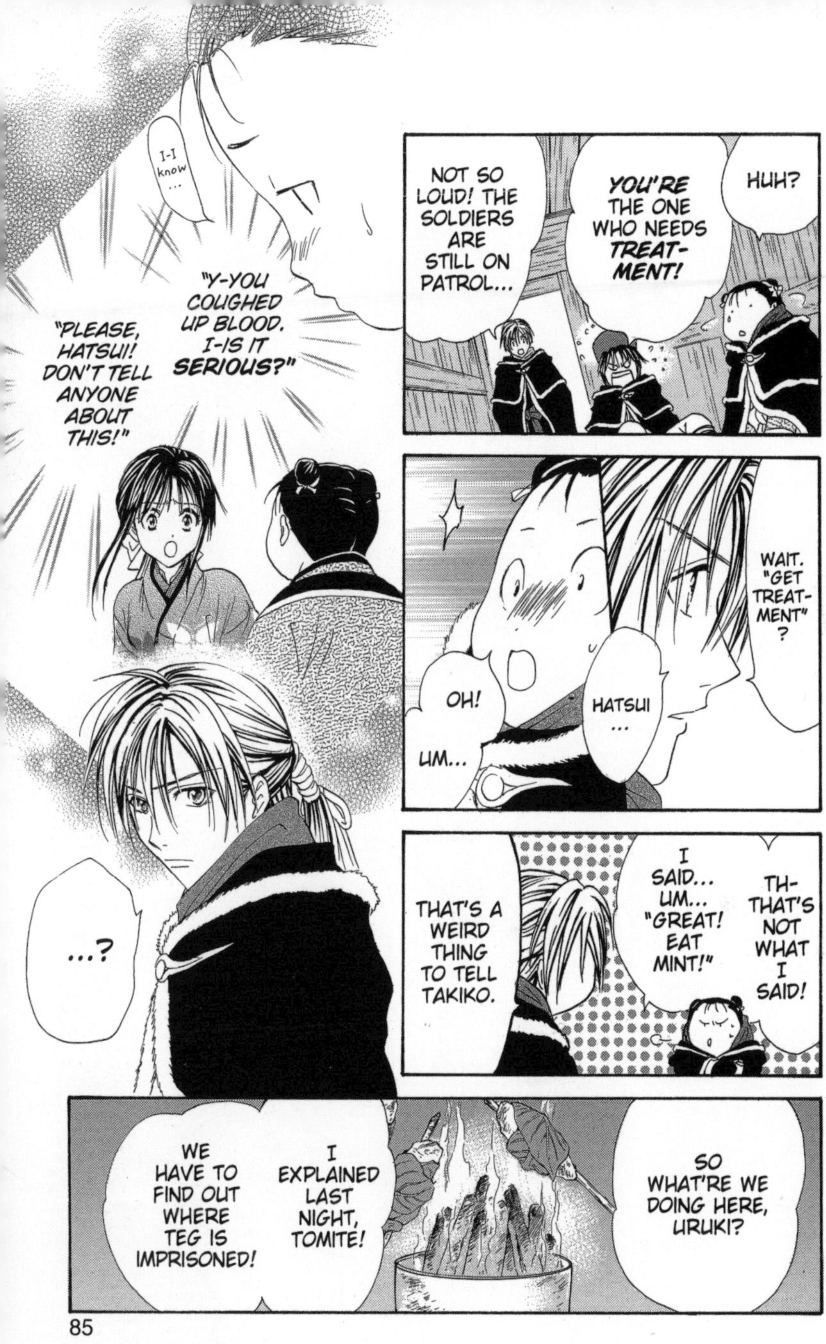
HUH?
YOU'RE THE ONE WHO NEEDS TREATMENT!
NOT SO LOUD! THE SOLDIERS ARE STILL ON PATROL...
WAIT. "GET TREATMENT"?
HATSUI...
OH!
UM...
TH-THAT'S NOT WHAT I SAID!
I SAID... UM... "GREAT! EAT MINT!"
THAT'S A WEIRD THING TO TELL TAKIKO.
I-I know...
"Y-YOU COUGHED UP BLOOD. I-IS IT SERIOUS?"
"PLEASE, HATSUI! DON'T TELL ANYONE ABOUT THIS!"
...?
SO WHAT'RE WE DOING HERE, URUKI?
I EXPLAINED LAST NIGHT, TOMITE!
WE HAVE TO FIND OUT WHERE TEG IS IMPRISONED!

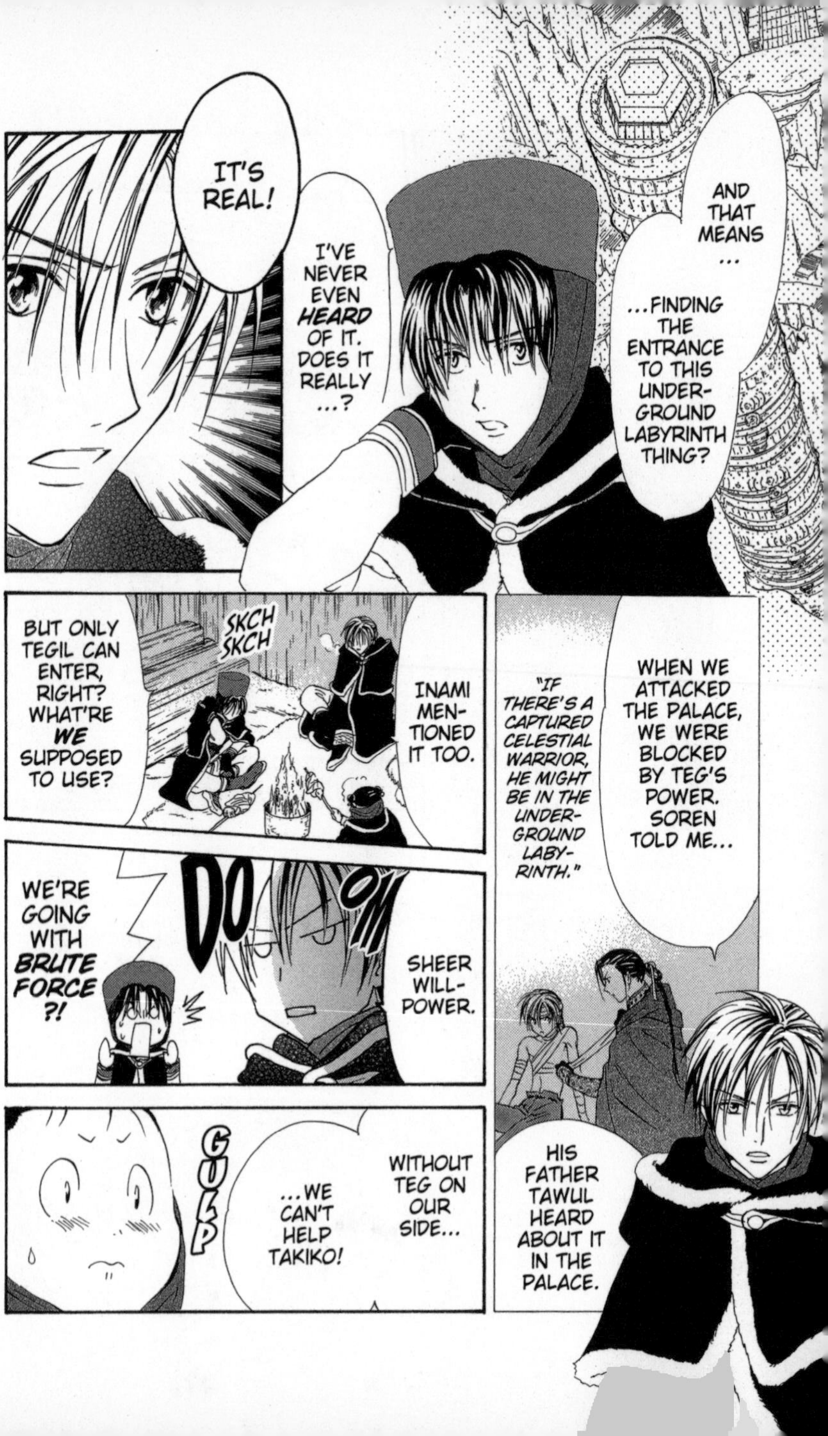
AND THAT MEANS ...
...FINDING THE ENTRANCE TO THIS UNDER-GROUND LABYRINTH THING?
I'VE NEVER EVEN HEARD OF IT. DOES IT REALLY ...?
IT'S REAL!
WHEN WE ATTACKED THE PALACE, WE WERE BLOCKED BY TEG'S POWER. SOREN TOLD ME...
"IF THERE'S A CAPTURED CELESTIAL WARRIOR, HE MIGHT BE IN THE UNDER-GROUND LABY-RINTH."
HIS FATHER TAWUL HEARD ABOUT IT IN THE PALACE.
INAMI MEN-TIONED IT TOO.
SKCH SKCH
BUT ONLY TEGIL CAN ENTER, RIGHT? WHAT'RE WE SUPPOSED TO USE?
SHEER WILL-POWER.
DOOM
WE'RE GOING WITH BRUTE FORCE ?!
WITHOUT TEG ON OUR SIDE...
...WE CAN'T HELP TAKIKO!
GULP

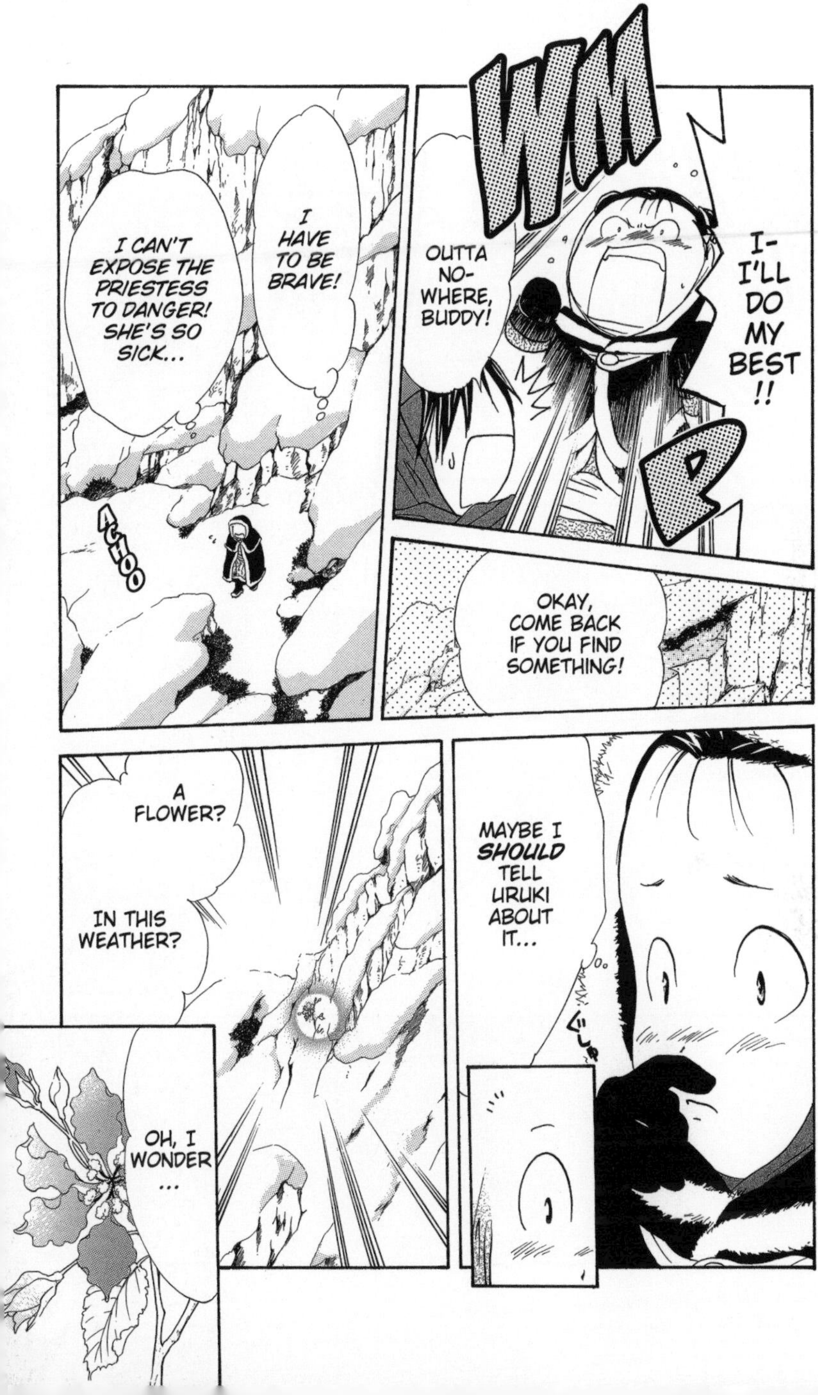
WM
I-I'LL DO MY BEST!!
OUTTA NO-WHERE, BUDDY!
P
OKAY, COME BACK IF YOU FIND SOMETHING!
I HAVE TO BE BRAVE!
I CAN'T EXPOSE THE PRIESTESS TO DANGER! SHE'S SO SICK...
ACHOO
MAYBE I SHOULD TELL URUKI ABOUT IT...
A FLOWER?
IN THIS WEATHER?
OH, I WONDER ...

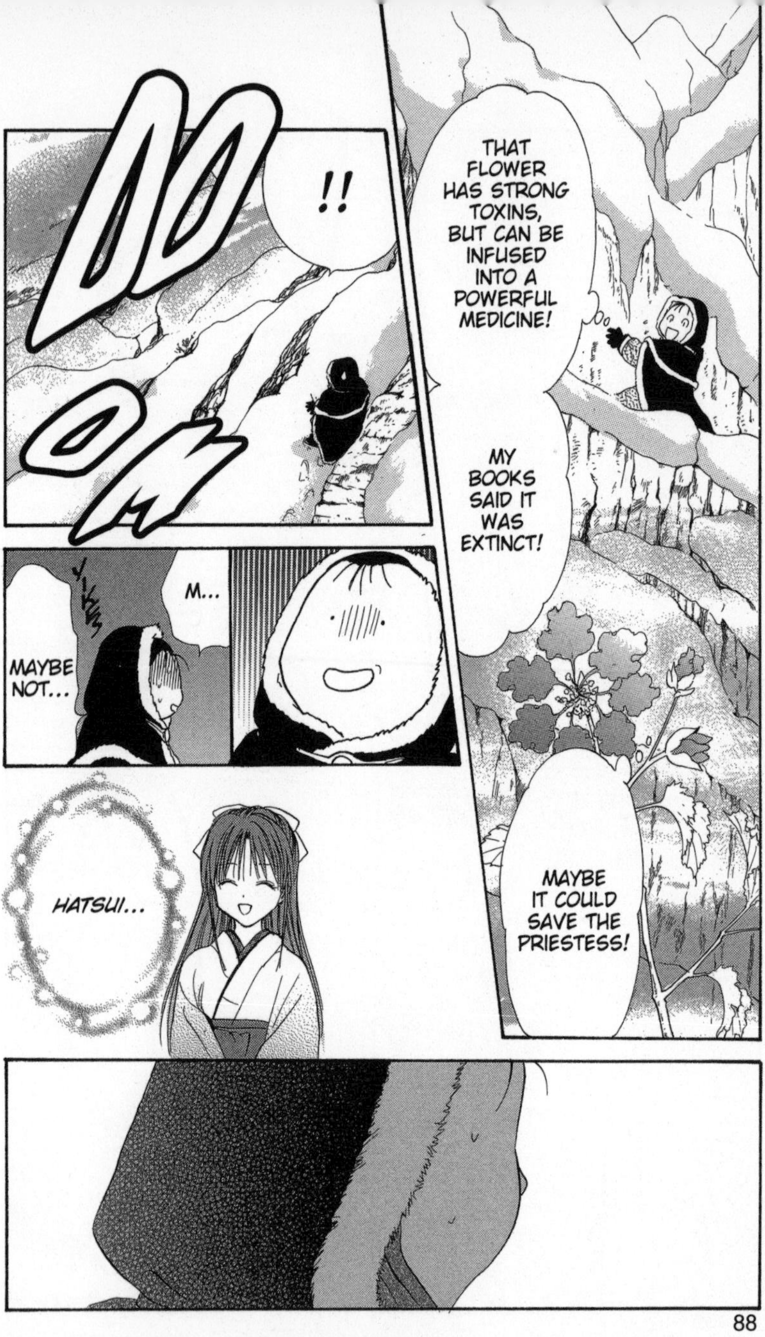
THAT FLOWER HAS STRONG TOXINS, BUT CAN BE INFUSED INTO A POWERFUL MEDICINE!
MY BOOKS SAID IT WAS EXTINCT!
MAYBE IT COULD SAVE THE PRIESTESS!
!!
MOM
M...
YIKES
MAYBE NOT...
HATSUI...

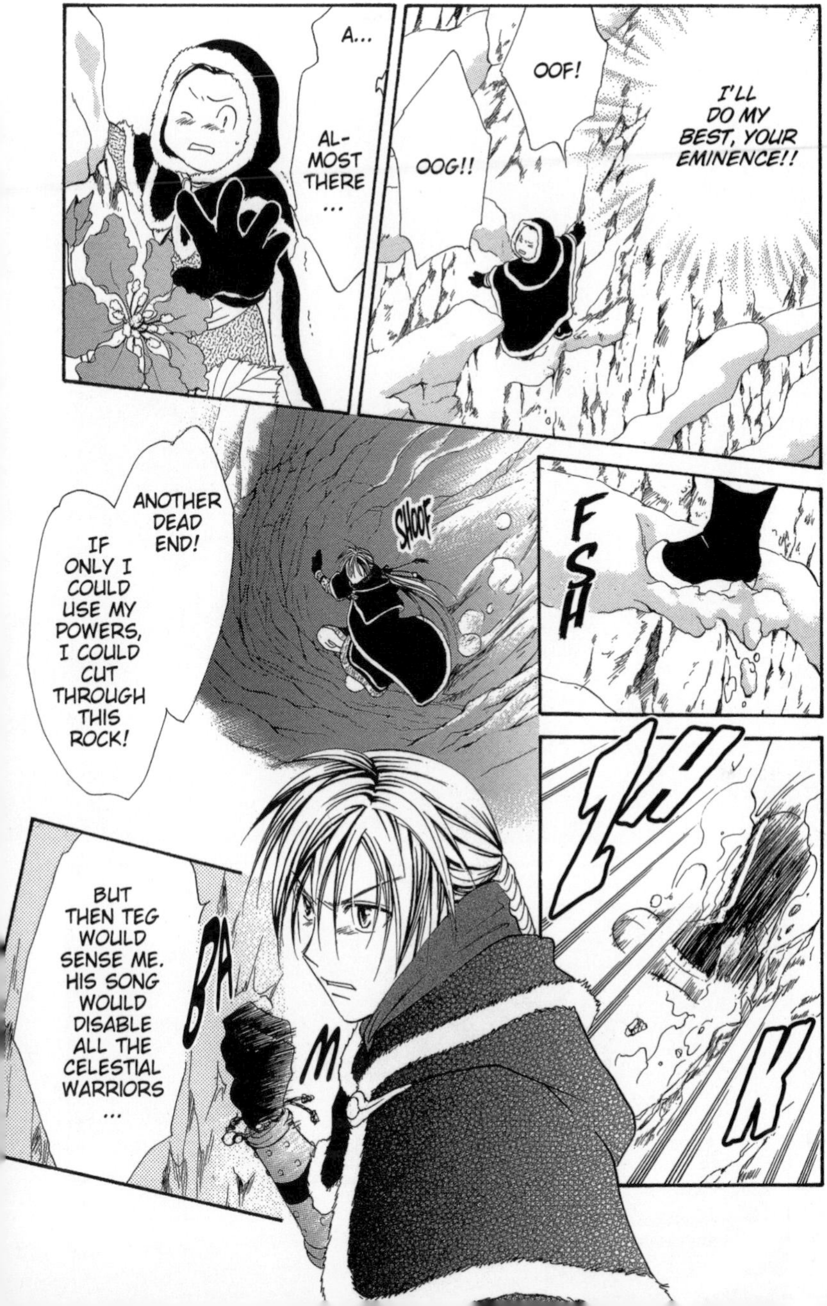

I'LL DO MY BEST, YOUR EMINENCE!!
OOF!
OOG!!
A...
ALMOST THERE...
FSH
SHOOF
ANOTHER DEAD END!
IF ONLY I COULD USE MY POWERS, I COULD CUT THROUGH THIS ROCK!
THK
BAM
BUT THEN TEG WOULD SENSE ME. HIS SONG WOULD DISABLE ALL THE CELESTIAL WARRIORS...

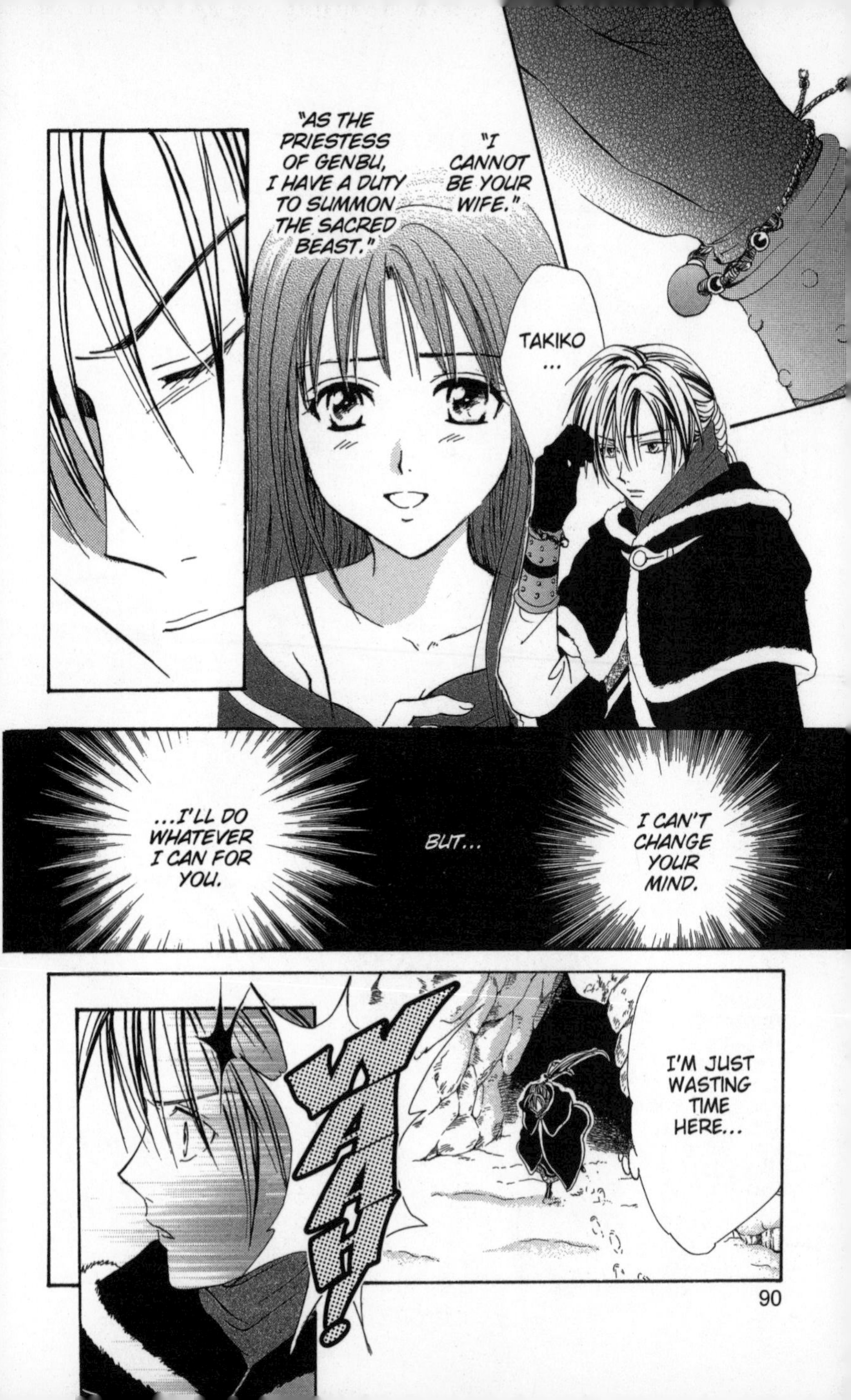
"I CANNOT BE YOUR WIFE."
"AS THE PRIESTESS OF GENBU, I HAVE A DUTY TO SUMMON THE SACRED BEAST."
TAKIKO ...
I CAN'T CHANGE YOUR MIND.
BUT...
...I'LL DO WHATEVER I CAN FOR YOU.
I'M JUST WASTING TIME HERE...

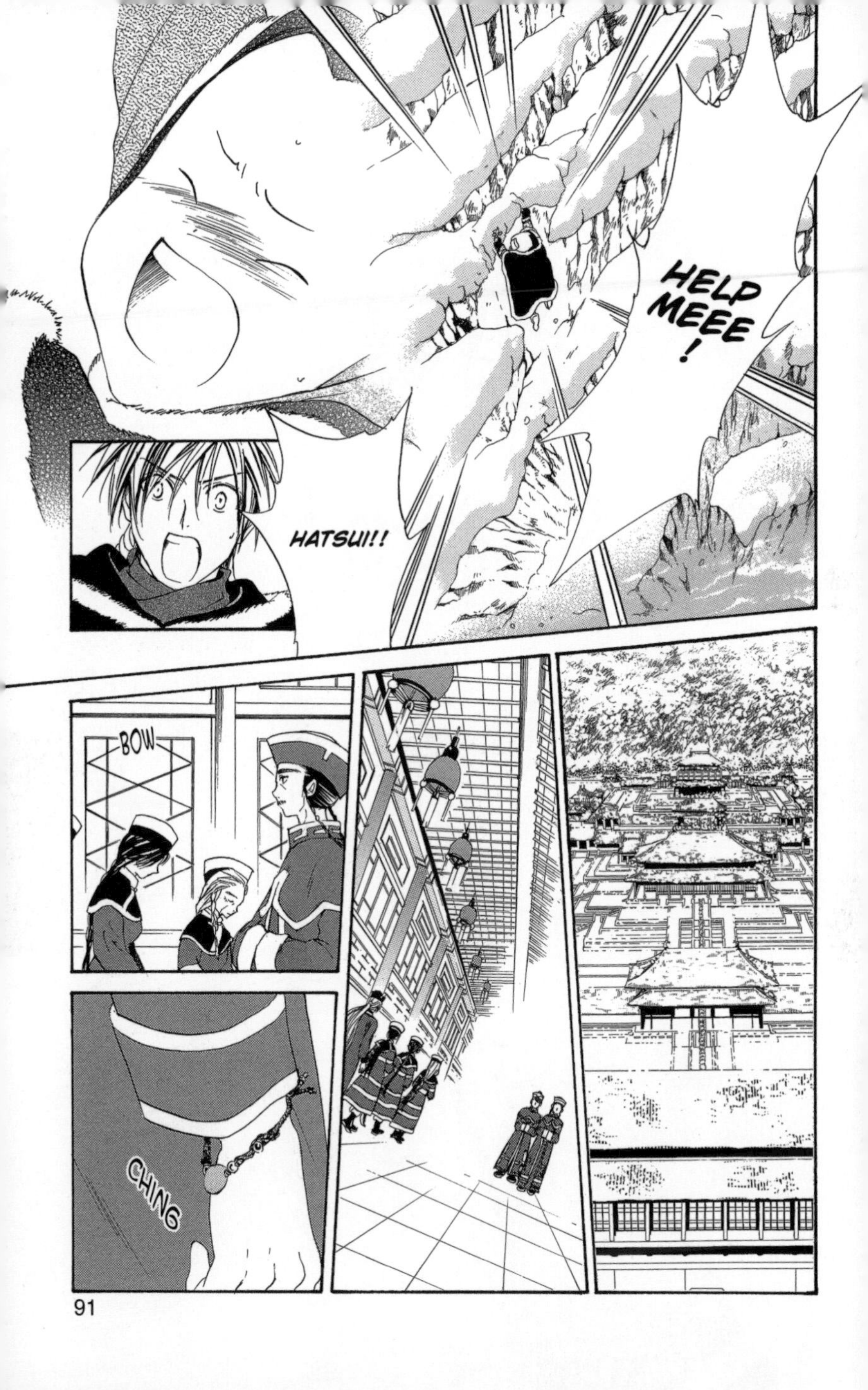
HELP MEEE!
HATSUI!!
BOW
CHING

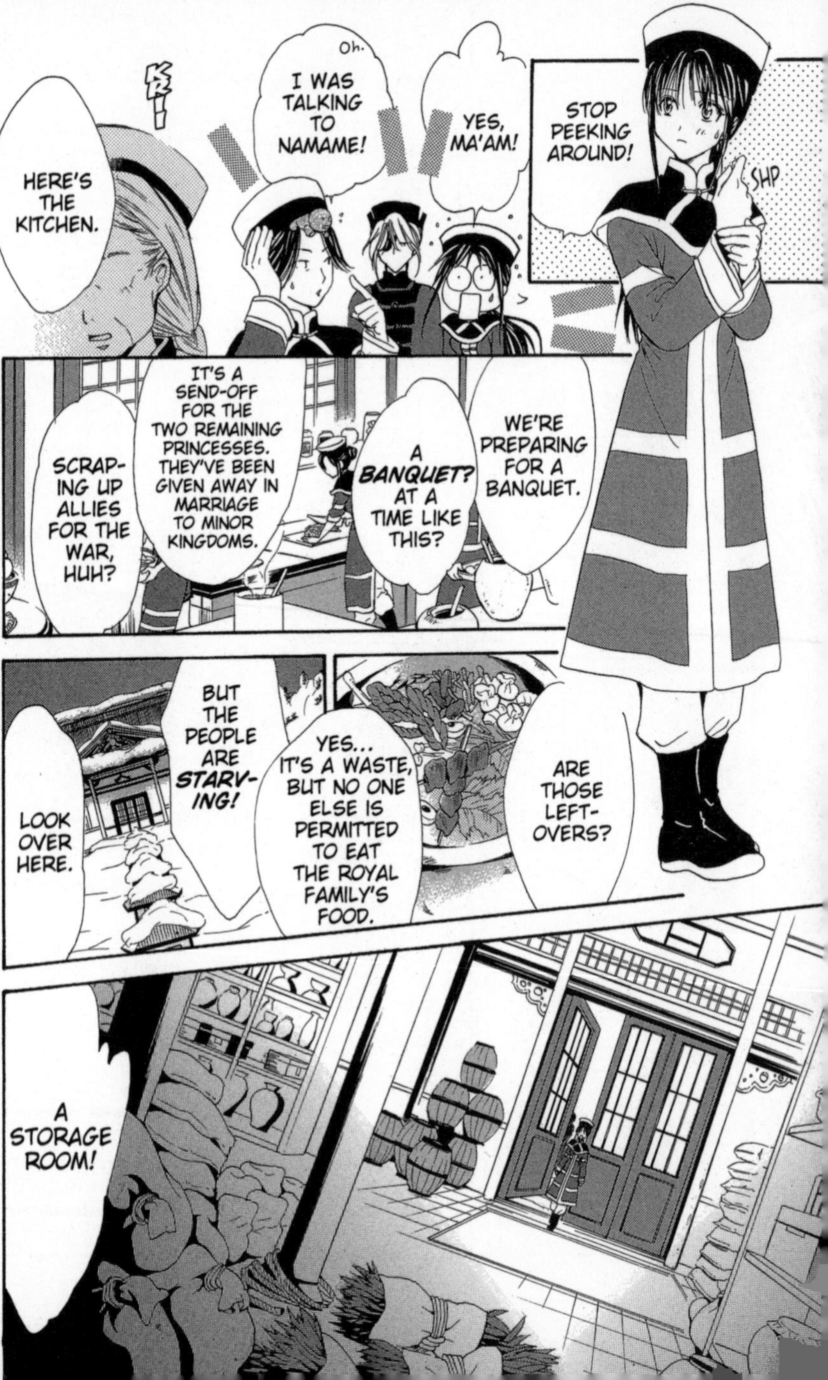
STOP PEEKING AROUND!
SHP
YES, MA'AM!
Oh.
I WAS TALKING TO NAMAME!
KRI
HERE'S THE KITCHEN.
WE'RE PREPARING FOR A BANQUET.
A BANQUET? AT A TIME LIKE THIS?
IT'S A SEND-OFF FOR THE TWO REMAINING PRINCESSES. THEY'VE BEEN GIVEN AWAY IN MARRIAGE TO MINOR KINGDOMS.
SCRAPING UP ALLIES FOR THE WAR, HUH?
ARE THOSE LEFT-OVERS?
YES... IT'S A WASTE, BUT NO ONE ELSE IS PERMITTED TO EAT THE ROYAL FAMILY'S FOOD.
BUT THE PEOPLE ARE STARVING!
LOOK OVER HERE.
A STORAGE ROOM!

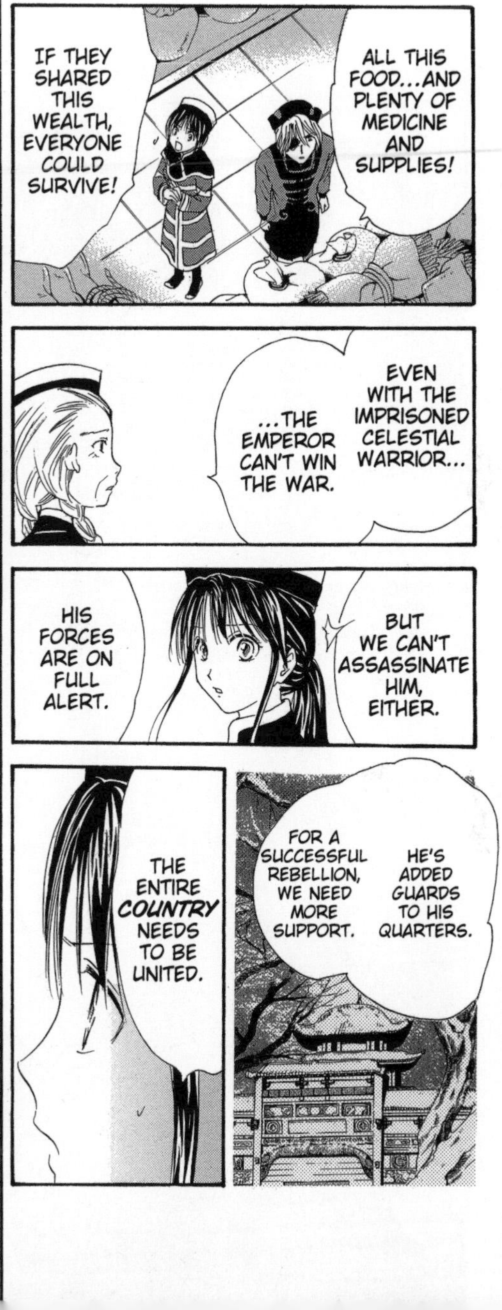
ALL THIS FOOD...AND PLENTY OF MEDICINE AND SUPPLIES!
IF THEY SHARED THIS WEALTH, EVERYONE COULD SURVIVE!
EVEN WITH THE IMPRISONED CELESTIAL WARRIOR...
...THE EMPEROR CAN'T WIN THE WAR.
BUT WE CAN'T ASSASSINATE HIM, EITHER.
HIS FORCES ARE ON FULL ALERT.
HE'S ADDED GUARDS TO HIS QUARTERS.
FOR A SUCCESSFUL REBELLION, WE NEED MORE SUPPORT.
THE ENTIRE *COUNTRY* NEEDS TO BE UNITED.

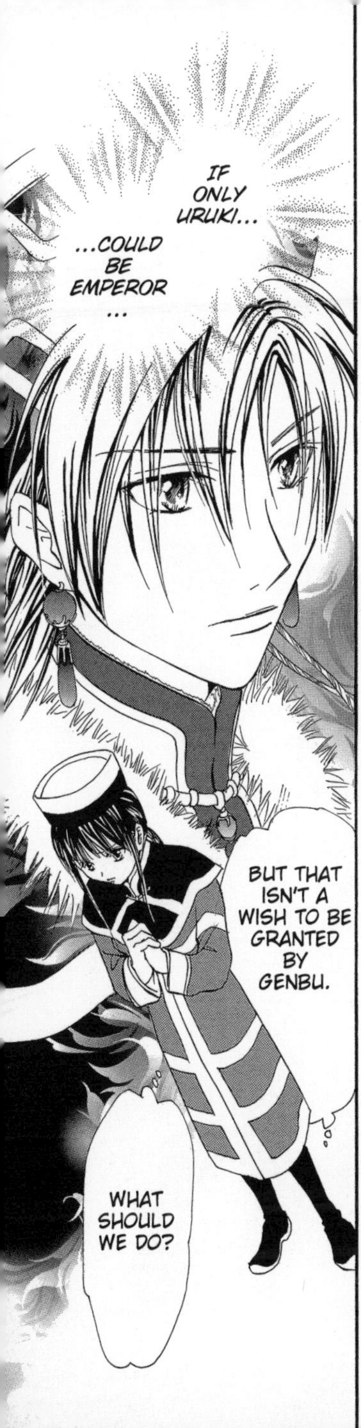
IF ONLY URUKI...
...COULD BE EMPEROR...
BUT THAT ISN'T A WISH TO BE GRANTED BY GENBU.
WHAT SHOULD WE DO?

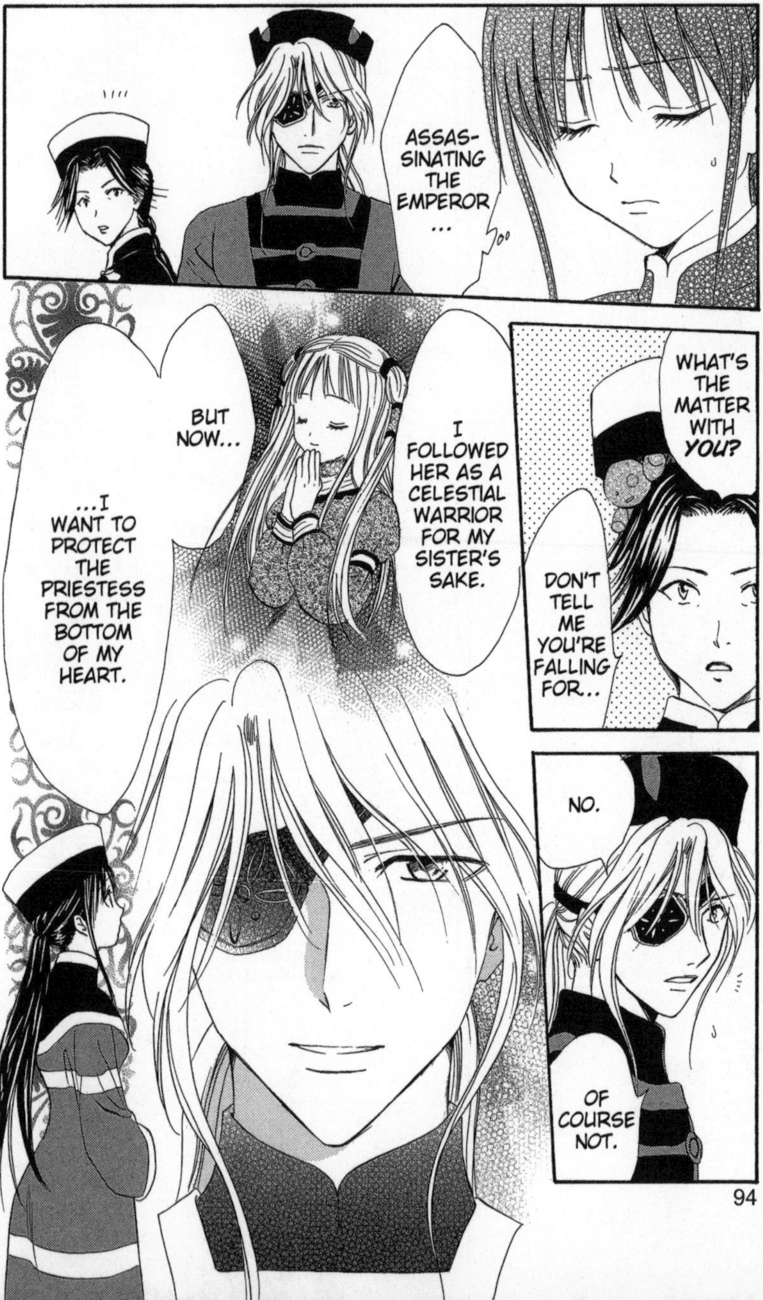
ASSAS-SINATING THE EMPEROR...
WHAT'S THE MATTER WITH *YOU?*
DON'T TELL ME YOU'RE FALLING FOR...
NO.
OF COURSE NOT.
I FOLLOWED HER AS A CELESTIAL WARRIOR FOR MY SISTER'S SAKE.
BUT NOW...
...I WANT TO PROTECT THE PRIESTESS FROM THE BOTTOM OF MY HEART.

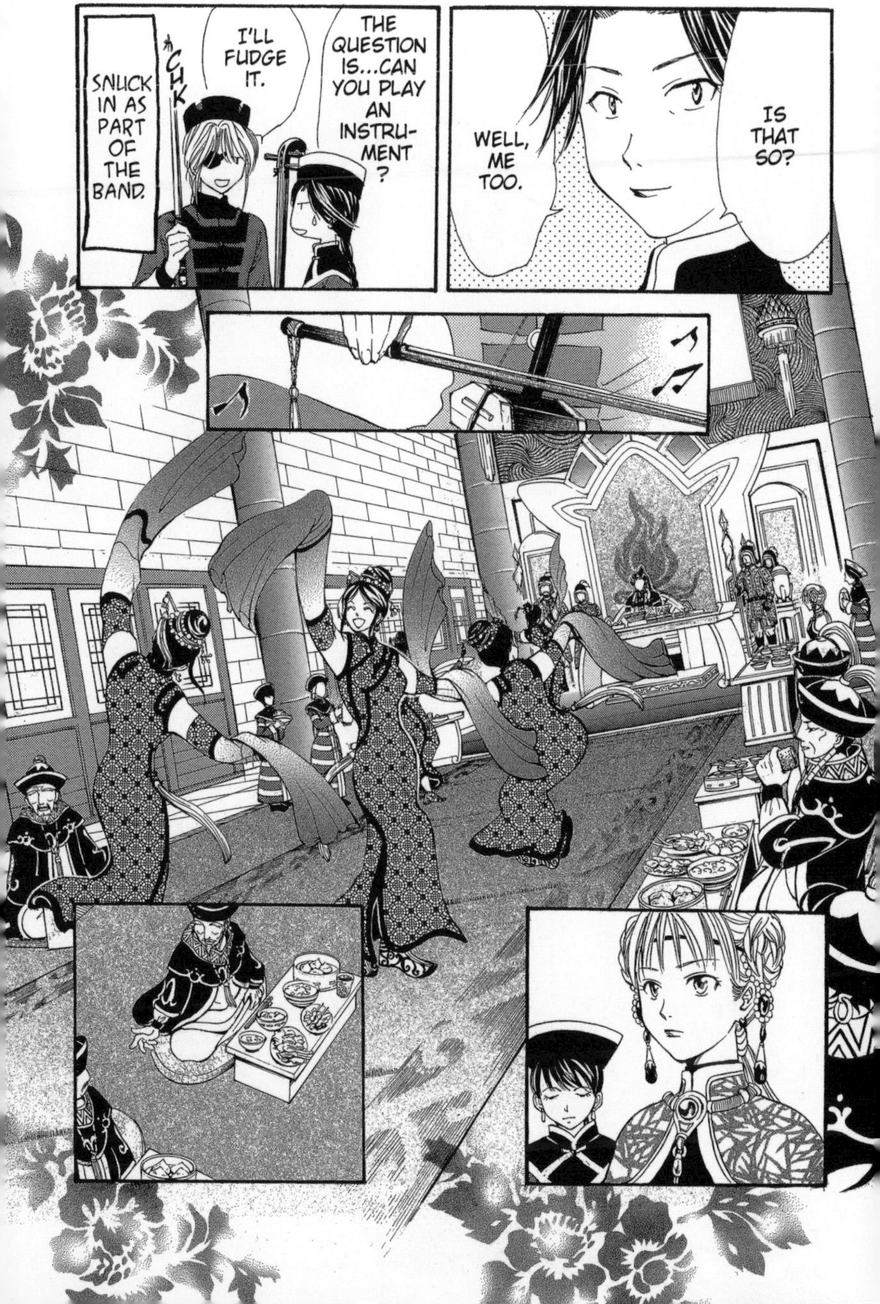
IS THAT SO?
WELL, ME TOO.
THE QUESTION IS...CAN YOU PLAY AN INSTRUMENT?
I'LL FUDGE IT.
CHK
SNUCK IN AS PART OF THE BAND.

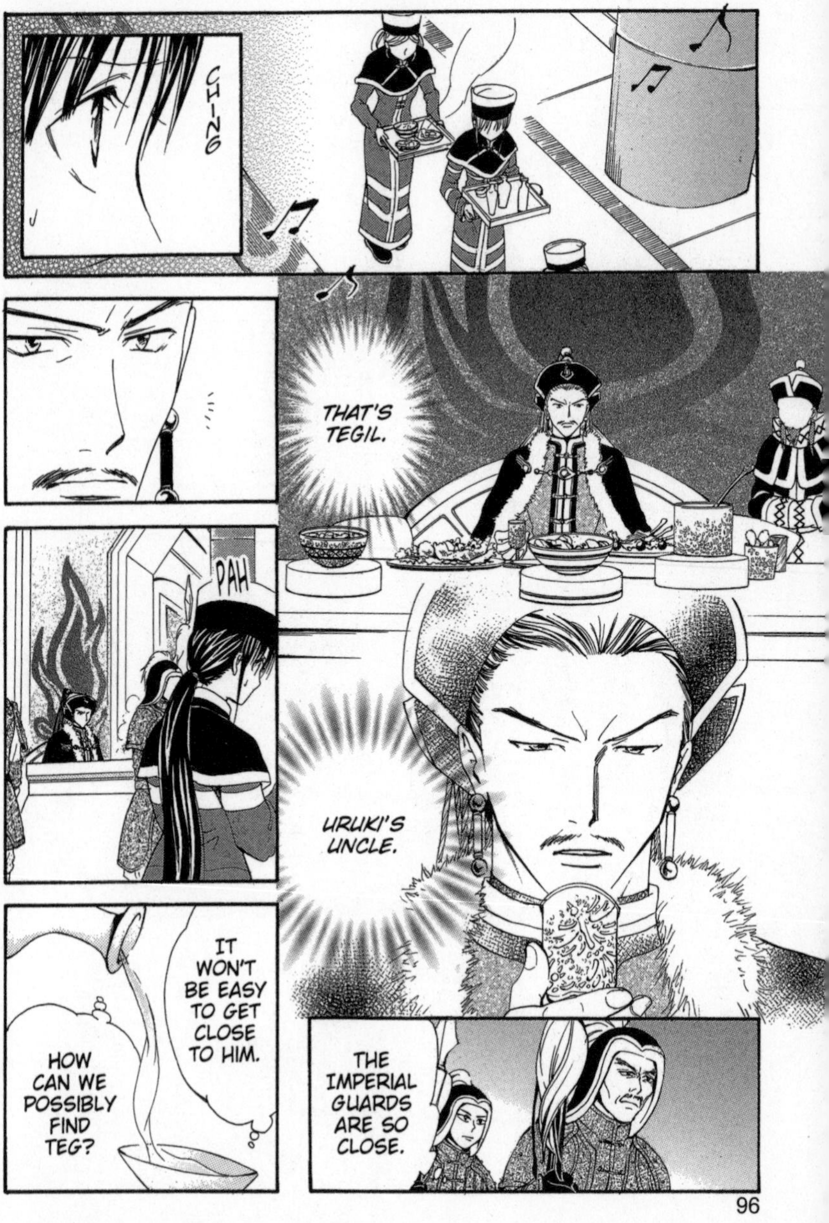
CHING
THAT'S TEGIL.
URUKI'S UNCLE.
PAH
THE IMPERIAL GUARDS ARE SO CLOSE.
IT WON'T BE EASY TO GET CLOSE TO HIM.
HOW CAN WE POSSIBLY FIND TEG?

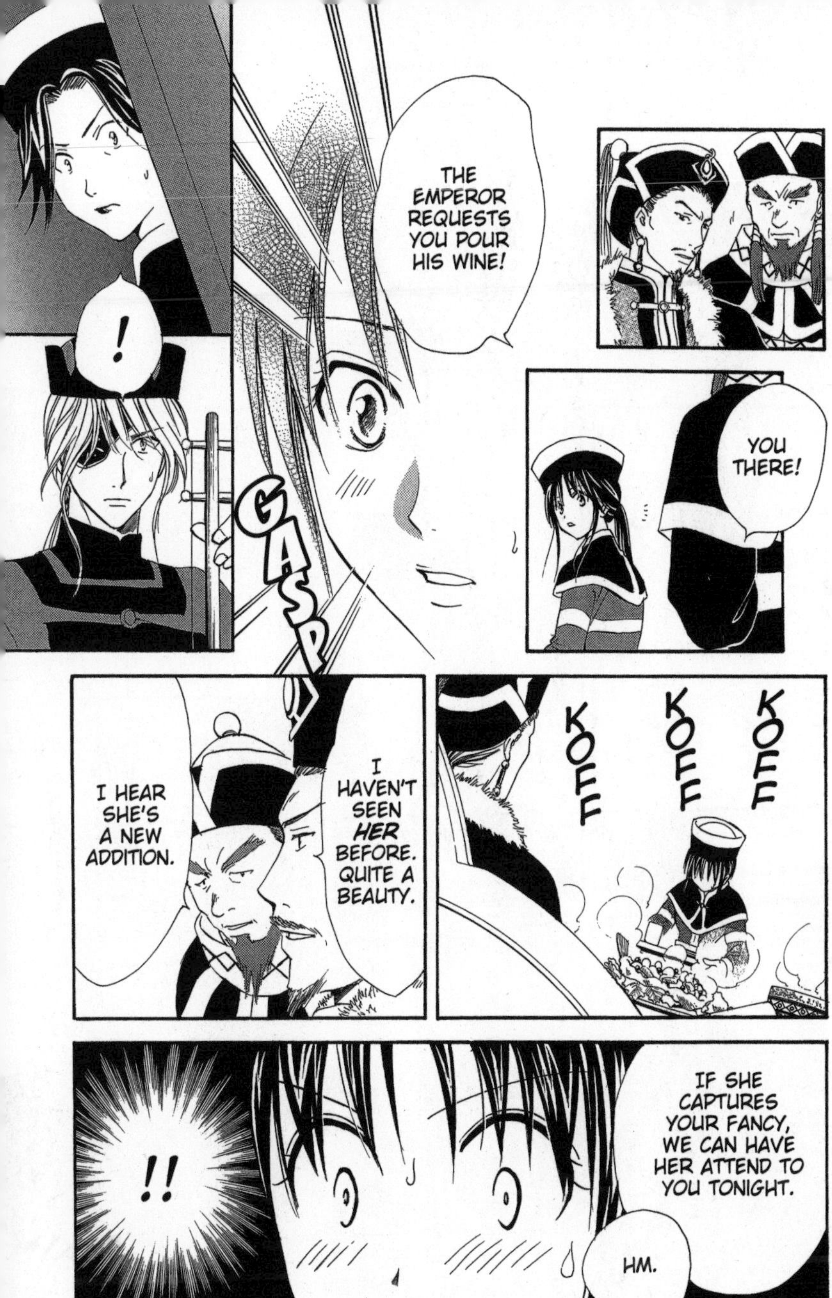
YOU THERE!
THE EMPEROR REQUESTS YOU POUR HIS WINE!
GASP
!
KOFF KOFF KOFF
I HAVEN'T SEEN *HER* BEFORE. QUITE A BEAUTY.
I HEAR SHE'S A NEW ADDITION.
IF SHE CAPTURES YOUR FANCY, WE CAN HAVE HER ATTEND TO YOU TONIGHT.
HM.
!!

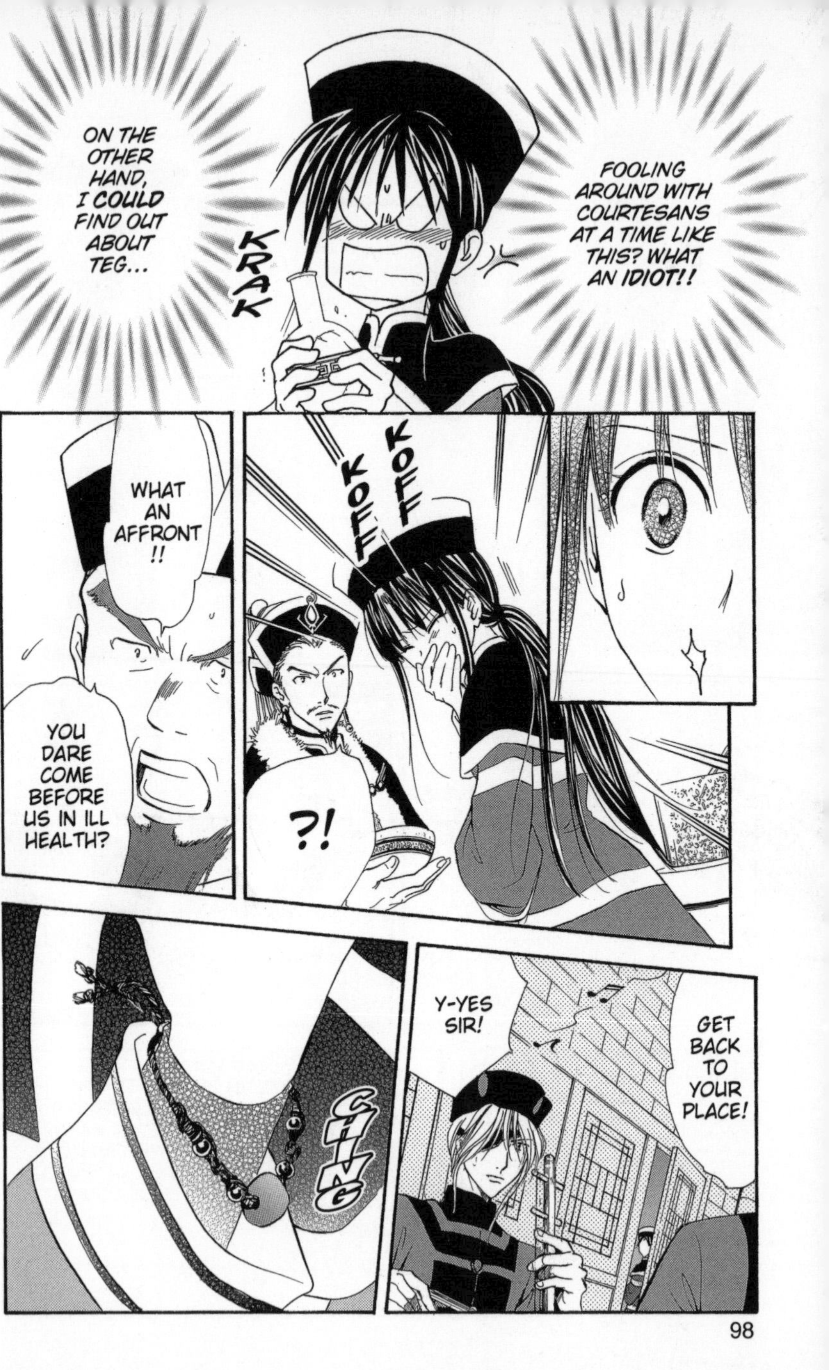
FOOLING AROUND WITH COURTESANS AT A TIME LIKE THIS? WHAT AN IDIOT!!
KRAK
ON THE OTHER HAND, I COULD FIND OUT ABOUT TEG...
KOFF KOFF
?!
WHAT AN AFFRONT!!
YOU DARE COME BEFORE US IN ILL HEALTH?
GET BACK TO YOUR PLACE!
Y-YES SIR!
CHING

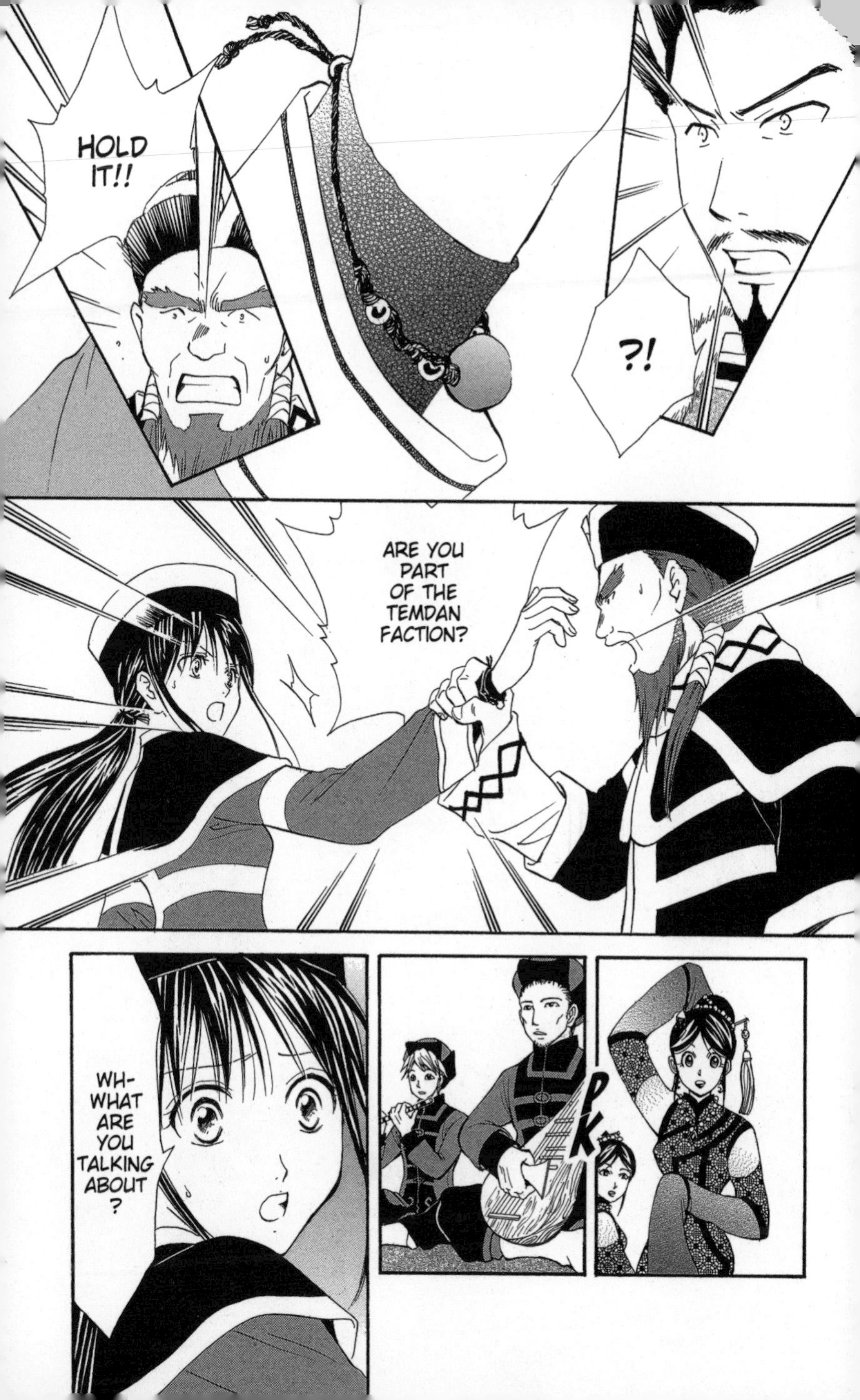
?!
HOLD IT!!
ARE YOU PART OF THE TEMDAN FACTION?
PK
WH- WHAT ARE YOU TALKING ABOUT?

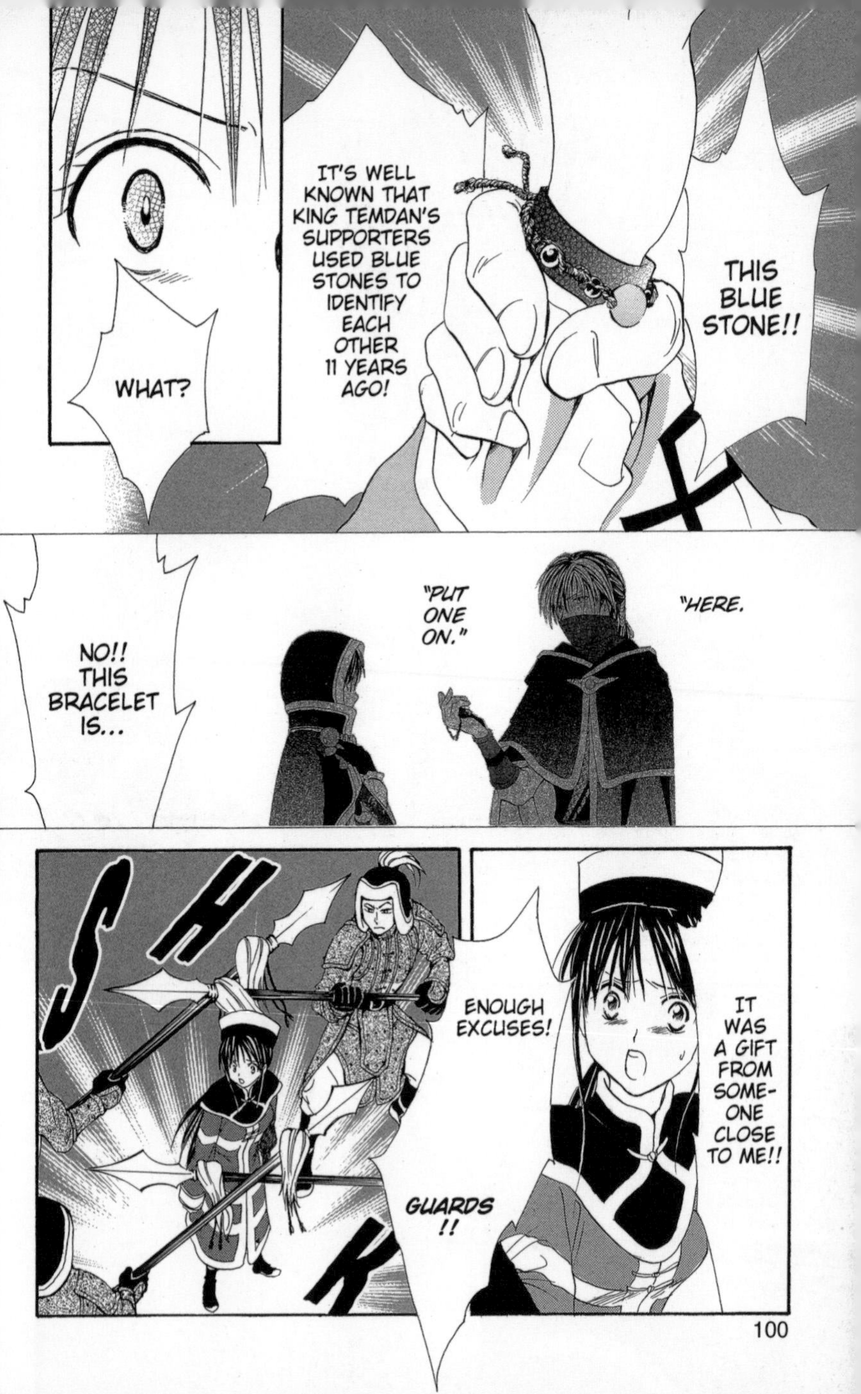
THIS BLUE STONE!!
IT'S WELL KNOWN THAT KING TEMDAN'S SUPPORTERS USED BLUE STONES TO IDENTIFY EACH OTHER 11 YEARS AGO!
WHAT?
"HERE.
"PUT ONE ON."
NO!! THIS BRACELET IS...
IT WAS A GIFT FROM SOME-ONE CLOSE TO ME!!
ENOUGH EXCUSES!
GUARDS !!
SHK

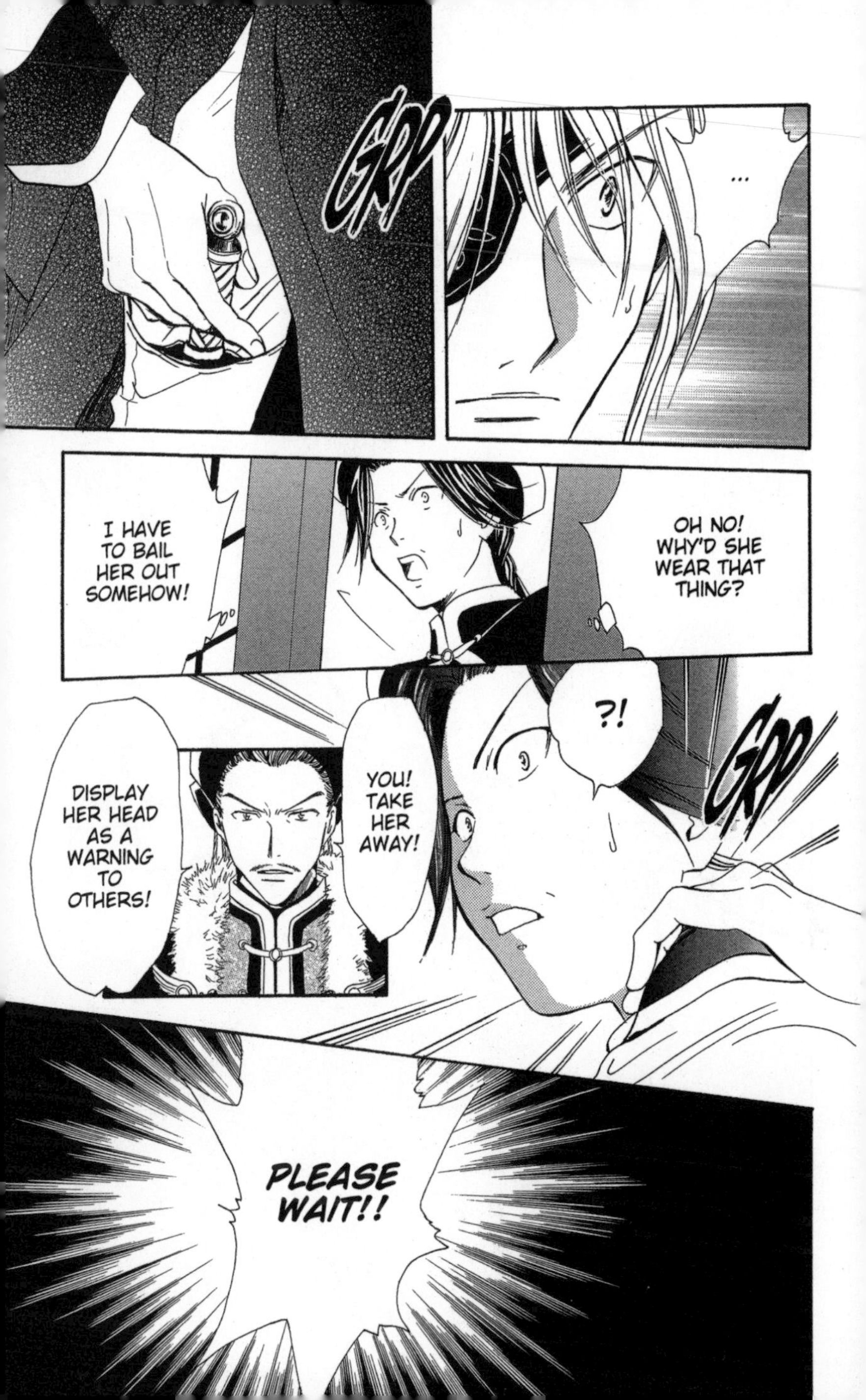
...
GRP
OH NO! WHY'D SHE WEAR THAT THING?
I HAVE TO BAIL HER OUT SOMEHOW!
GRP
?!
YOU! TAKE HER AWAY!
DISPLAY HER HEAD AS A WARNING TO OTHERS!
PLEASE WAIT!!

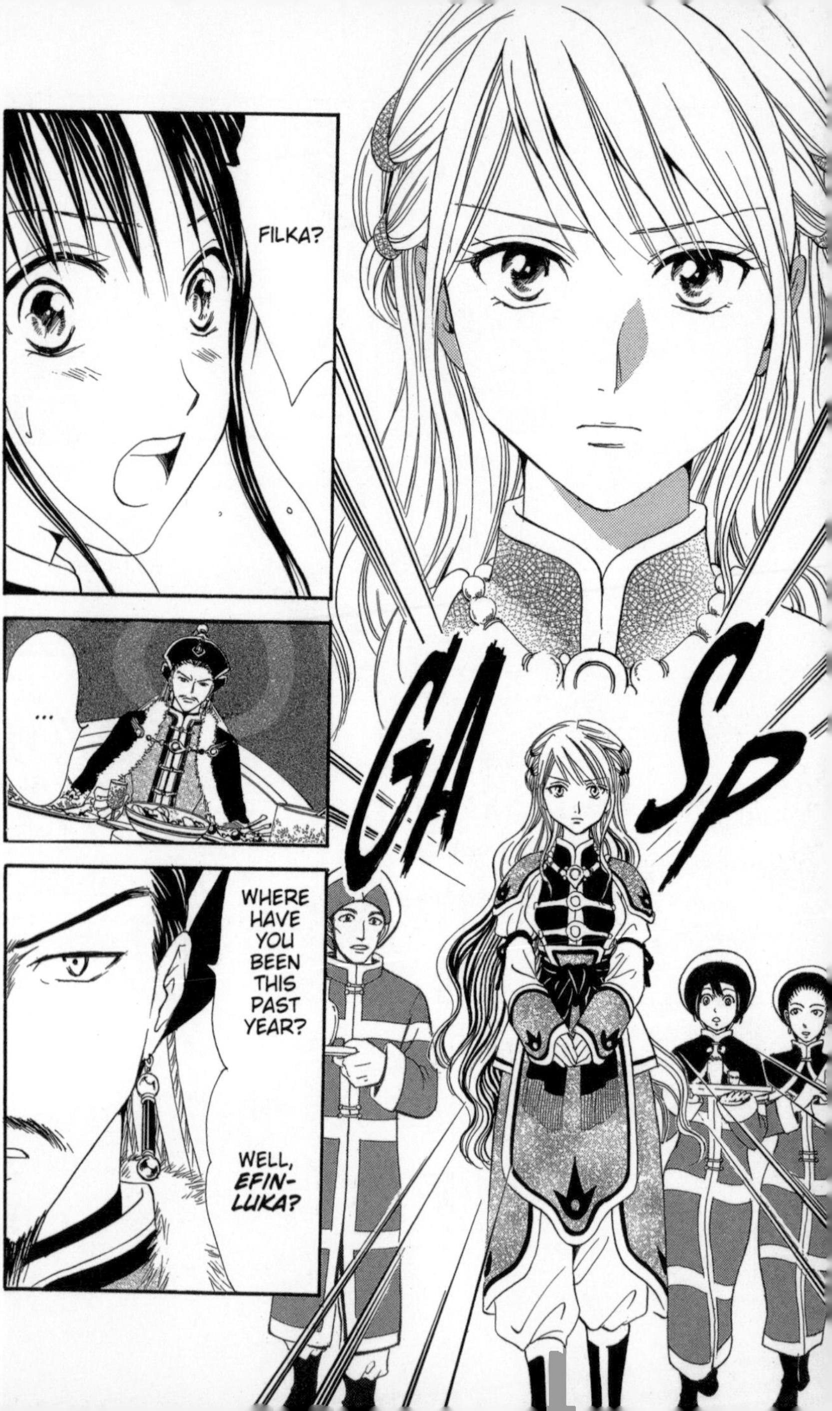
GASP
FILKA?
...
WHERE HAVE YOU BEEN THIS PAST YEAR?
WELL, *EFIN-LUKA?*

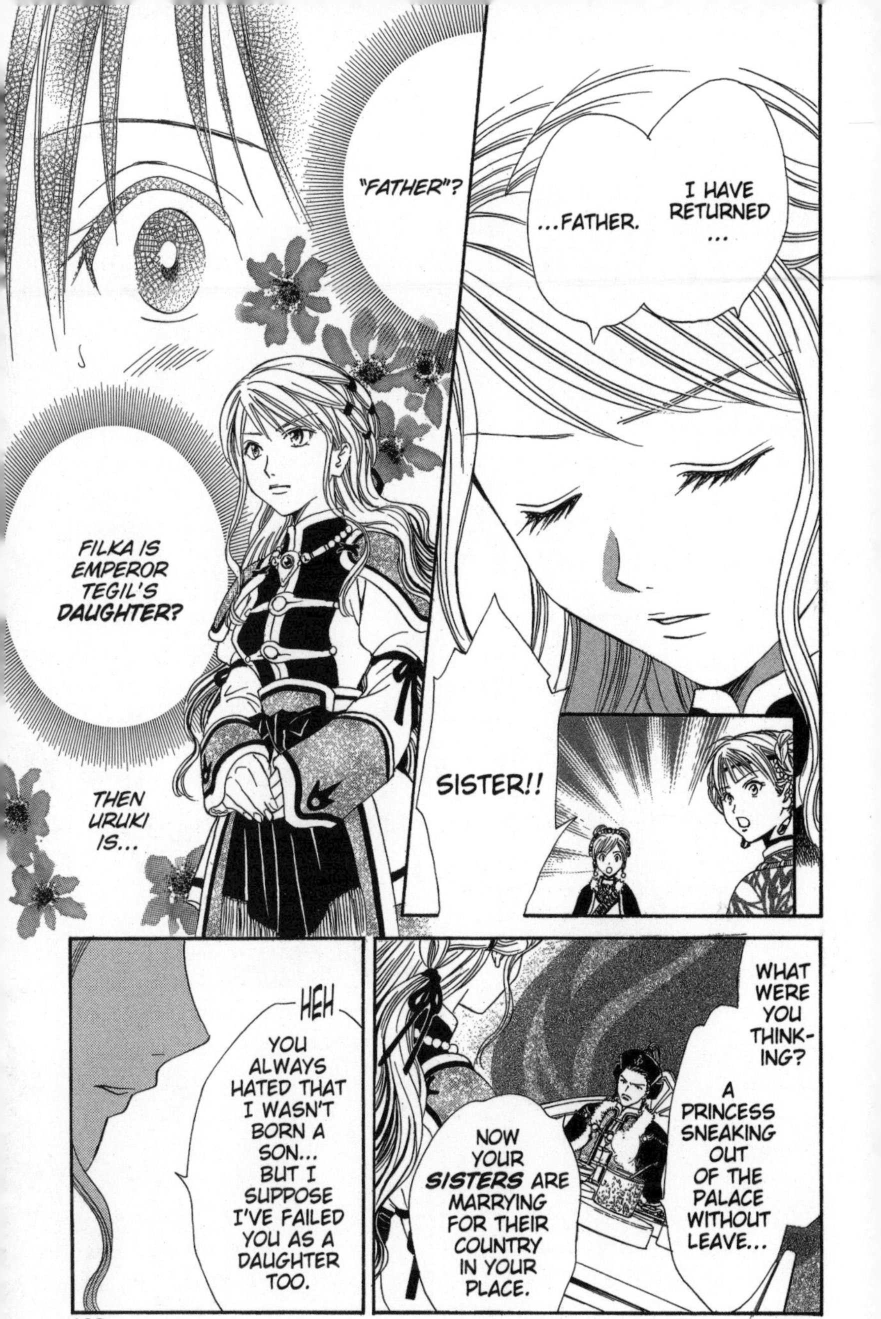
I HAVE RETURNED ...
...FATHER.
SISTER!!
"FATHER"?
FILKA IS EMPEROR TEGIL'S DAUGHTER?
THEN URUKI IS...
WHAT WERE YOU THINKING?
A PRINCESS SNEAKING OUT OF THE PALACE WITHOUT LEAVE...
NOW YOUR SISTERS ARE MARRYING FOR THEIR COUNTRY IN YOUR PLACE.
HEH
YOU ALWAYS HATED THAT I WASN'T BORN A SON... BUT I SUPPOSE I'VE FAILED YOU AS A DAUGHTER TOO.

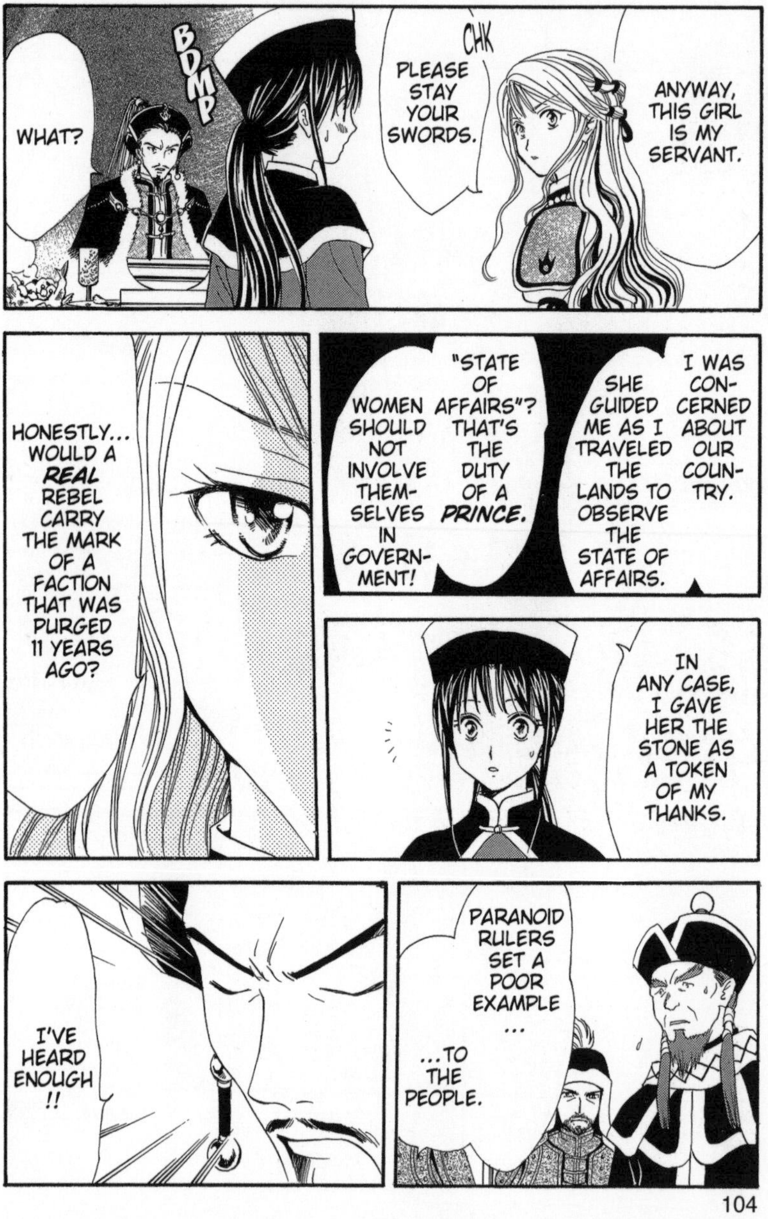
ANYWAY, THIS GIRL IS MY SERVANT.
CHK
PLEASE STAY YOUR SWORDS.
BDMP
WHAT?
I WAS CONCERNED ABOUT OUR COUNTRY.
SHE GUIDED ME AS I TRAVELED THE LANDS TO OBSERVE THE STATE OF AFFAIRS.
"STATE OF AFFAIRS"? THAT'S THE DUTY OF A *PRINCE.*
WOMEN SHOULD NOT INVOLVE THEMSELVES IN GOVERNMENT!
IN ANY CASE, I GAVE HER THE STONE AS A TOKEN OF MY THANKS.
HONESTLY... WOULD A *REAL* REBEL CARRY THE MARK OF A FACTION THAT WAS PURGED 11 YEARS AGO?
PARANOID RULERS SET A POOR EXAMPLE ...
...TO THE PEOPLE.
I'VE HEARD ENOUGH!!

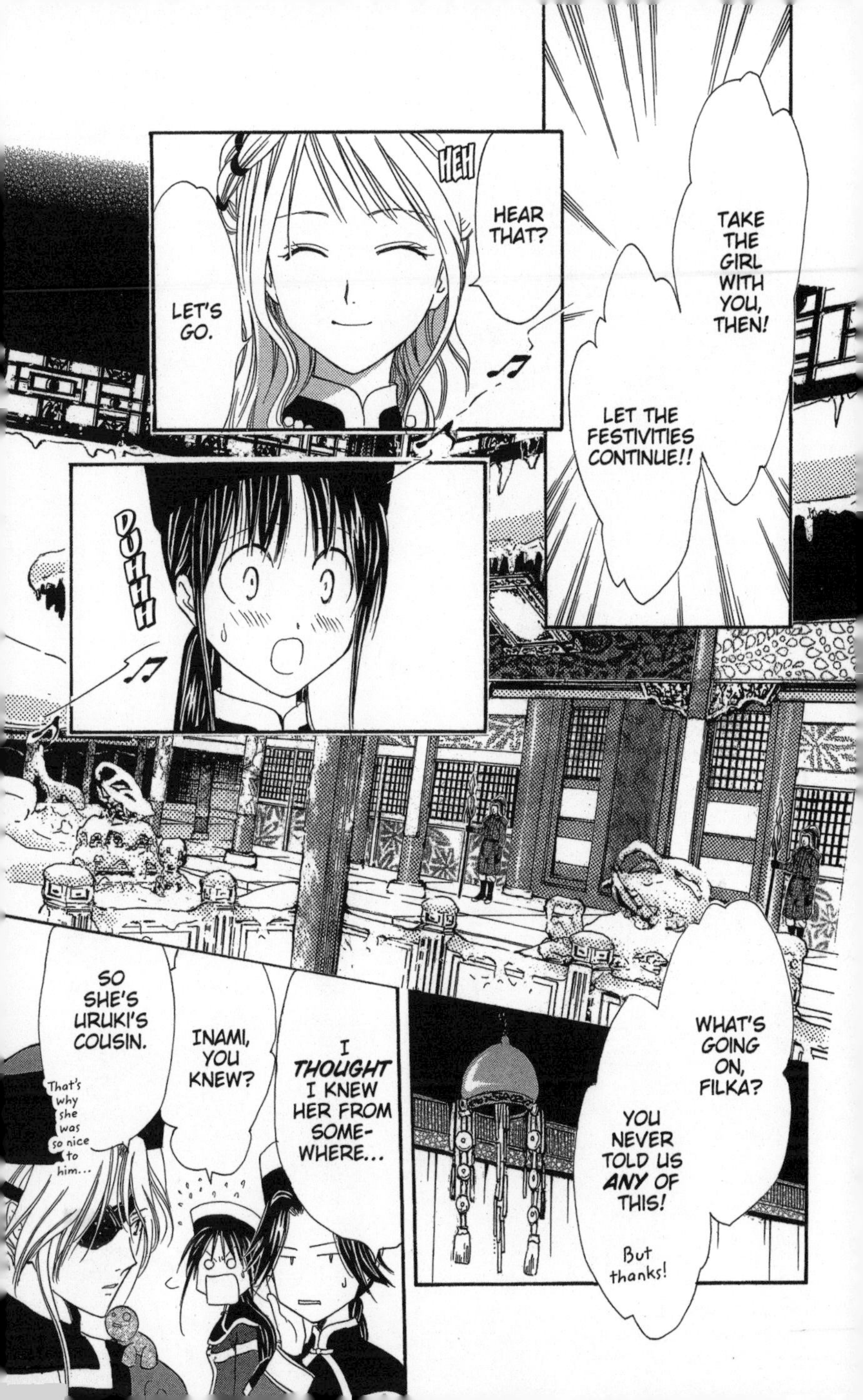
TAKE THE GIRL WITH YOU, THEN!
LET THE FESTIVITIES CONTINUE!!
HEH
HEAR THAT?
LET'S GO.
DUHHH
WHAT'S GOING ON, FILKA?
YOU NEVER TOLD US *ANY* OF THIS!
But thanks!
I *THOUGHT* I KNEW HER FROM SOME-WHERE...
INAMI, YOU KNEW?
SO SHE'S URUKI'S COUSIN.
That's why she was so nice to him...

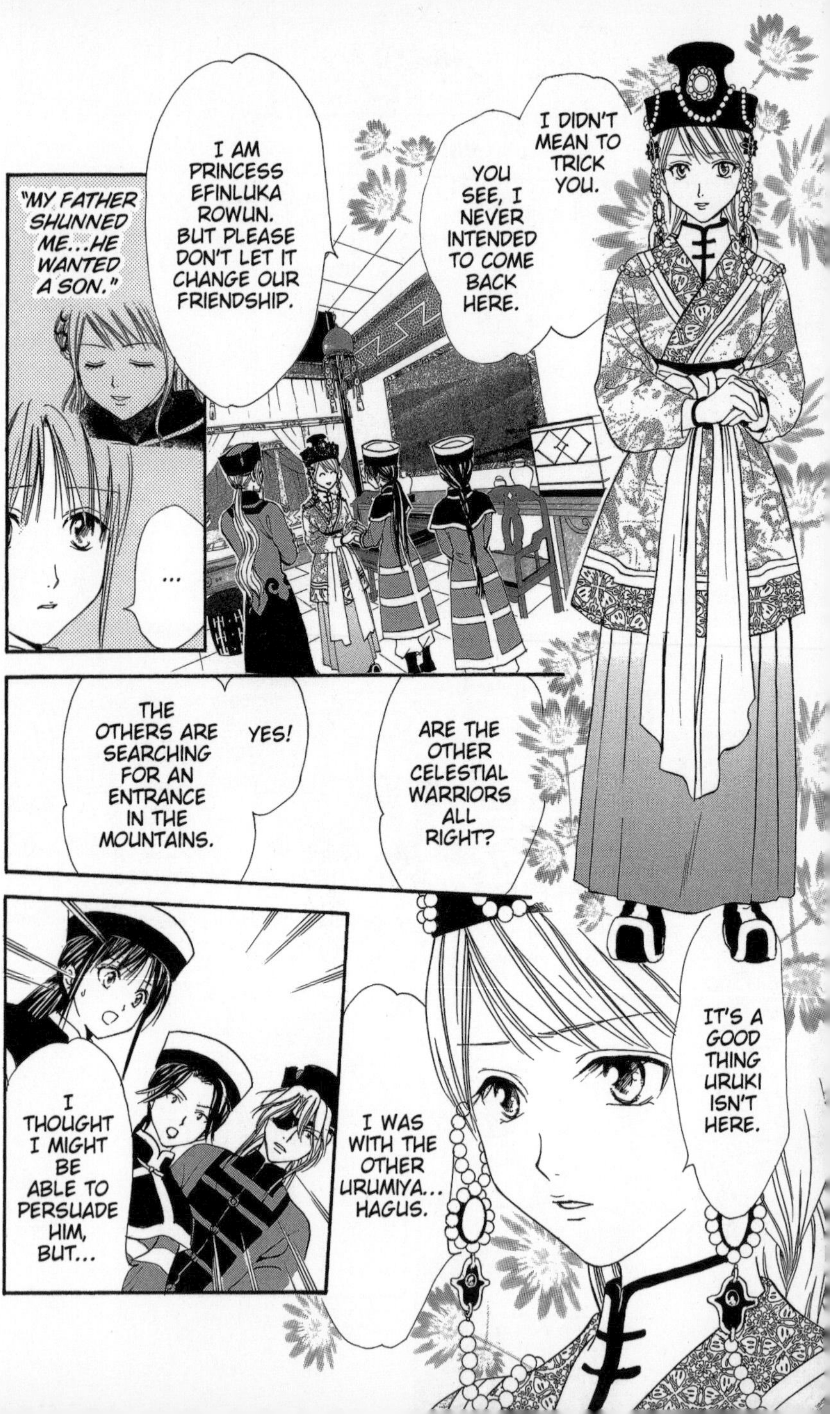
I DIDN'T MEAN TO TRICK YOU.
YOU SEE, I NEVER INTENDED TO COME BACK HERE.
I AM PRINCESS EFINLUKA ROWUN. BUT PLEASE DON'T LET IT CHANGE OUR FRIENDSHIP.
"MY FATHER SHUNNED ME...HE WANTED A SON."
...
ARE THE OTHER CELESTIAL WARRIORS ALL RIGHT?
YES!
THE OTHERS ARE SEARCHING FOR AN ENTRANCE IN THE MOUNTAINS.
IT'S A GOOD THING URUKI ISN'T HERE.
I WAS WITH THE OTHER URUMIYA... HAGUS.
I THOUGHT I MIGHT BE ABLE TO PERSUADE HIM, BUT...

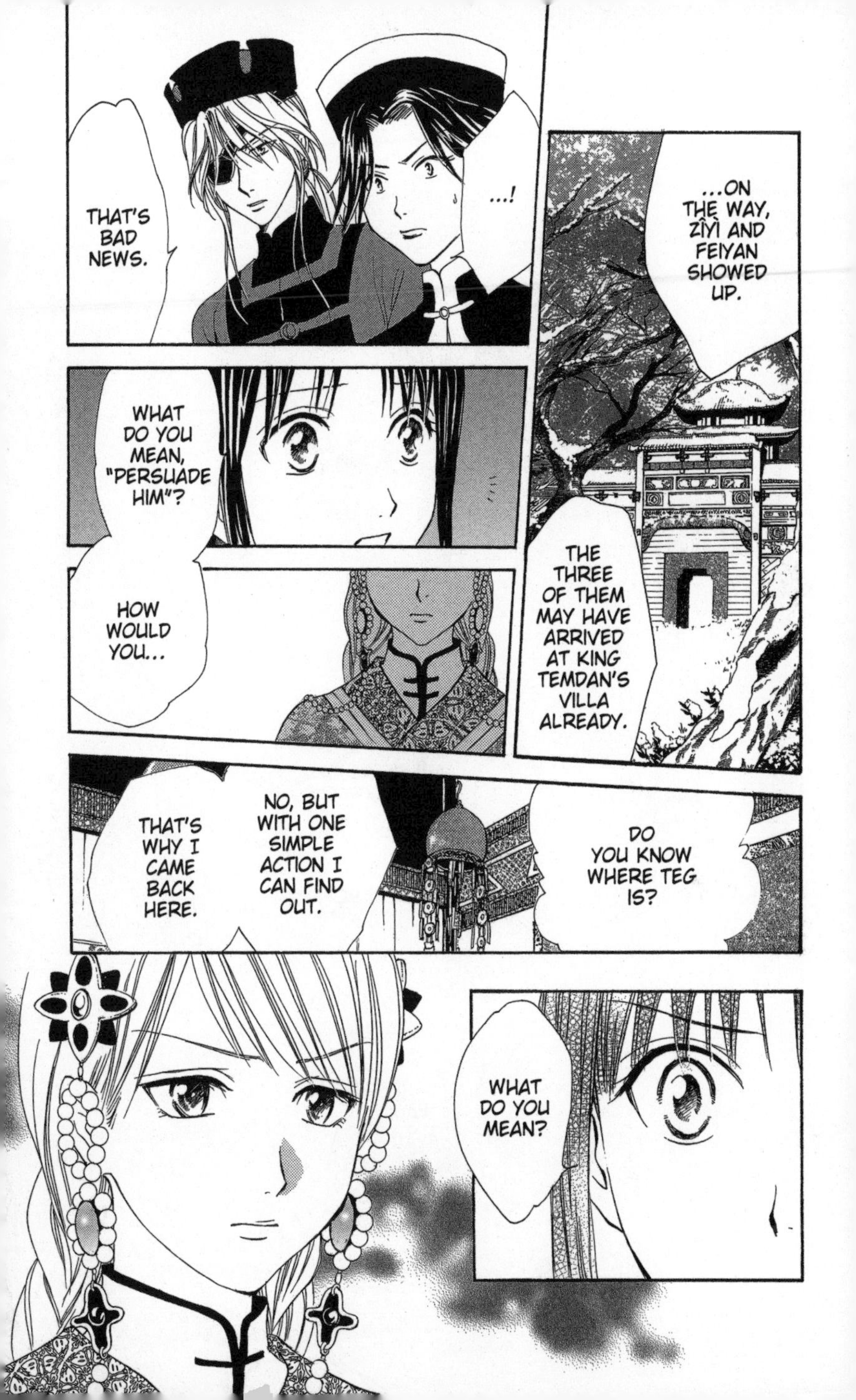

...ON THE WAY, ZÎYÌ AND FEIYAN SHOWED UP.
THE THREE OF THEM MAY HAVE ARRIVED AT KING TEMDAN'S VILLA ALREADY.
...!
THAT'S BAD NEWS.
WHAT DO YOU MEAN, "PERSUADE HIM"?
HOW WOULD YOU...
DO YOU KNOW WHERE TEG IS?
NO, BUT WITH ONE SIMPLE ACTION I CAN FIND OUT.
THAT'S WHY I CAME BACK HERE.
WHAT DO YOU MEAN?

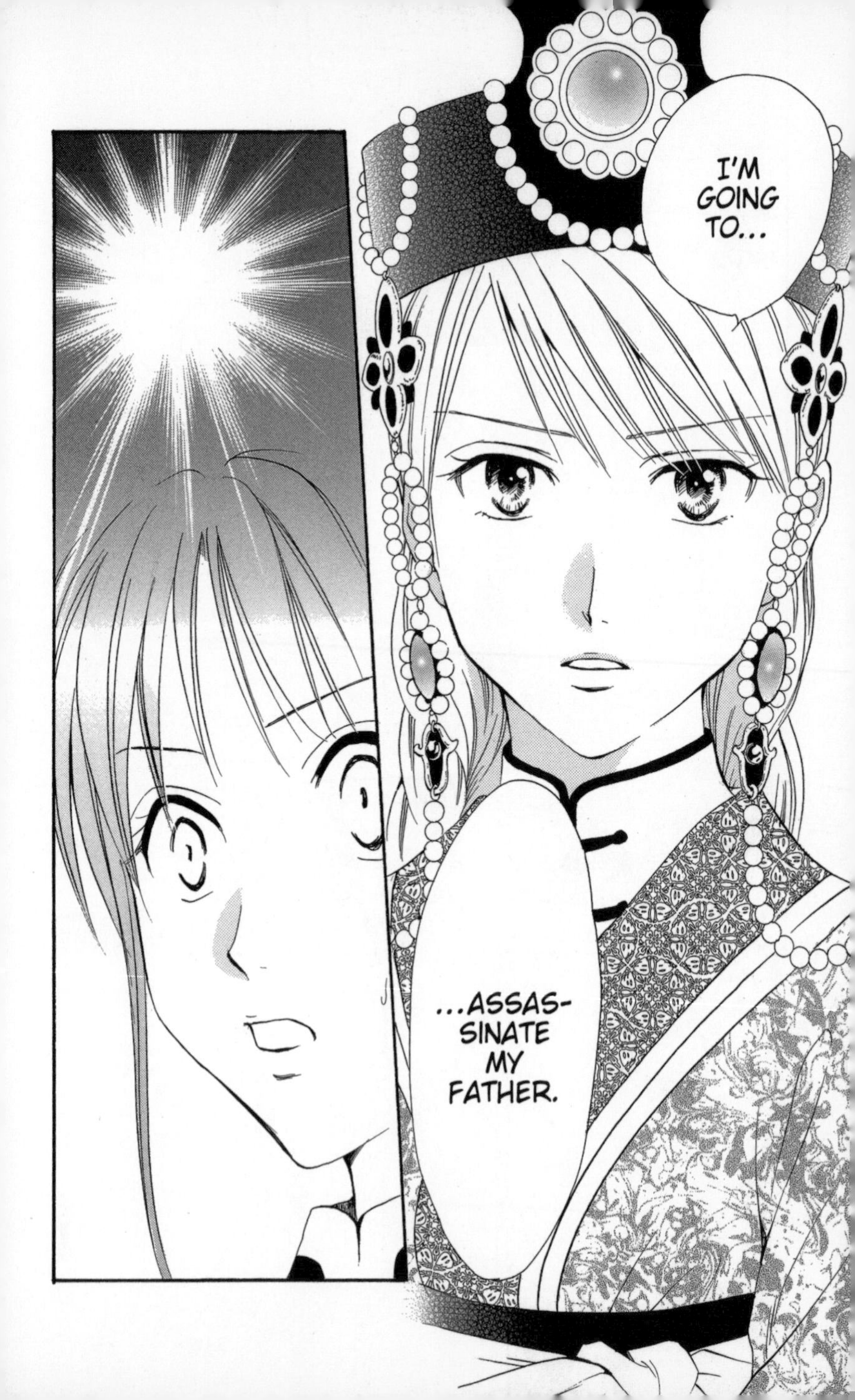
I'M GOING TO...
...ASSAS-SINATE MY FATHER.

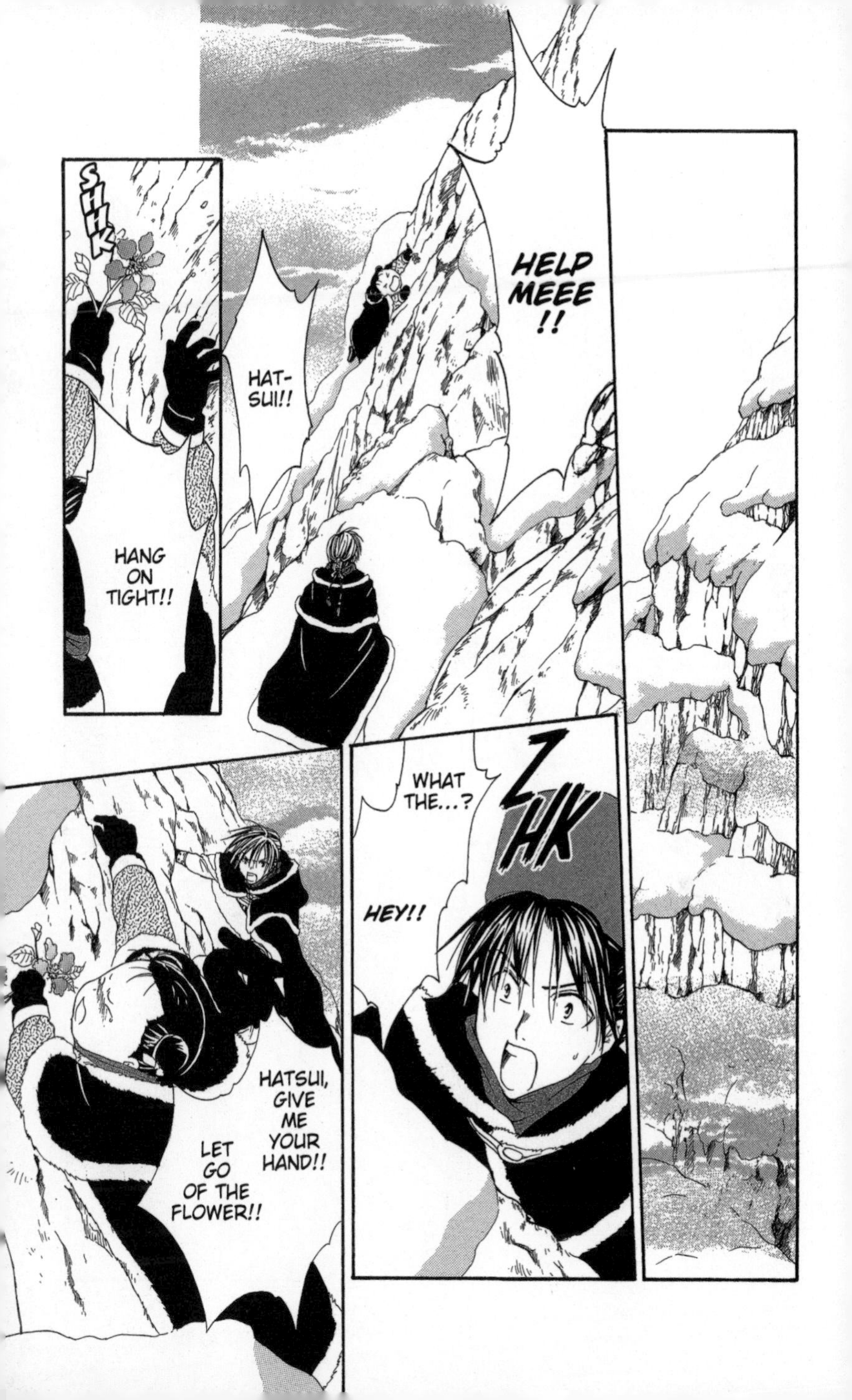
HELP MEEE!!
HAT-SUI!!
SHHK
HANG ON TIGHT!!
WHAT THE...?
ZHK
HEY!!
HATSUI, GIVE ME YOUR HAND!!
LET GO OF THE FLOWER!!

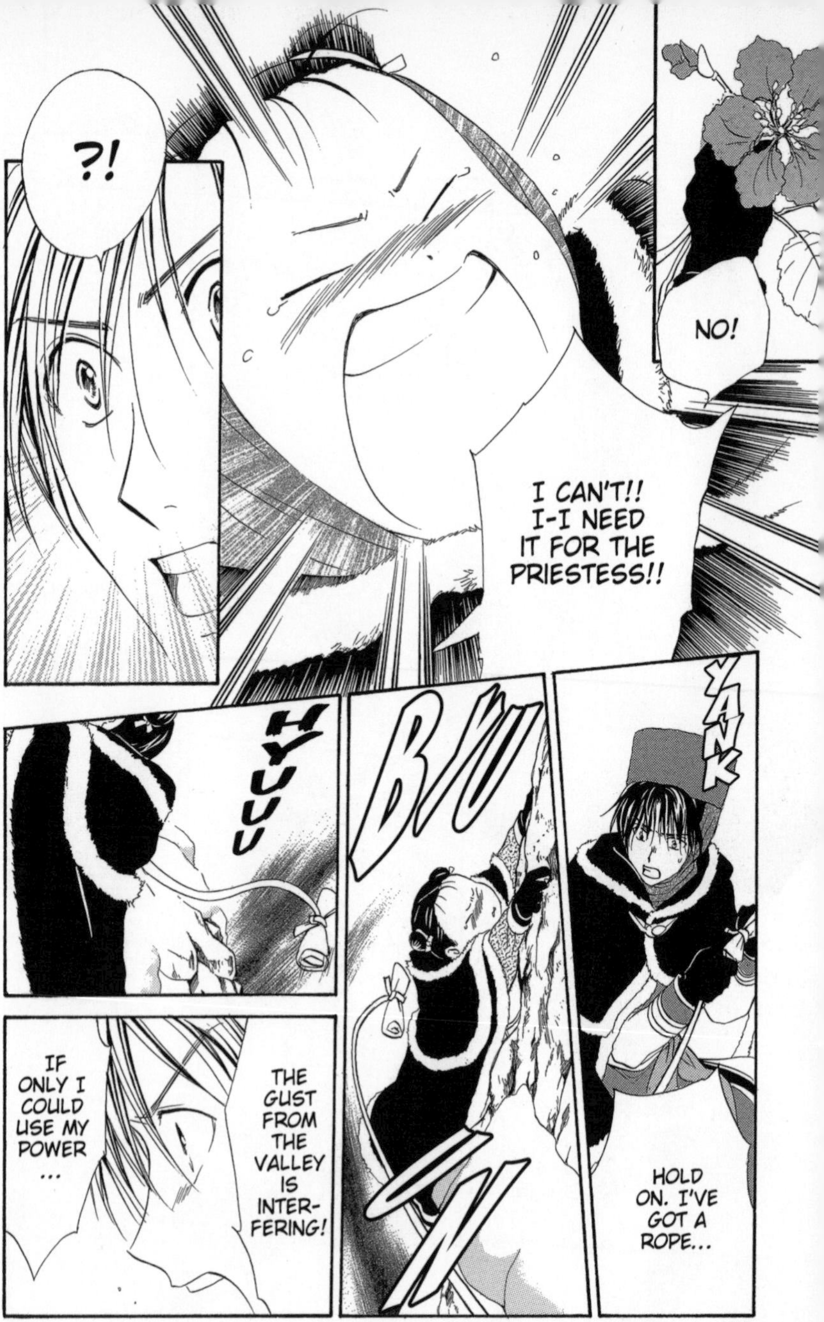
NO!
I CAN'T!! I-I NEED IT FOR THE PRIESTESS!!
?!
YANK
HOLD ON. I'VE GOT A ROPE...
BYU
HYUUUU
THE GUST FROM THE VALLEY IS INTER- FERING!
IF ONLY I COULD USE MY POWER ...

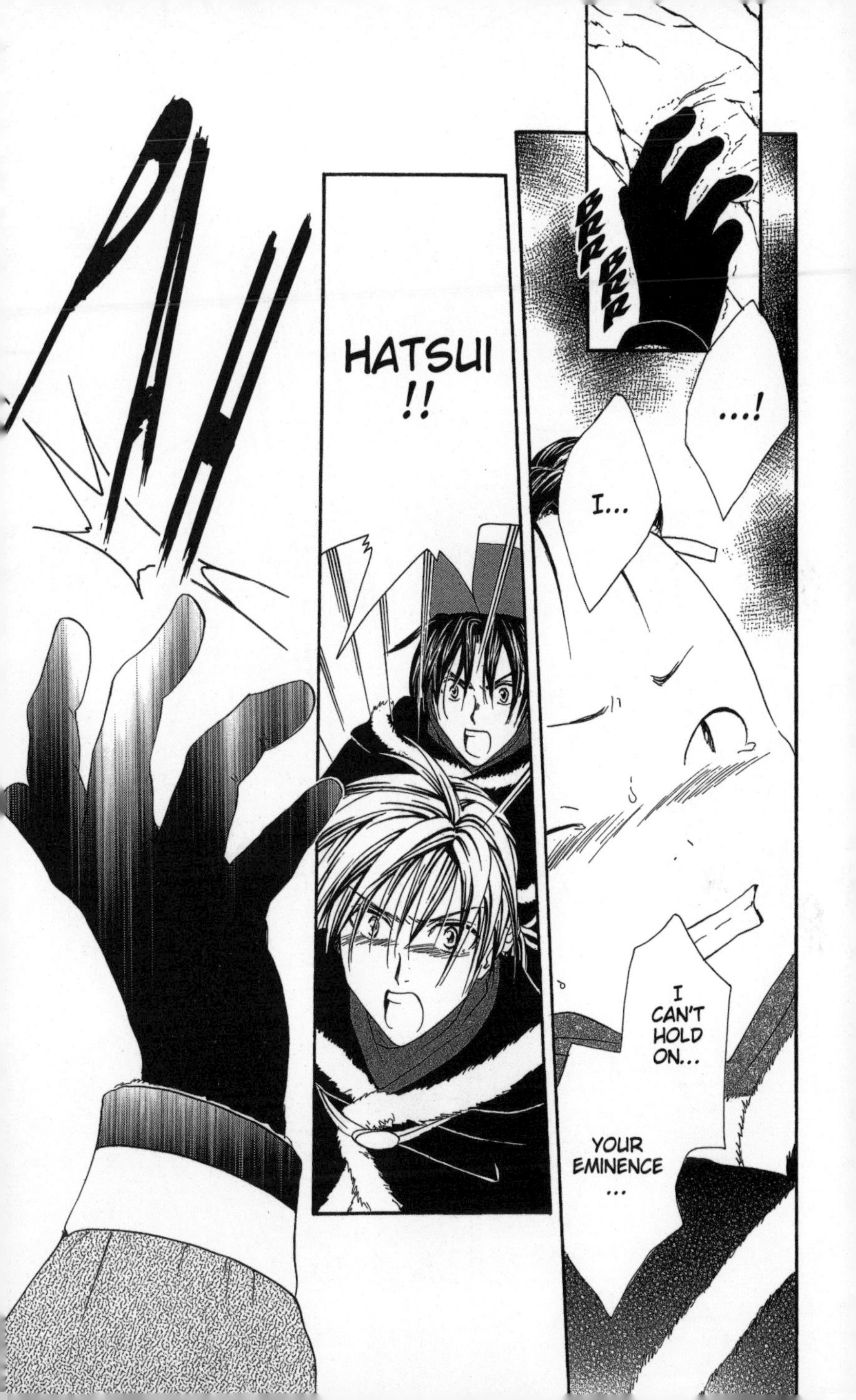
BRR BRR
...!
I...
I CAN'T HOLD ON...
YOUR EMINENCE ...
HATSUI !!
PAH

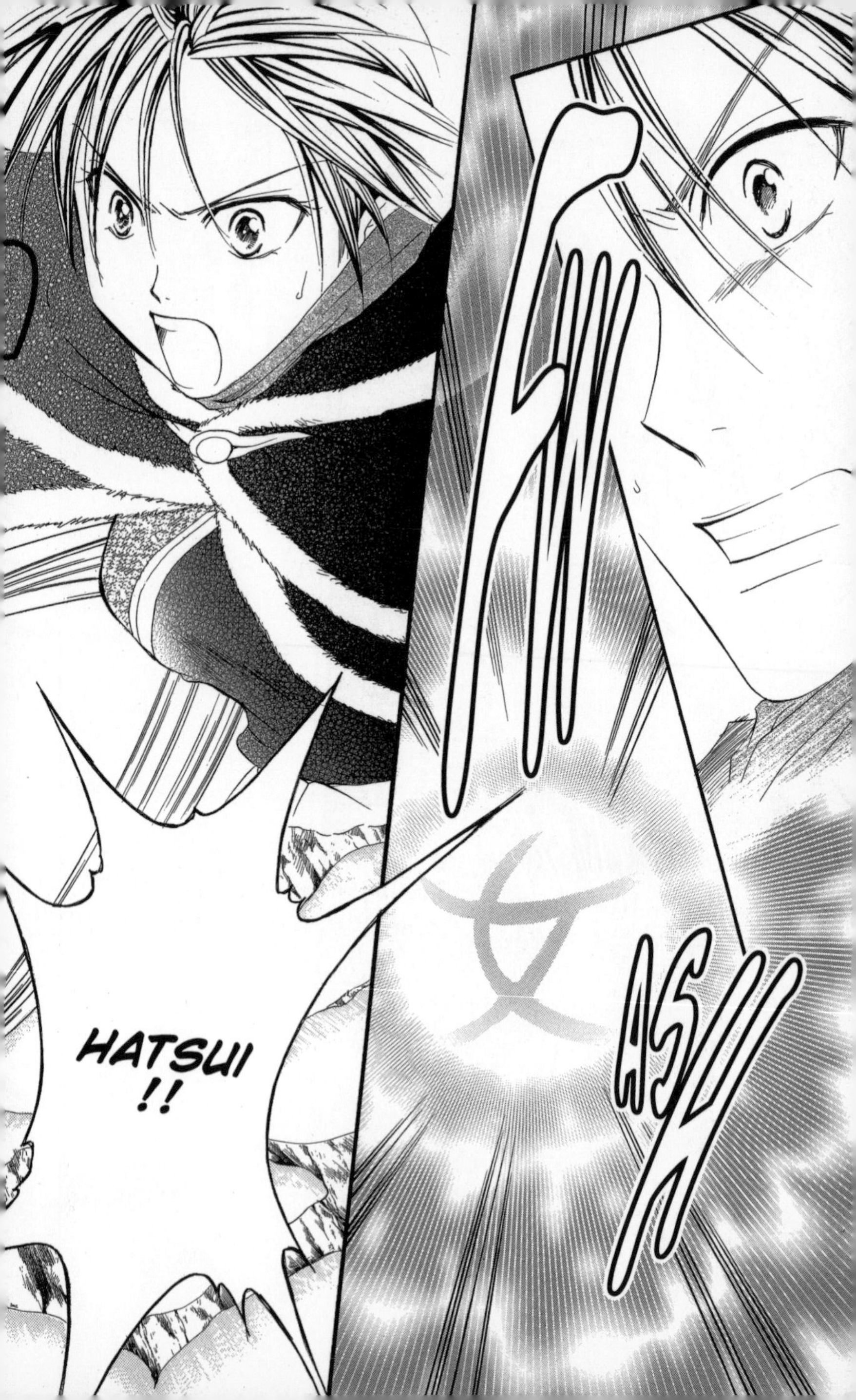
HATSUI !!

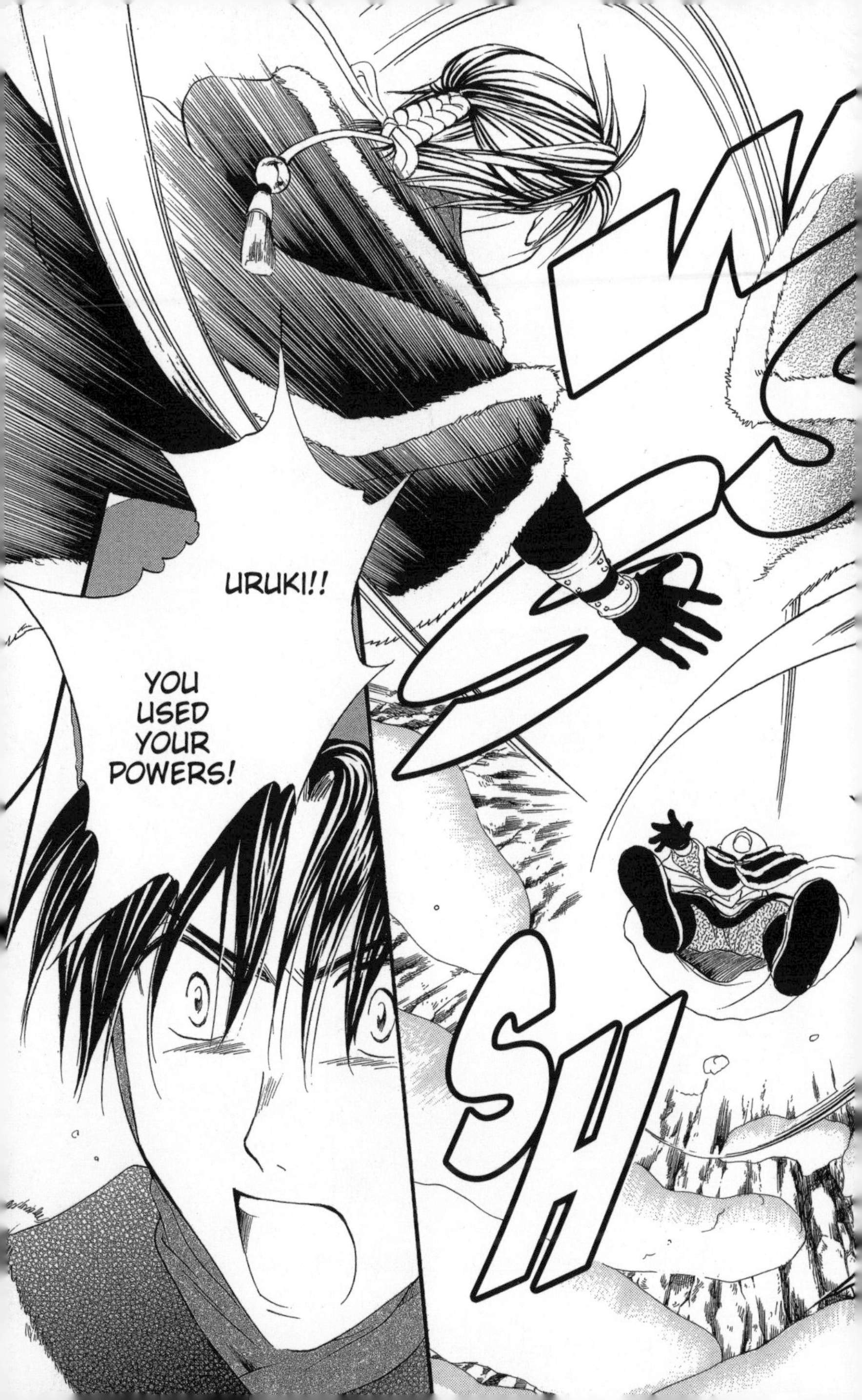
WH
S
URUKI!!
YOU USED YOUR POWERS!
SH

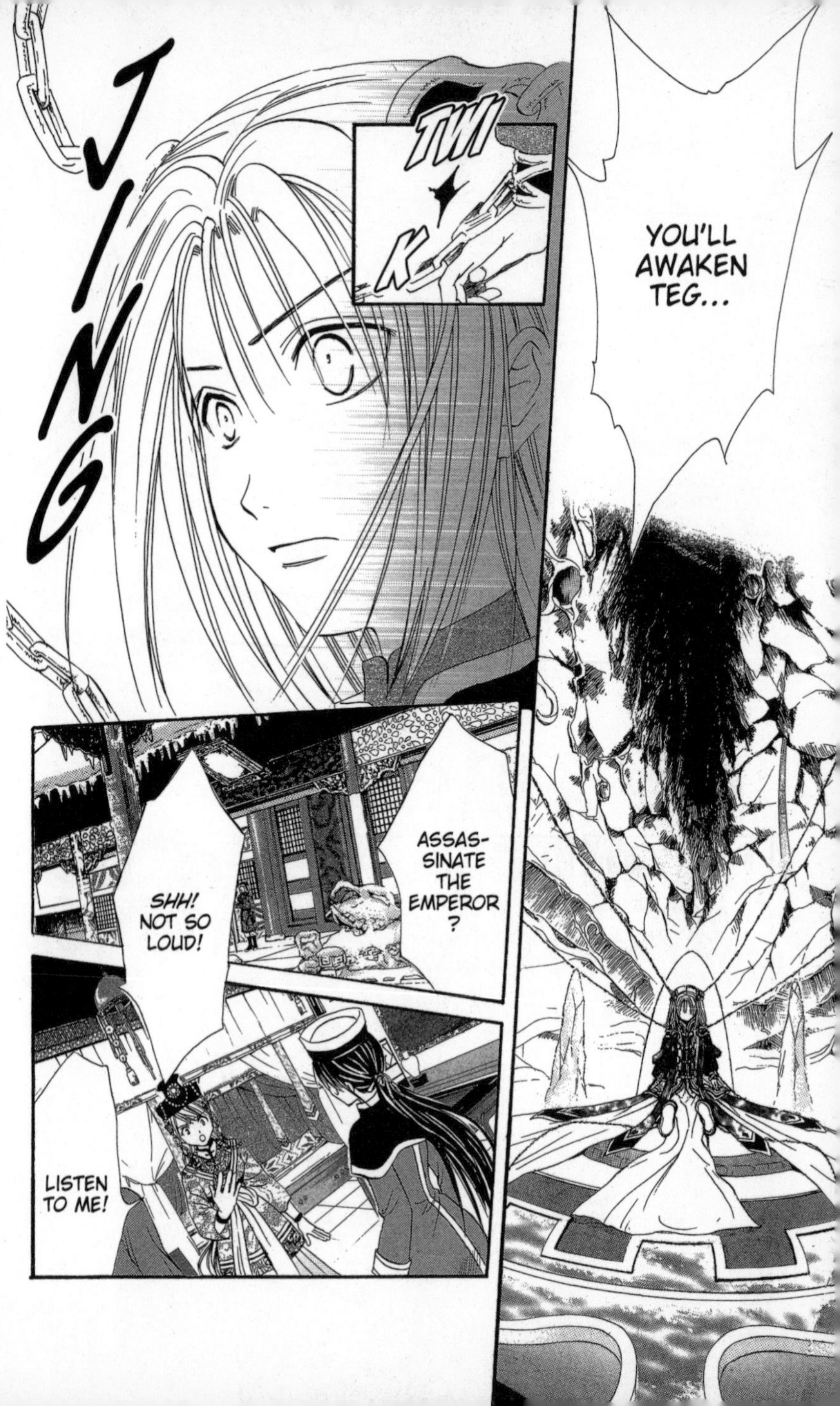
YOU'LL AWAKEN TEG...
JING
TWIK
ASSAS-SINATE THE EMPEROR?
SHH! NOT SO LOUD!
LISTEN TO ME!

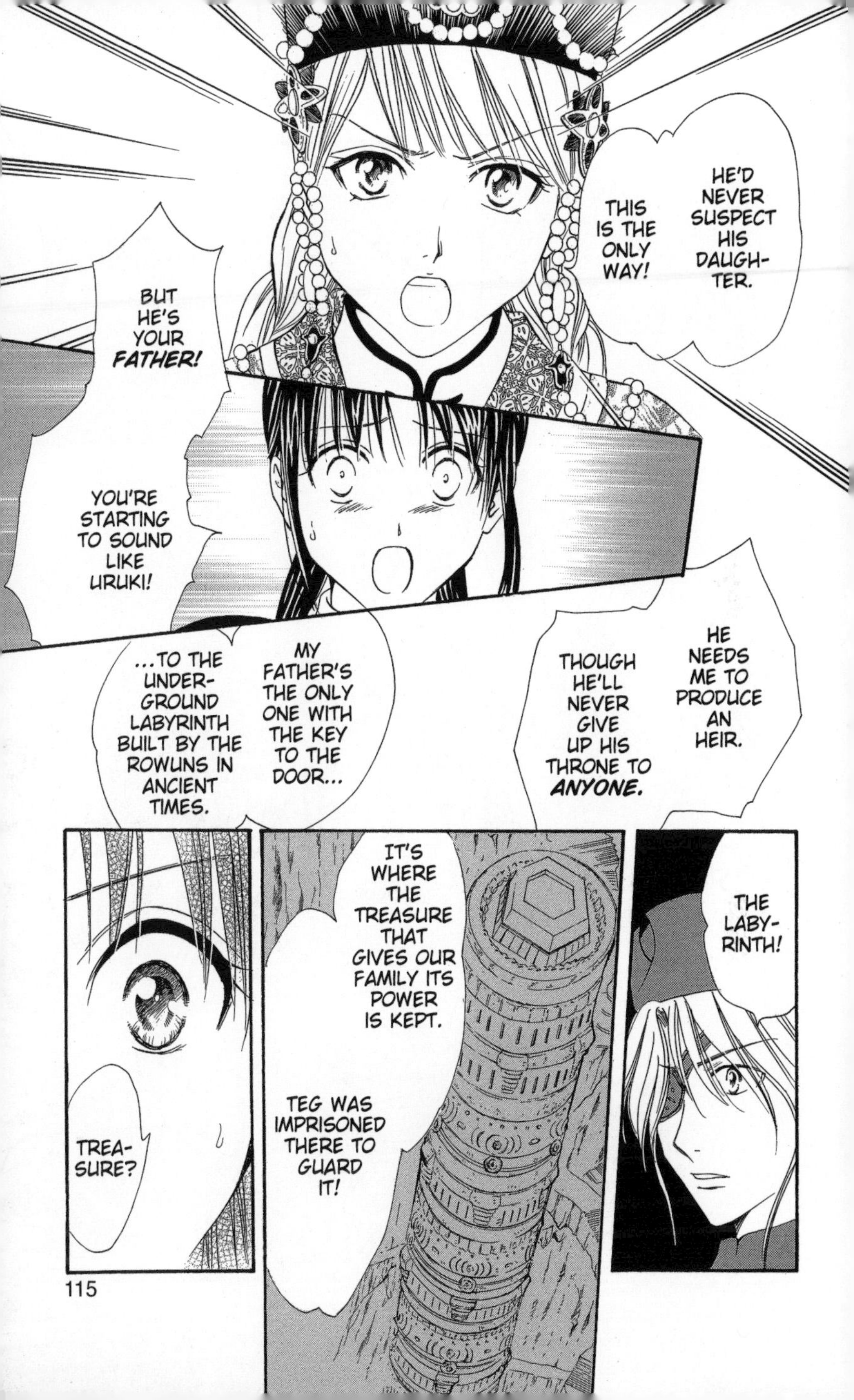
HE'D NEVER SUSPECT HIS DAUGHTER.
THIS IS THE ONLY WAY!
BUT HE'S YOUR *FATHER!*
YOU'RE STARTING TO SOUND LIKE URUKI!
HE NEEDS ME TO PRODUCE AN HEIR.
THOUGH HE'LL NEVER GIVE UP HIS THRONE TO *ANYONE.*
MY FATHER'S THE ONLY ONE WITH THE KEY TO THE DOOR...
...TO THE UNDERGROUND LABYRINTH BUILT BY THE ROWUNS IN ANCIENT TIMES.
THE LABYRINTH!
IT'S WHERE THE TREASURE THAT GIVES OUR FAMILY ITS POWER IS KEPT.
TEG WAS IMPRISONED THERE TO GUARD IT!
TREASURE?

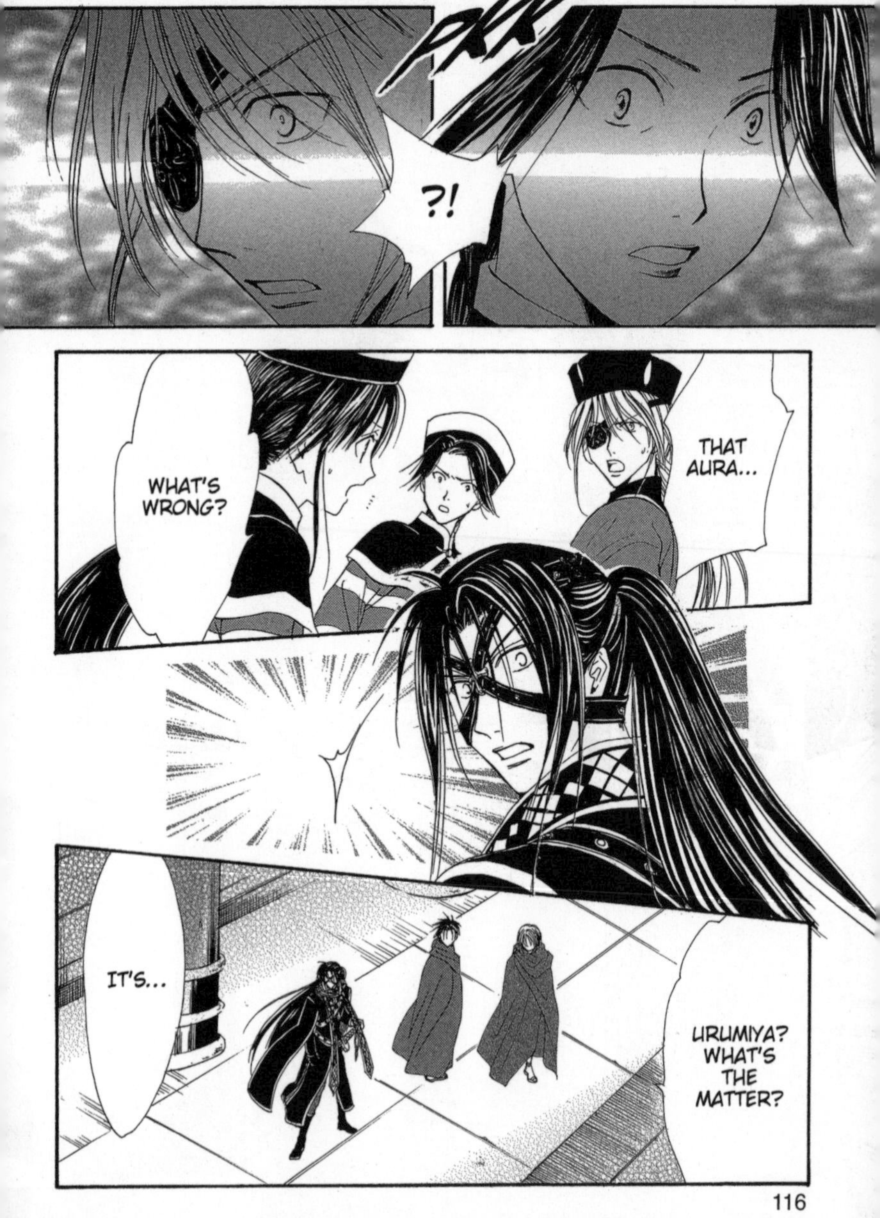
PKK
?!
THAT AURA...
WHAT'S WRONG?
URUMIYA? WHAT'S THE MATTER?
IT'S...

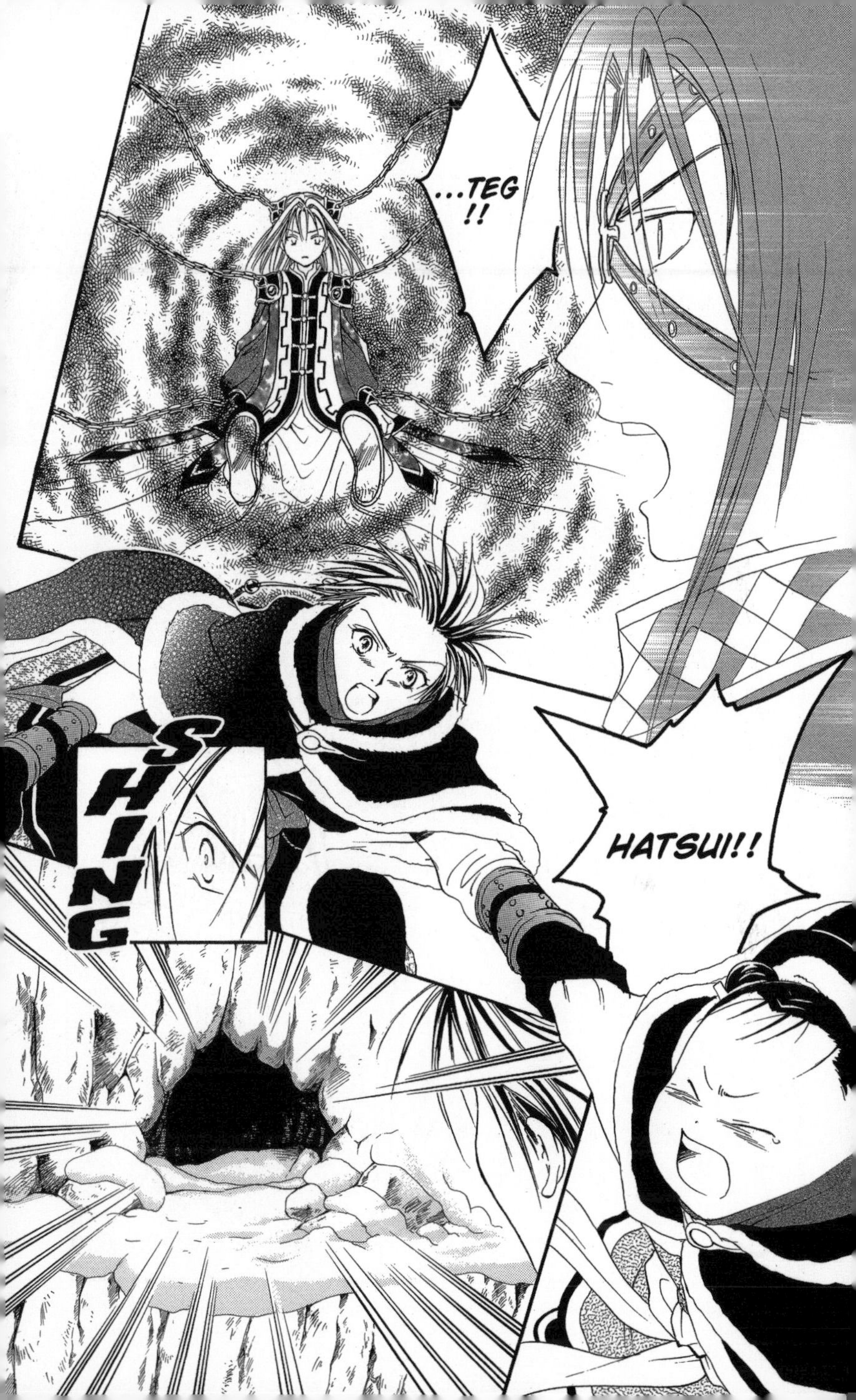
...TEG !!
SHING
HATSUI!!

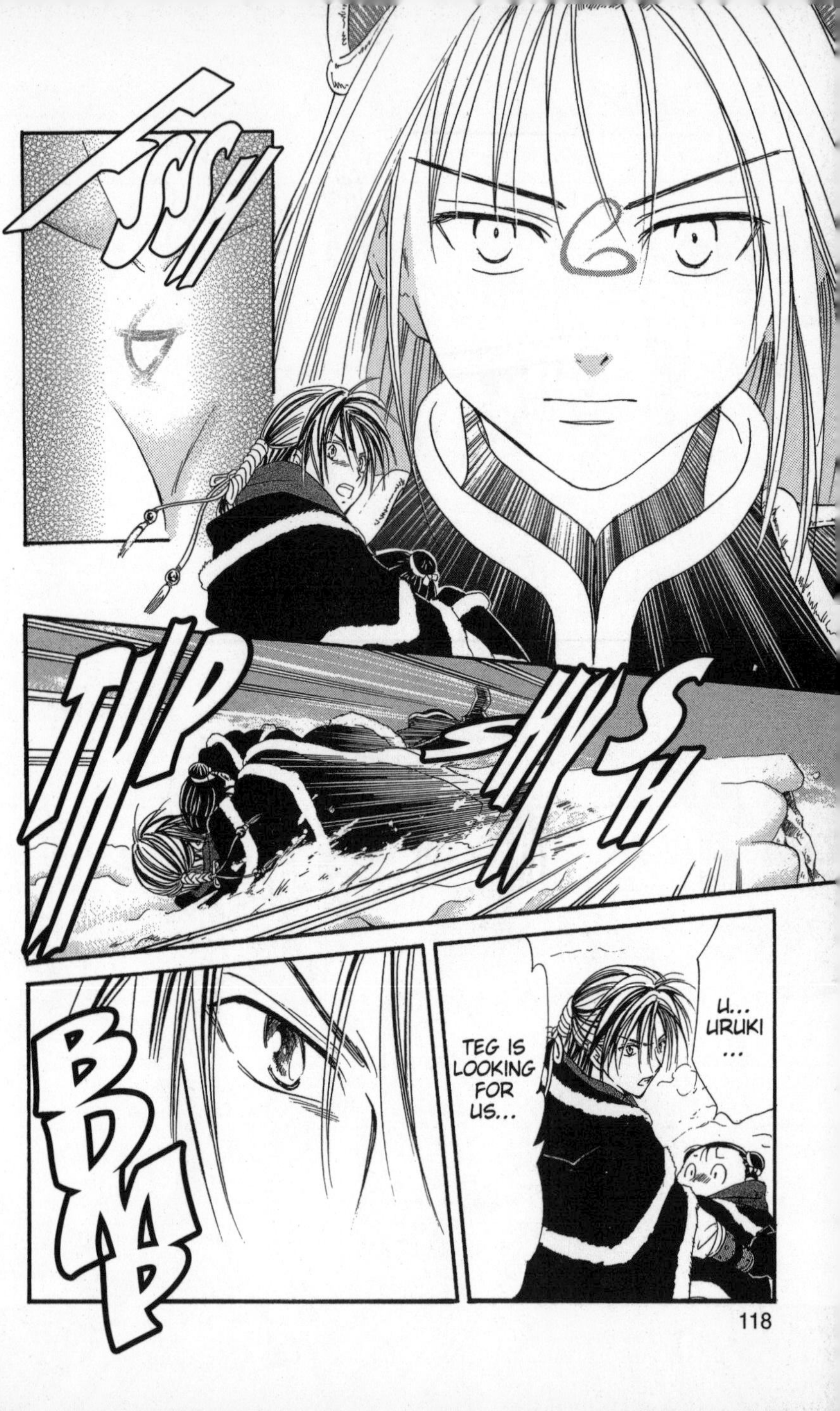
FSSH
SHSH
THP
U... URUKI...
TEG IS LOOKING FOR US...
BDUMP

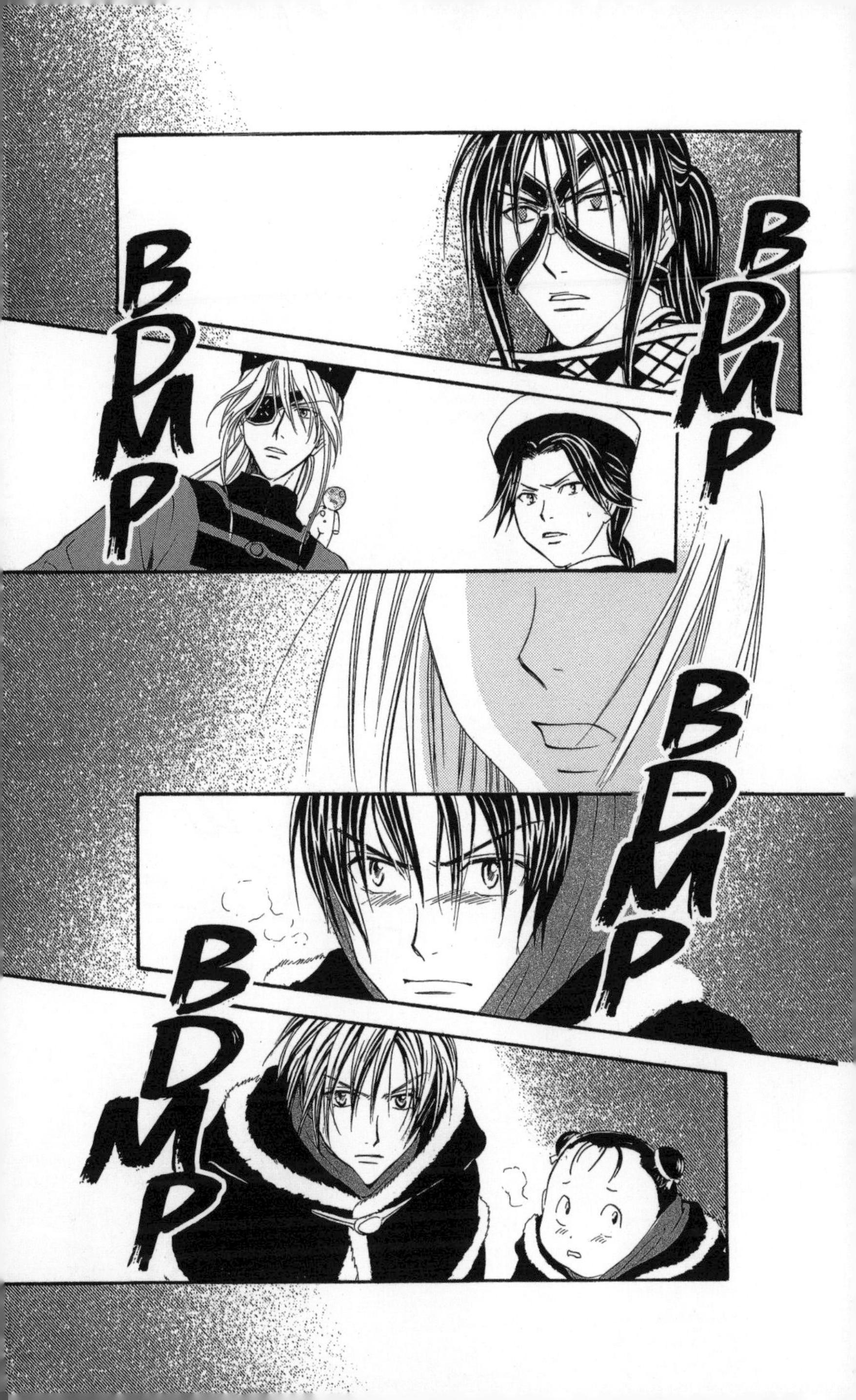
BDMP
BDMP
BDMP
BDMP

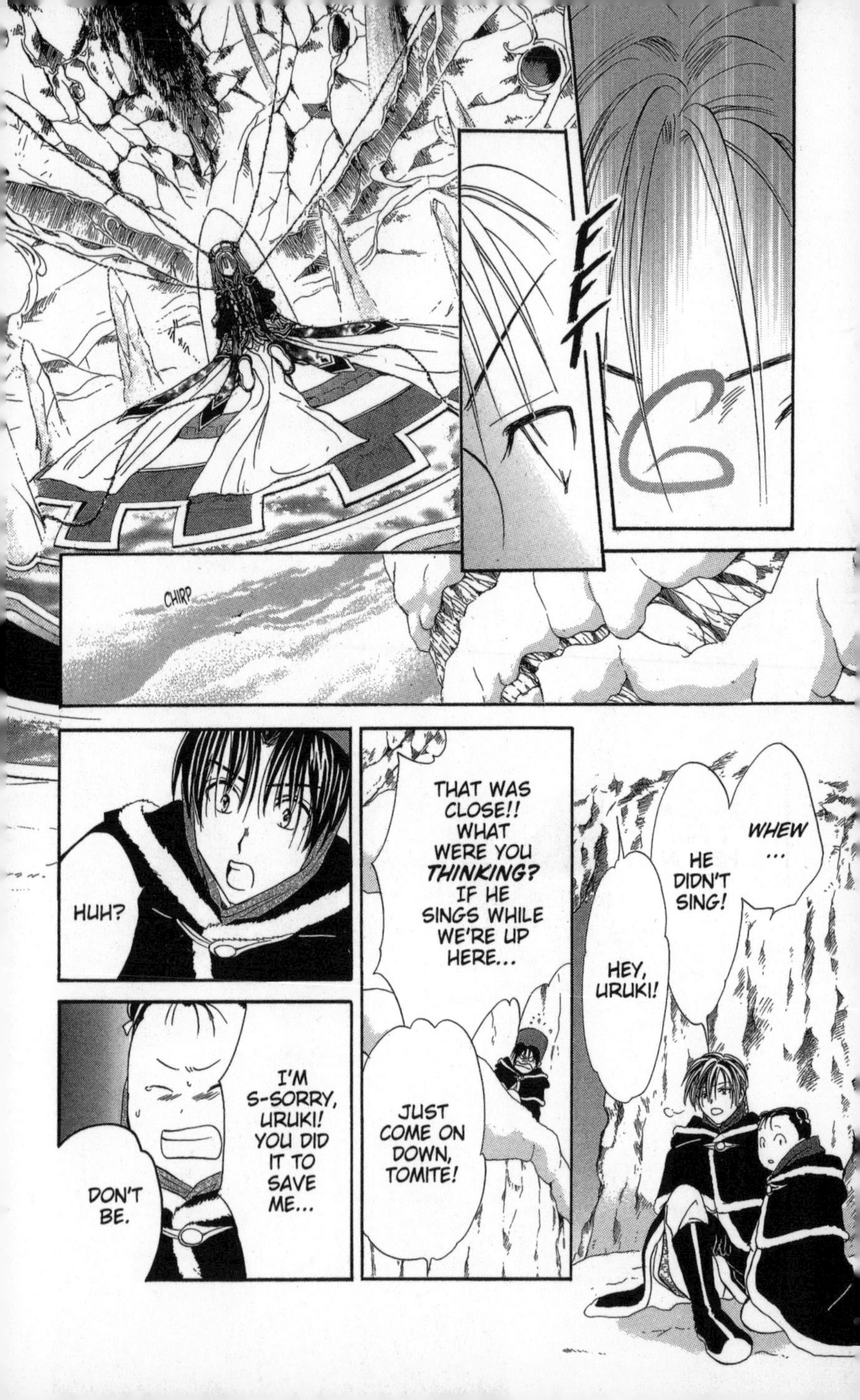
FFT
CHIRP
WHEW...
HE DIDN'T SING!
HEY, URUKI!
THAT WAS CLOSE!! WHAT WERE YOU *THINKING?* IF HE SINGS WHILE WE'RE UP HERE...
JUST COME ON DOWN, TOMITE!
HUH?
I'M S-SORRY, URUKI! YOU DID IT TO SAVE ME...
DON'T BE.

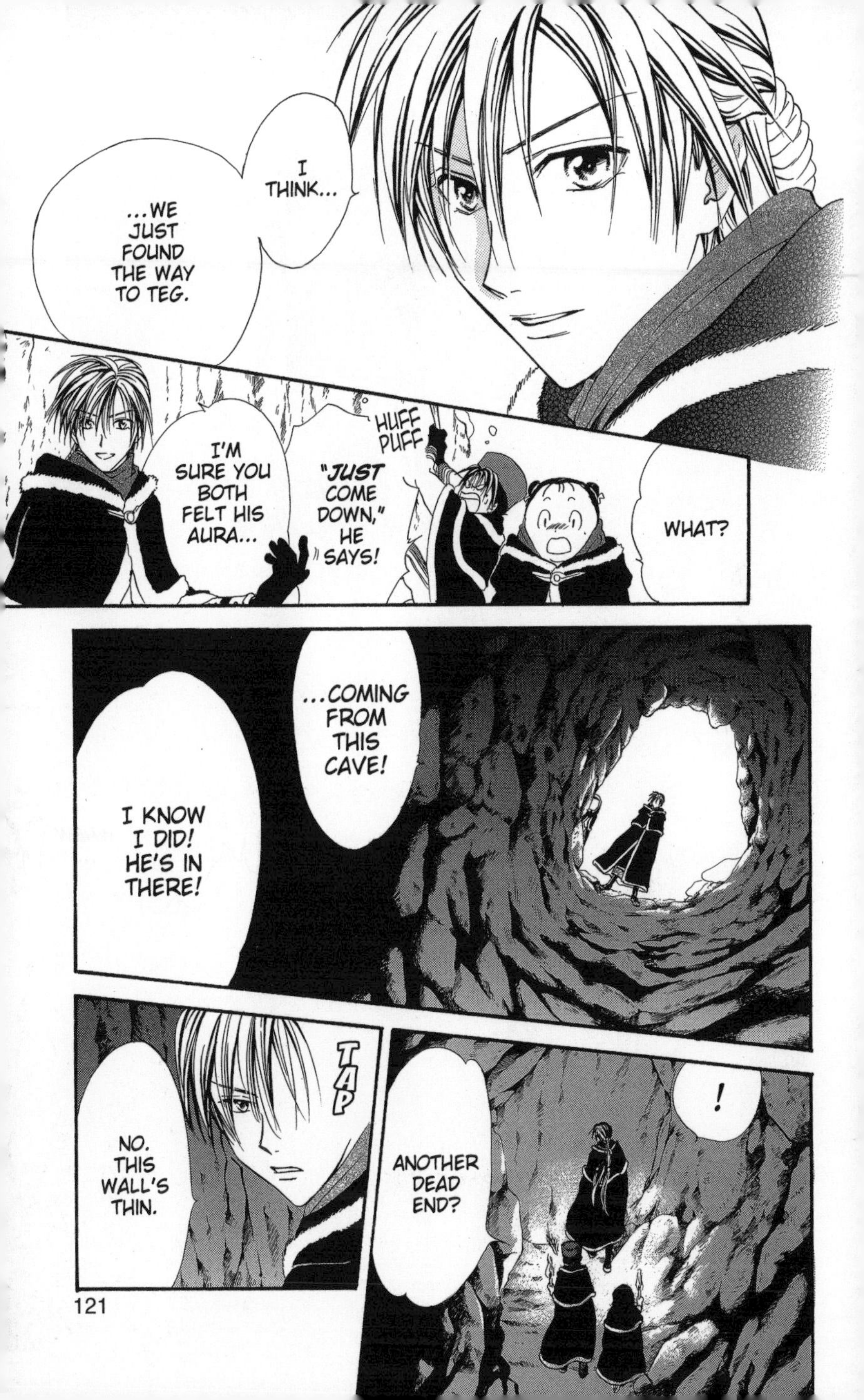
I THINK...
...WE JUST FOUND THE WAY TO TEG.
WHAT?
HUFF PUFF
"*JUST* COME DOWN," HE SAYS!
I'M SURE YOU BOTH FELT HIS AURA...
...COMING FROM THIS CAVE!
I KNOW I DID! HE'S IN THERE!
!
ANOTHER DEAD END?
TAP
NO. THIS WALL'S THIN.

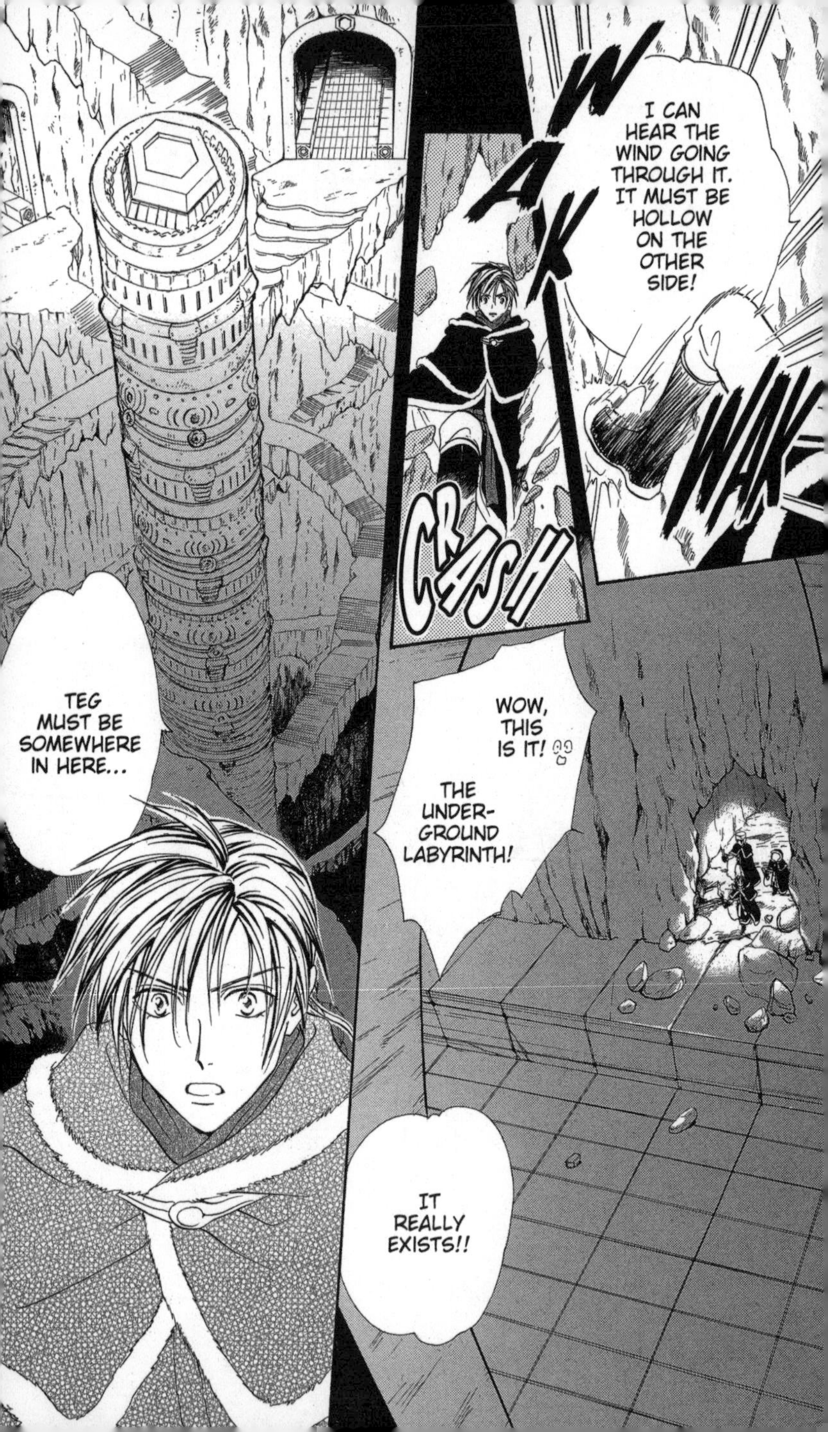
WAK
I CAN HEAR THE WIND GOING THROUGH IT. IT MUST BE HOLLOW ON THE OTHER SIDE!
WAK
CRASH
WOW, THIS IS IT!
THE UNDER-GROUND LABYRINTH!
IT REALLY EXISTS!!
TEG MUST BE SOMEWHERE IN HERE...

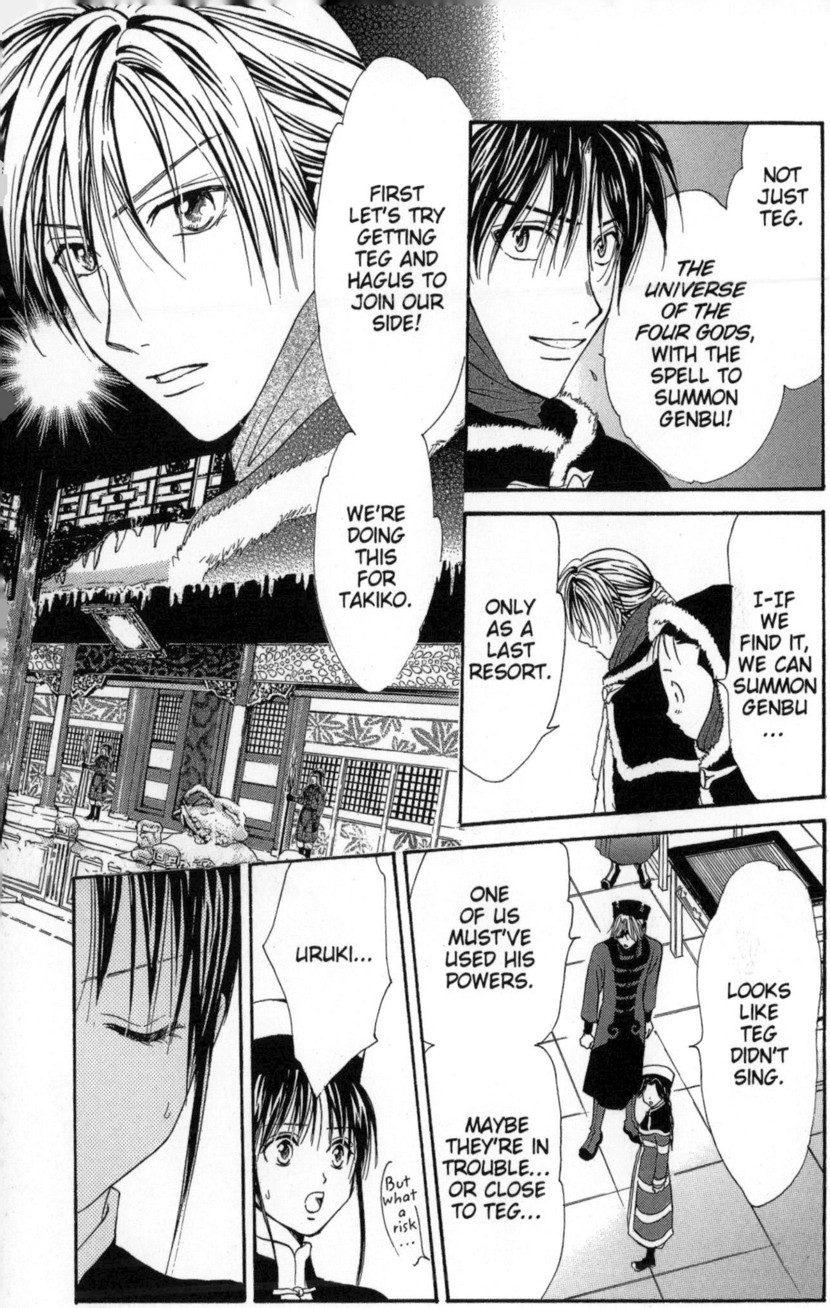
NOT JUST TEG.
THE UNIVERSE OF THE FOUR GODS, WITH THE SPELL TO SUMMON GENBU!
I-IF WE FIND IT, WE CAN SUMMON GENBU ...
ONLY AS A LAST RESORT.
FIRST LET'S TRY GETTING TEG AND HAGUS TO JOIN OUR SIDE!
WE'RE DOING THIS FOR TAKIKO.
LOOKS LIKE TEG DIDN'T SING.
ONE OF US MUST'VE USED HIS POWERS.
MAYBE THEY'RE IN TROUBLE... OR CLOSE TO TEG...
URUKI...
But what a risk ...

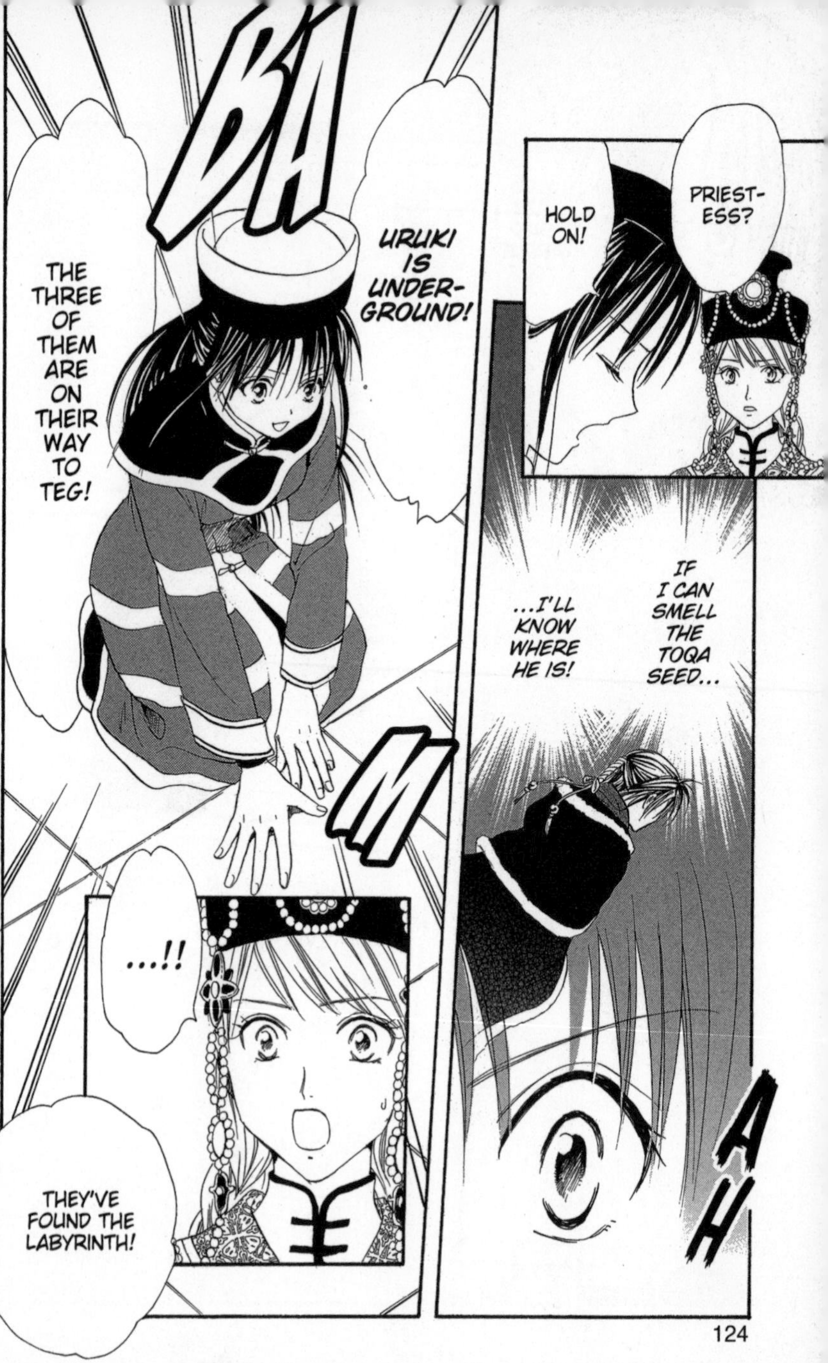
PRIEST-ESS?
HOLD ON!
IF I CAN SMELL THE TOQA SEED...
...I'LL KNOW WHERE HE IS!
AH
BA
URUKI IS UNDER-GROUND!
THE THREE OF THEM ARE ON THEIR WAY TO TEG!
M
...!!
THEY'VE FOUND THE LABYRINTH!

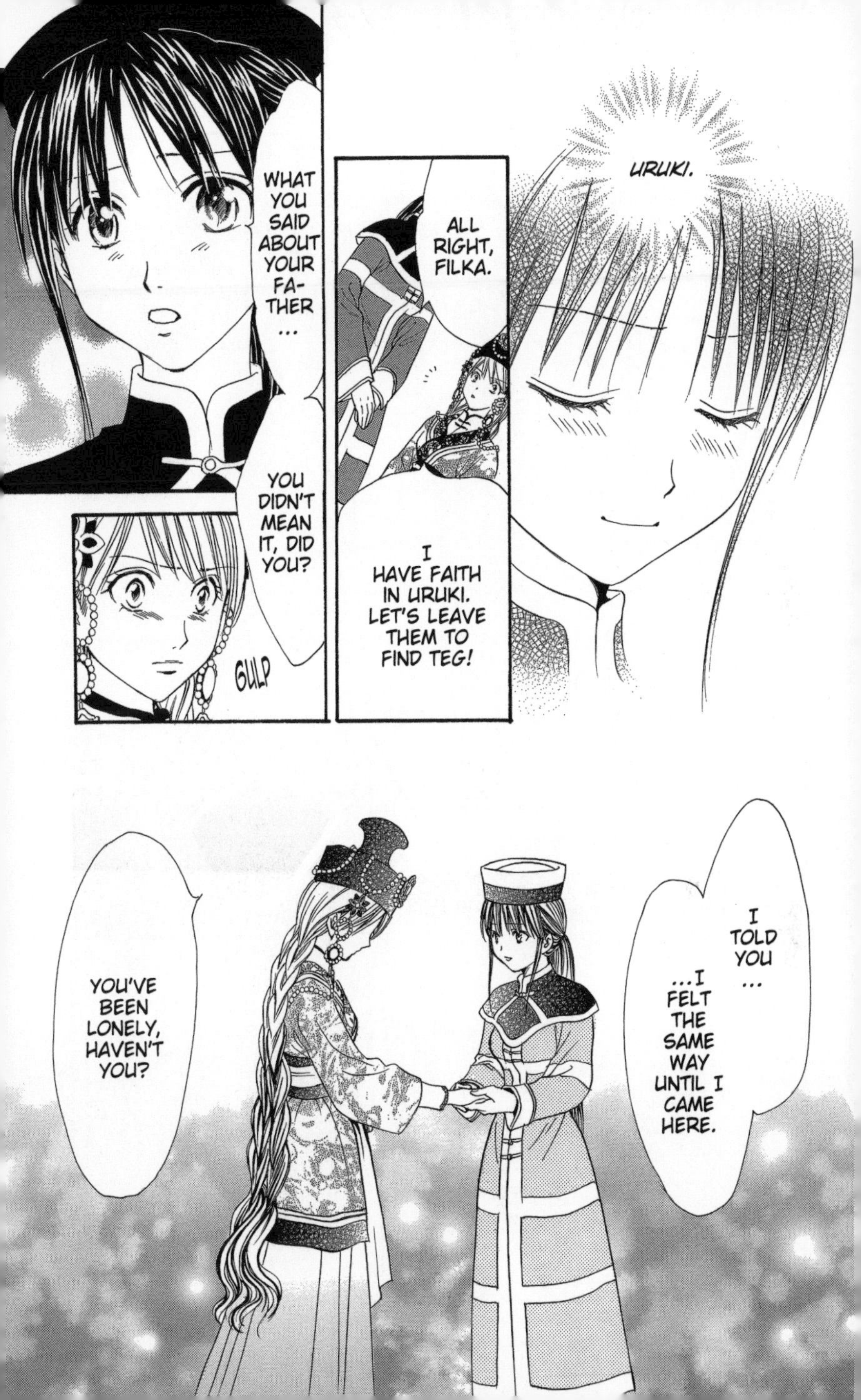
URUKI.
ALL RIGHT, FILKA.
I HAVE FAITH IN URUKI. LET'S LEAVE THEM TO FIND TEG!
WHAT YOU SAID ABOUT YOUR FA-THER...
YOU DIDN'T MEAN IT, DID YOU?
GULP
I TOLD YOU...
...I FELT THE SAME WAY UNTIL I CAME HERE.
YOU'VE BEEN LONELY, HAVEN'T YOU?

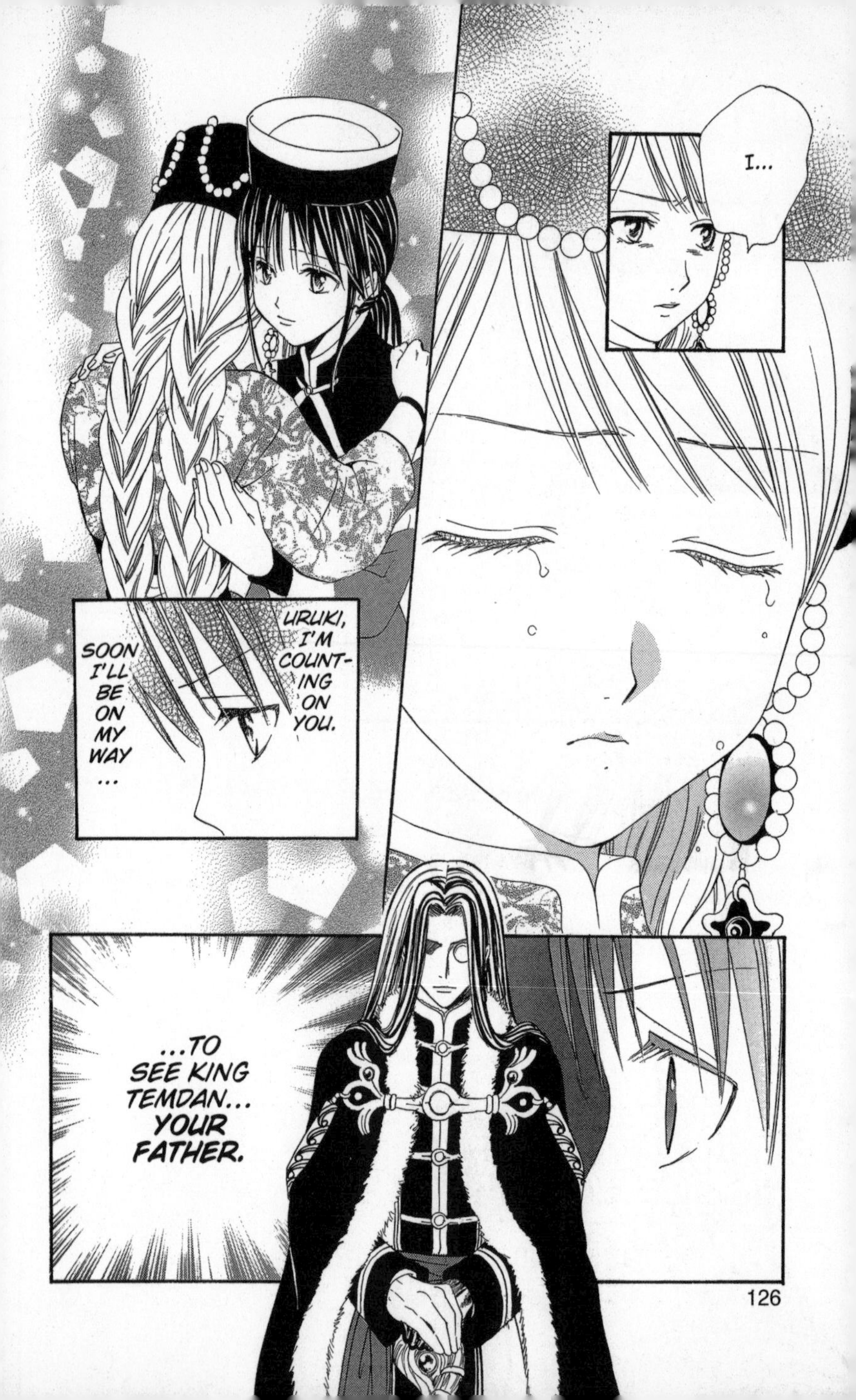
I...
URUKI, I'M COUNTING ON YOU.
SOON I'LL BE ON MY WAY...
...TO SEE KING TEMDAN... YOUR FATHER.

PRINCE OF SORROWFUL WIND

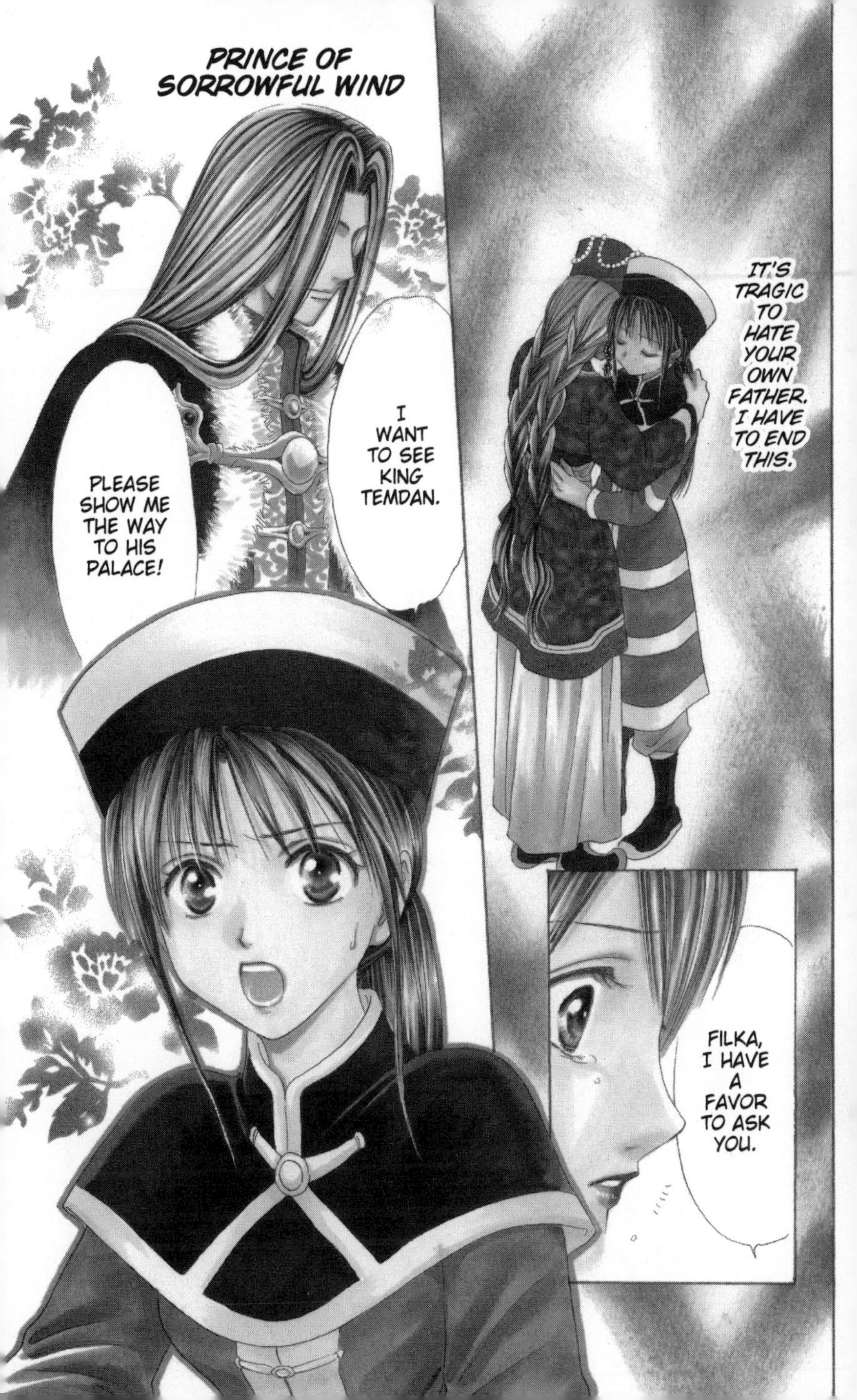
IT'S TRAGIC TO HATE YOUR OWN FATHER. I HAVE TO END THIS.
FILKA, I HAVE A FAVOR TO ASK YOU.
I WANT TO SEE KING TEMDAN.
PLEASE SHOW ME THE WAY TO HIS PALACE!

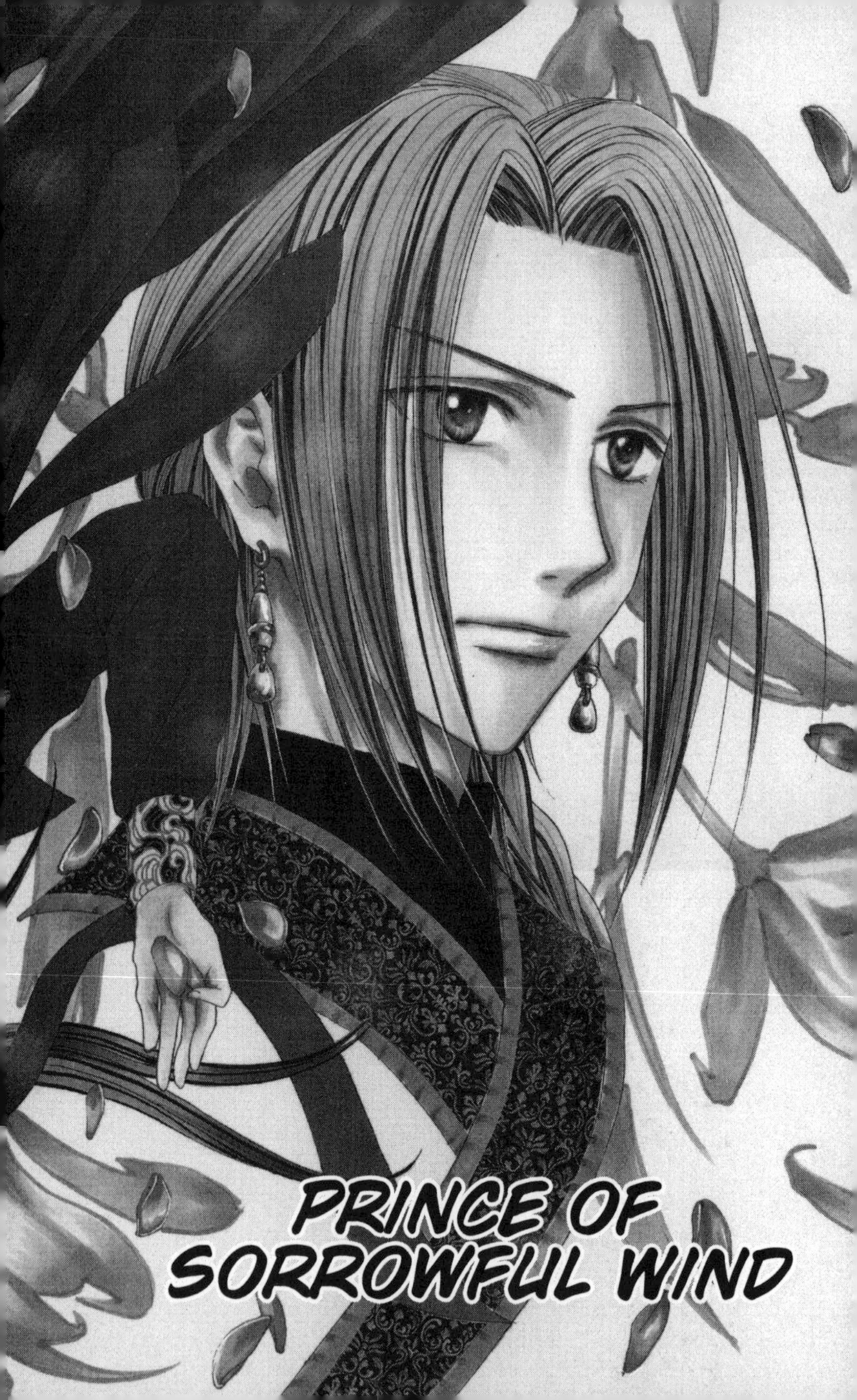
PRINCE OF
SORROWFUL WIND

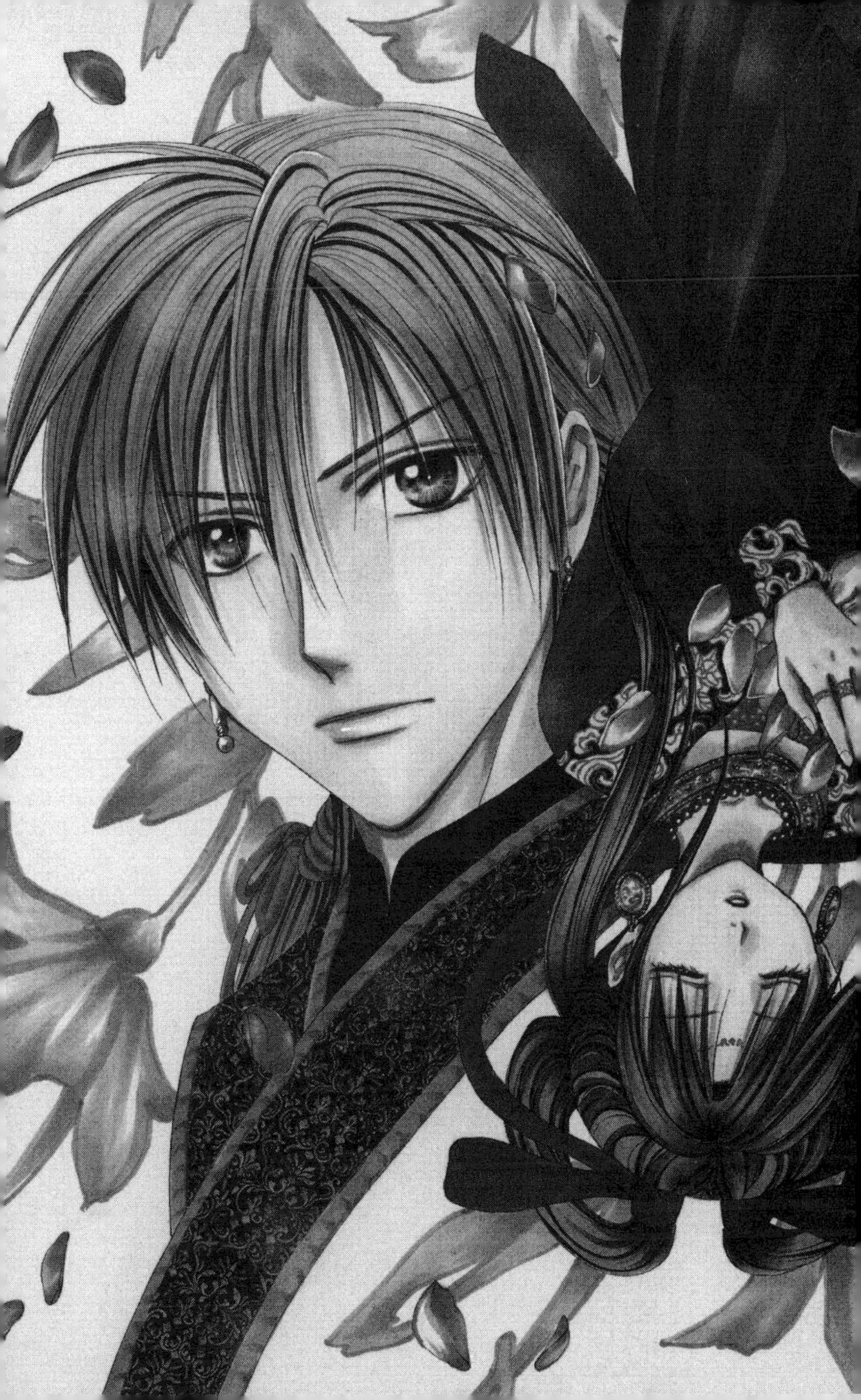

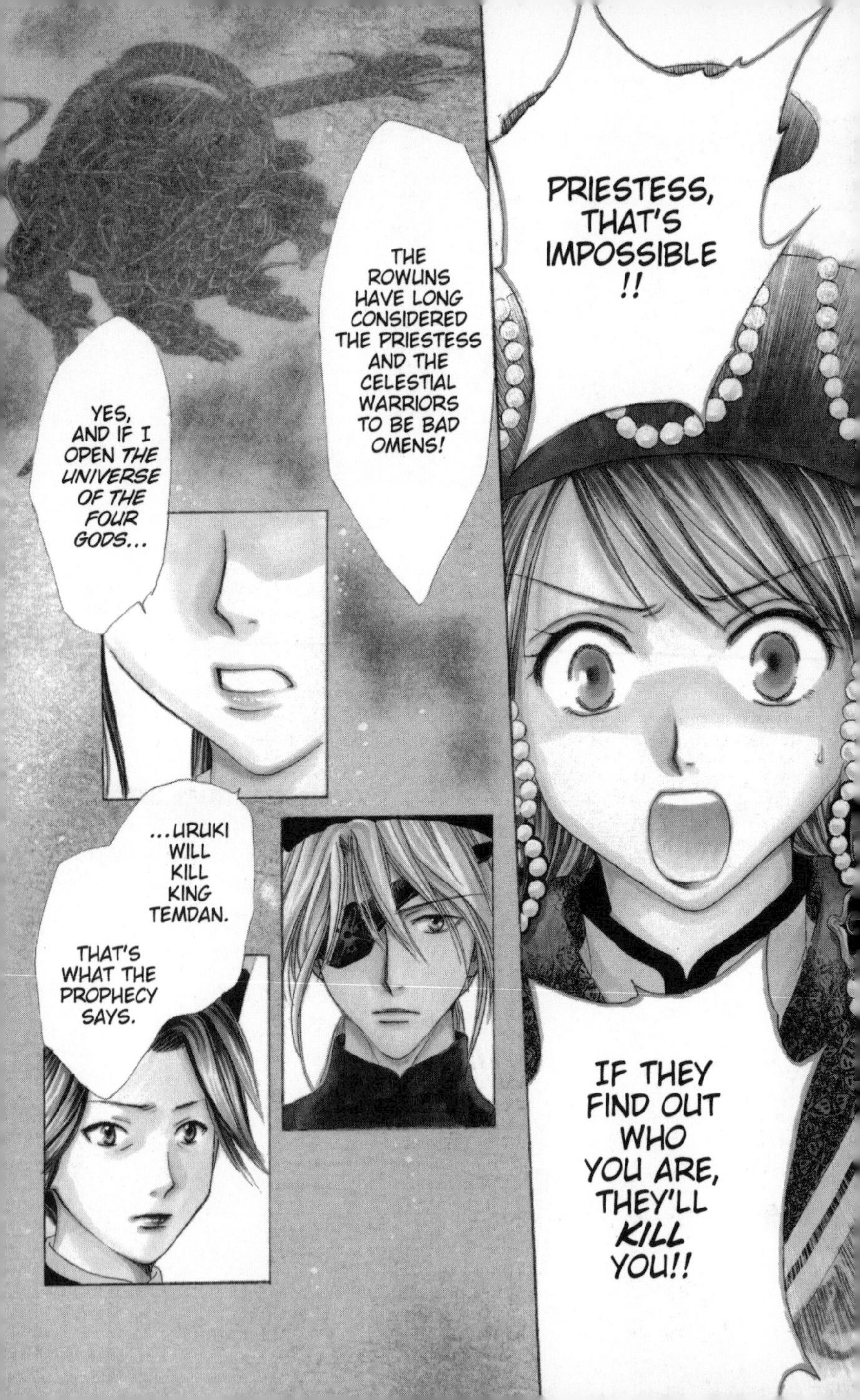
PRIESTESS, THAT'S IMPOSSIBLE!!
IF THEY FIND OUT WHO YOU ARE, THEY'LL *KILL* YOU!!
THE ROWUNS HAVE LONG CONSIDERED THE PRIESTESS AND THE CELESTIAL WARRIORS TO BE BAD OMENS!
YES, AND IF I OPEN *THE UNIVERSE OF THE FOUR GODS*...
...URUKI WILL KILL KING TEMDAN.
THAT'S WHAT THE PROPHECY SAYS.

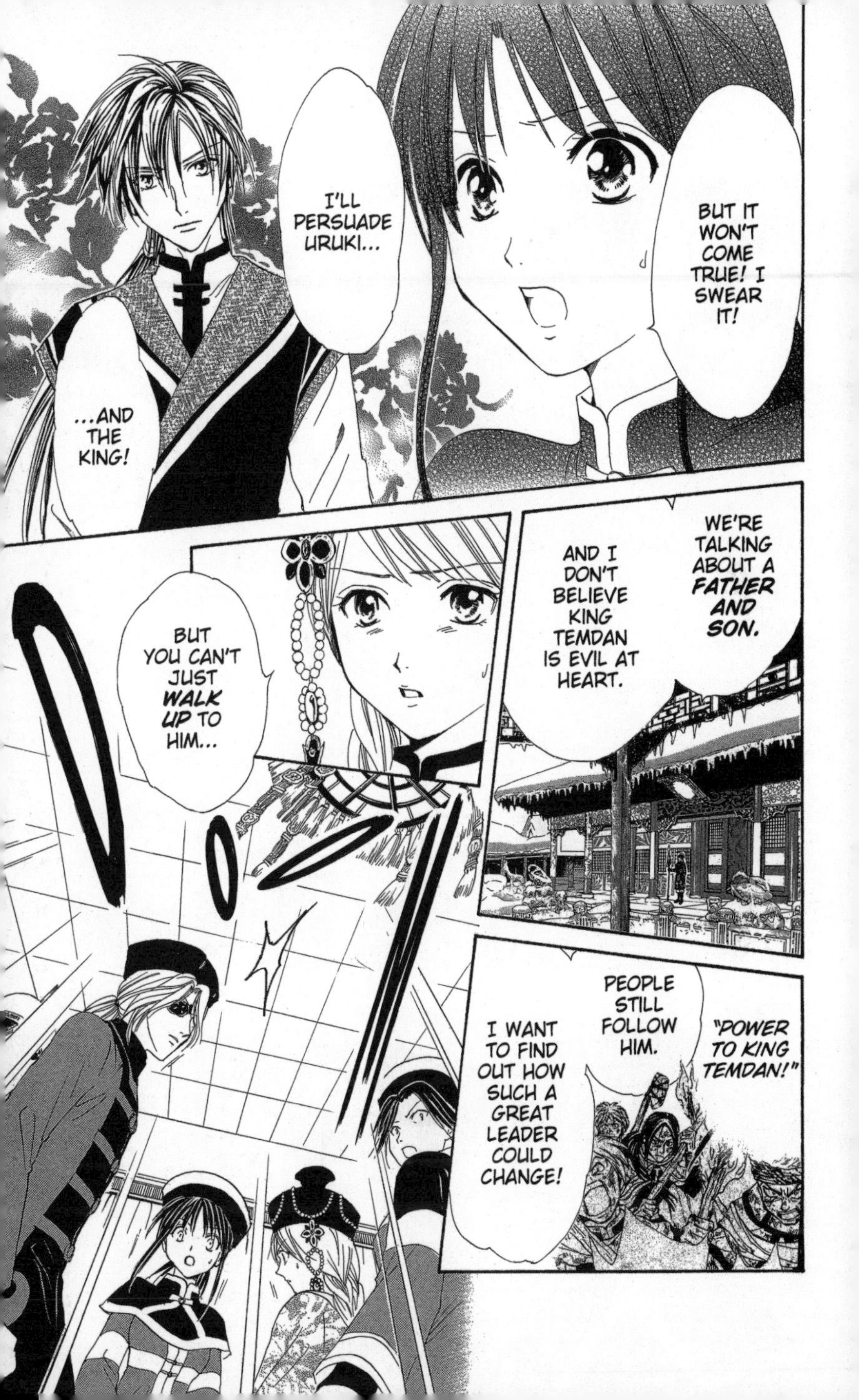
BUT IT WON'T COME TRUE! I SWEAR IT!
I'LL PERSUADE URUKI...
...AND THE KING!
WE'RE TALKING ABOUT A FATHER AND SON.
AND I DON'T BELIEVE KING TEMDAN IS EVIL AT HEART.
BUT YOU CAN'T JUST WALK UP TO HIM...
"POWER TO KING TEMDAN!"
PEOPLE STILL FOLLOW HIM.
I WANT TO FIND OUT HOW SUCH A GREAT LEADER COULD CHANGE!

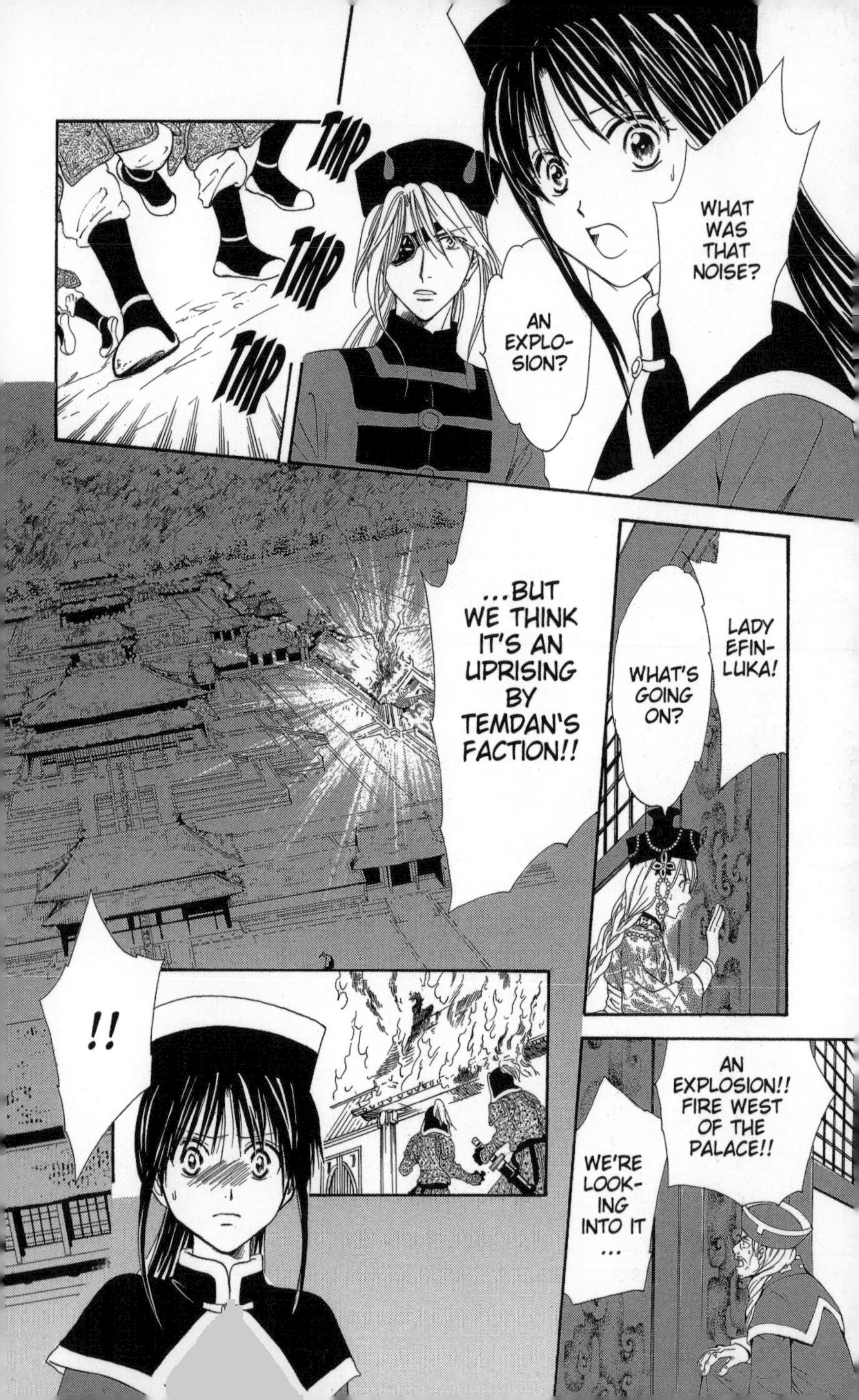
WHAT WAS THAT NOISE?
AN EXPLOSION?
TMP
TMP
TMP
LADY EFIN-LUKA!
WHAT'S GOING ON?
AN EXPLOSION!! FIRE WEST OF THE PALACE!!
WE'RE LOOK-ING INTO IT...
...BUT WE THINK IT'S AN UPRISING BY TEMDAN'S FACTION!!
!!

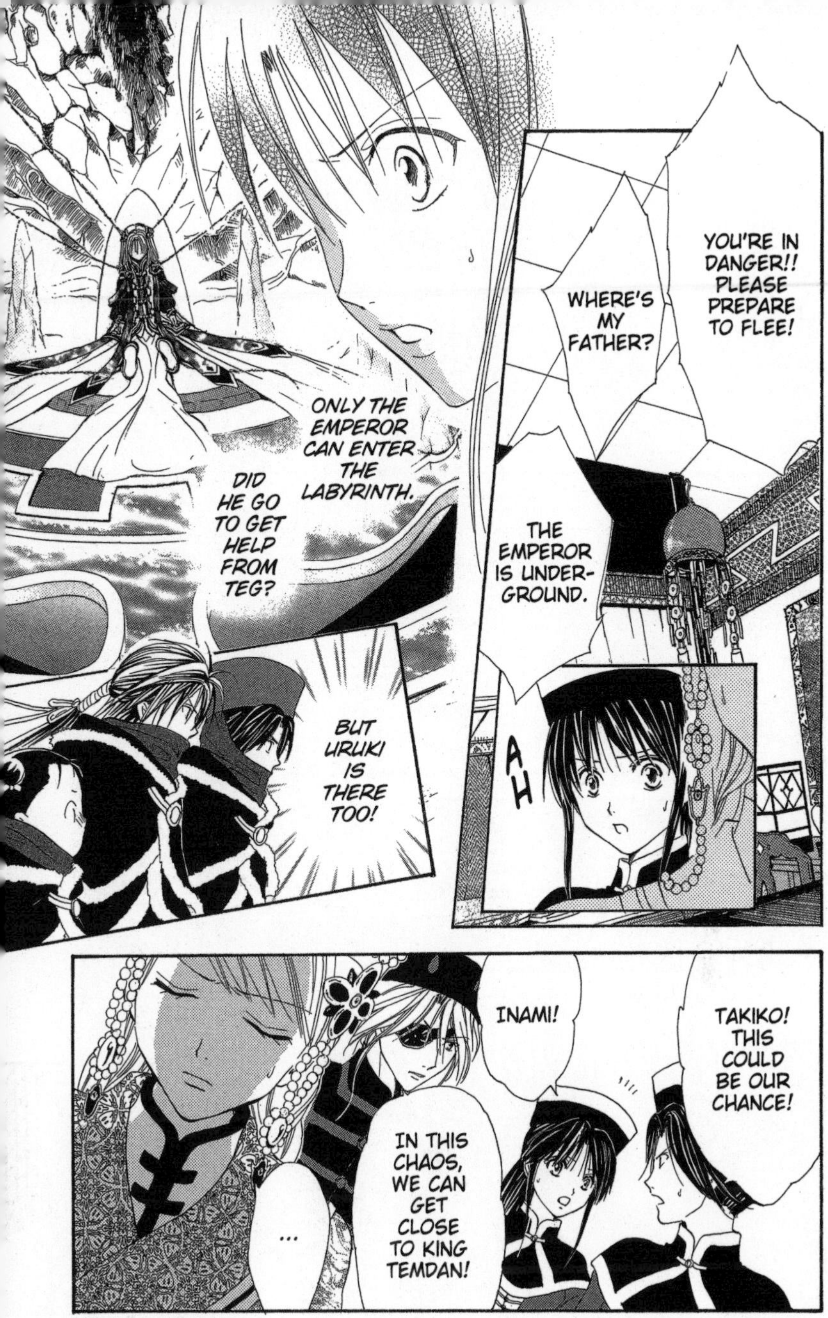
YOU'RE IN DANGER!! PLEASE PREPARE TO FLEE!
WHERE'S MY FATHER?
THE EMPEROR IS UNDERGROUND.
AH
ONLY THE EMPEROR CAN ENTER THE LABYRINTH.
DID HE GO TO GET HELP FROM TEG?
BUT URUKI IS THERE TOO!
TAKIKO! THIS COULD BE OUR CHANCE!
INAMI!
IN THIS CHAOS, WE CAN GET CLOSE TO KING TEMDAN!
...

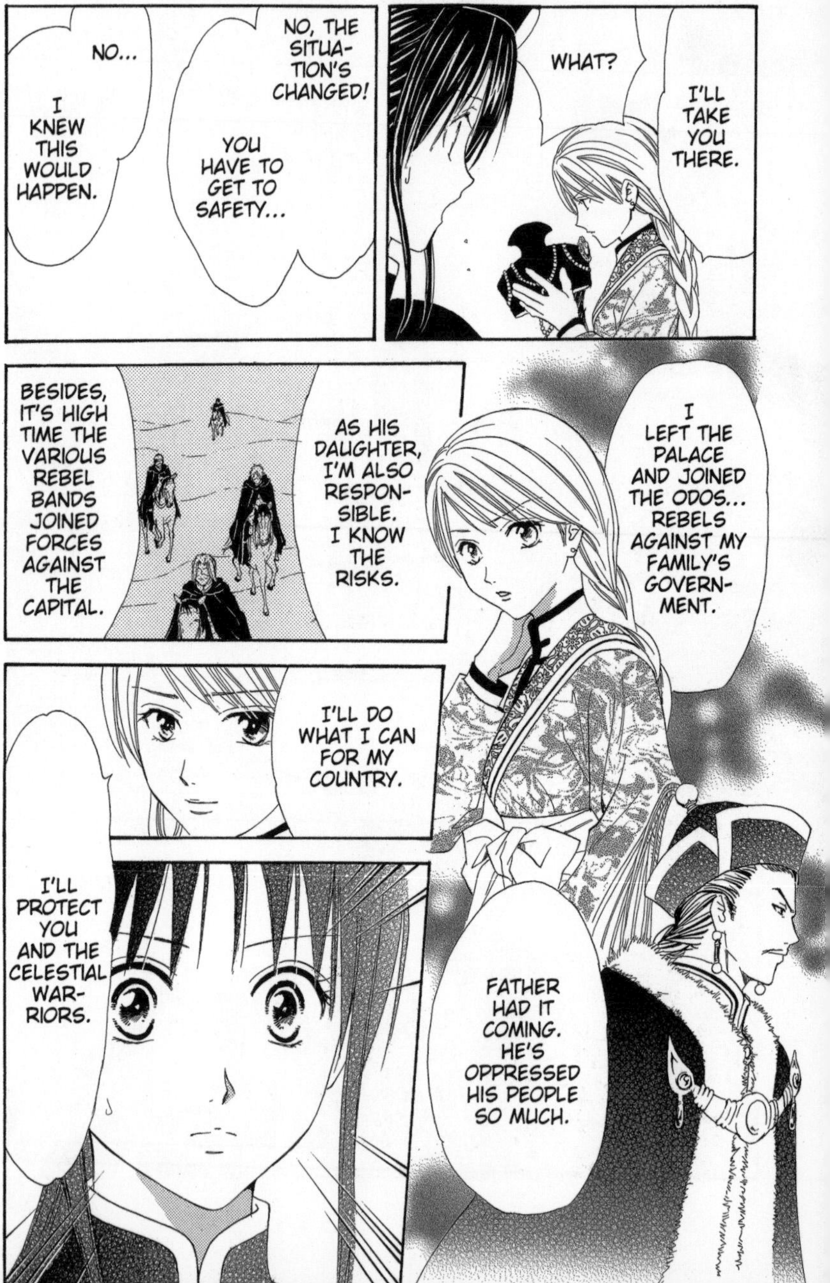
WHAT?
I'LL TAKE YOU THERE.
NO, THE SITUA-TION'S CHANGED!
YOU HAVE TO GET TO SAFETY...
NO...
I KNEW THIS WOULD HAPPEN.
I LEFT THE PALACE AND JOINED THE ODOS... REBELS AGAINST MY FAMILY'S GOVERN-MENT.
FATHER HAD IT COMING. HE'S OPPRESSED HIS PEOPLE SO MUCH.
AS HIS DAUGHTER, I'M ALSO RESPON-SIBLE. I KNOW THE RISKS.
BESIDES, IT'S HIGH TIME THE VARIOUS REBEL BANDS JOINED FORCES AGAINST THE CAPITAL.
I'LL DO WHAT I CAN FOR MY COUNTRY.
I'LL PROTECT YOU AND THE CELESTIAL WAR-RIORS.

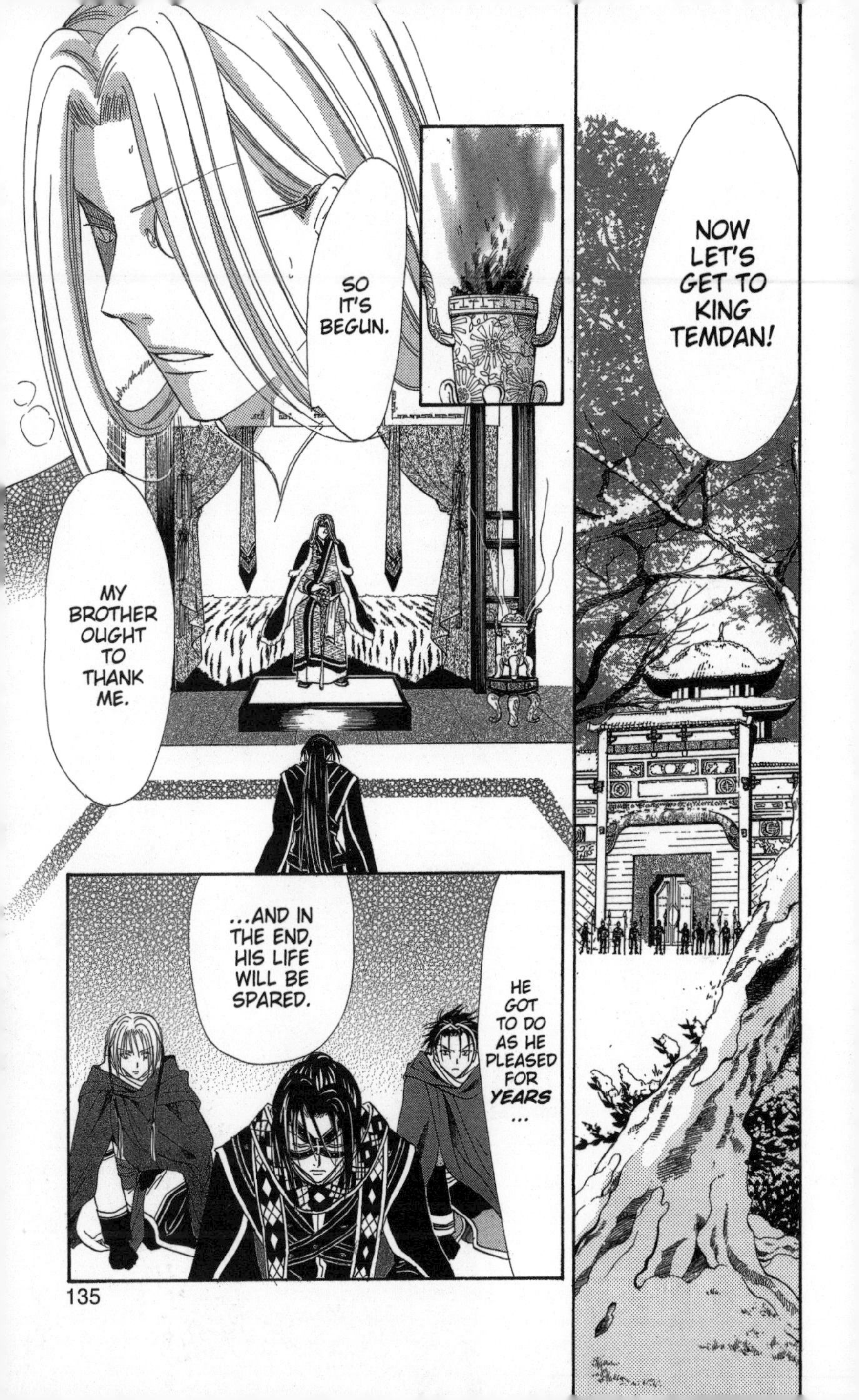
NOW LET'S GET TO KING TEMDAN!
SO IT'S BEGUN.
MY BROTHER OUGHT TO THANK ME.
HE GOT TO DO AS HE PLEASED FOR *YEARS*...
...AND IN THE END, HIS LIFE WILL BE SPARED.

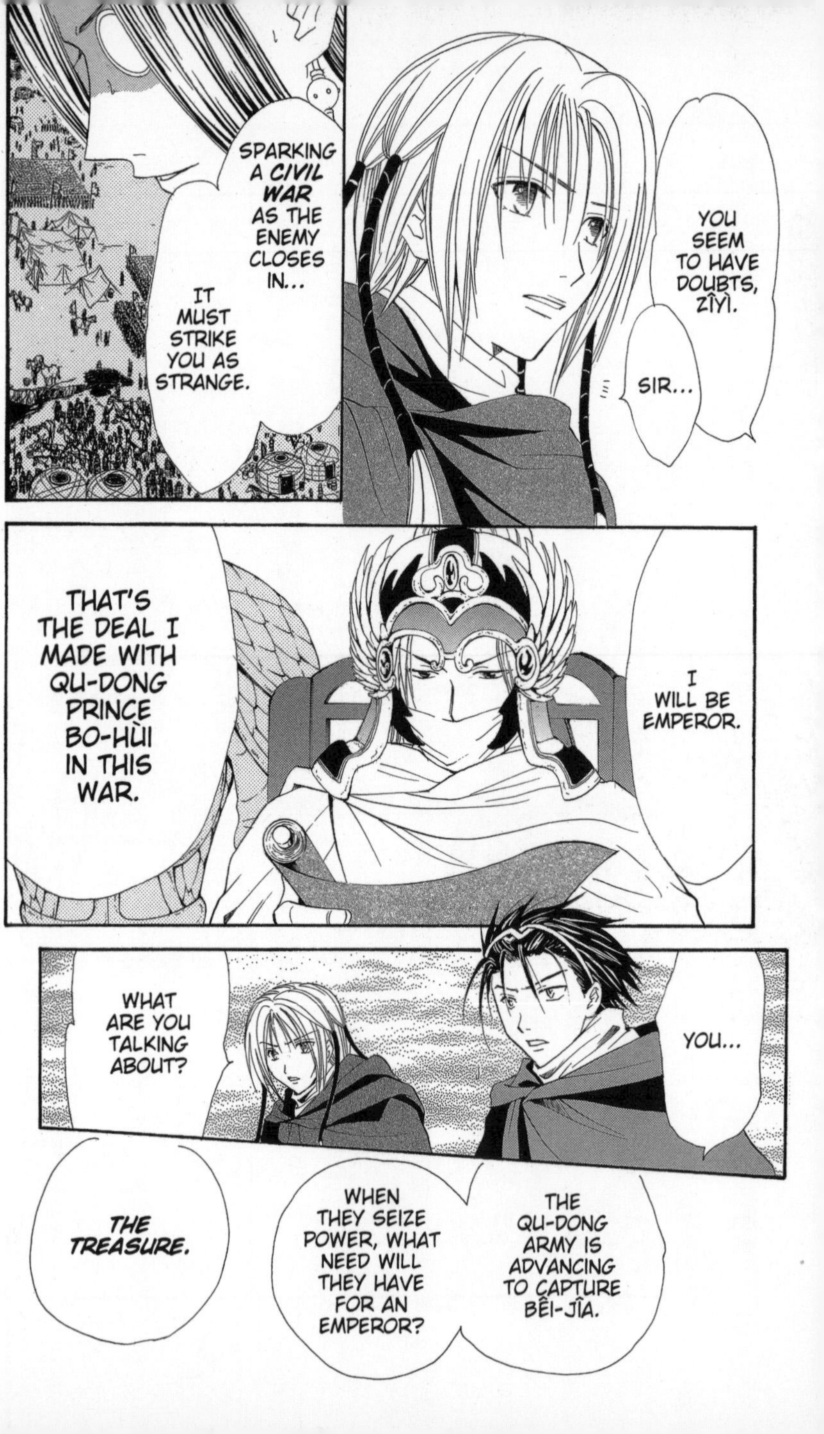
YOU SEEM TO HAVE DOUBTS, ZÎYÌ.
SIR...
SPARKING A *CIVIL WAR* AS THE ENEMY CLOSES IN...
IT MUST STRIKE YOU AS STRANGE.
I WILL BE EMPEROR.
THAT'S THE DEAL I MADE WITH QU-DONG PRINCE BO-HÙI IN THIS WAR.
YOU...
WHAT ARE YOU TALKING ABOUT?
THE QU-DONG ARMY IS ADVANCING TO CAPTURE BÊI-JÎA.
WHEN THEY SEIZE POWER, WHAT NEED WILL THEY HAVE FOR AN EMPEROR?
THE TREASURE.

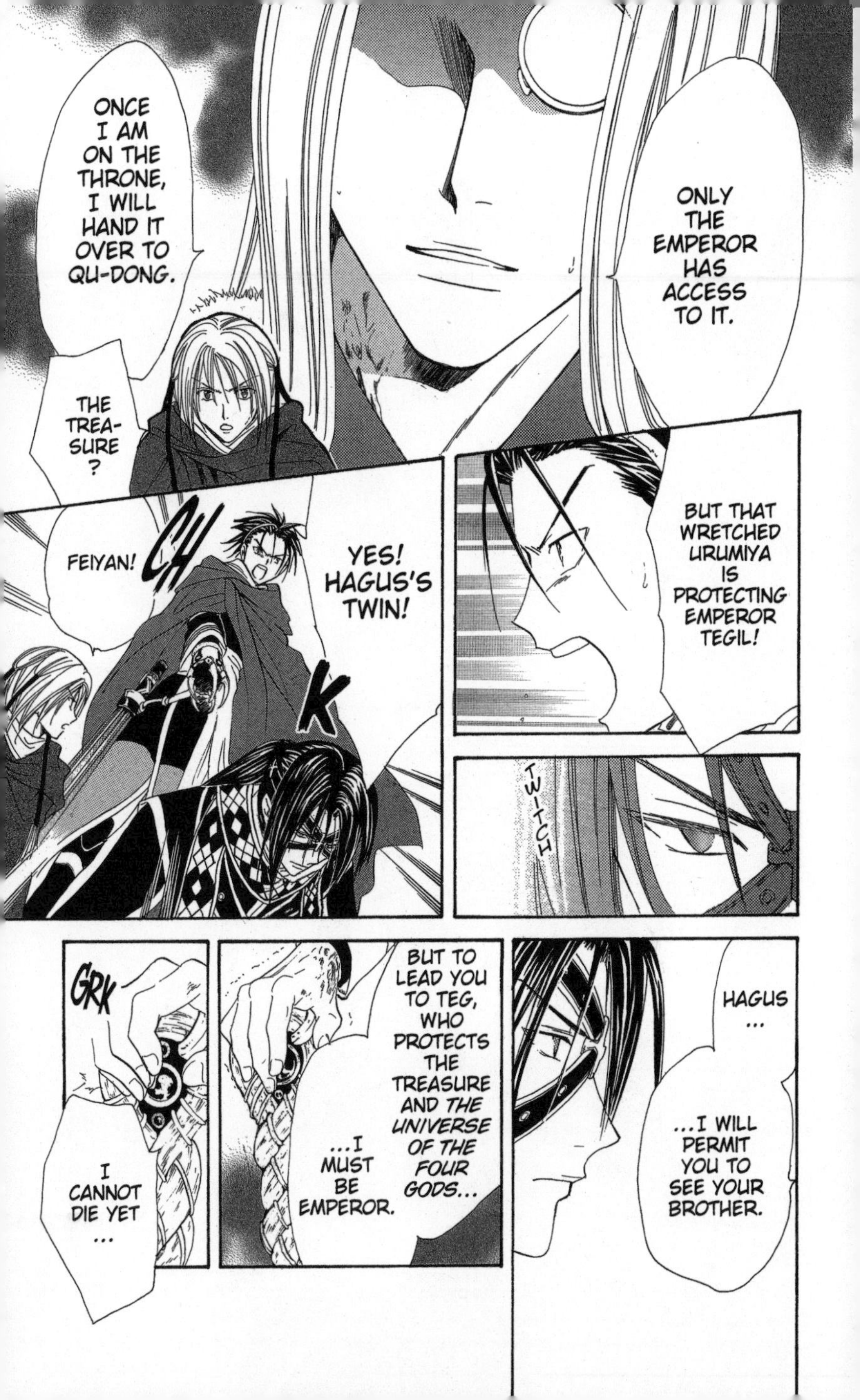
ONLY THE EMPEROR HAS ACCESS TO IT.
ONCE I AM ON THE THRONE, I WILL HAND IT OVER TO QU-DONG.
THE TREASURE?
BUT THAT WRETCHED URUMIYA IS PROTECTING EMPEROR TEGIL!
TWITCH
YES! HAGUS'S TWIN!
CHK
FEIYAN!
HAGUS...
...I WILL PERMIT YOU TO SEE YOUR BROTHER.
BUT TO LEAD YOU TO TEG, WHO PROTECTS THE TREASURE AND *THE UNIVERSE OF THE FOUR GODS*...
...I MUST BE EMPEROR.
GRK
I CANNOT DIE YET...

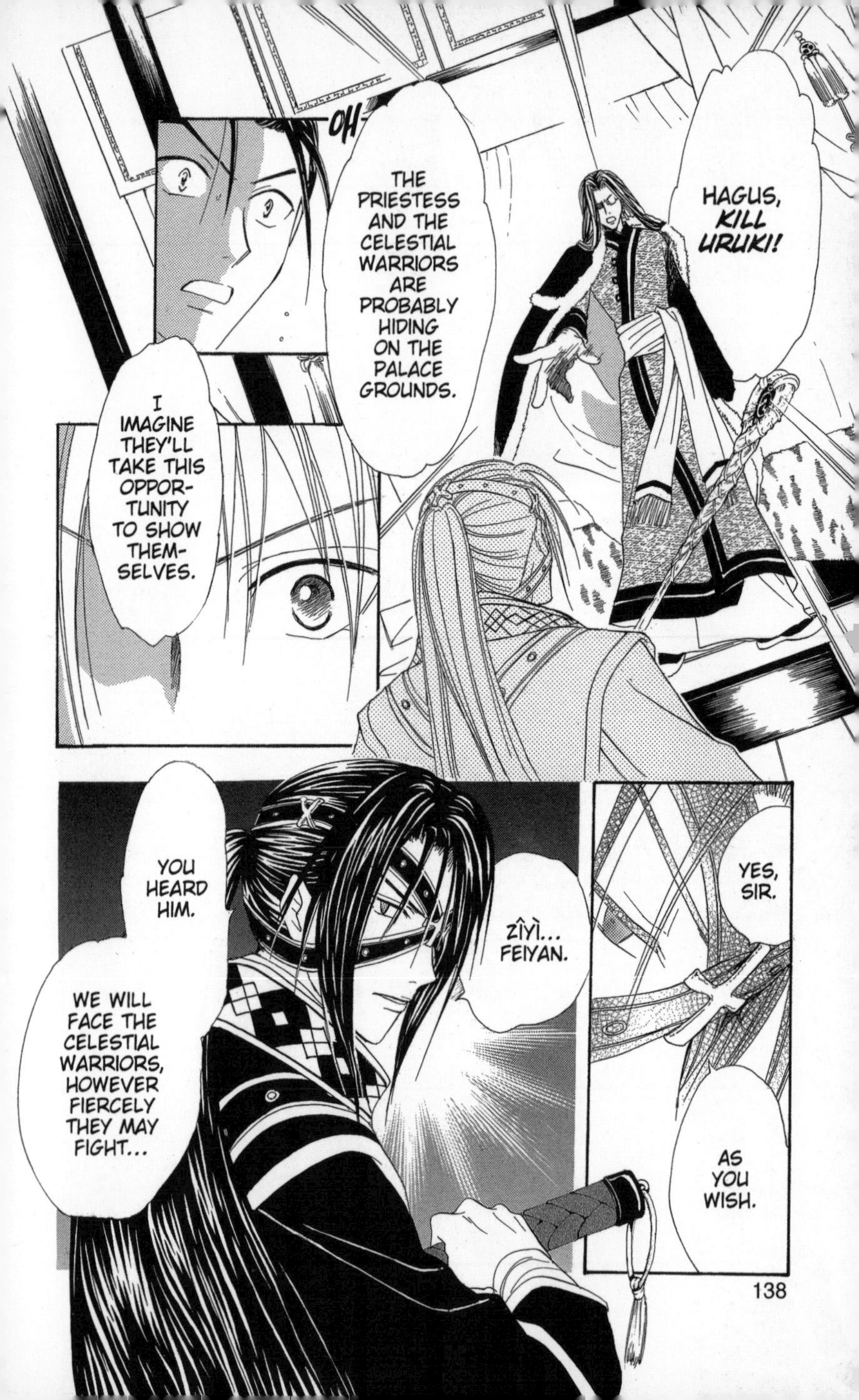
HAGUS, KILL URUKI!
OH-
THE PRIESTESS AND THE CELESTIAL WARRIORS ARE PROBABLY HIDING ON THE PALACE GROUNDS.
I IMAGINE THEY'LL TAKE THIS OPPOR-TUNITY TO SHOW THEM-SELVES.
YOU HEARD HIM.
ZÎYÌ... FEIYAN.
WE WILL FACE THE CELESTIAL WARRIORS, HOWEVER FIERCELY THEY MAY FIGHT...
YES, SIR.
AS YOU WISH.

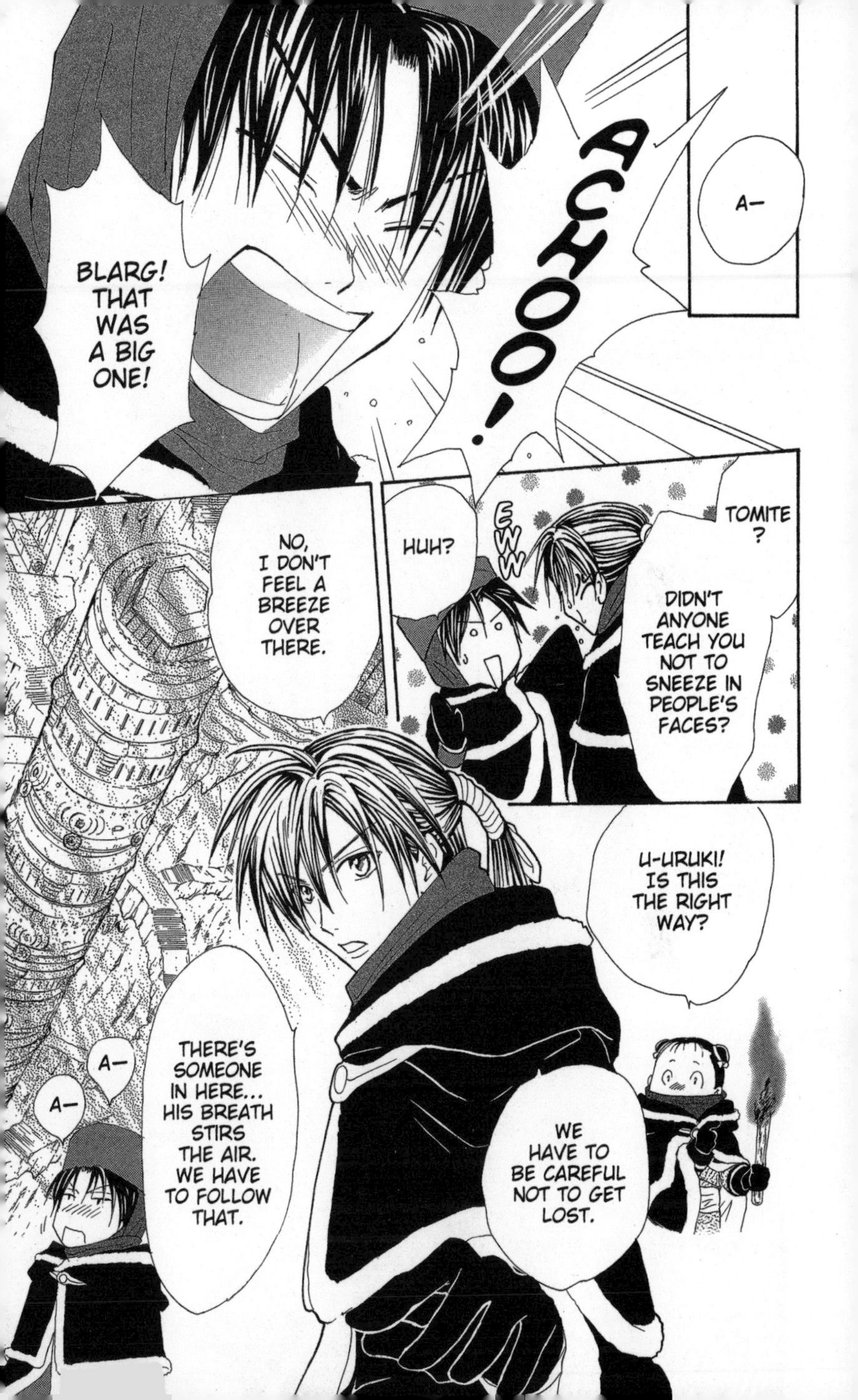
A—
ACHOO!
BLARG! THAT WAS A BIG ONE!
TOMITE?
DIDN'T ANYONE TEACH YOU NOT TO SNEEZE IN PEOPLE'S FACES?
EWW
HUH?
NO, I DON'T FEEL A BREEZE OVER THERE.
U-URUKI! IS THIS THE RIGHT WAY?
WE HAVE TO BE CAREFUL NOT TO GET LOST.
THERE'S SOMEONE IN HERE... HIS BREATH STIRS THE AIR. WE HAVE TO FOLLOW THAT.
A—
A—

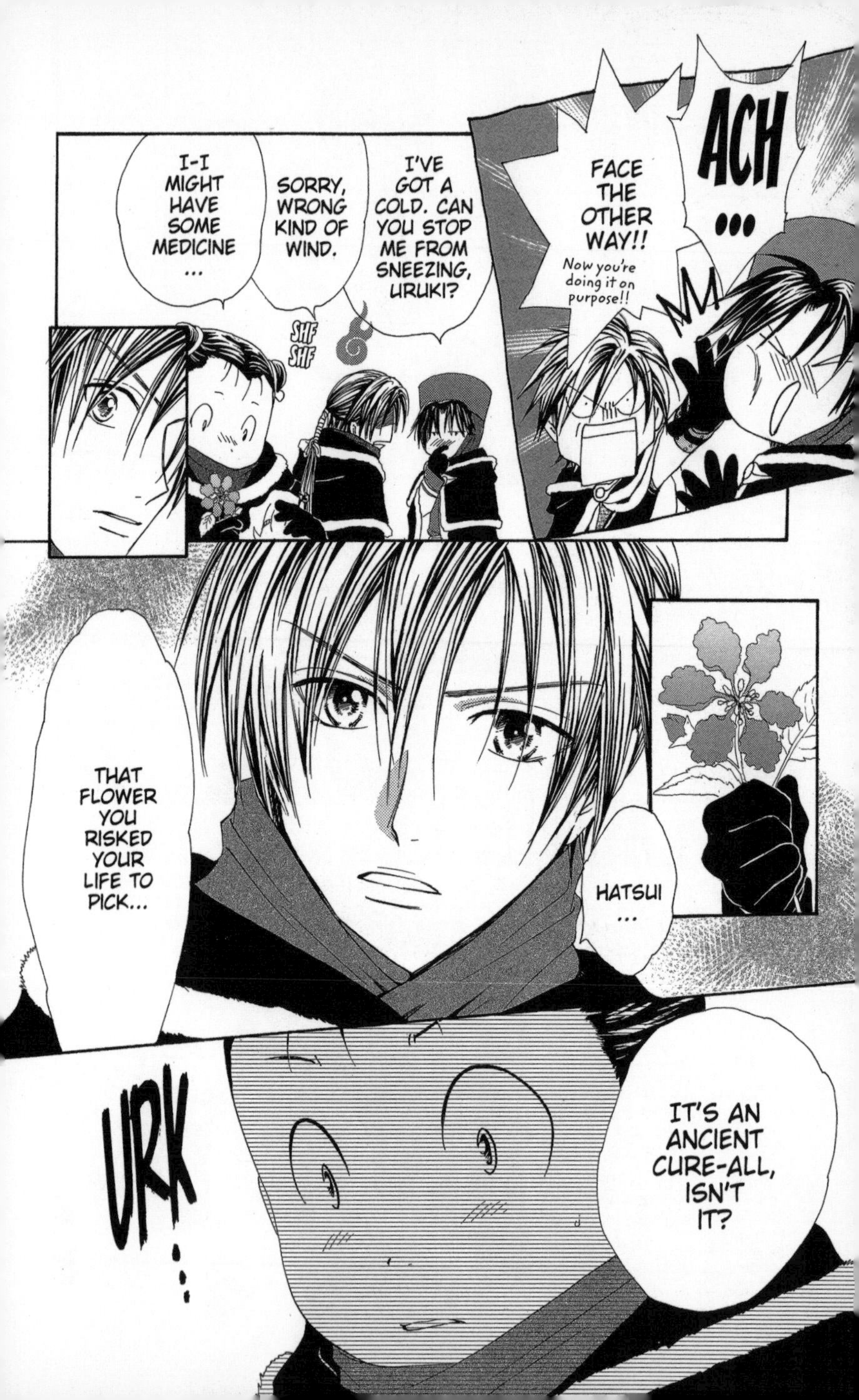
ACH...
FACE THE OTHER WAY!!
Now you're doing it on purpose!!
I'VE GOT A COLD. CAN YOU STOP ME FROM SNEEZING, URUKI?
SHF SHF
SORRY, WRONG KIND OF WIND.
I-I MIGHT HAVE SOME MEDICINE...
HATSUI...
THAT FLOWER YOU RISKED YOUR LIFE TO PICK...
IT'S AN ANCIENT CURE-ALL, ISN'T IT?
URK...

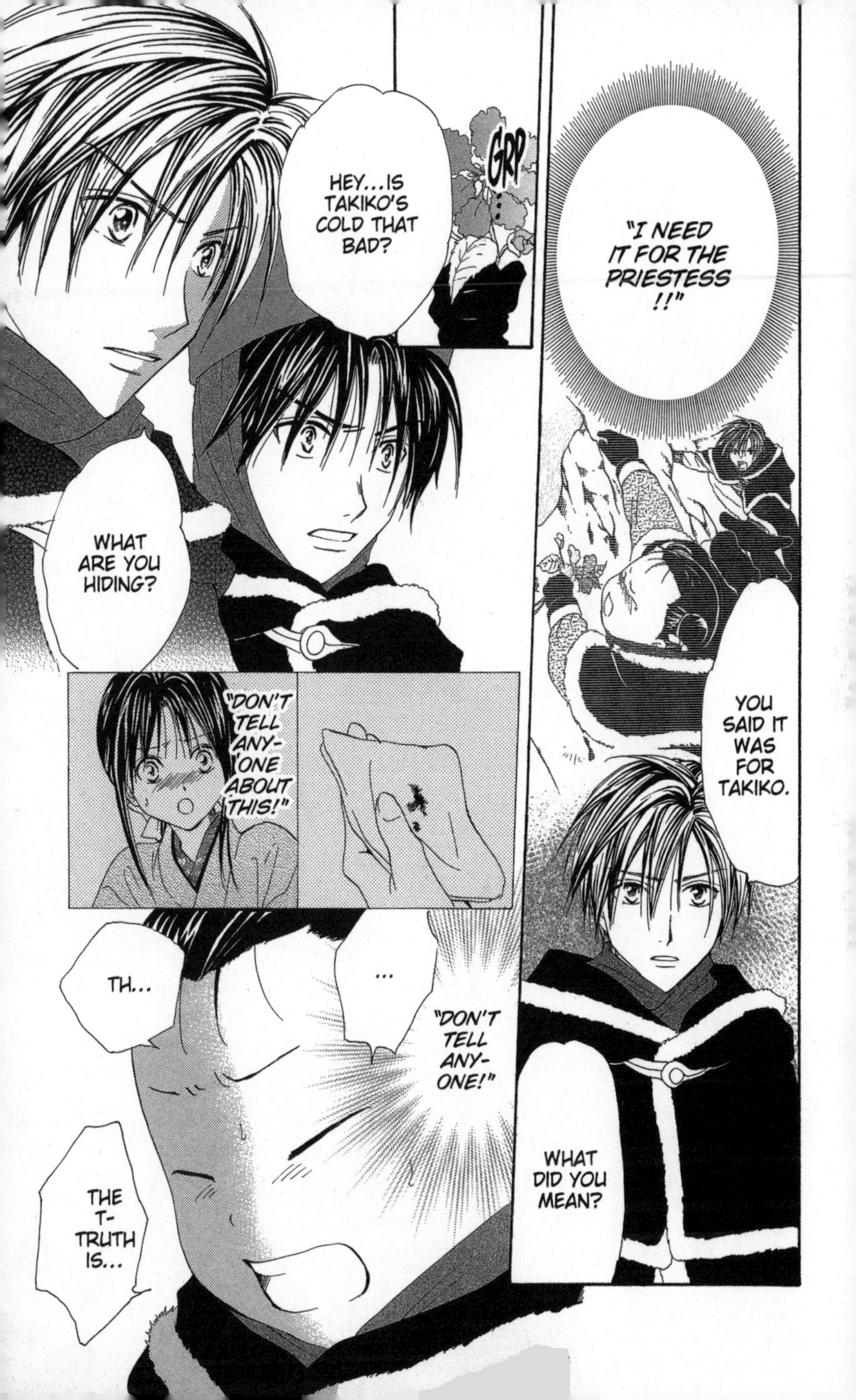
"I NEED IT FOR THE PRIESTESS!!"
YOU SAID IT WAS FOR TAKIKO.
WHAT DID YOU MEAN?
GRP
...
HEY...IS TAKIKO'S COLD THAT BAD?
WHAT ARE YOU HIDING?
"DON'T TELL ANY-ONE ABOUT THIS!"
...
"DON'T TELL ANY-ONE!"
TH...
THE T-TRUTH IS...

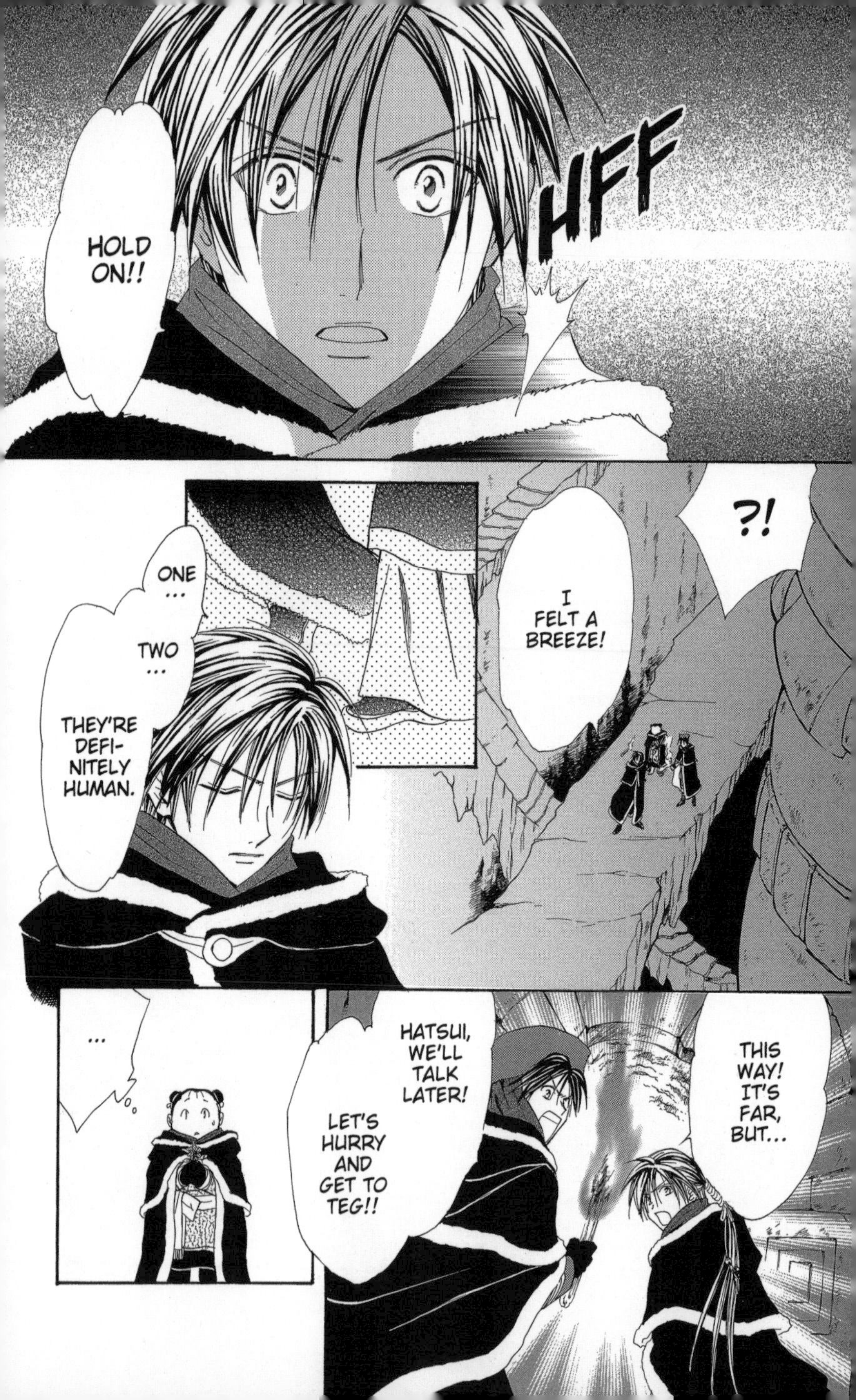
HFF
HOLD ON!!
?!
I FELT A BREEZE!
ONE...
TWO...
THEY'RE DEFI-NITELY HUMAN.
THIS WAY! IT'S FAR, BUT...
HATSUI, WE'LL TALK LATER!
LET'S HURRY AND GET TO TEG!!
...

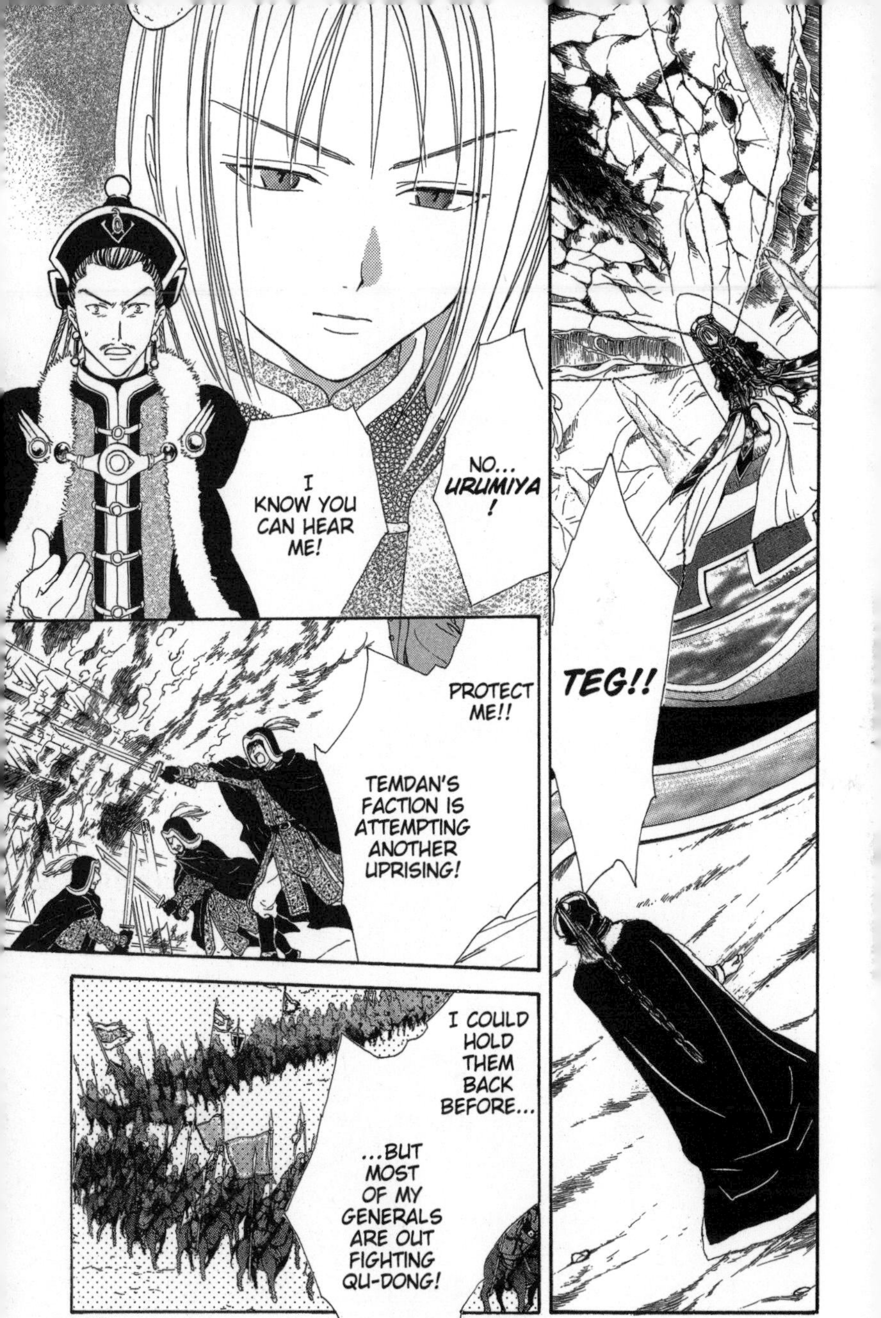
TEG!!
NO... URUMIYA!
I KNOW YOU CAN HEAR ME!
PROTECT ME!!
TEMDAN'S FACTION IS ATTEMPTING ANOTHER UPRISING!
I COULD HOLD THEM BACK BEFORE...
...BUT MOST OF MY GENERALS ARE OUT FIGHTING QU-DONG!

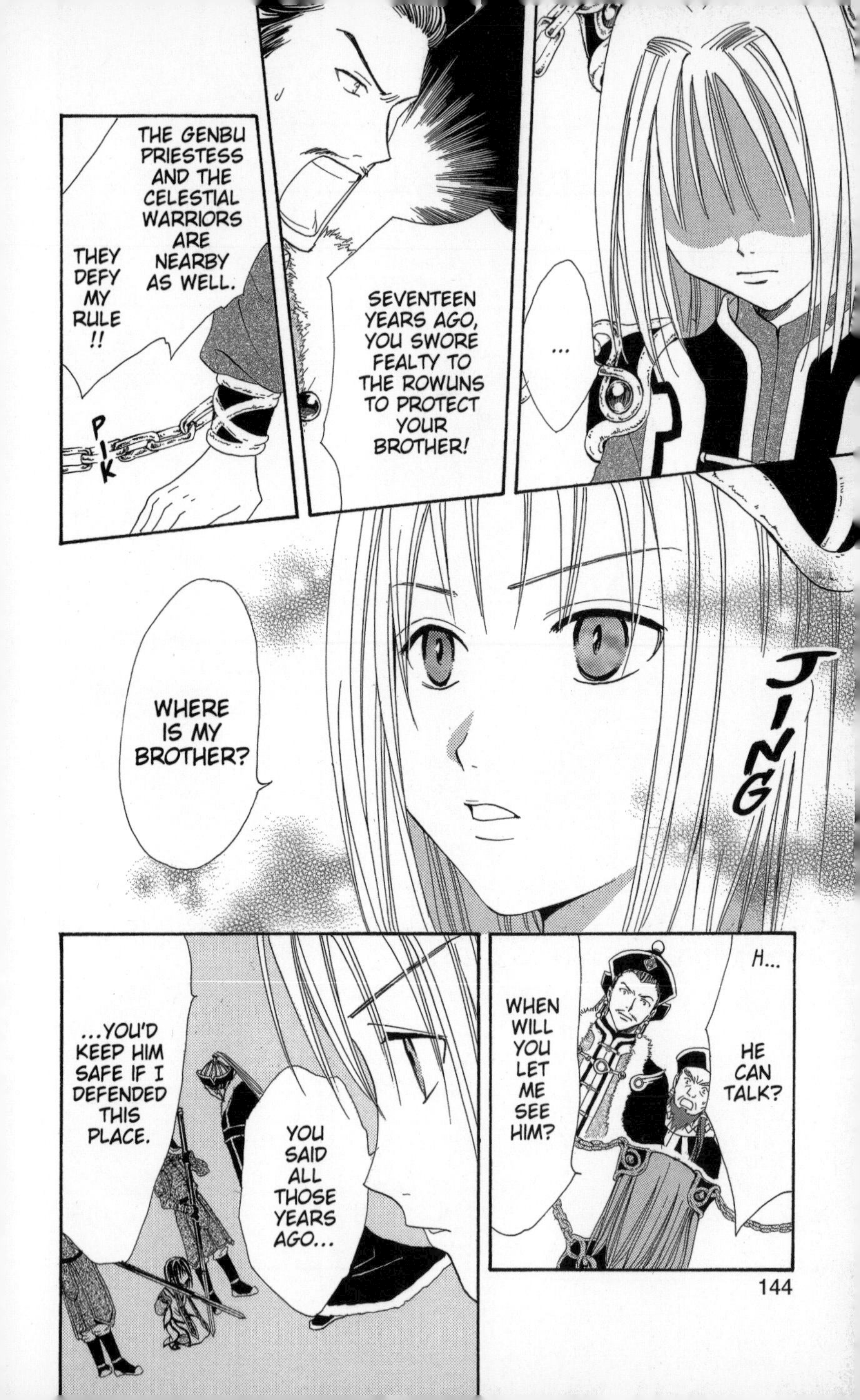
...
SEVENTEEN YEARS AGO, YOU SWORE FEALTY TO THE ROWUNS TO PROTECT YOUR BROTHER!
THE GENBU PRIESTESS AND THE CELESTIAL WARRIORS ARE NEARBY AS WELL.
THEY DEFY MY RULE !!
PIK
JING
WHERE IS MY BROTHER?
H...
HE CAN TALK?
WHEN WILL YOU LET ME SEE HIM?
YOU SAID ALL THOSE YEARS AGO...
...YOU'D KEEP HIM SAFE IF I DEFENDED THIS PLACE.

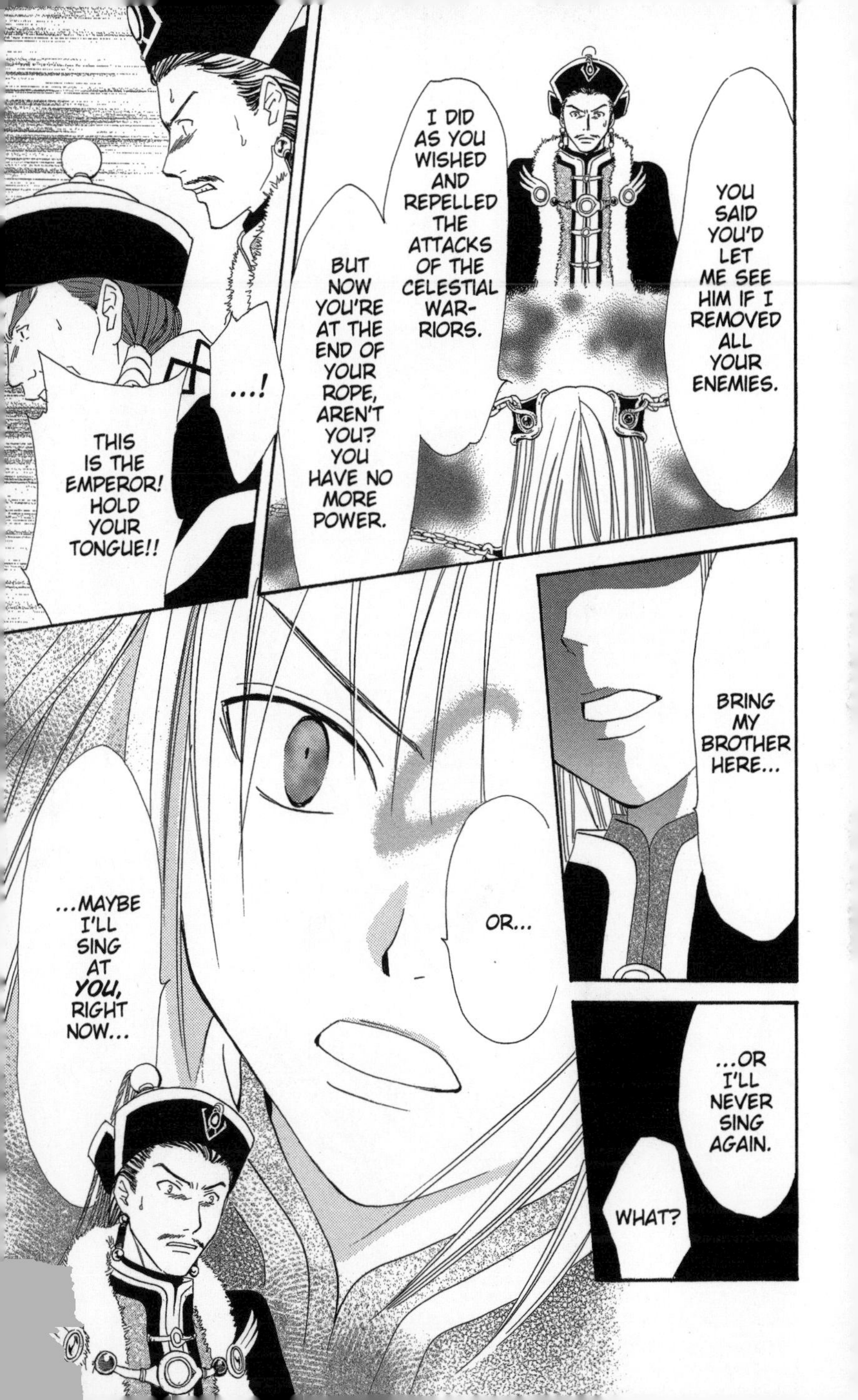
YOU SAID YOU'D LET ME SEE HIM IF I REMOVED ALL YOUR ENEMIES.
I DID AS YOU WISHED AND REPELLED THE ATTACKS OF THE CELESTIAL WAR-RIORS.
BUT NOW YOU'RE AT THE END OF YOUR ROPE, AREN'T YOU? YOU HAVE NO MORE POWER.
...!
THIS IS THE EMPEROR! HOLD YOUR TONGUE!!
BRING MY BROTHER HERE...
...OR I'LL NEVER SING AGAIN.
WHAT?
OR...
...MAYBE I'LL SING AT *YOU*, RIGHT NOW...

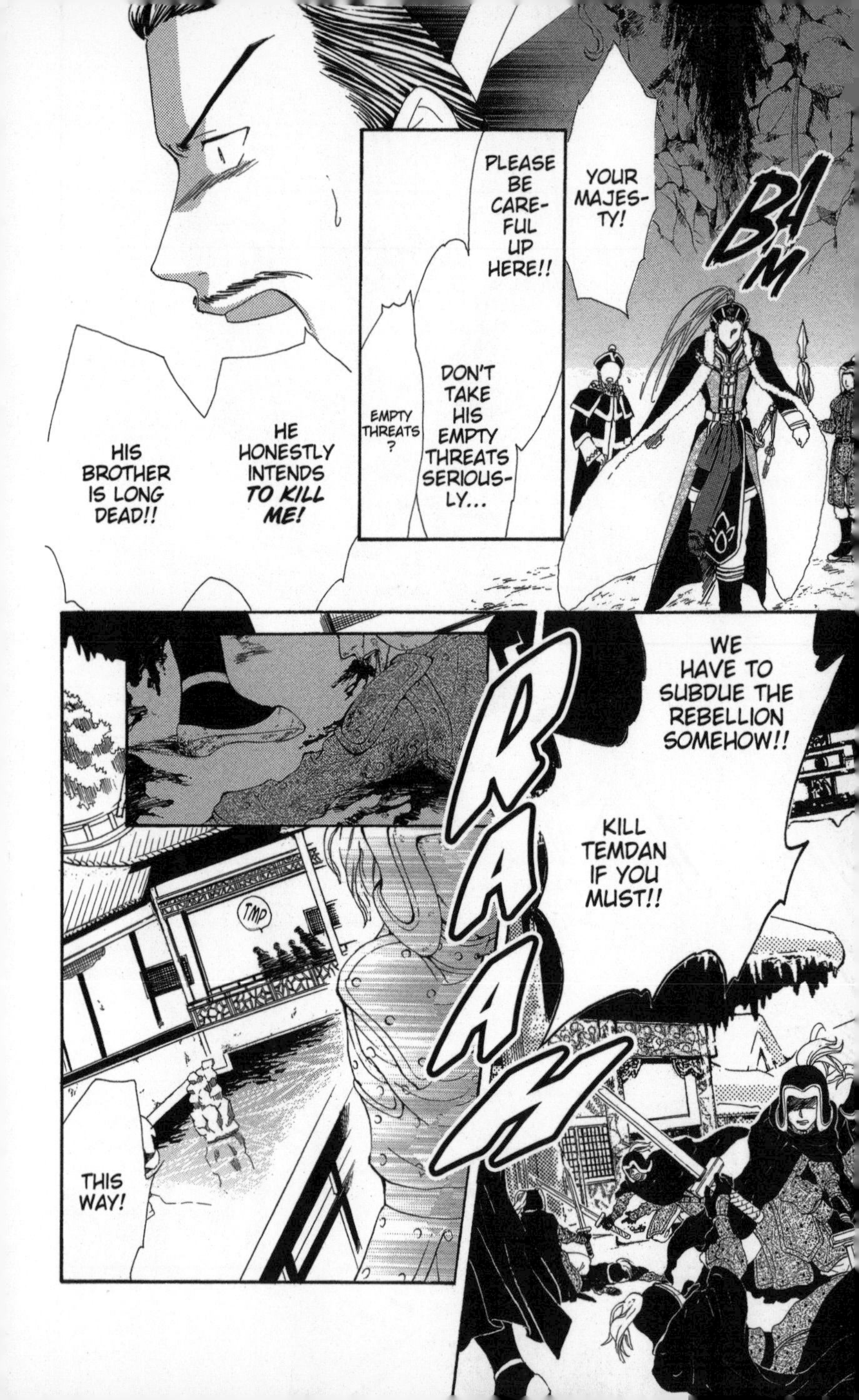
BAM
YOUR MAJESTY!
PLEASE BE CAREFUL UP HERE!!
DON'T TAKE HIS EMPTY THREATS SERIOUSLY...
EMPTY THREATS?
HE HONESTLY INTENDS *TO KILL ME!*
HIS BROTHER IS LONG DEAD!!
WE HAVE TO SUBDUE THE REBELLION SOMEHOW!!
KILL TEMDAN IF YOU MUST!!
DRAAAH
TMP
THIS WAY!

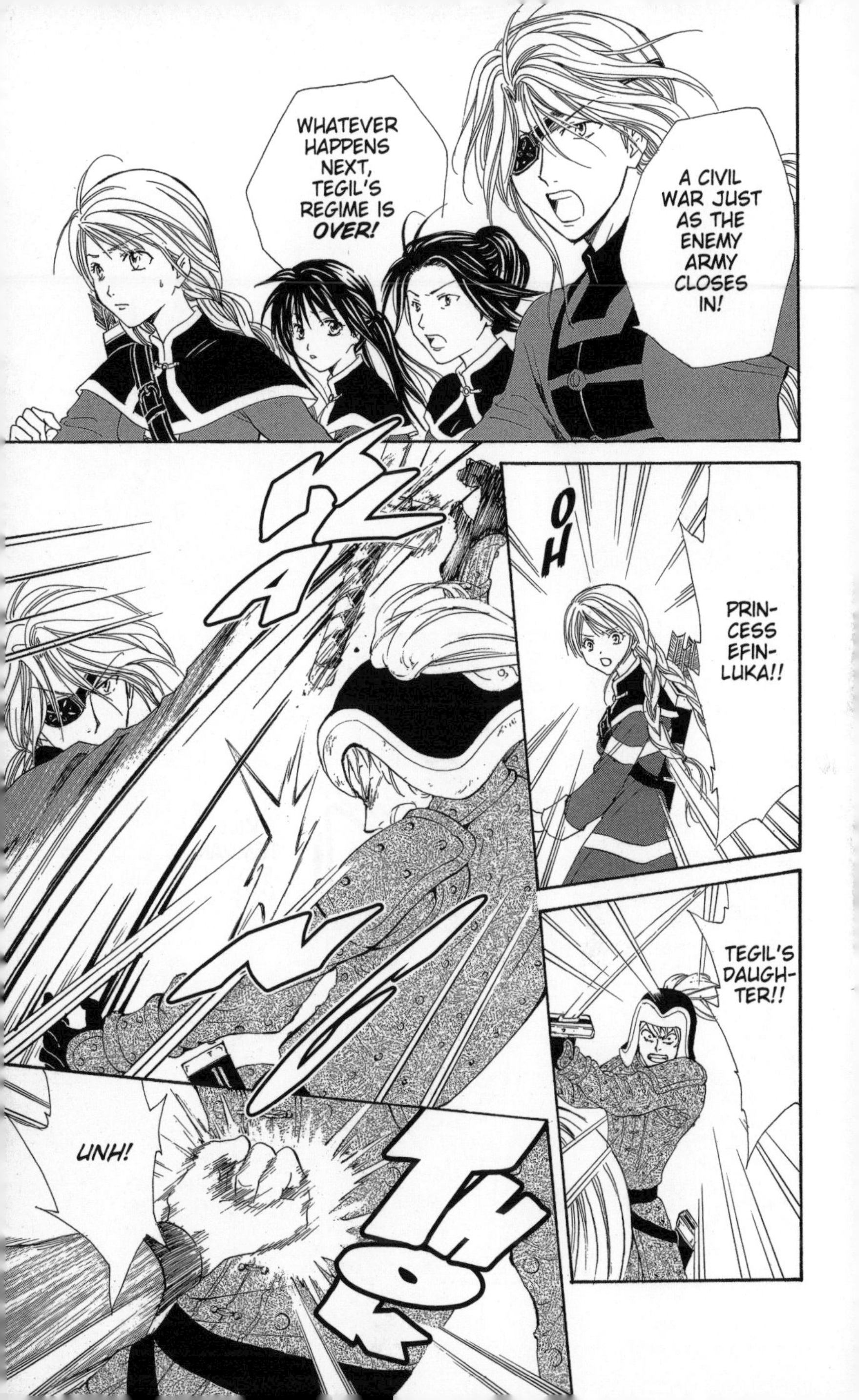

A CIVIL WAR JUST AS THE ENEMY ARMY CLOSES IN!
WHATEVER HAPPENS NEXT, TEGIL'S REGIME IS *OVER!*
OH
PRIN-CESS EFIN-LUKA!!
TEGIL'S DAUGH-TER!!
UNH!

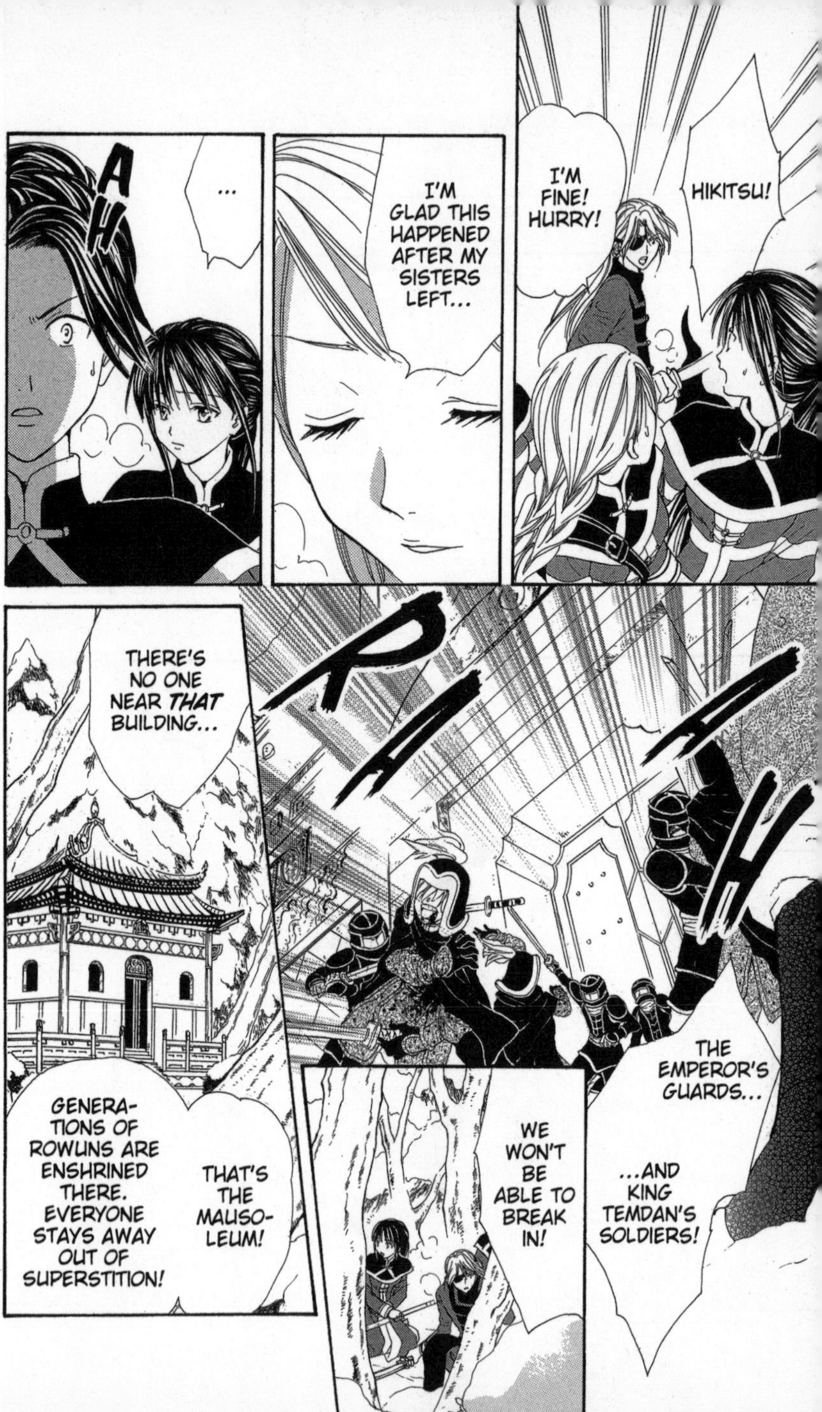
HIKITSU!
I'M FINE! HURRY!
I'M GLAD THIS HAPPENED AFTER MY SISTERS LEFT...
AH
...
RAAH
THE EMPEROR'S GUARDS...
...AND KING TEMDAN'S SOLDIERS!
WE WON'T BE ABLE TO BREAK IN!
THERE'S NO ONE NEAR *THAT* BUILDING...
THAT'S THE MAUSO-LEUM!
GENERA-TIONS OF ROWUNS ARE ENSHRINED THERE. EVERYONE STAYS AWAY OUT OF SUPERSTITION!

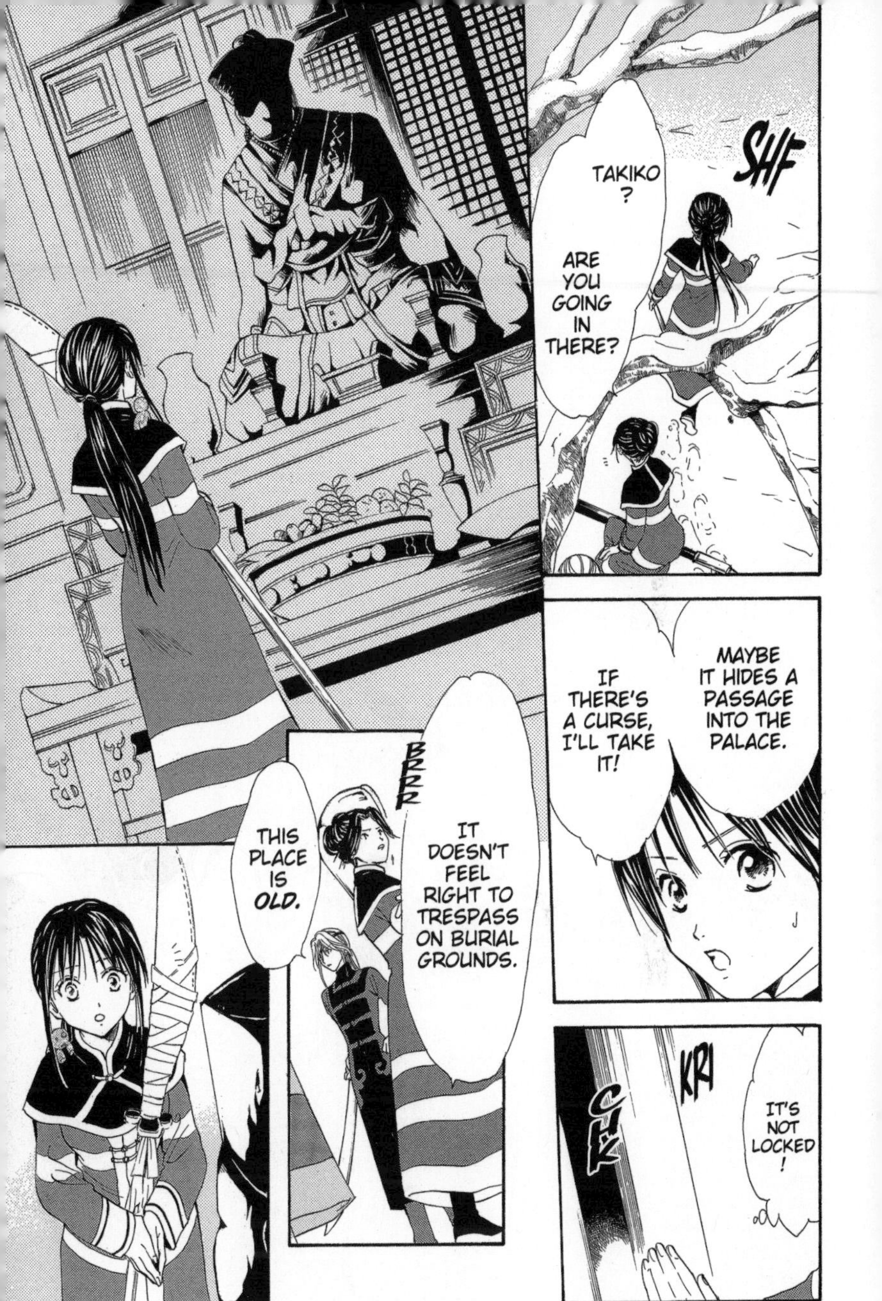
SHF
TAKIKO?
ARE YOU GOING IN THERE?
MAYBE IT HIDES A PASSAGE INTO THE PALACE.
IF THERE'S A CURSE, I'LL TAKE IT!
BRRR
IT DOESN'T FEEL RIGHT TO TRESPASS ON BURIAL GROUNDS.
THIS PLACE IS *OLD.*
KRI
CHK
IT'S NOT LOCKED!

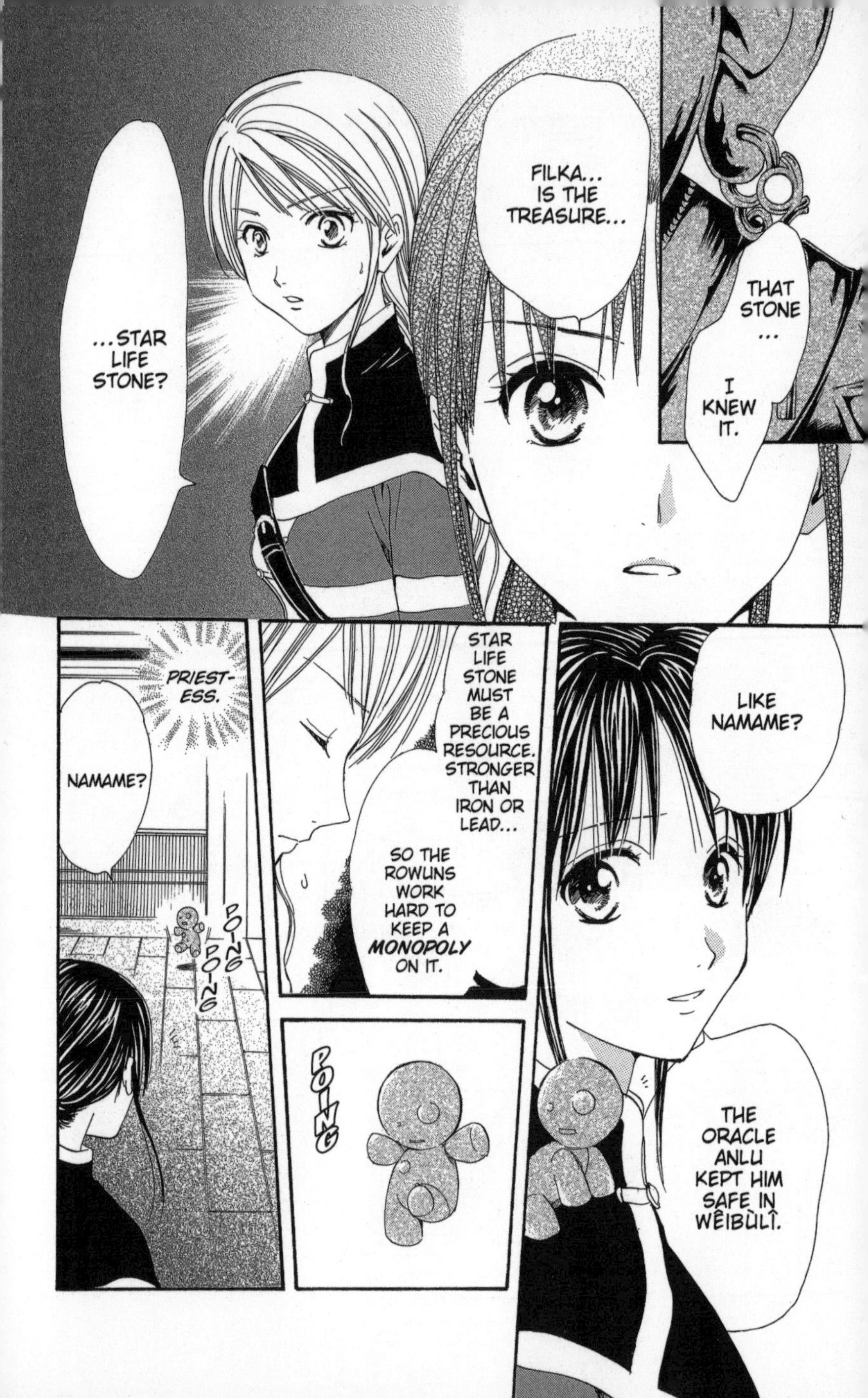
THAT STONE ...
I KNEW IT.
FILKA... IS THE TREASURE...
...STAR LIFE STONE?
STAR LIFE STONE MUST BE A PRECIOUS RESOURCE. STRONGER THAN IRON OR LEAD...
SO THE ROWLINS WORK HARD TO KEEP A ***MONOPOLY*** ON IT.
PRIEST-ESS.
NAMAME?
POING POING
POING
LIKE NAMAME?
THE ORACLE ANLU KEPT HIM SAFE IN WÊIBÙLÎ.

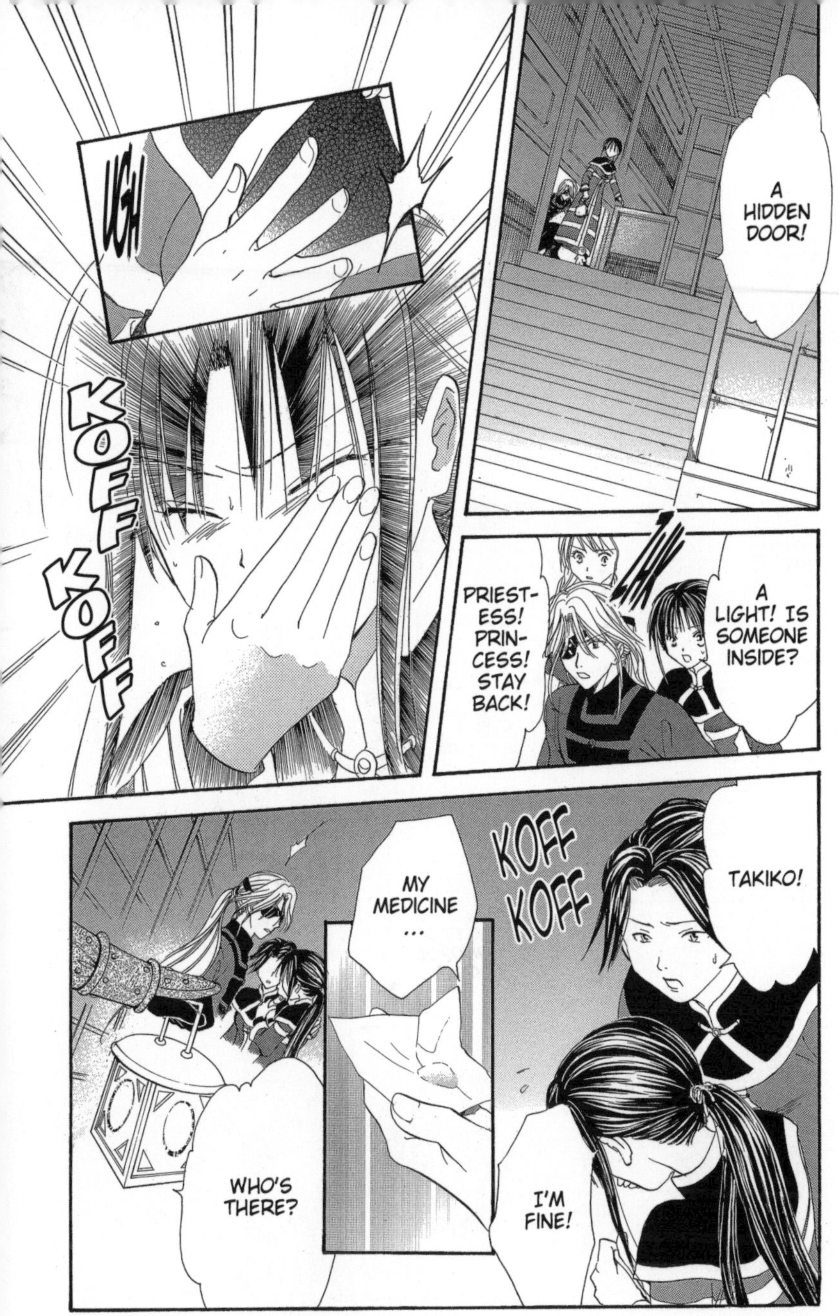
A HIDDEN DOOR!
A LIGHT! IS SOMEONE INSIDE?
PRIEST-ESS! PRIN-CESS! STAY BACK!
UGH
KOFF KOFF
KOFF KOFF
TAKIKO!
KOFF KOFF
MY MEDICINE ...
I'M FINE!
WHO'S THERE?

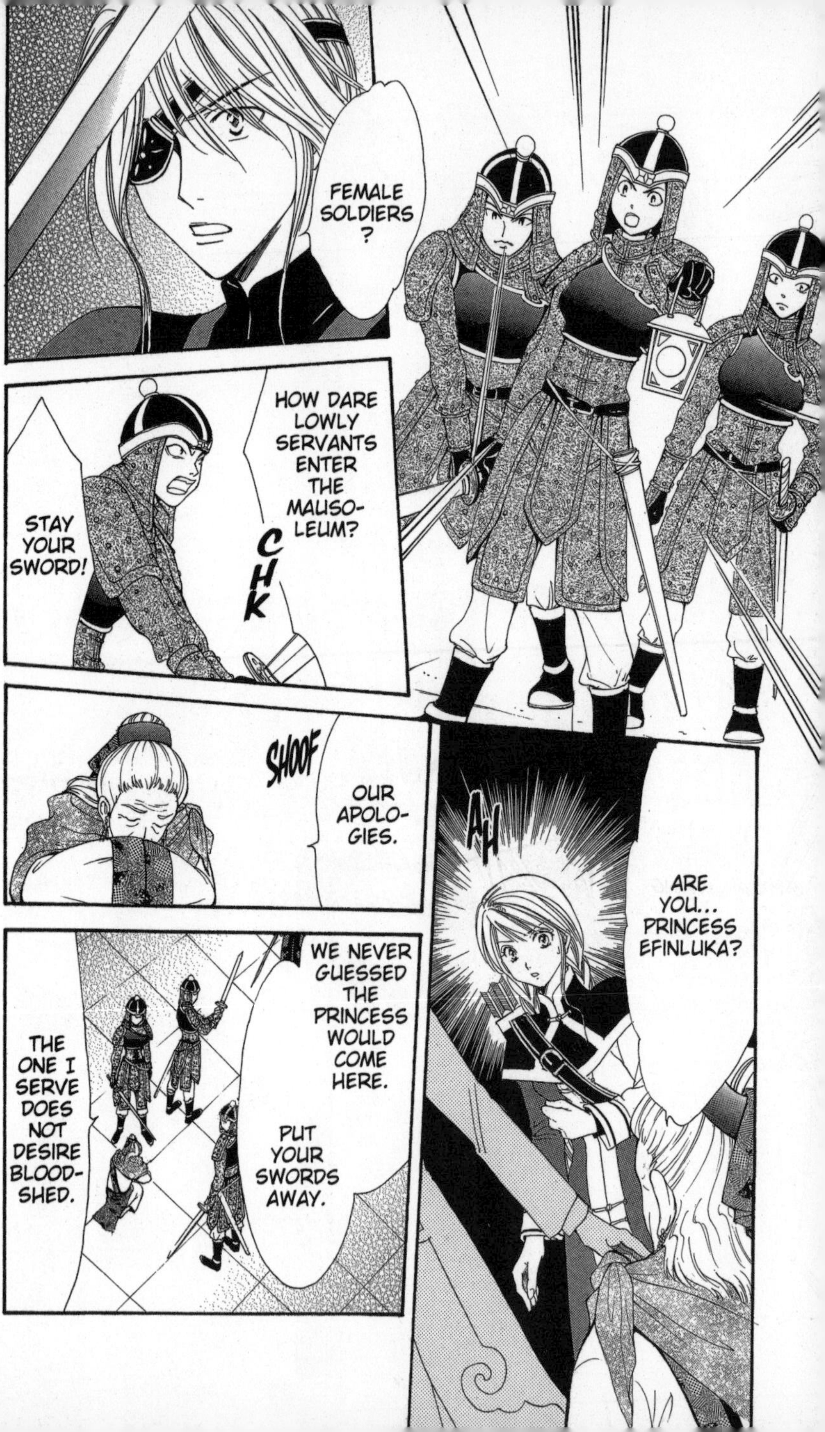
FEMALE SOLDIERS?
HOW DARE LOWLY SERVANTS ENTER THE MAUSOLEUM?
CHK
STAY YOUR SWORD!
AH
ARE YOU... PRINCESS EFINLUKA?
SHOOF
OUR APOLOGIES.
WE NEVER GUESSED THE PRINCESS WOULD COME HERE.
PUT YOUR SWORDS AWAY.
THE ONE I SERVE DOES NOT DESIRE BLOODSHED.

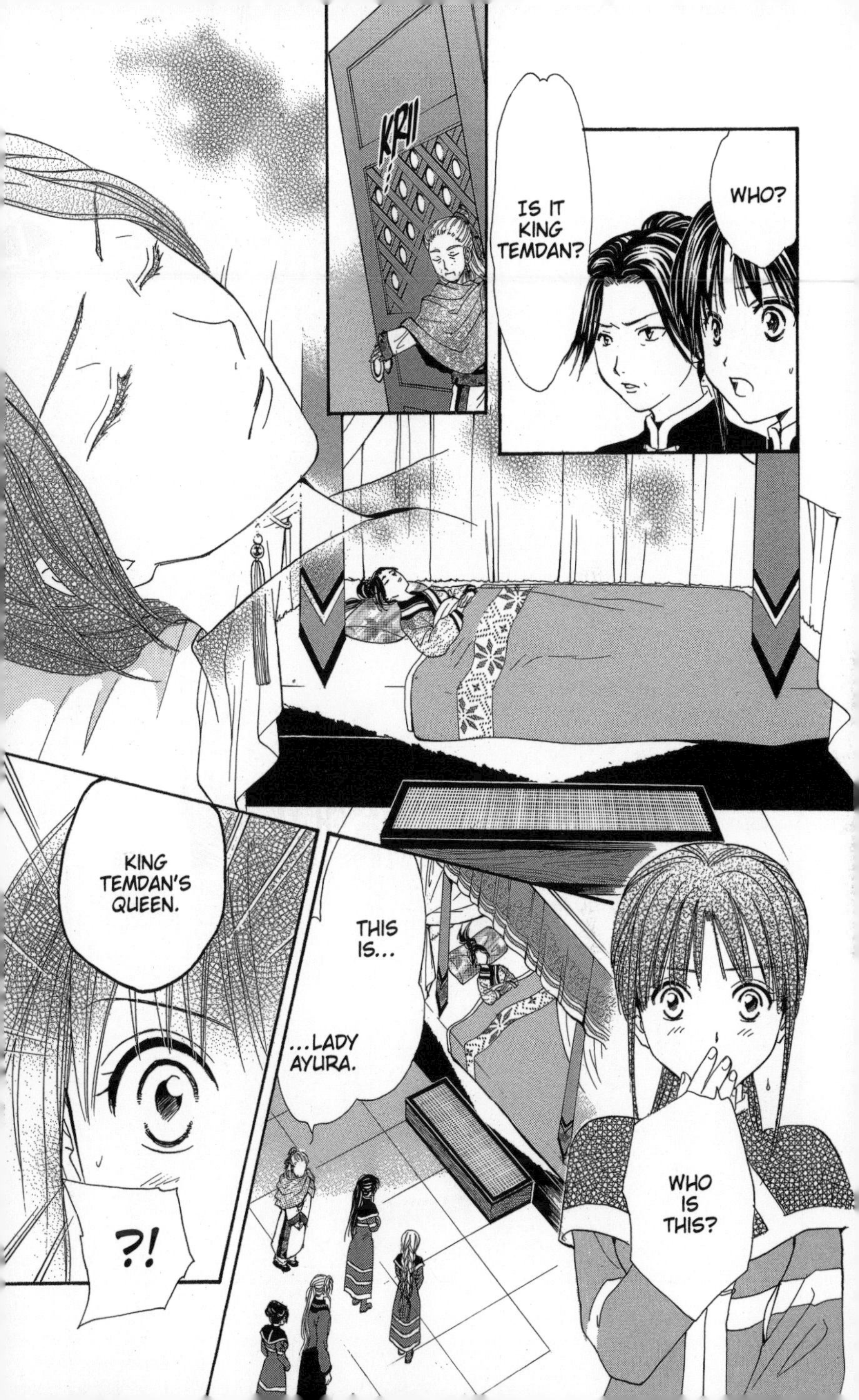
WHO?
IS IT KING TEMDAN?
KRII
WHO IS THIS?
THIS IS...
...LADY AYURA.
KING TEMDAN'S QUEEN.
?!

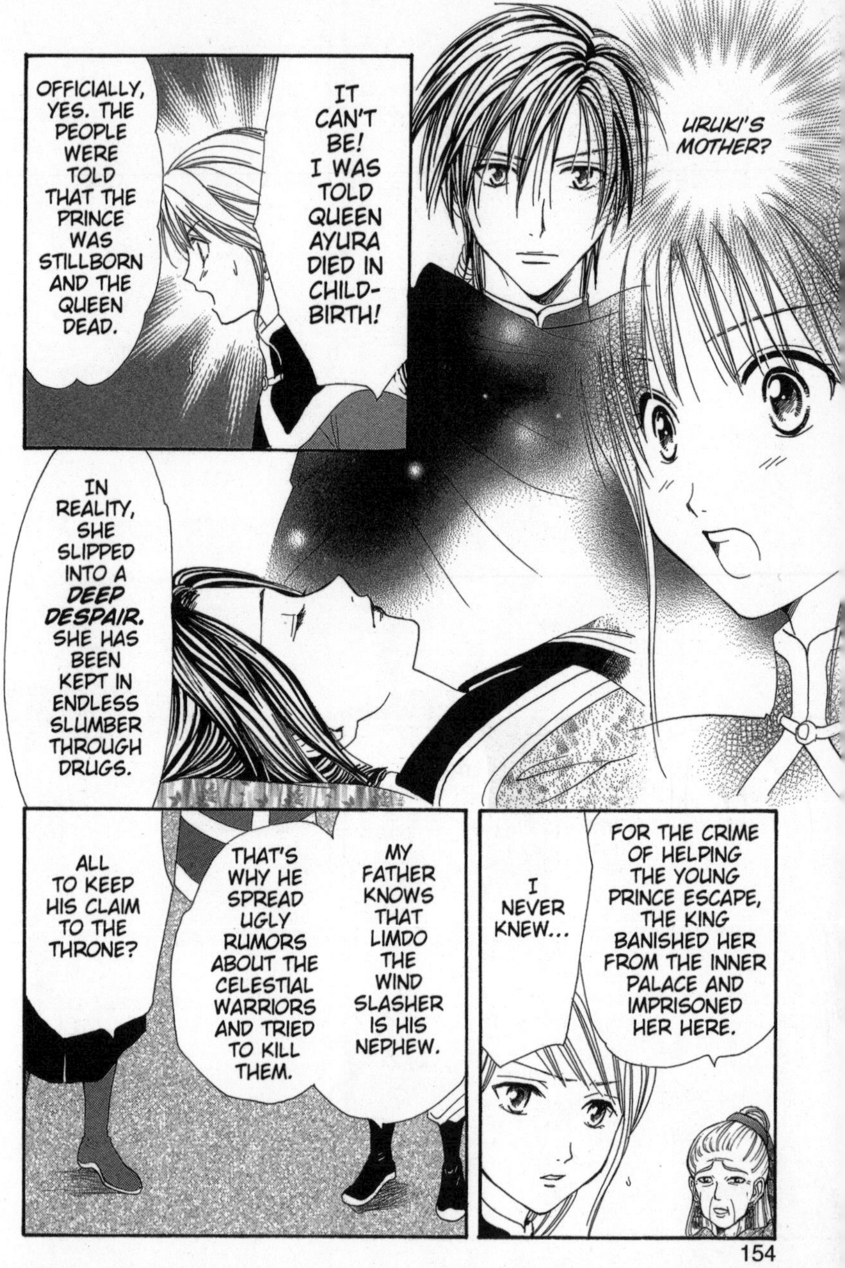
URUKI'S MOTHER?
IT CAN'T BE! I WAS TOLD QUEEN AYURA DIED IN CHILD-BIRTH!
OFFICIALLY, YES. THE PEOPLE WERE TOLD THAT THE PRINCE WAS STILLBORN AND THE QUEEN DEAD.
IN REALITY, SHE SLIPPED INTO A ***DEEP DESPAIR.*** SHE HAS BEEN KEPT IN ENDLESS SLUMBER THROUGH DRUGS.
FOR THE CRIME OF HELPING THE YOUNG PRINCE ESCAPE, THE KING BANISHED HER FROM THE INNER PALACE AND IMPRISONED HER HERE.
I NEVER KNEW...
MY FATHER KNOWS THAT LIMDO THE WIND SLASHER IS HIS NEPHEW.
THAT'S WHY HE SPREAD UGLY RUMORS ABOUT THE CELESTIAL WARRIORS AND TRIED TO KILL THEM.
ALL TO KEEP HIS CLAIM TO THE THRONE?

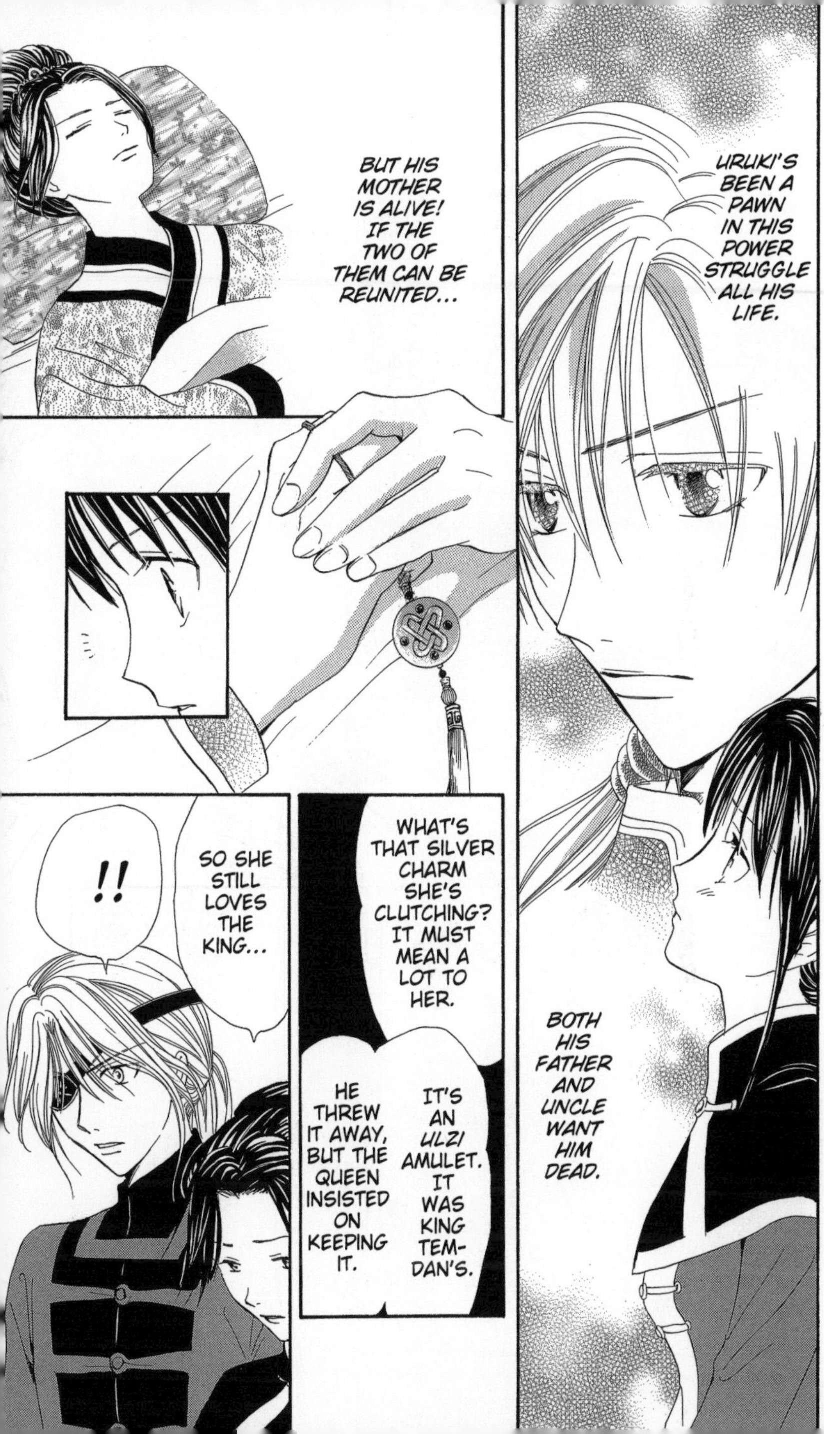
URUKI'S BEEN A PAWN IN THIS POWER STRUGGLE ALL HIS LIFE.
BOTH HIS FATHER AND UNCLE WANT HIM DEAD.
BUT HIS MOTHER IS ALIVE! IF THE TWO OF THEM CAN BE REUNITED...
WHAT'S THAT SILVER CHARM SHE'S CLUTCHING? IT MUST MEAN A LOT TO HER.
IT'S AN ULZI AMULET. IT WAS KING TEM-DAN'S.
HE THREW IT AWAY, BUT THE QUEEN INSISTED ON KEEPING IT.
SO SHE STILL LOVES THE KING...
!!

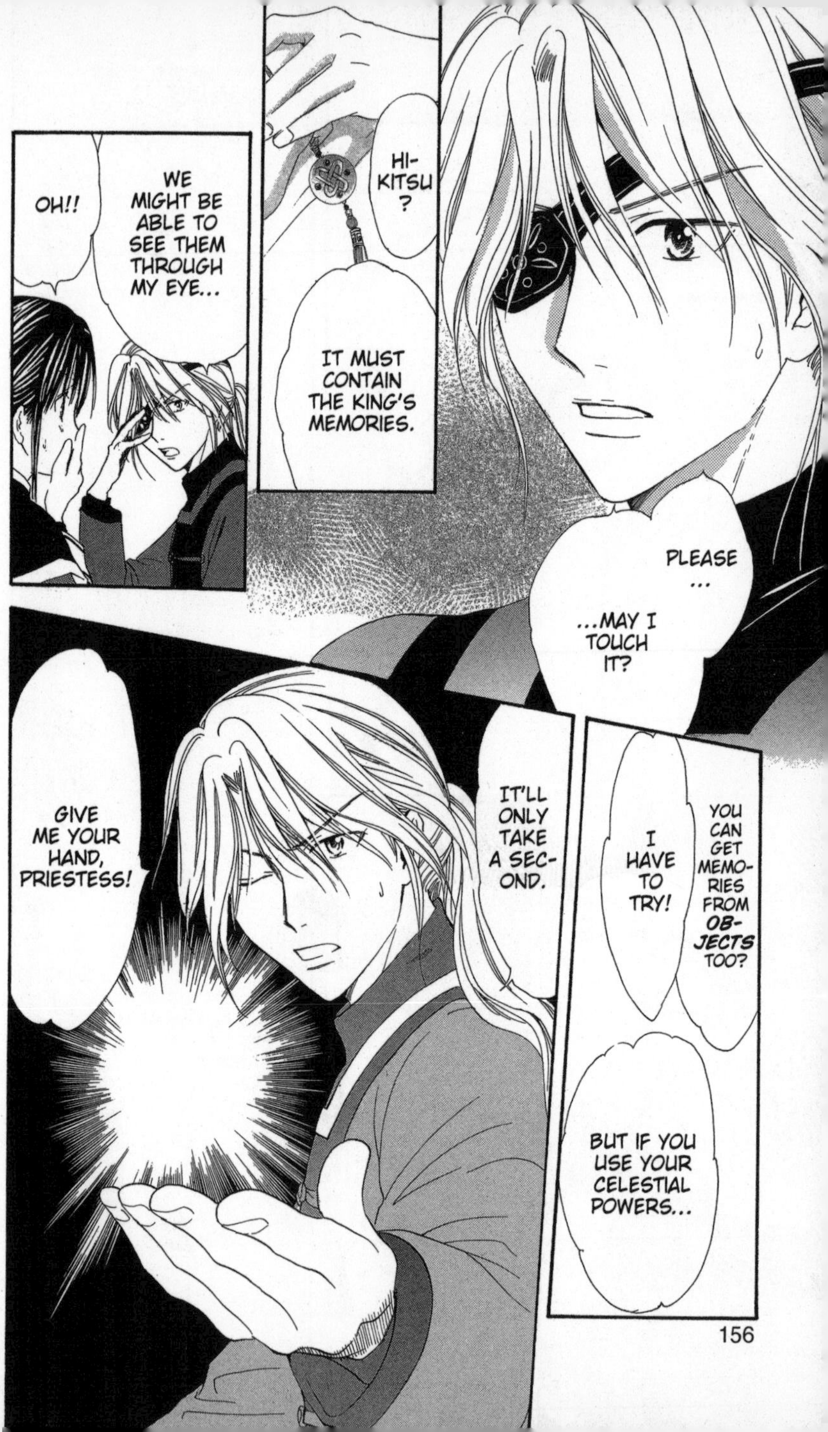
HI-KITSU?
IT MUST CONTAIN THE KING'S MEMORIES.
WE MIGHT BE ABLE TO SEE THEM THROUGH MY EYE...
OH!!
PLEASE...
...MAY I TOUCH IT?
YOU CAN GET MEMORIES FROM ***OBJECTS*** TOO?
I HAVE TO TRY!
BUT IF YOU USE YOUR CELESTIAL POWERS...
IT'LL ONLY TAKE A SECOND.
GIVE ME YOUR HAND, PRIESTESS!

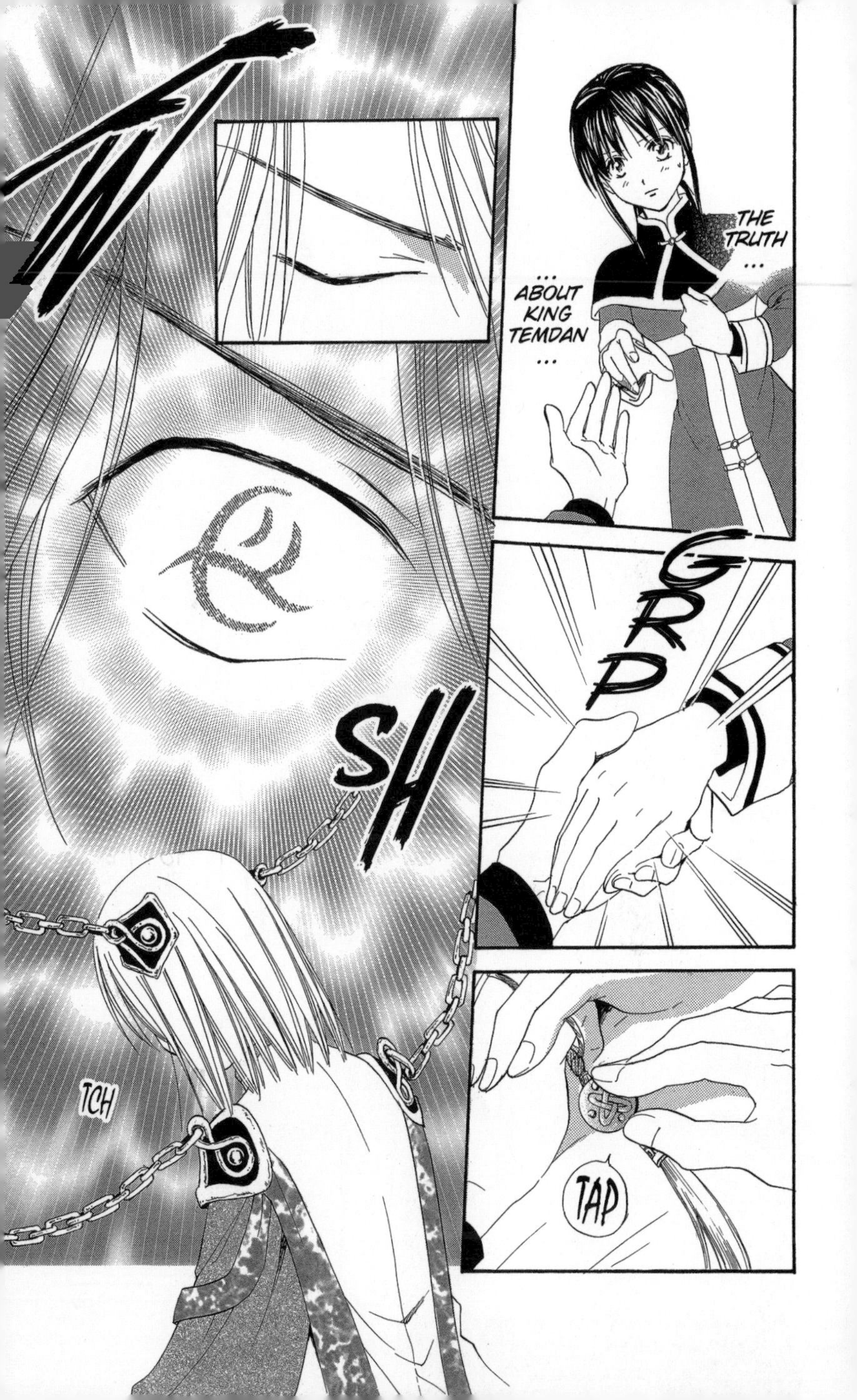

THE TRUTH ...
... ABOUT KING TEMDAN ...
GRP
TAP
SH
TCH

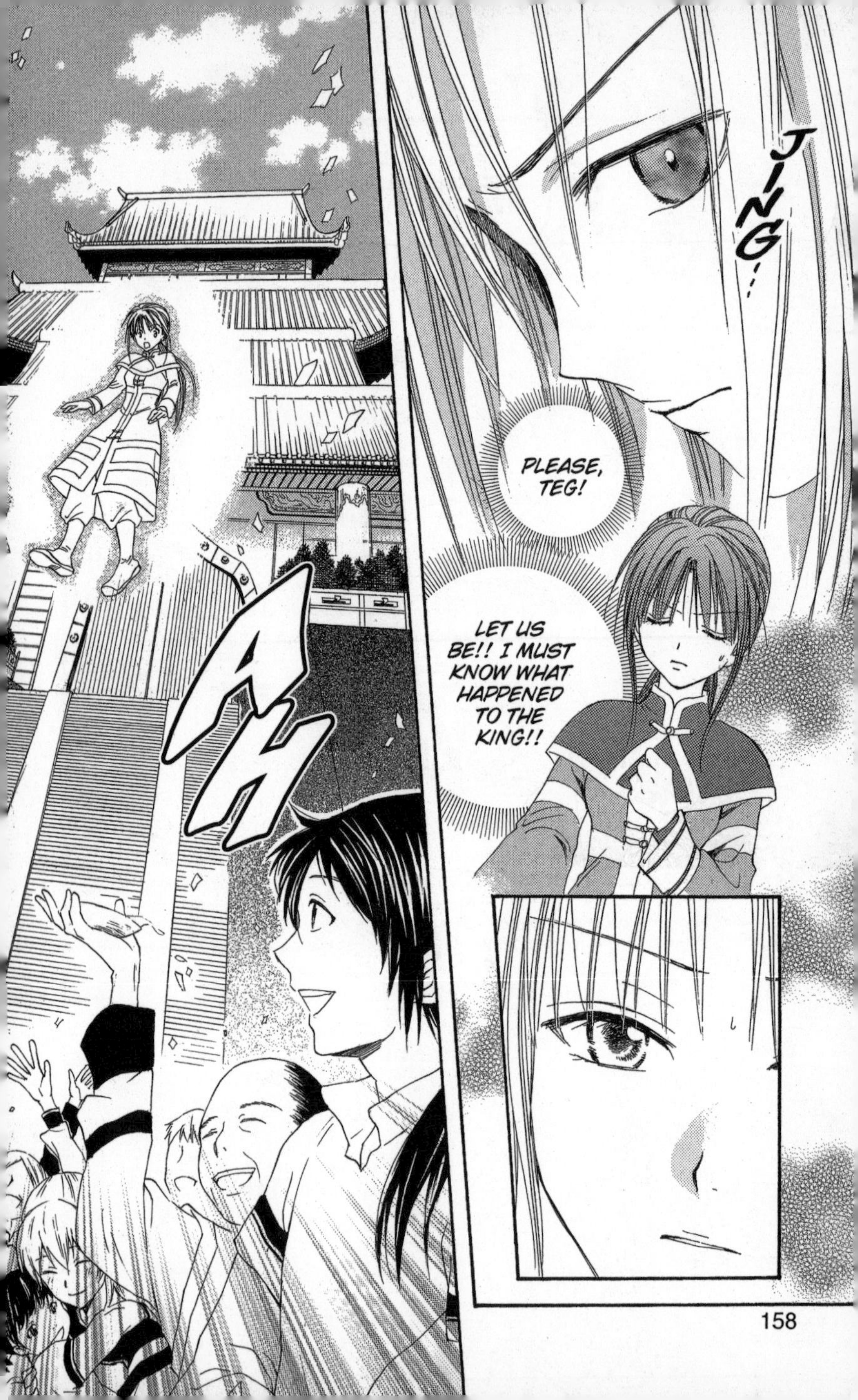
JING!!
PLEASE, TEG!
LET US BE!! I MUST KNOW WHAT HAPPENED TO THE KING!!
AH

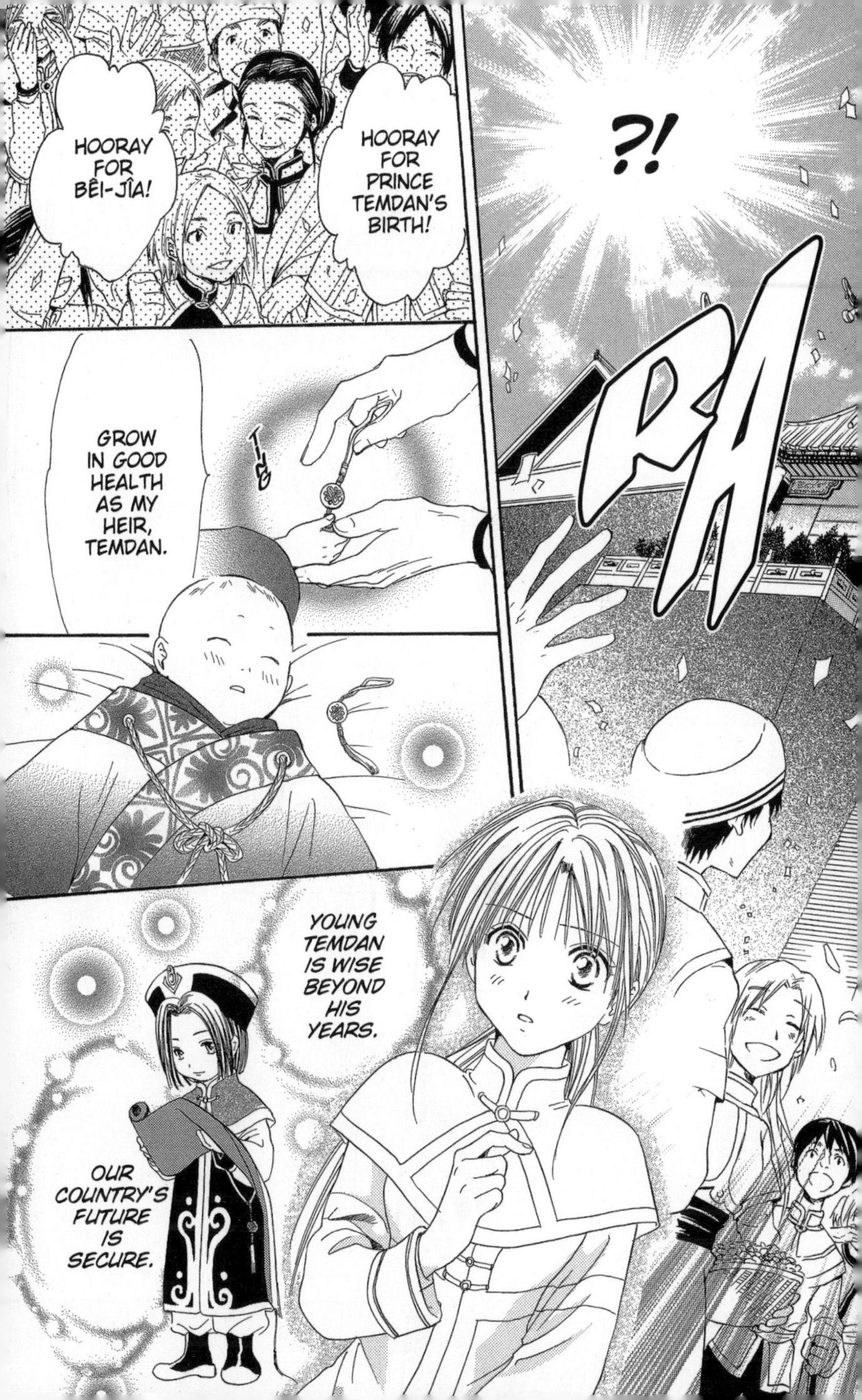
?!
PA
HOORAY FOR PRINCE TEMDAN'S BIRTH!
HOORAY FOR BÊI-JÎA!
GROW IN GOOD HEALTH AS MY HEIR, TEMDAN.
TING
YOUNG TEMDAN IS WISE BEYOND HIS YEARS.
OUR COUNTRY'S FUTURE IS SECURE.

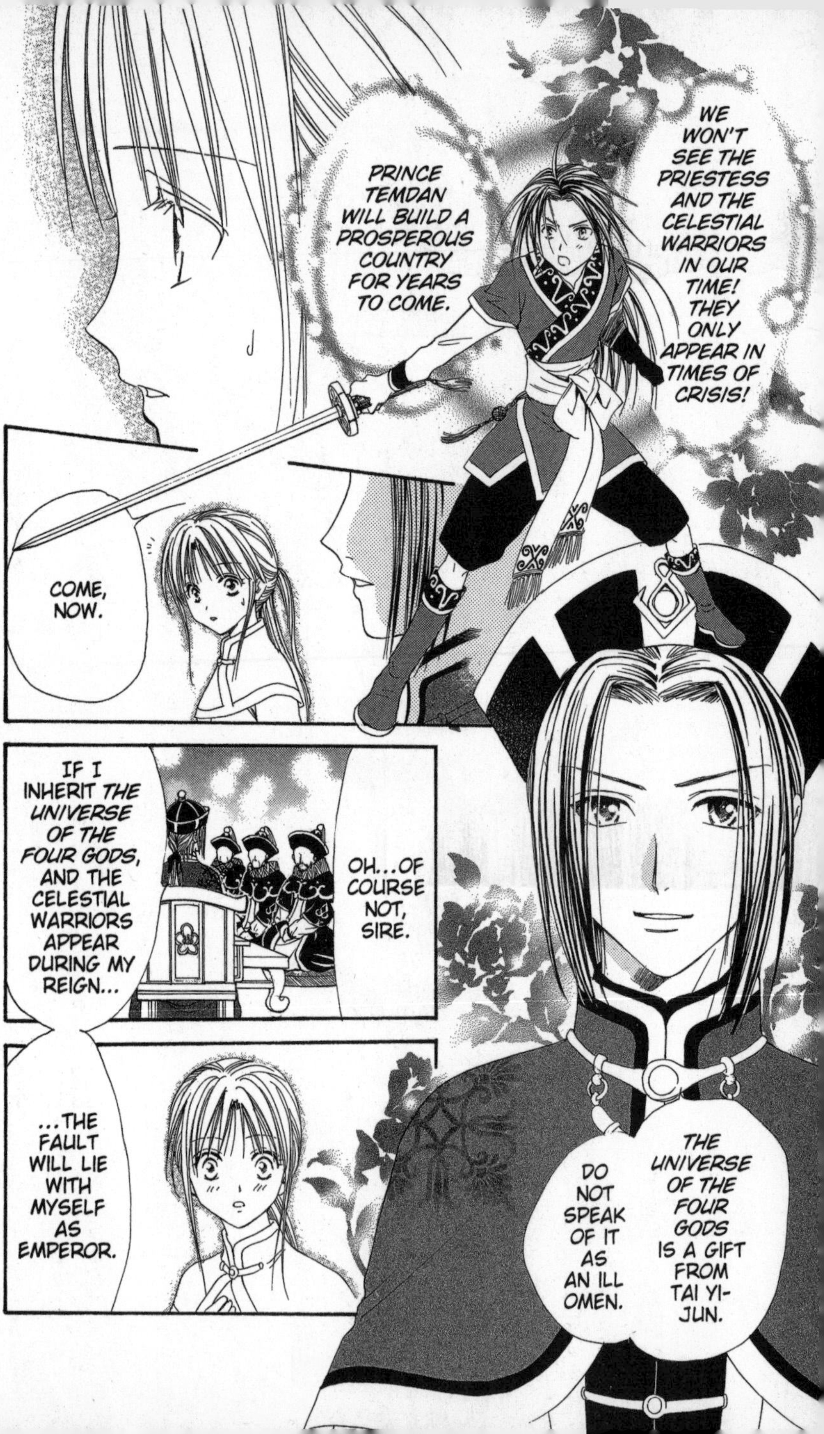

WE WON'T SEE THE PRIESTESS AND THE CELESTIAL WARRIORS IN OUR TIME! THEY ONLY APPEAR IN TIMES OF CRISIS!
PRINCE TEMDAN WILL BUILD A PROSPEROUS COUNTRY FOR YEARS TO COME.
COME, NOW.
THE UNIVERSE OF THE FOUR GODS IS A GIFT FROM TAI YI-JUN.
DO NOT SPEAK OF IT AS AN ILL OMEN.
OH...OF COURSE NOT, SIRE.
IF I INHERIT *THE UNIVERSE OF THE FOUR GODS*, AND THE CELESTIAL WARRIORS APPEAR DURING MY REIGN...
...THE FAULT WILL LIE WITH MYSELF AS EMPEROR.

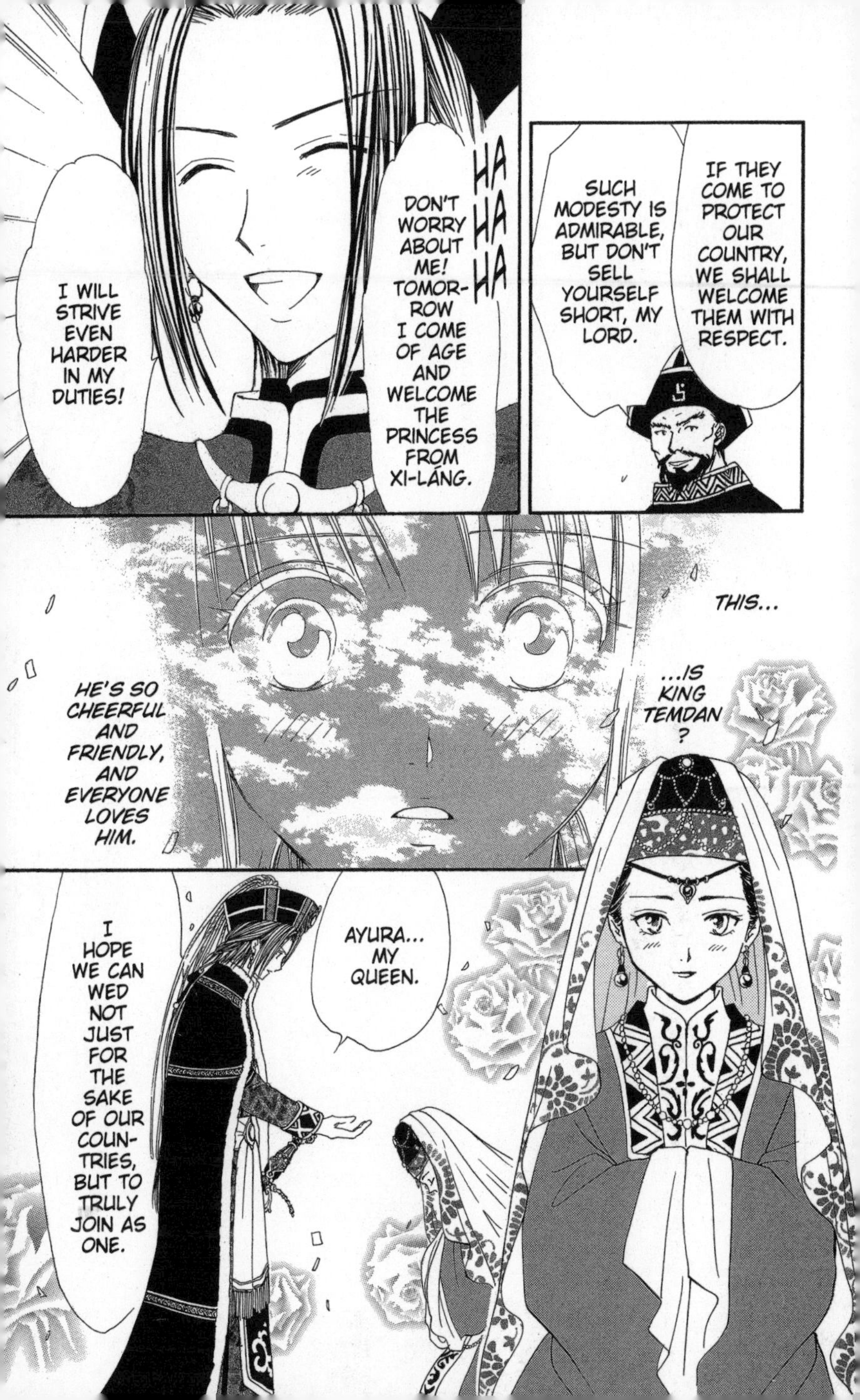
IF THEY COME TO PROTECT OUR COUNTRY, WE SHALL WELCOME THEM WITH RESPECT.
SUCH MODESTY IS ADMIRABLE, BUT DON'T SELL YOURSELF SHORT, MY LORD.
HA HA HA
DON'T WORRY ABOUT ME! TOMORROW I COME OF AGE AND WELCOME THE PRINCESS FROM XI-LÁNG.
I WILL STRIVE EVEN HARDER IN MY DUTIES!
THIS...
...IS KING TEMDAN?
HE'S SO CHEERFUL AND FRIENDLY, AND EVERYONE LOVES HIM.
AYURA... MY QUEEN.
I HOPE WE CAN WED NOT JUST FOR THE SAKE OF OUR COUNTRIES, BUT TO TRULY JOIN AS ONE.

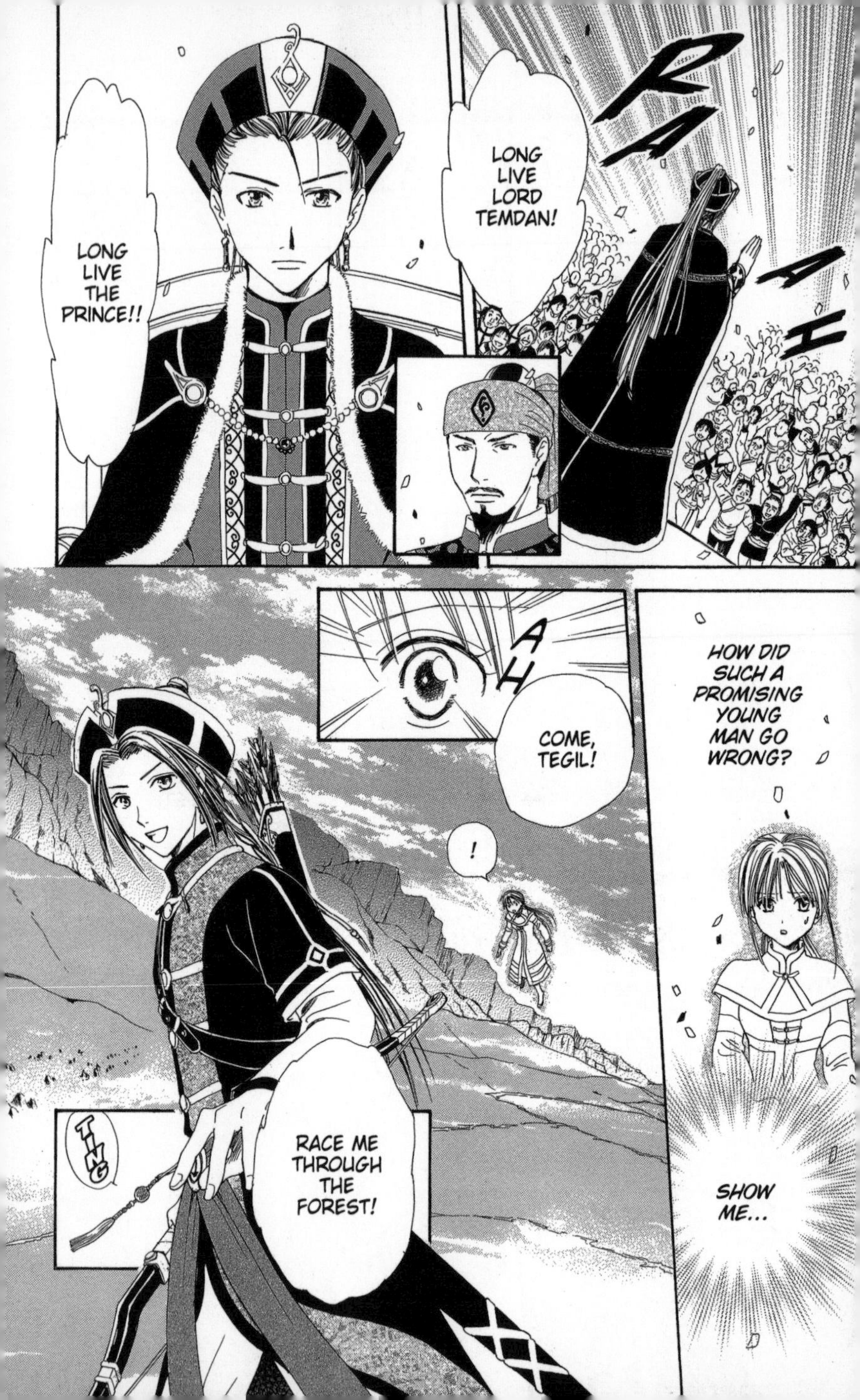
RAAAH
LONG LIVE LORD TEMDAN!
LONG LIVE THE PRINCE!!
HOW DID SUCH A PROMISING YOUNG MAN GO WRONG?
SHOW ME...
AH
COME, TEGIL!
!
RACE ME THROUGH THE FOREST!
TING

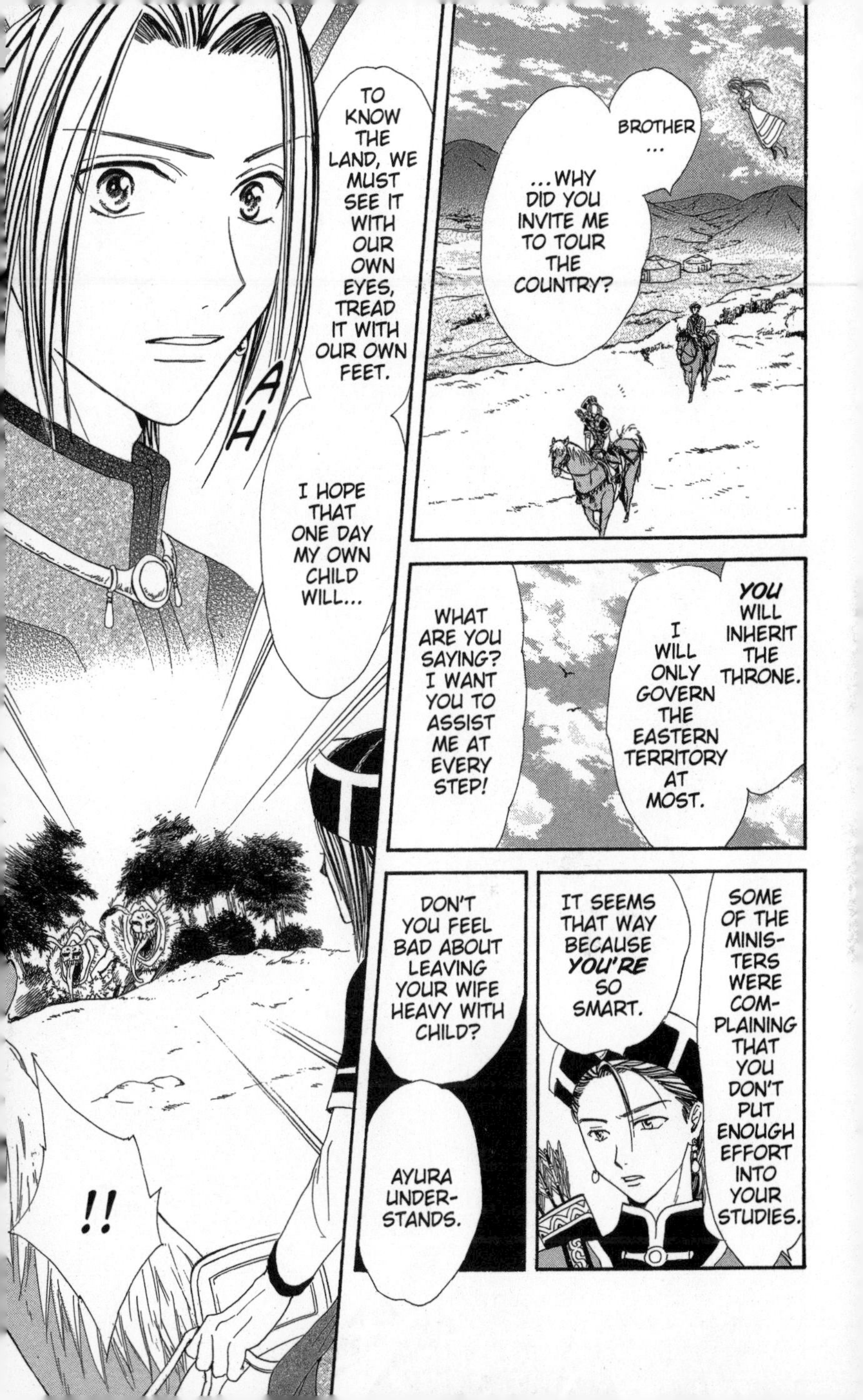

BROTHER ...
...WHY DID YOU INVITE ME TO TOUR THE COUNTRY?
YOU WILL INHERIT THE THRONE.
I WILL ONLY GOVERN THE EASTERN TERRITORY AT MOST.
WHAT ARE YOU SAYING? I WANT YOU TO ASSIST ME AT EVERY STEP!
SOME OF THE MINISTERS WERE COMPLAINING THAT YOU DON'T PUT ENOUGH EFFORT INTO YOUR STUDIES.
IT SEEMS THAT WAY BECAUSE *YOU'RE* SO SMART.
DON'T YOU FEEL BAD ABOUT LEAVING YOUR WIFE HEAVY WITH CHILD?
AYURA UNDERSTANDS.
TO KNOW THE LAND, WE MUST SEE IT WITH OUR OWN EYES, TREAD IT WITH OUR OWN FEET.
I HOPE THAT ONE DAY MY OWN CHILD WILL...
AH
!!

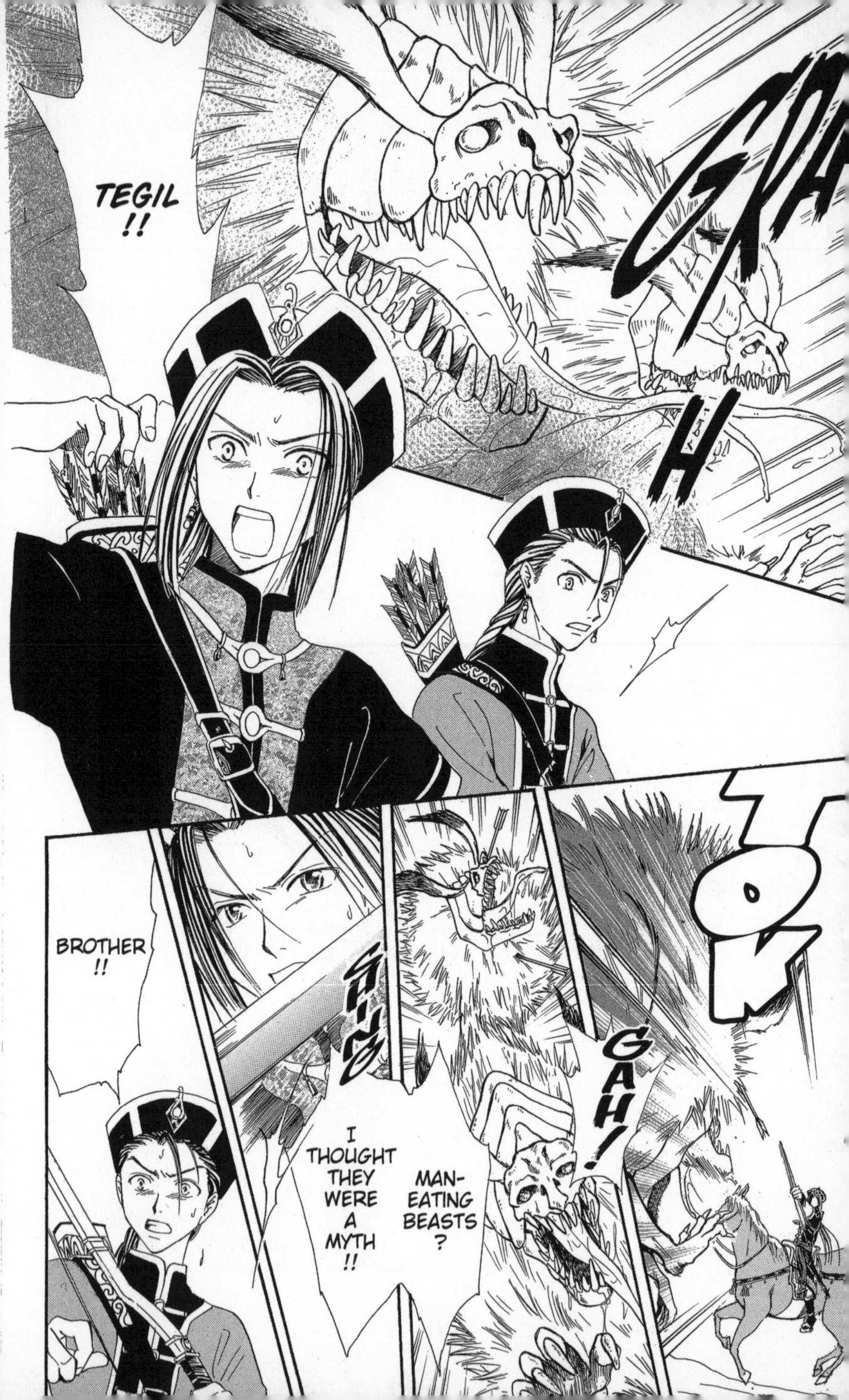
GRAH
TEGIL !!
TON
GAH!
SHING
MAN-EATING BEASTS ?
I THOUGHT THEY WERE A MYTH !!
BROTHER !!

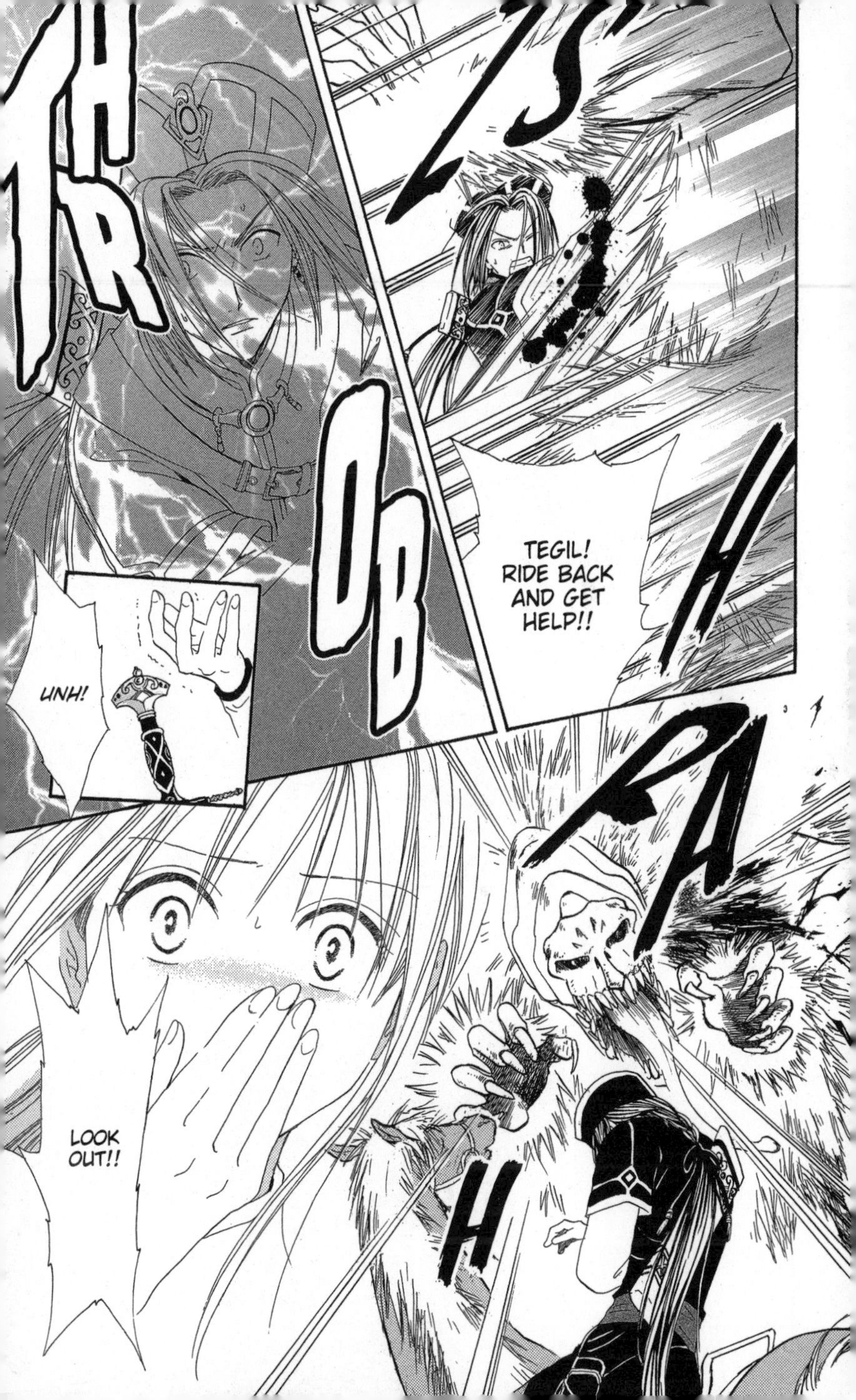

TEGIL! RIDE BACK AND GET HELP!!
UNH!
LOOK OUT!!

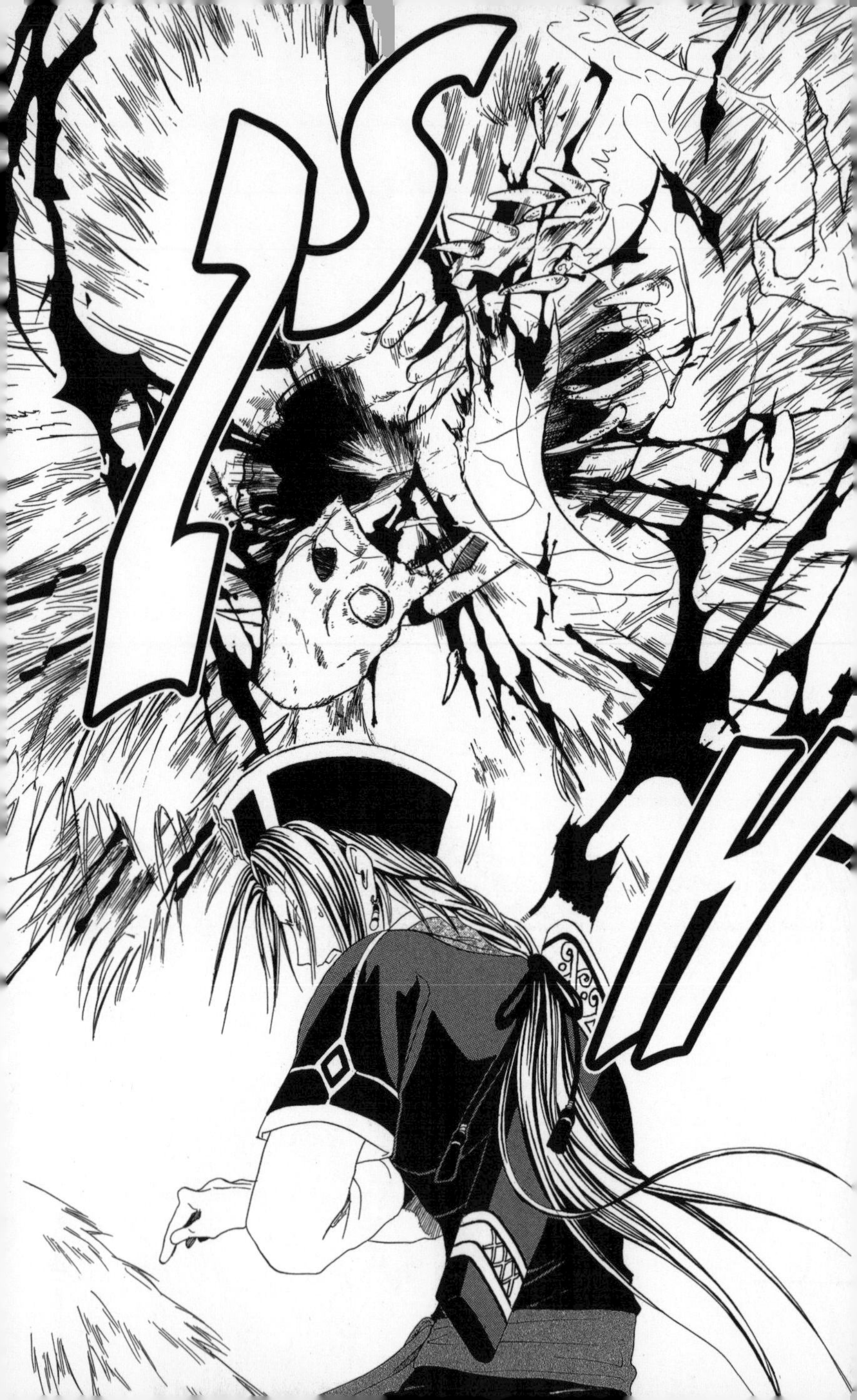
ZS
H

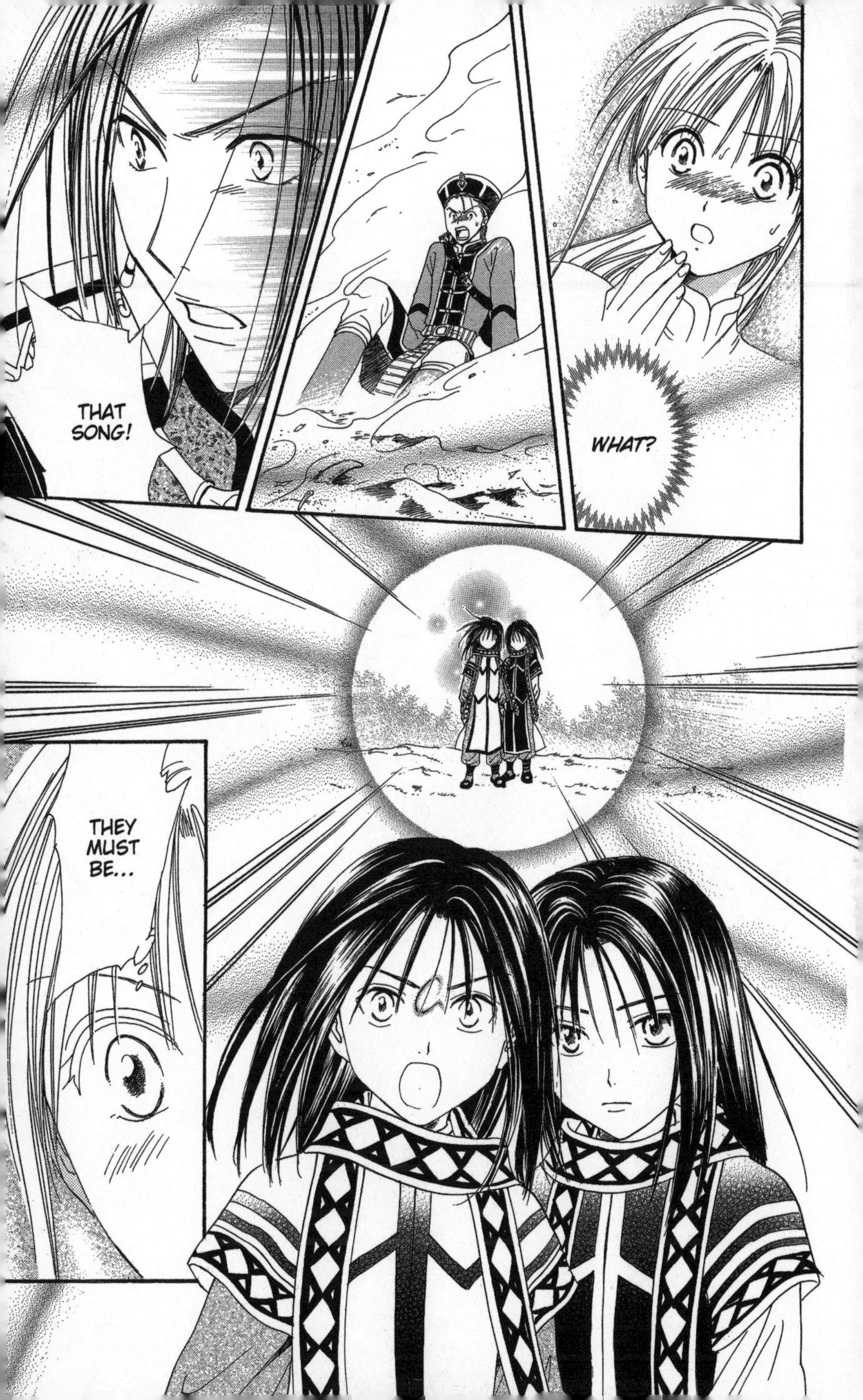
WHAT?
THAT SONG!
THEY MUST BE...

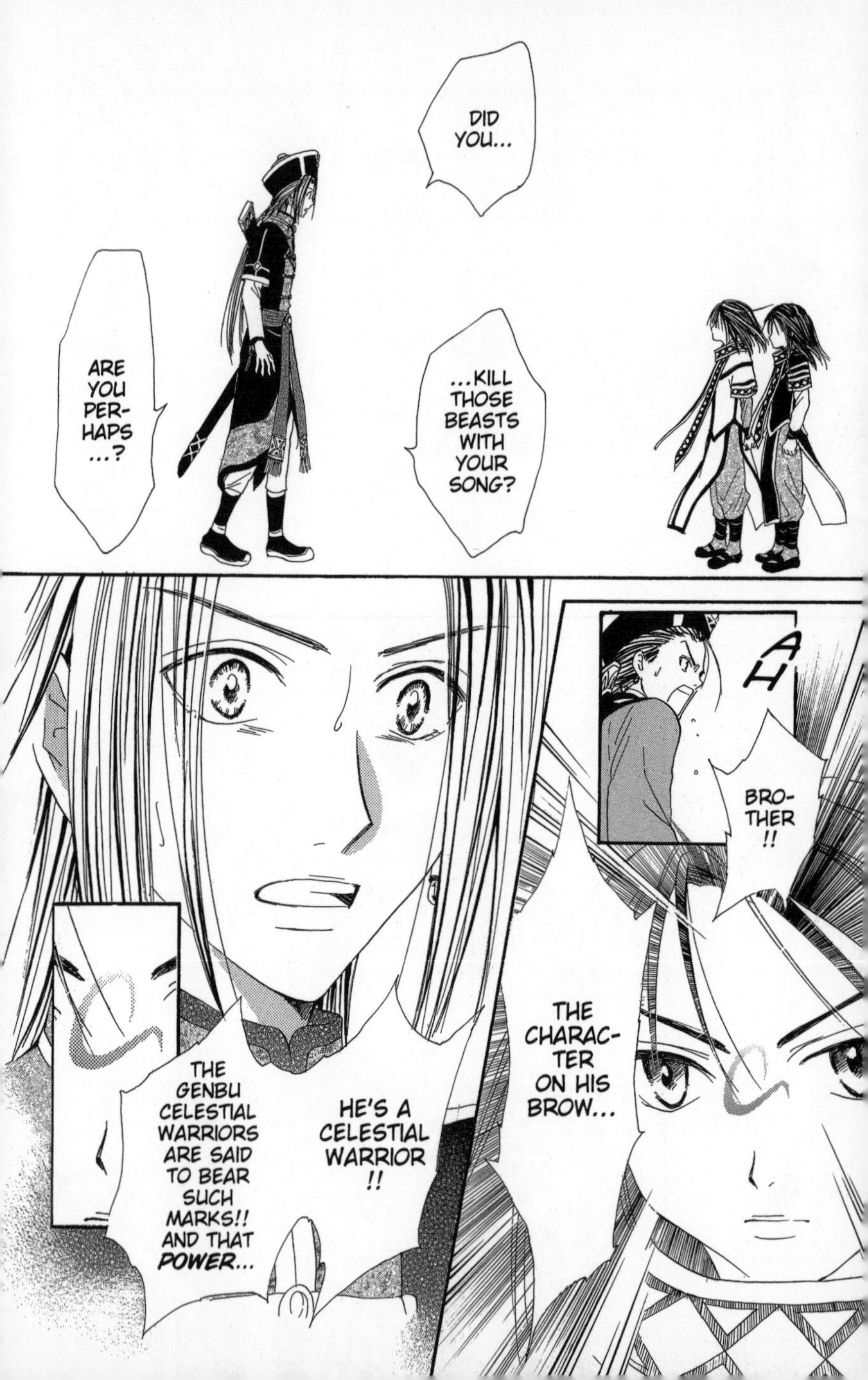
DID YOU...
...KILL THOSE BEASTS WITH YOUR SONG?
ARE YOU PER-HAPS ...?
AH
BRO-THER !!
THE CHARAC-TER ON HIS BROW...
HE'S A CELESTIAL WARRIOR !!
THE GENBU CELESTIAL WARRIORS ARE SAID TO BEAR SUCH MARKS!! AND THAT POWER...

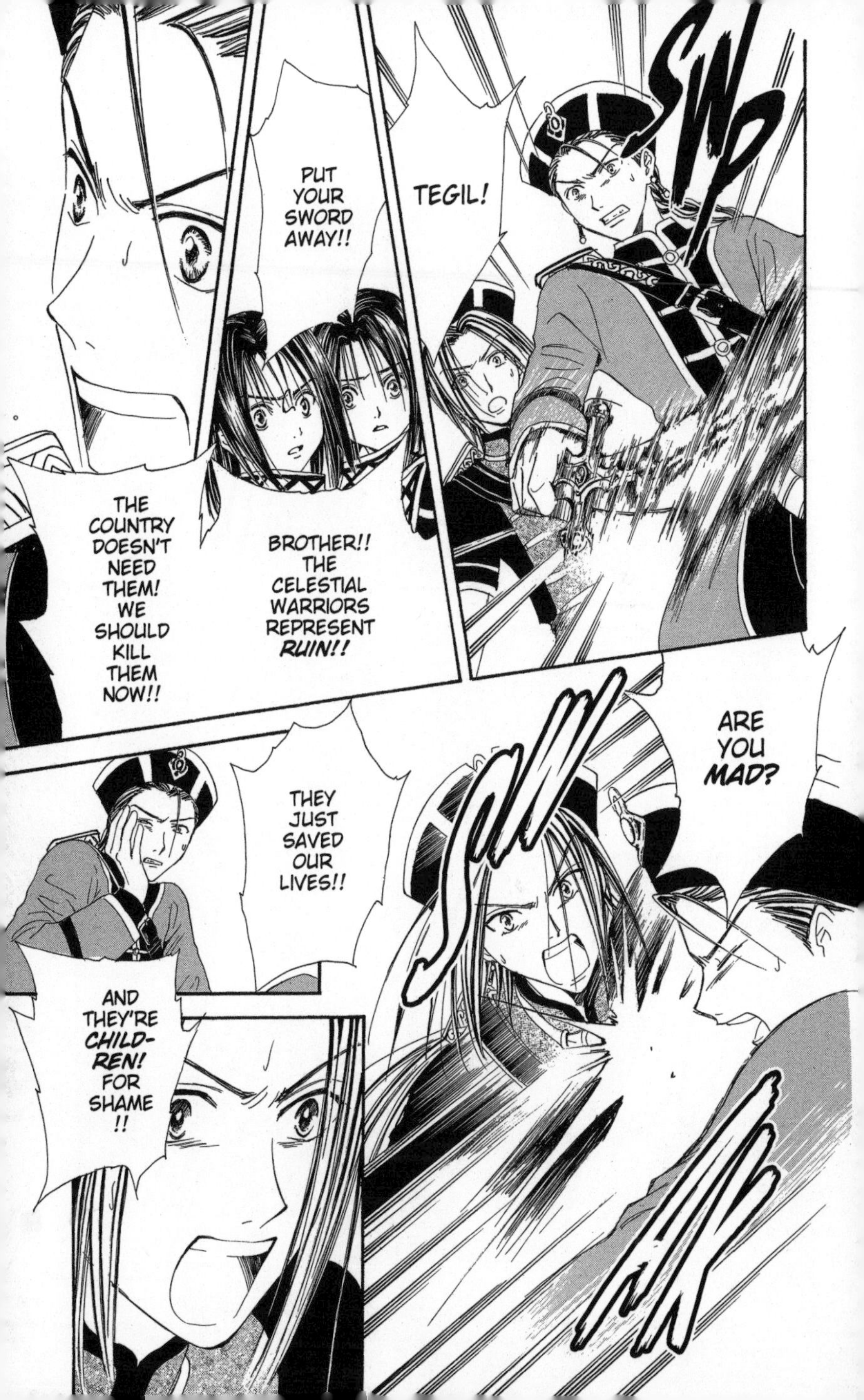

TEGIL!
PUT YOUR SWORD AWAY!!
BROTHER!! THE CELESTIAL WARRIORS REPRESENT *RUIN!!*
THE COUNTRY DOESN'T NEED THEM! WE SHOULD KILL THEM NOW!!
ARE YOU *MAD?*
THEY JUST SAVED OUR LIVES!!
AND THEY'RE *CHILD-REN!* FOR SHAME !!

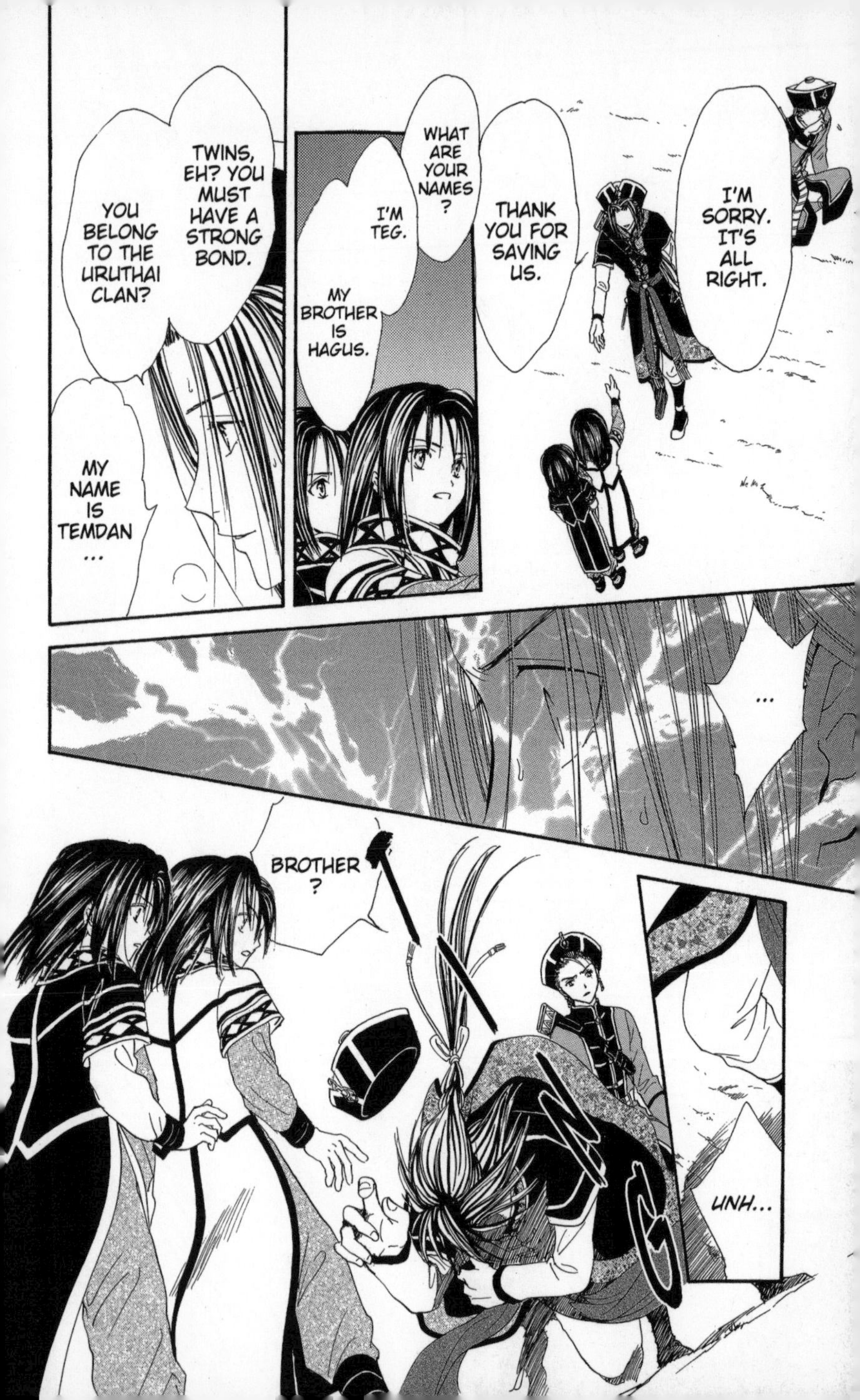
I'M SORRY. IT'S ALL RIGHT.
THANK YOU FOR SAVING US.
WHAT ARE YOUR NAMES?
I'M TEG.
MY BROTHER IS HAGUS.
TWINS, EH? YOU MUST HAVE A STRONG BOND.
YOU BELONG TO THE URUTHAI CLAN?
MY NAME IS TEMDAN...
...
UNH...
BROTHER?

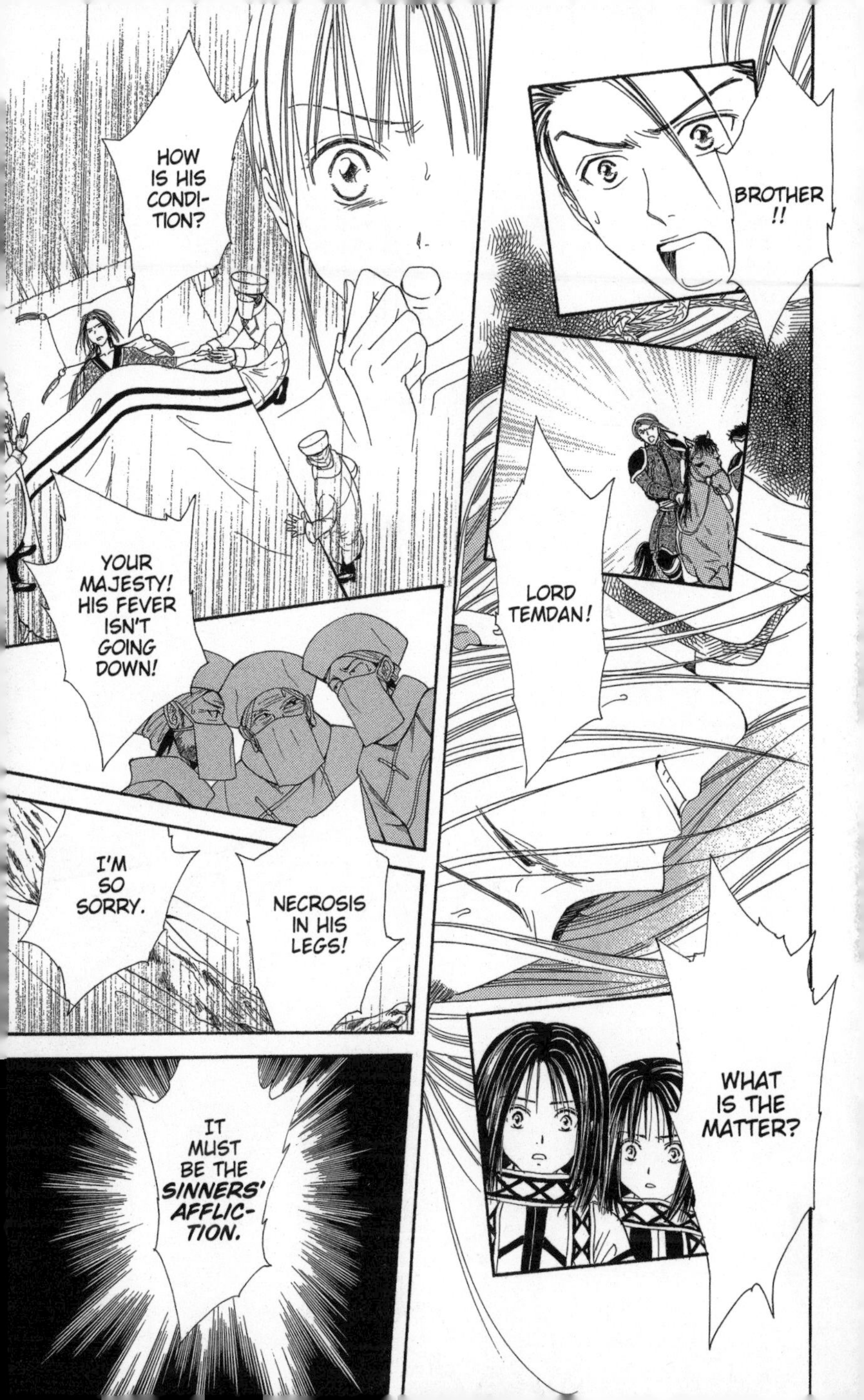
BROTHER !!
LORD TEMDAN!
WHAT IS THE MATTER?
HOW IS HIS CONDITION?
YOUR MAJESTY! HIS FEVER ISN'T GOING DOWN!
NECROSIS IN HIS LEGS!
I'M SO SORRY.
IT MUST BE THE *SINNERS' AFFLICTION.*

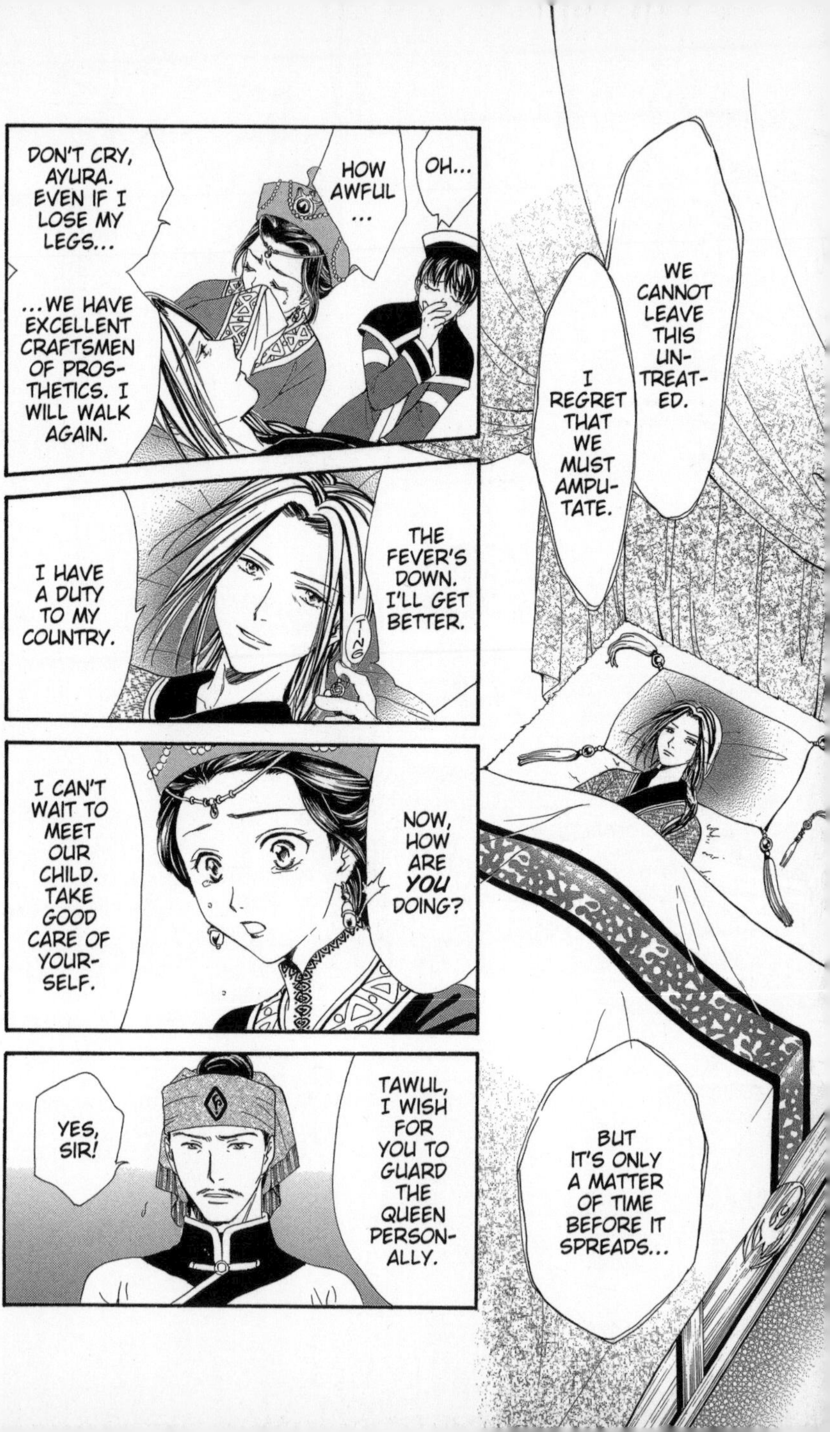
WE CANNOT LEAVE THIS UN-TREAT-ED.
I REGRET THAT WE MUST AMPU-TATE.
BUT IT'S ONLY A MATTER OF TIME BEFORE IT SPREADS...
OH...
HOW AWFUL...
DON'T CRY, AYURA. EVEN IF I LOSE MY LEGS...
...WE HAVE EXCELLENT CRAFTSMEN OF PROS-THETICS. I WILL WALK AGAIN.
THE FEVER'S DOWN. I'LL GET BETTER.
TING
I HAVE A DUTY TO MY COUNTRY.
NOW, HOW ARE *YOU* DOING?
I CAN'T WAIT TO MEET OUR CHILD. TAKE GOOD CARE OF YOUR-SELF.
TAWUL, I WISH FOR YOU TO GUARD THE QUEEN PERSON-ALLY.
YES, SIR!

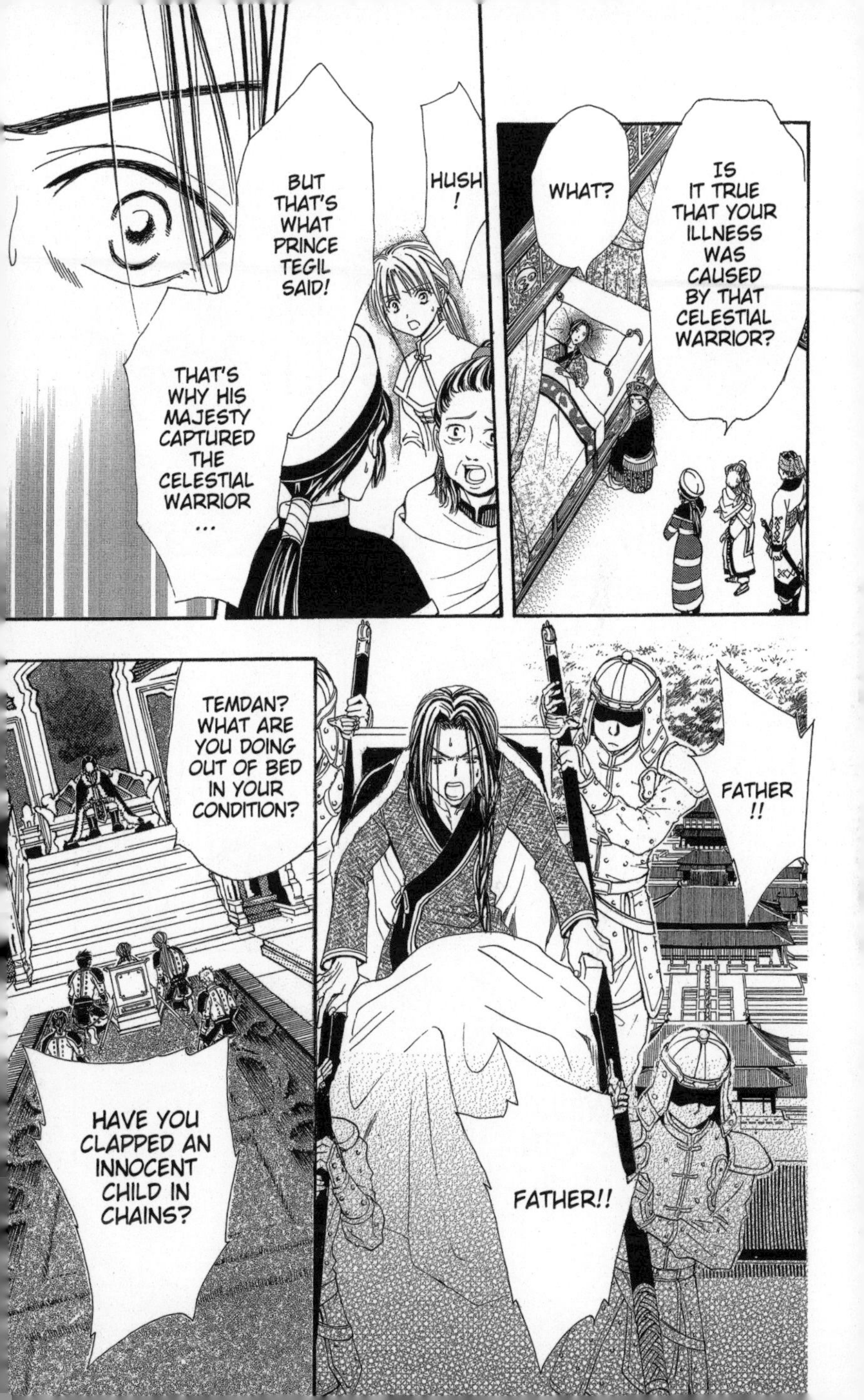
IS IT TRUE THAT YOUR ILLNESS WAS CAUSED BY THAT CELESTIAL WARRIOR?
WHAT?
HUSH!
BUT THAT'S WHAT PRINCE TEGIL SAID!
THAT'S WHY HIS MAJESTY CAPTURED THE CELESTIAL WARRIOR...
FATHER!!
FATHER!!
TEMDAN? WHAT ARE YOU DOING OUT OF BED IN YOUR CONDITION?
HAVE YOU CLAPPED AN INNOCENT CHILD IN CHAINS?

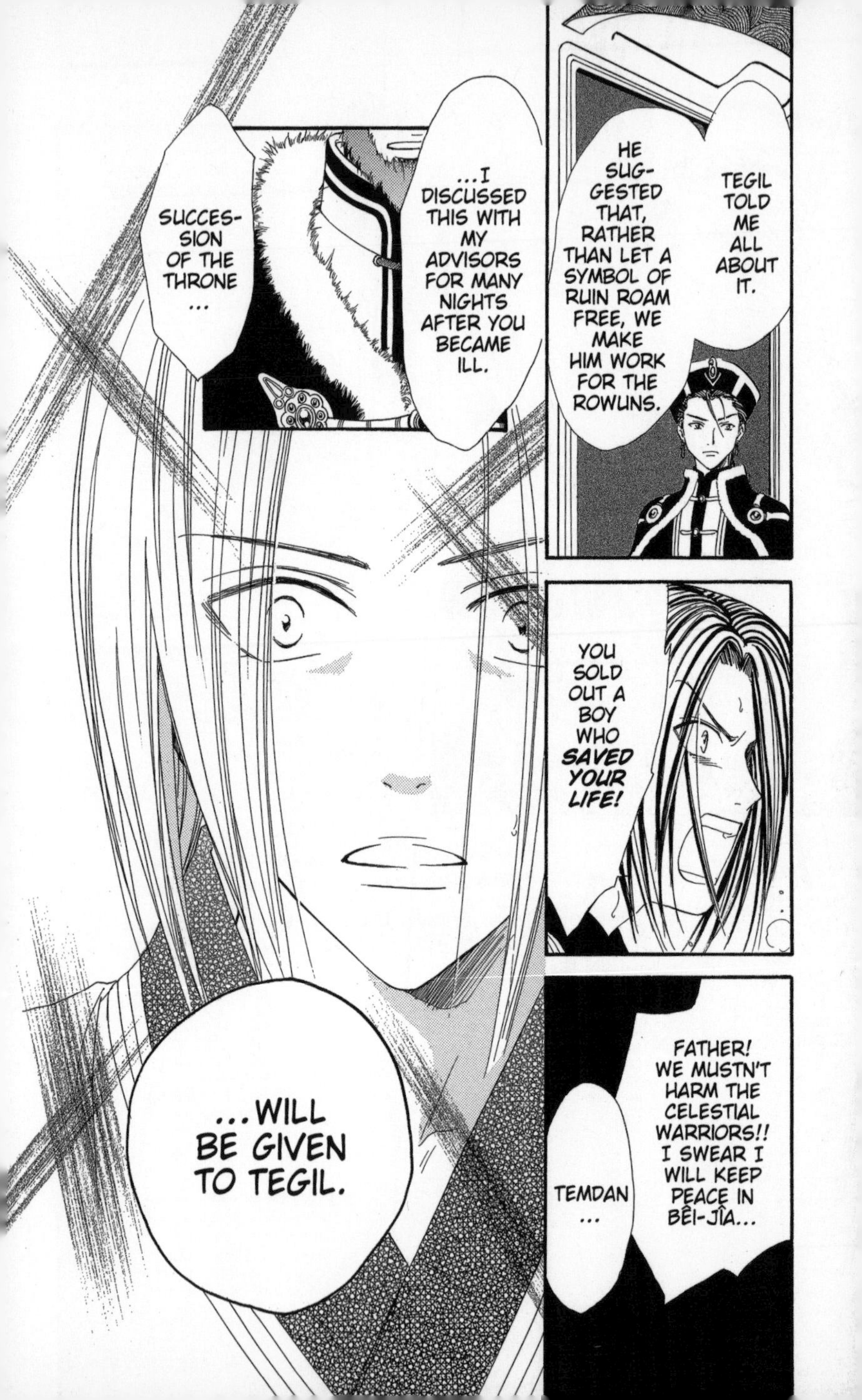
TEGIL TOLD ME ALL ABOUT IT.
HE SUGGESTED THAT, RATHER THAN LET A SYMBOL OF RUIN ROAM FREE, WE MAKE HIM WORK FOR THE ROWUNS.
YOU SOLD OUT A BOY WHO *SAVED YOUR LIFE!*
FATHER! WE MUSTN'T HARM THE CELESTIAL WARRIORS!! I SWEAR I WILL KEEP PEACE IN BÊI-JÎA...
TEMDAN...
...I DISCUSSED THIS WITH MY ADVISORS FOR MANY NIGHTS AFTER YOU BECAME ILL.
SUCCESSION OF THE THRONE...
...WILL BE GIVEN TO TEGIL.

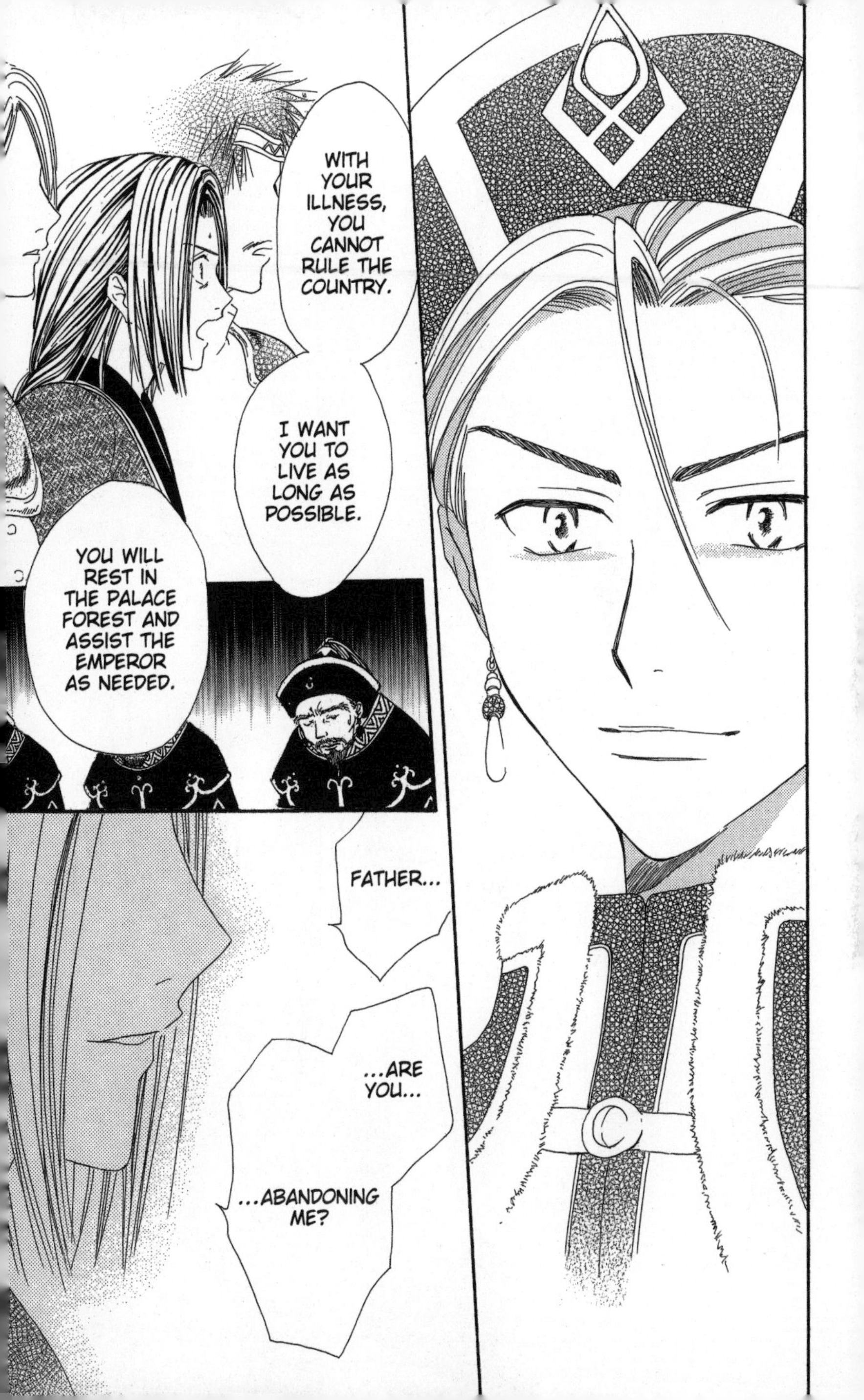
WITH YOUR ILLNESS, YOU CANNOT RULE THE COUNTRY.
I WANT YOU TO LIVE AS LONG AS POSSIBLE.
YOU WILL REST IN THE PALACE FOREST AND ASSIST THE EMPEROR AS NEEDED.
FATHER...
...ARE YOU...
...ABANDONING ME?

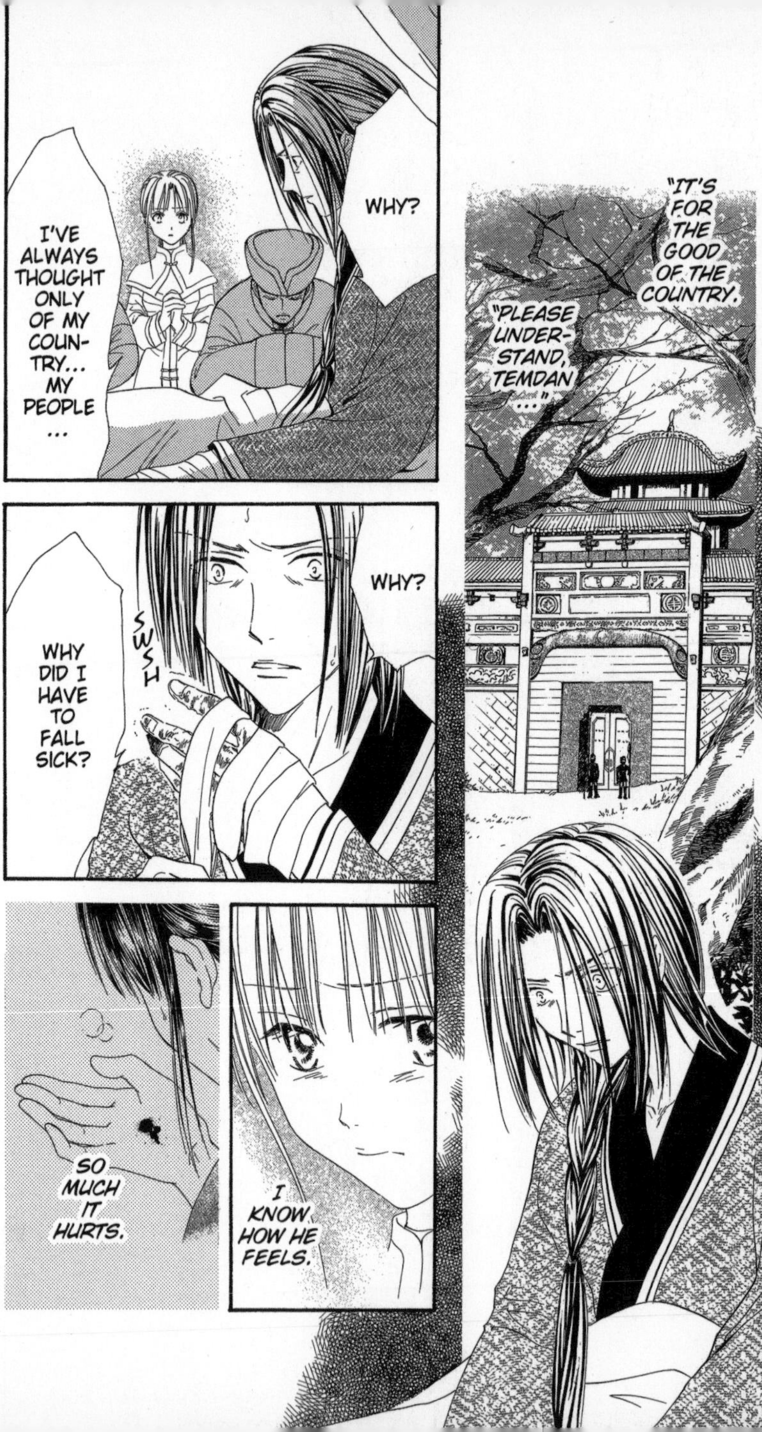
WHY?
I'VE ALWAYS THOUGHT ONLY OF MY COUNTRY... MY PEOPLE...
WHY?
SWSH
WHY DID I HAVE TO FALL SICK?
I KNOW HOW HE FEELS.
SO MUCH IT HURTS.
"IT'S FOR THE GOOD OF THE COUNTRY.
"PLEASE UNDERSTAND, TEMDAN..."

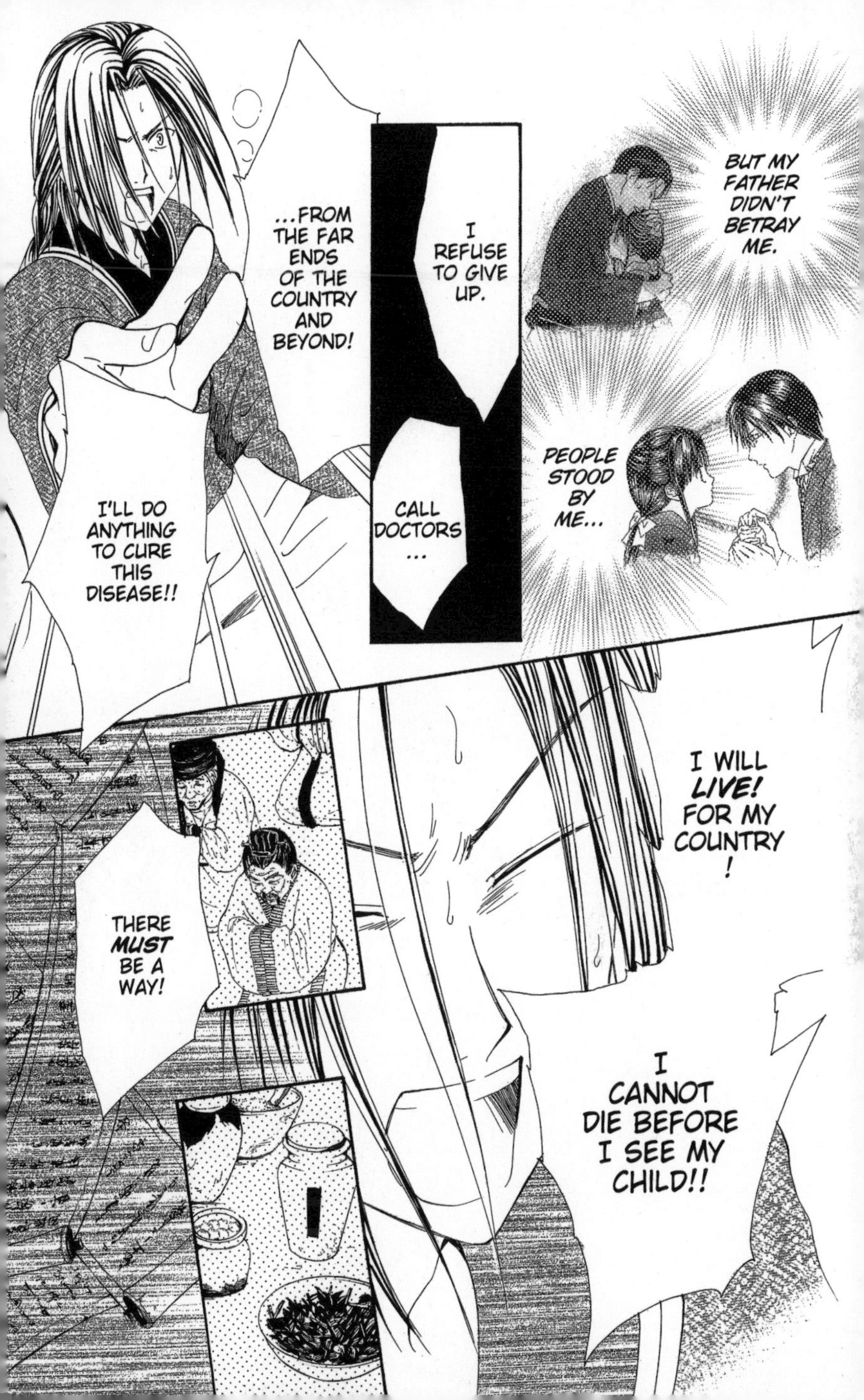
BUT MY FATHER DIDN'T BETRAY ME.
PEOPLE STOOD BY ME...
I REFUSE TO GIVE UP.
CALL DOCTORS ...
...FROM THE FAR ENDS OF THE COUNTRY AND BEYOND!
I'LL DO ANYTHING TO CURE THIS DISEASE!!
I WILL *LIVE!* FOR MY COUNTRY!
I CANNOT DIE BEFORE I SEE MY CHILD!!
THERE *MUST* BE A WAY!

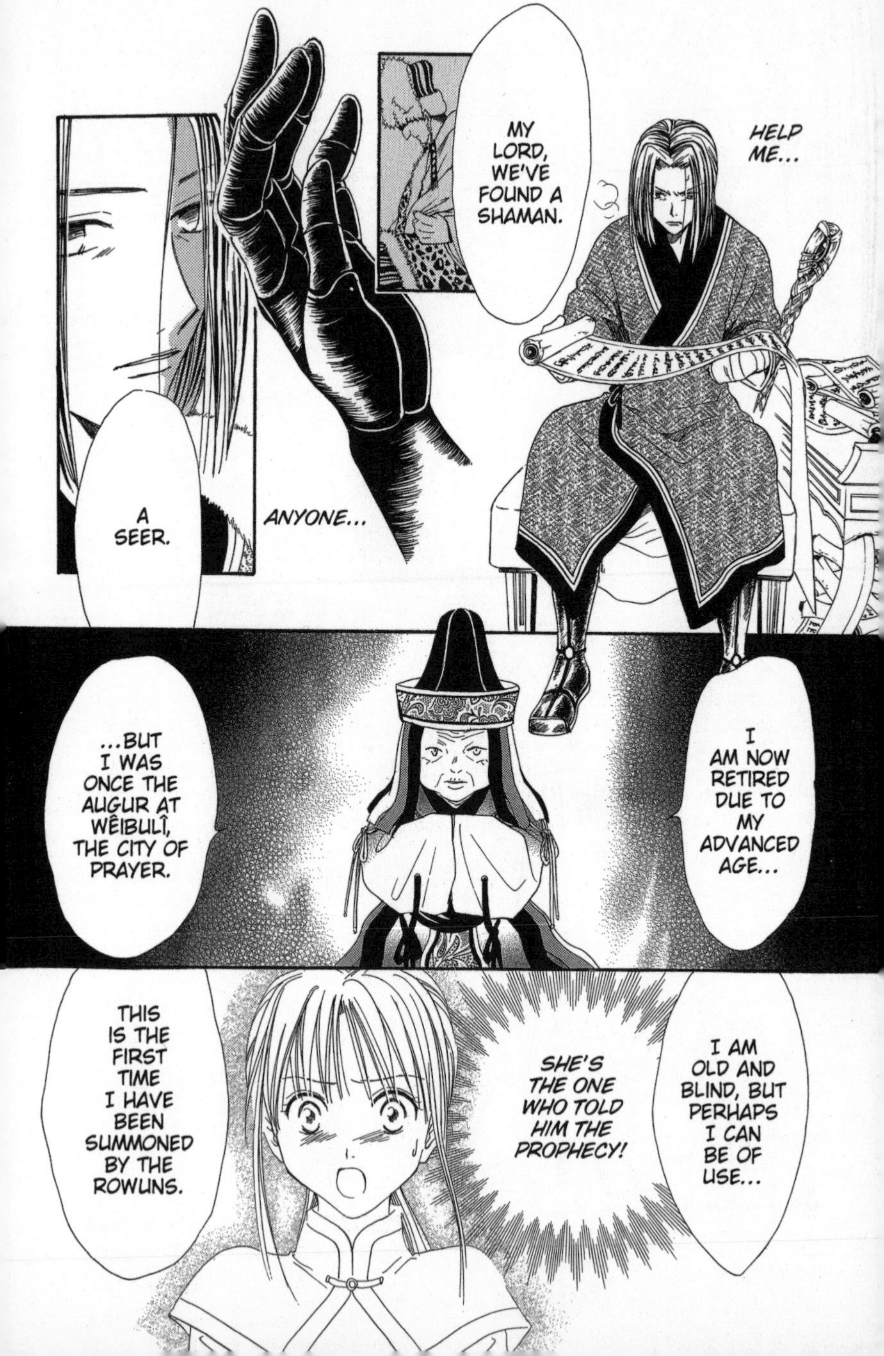
HELP ME...
MY LORD, WE'VE FOUND A SHAMAN.
ANYONE...
A SEER.
I AM NOW RETIRED DUE TO MY ADVANCED AGE...
...BUT I WAS ONCE THE AUGUR AT WÊIBULÎ, THE CITY OF PRAYER.
I AM OLD AND BLIND, BUT PERHAPS I CAN BE OF USE...
SHE'S THE ONE WHO TOLD HIM THE PROPHECY!
THIS IS THE FIRST TIME I HAVE BEEN SUMMONED BY THE ROWUNS.

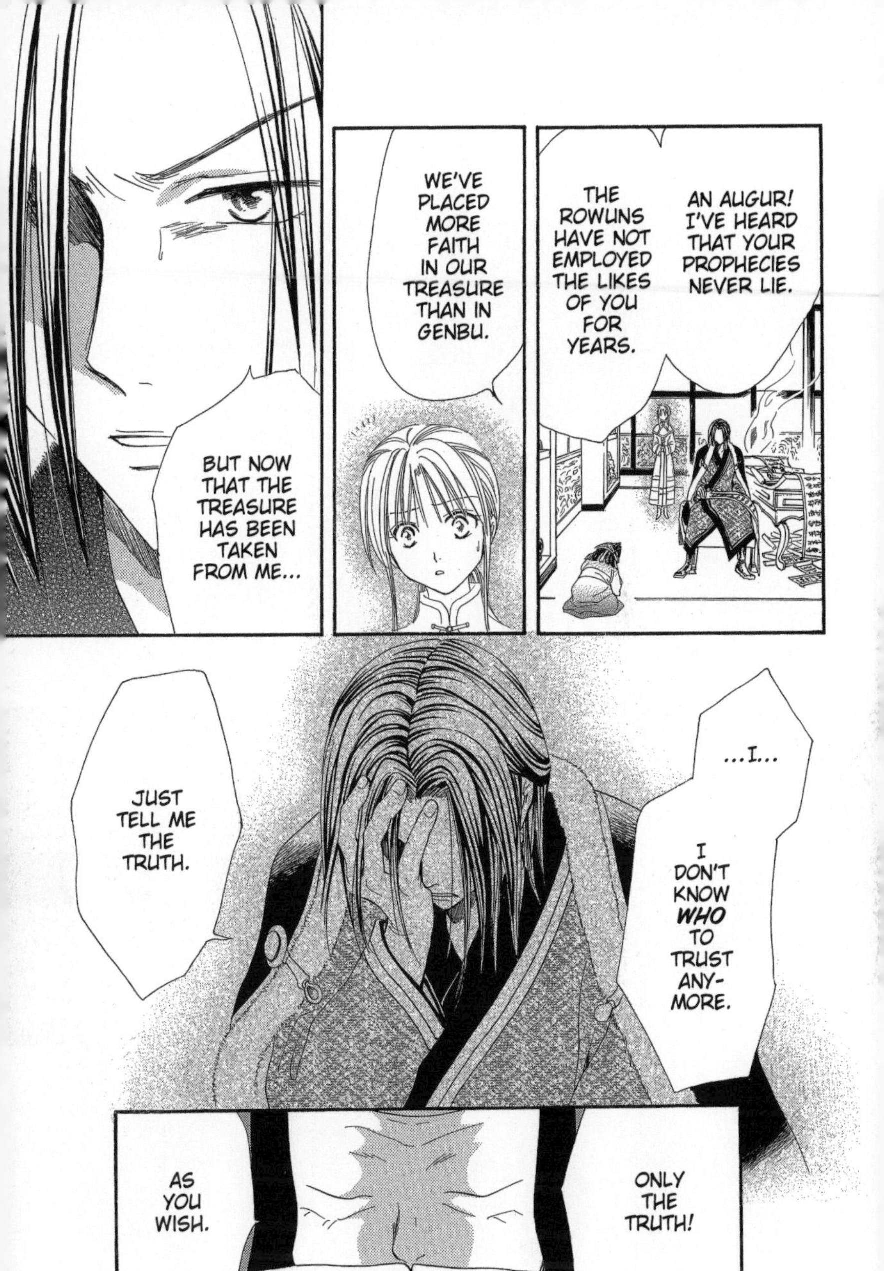
AN AUGUR! I'VE HEARD THAT YOUR PROPHECIES NEVER LIE.
THE ROWUNS HAVE NOT EMPLOYED THE LIKES OF YOU FOR YEARS.
WE'VE PLACED MORE FAITH IN OUR TREASURE THAN IN GENBU.
BUT NOW THAT THE TREASURE HAS BEEN TAKEN FROM ME...
...I...
I DON'T KNOW *WHO* TO TRUST ANY-MORE.
JUST TELL ME THE TRUTH.
ONLY THE TRUTH!
AS YOU WISH.

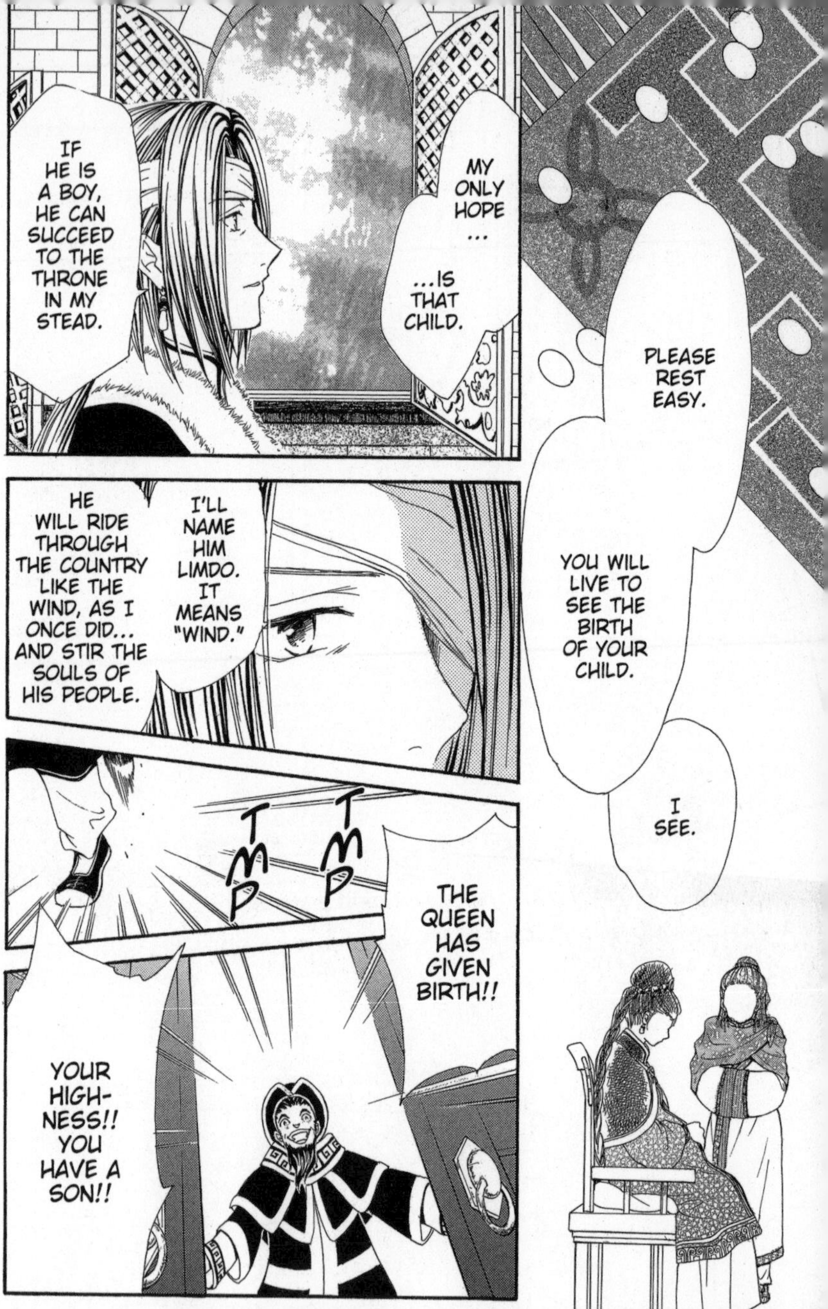
PLEASE REST EASY.
YOU WILL LIVE TO SEE THE BIRTH OF YOUR CHILD.
I SEE.
MY ONLY HOPE ...
...IS THAT CHILD.
IF HE IS A BOY, HE CAN SUCCEED TO THE THRONE IN MY STEAD.
I'LL NAME HIM LIMDO. IT MEANS "WIND."
HE WILL RIDE THROUGH THE COUNTRY LIKE THE WIND, AS I ONCE DID... AND STIR THE SOULS OF HIS PEOPLE.
TMP
TMP
THE QUEEN HAS GIVEN BIRTH!!
YOUR HIGHNESS!! YOU HAVE A SON!!

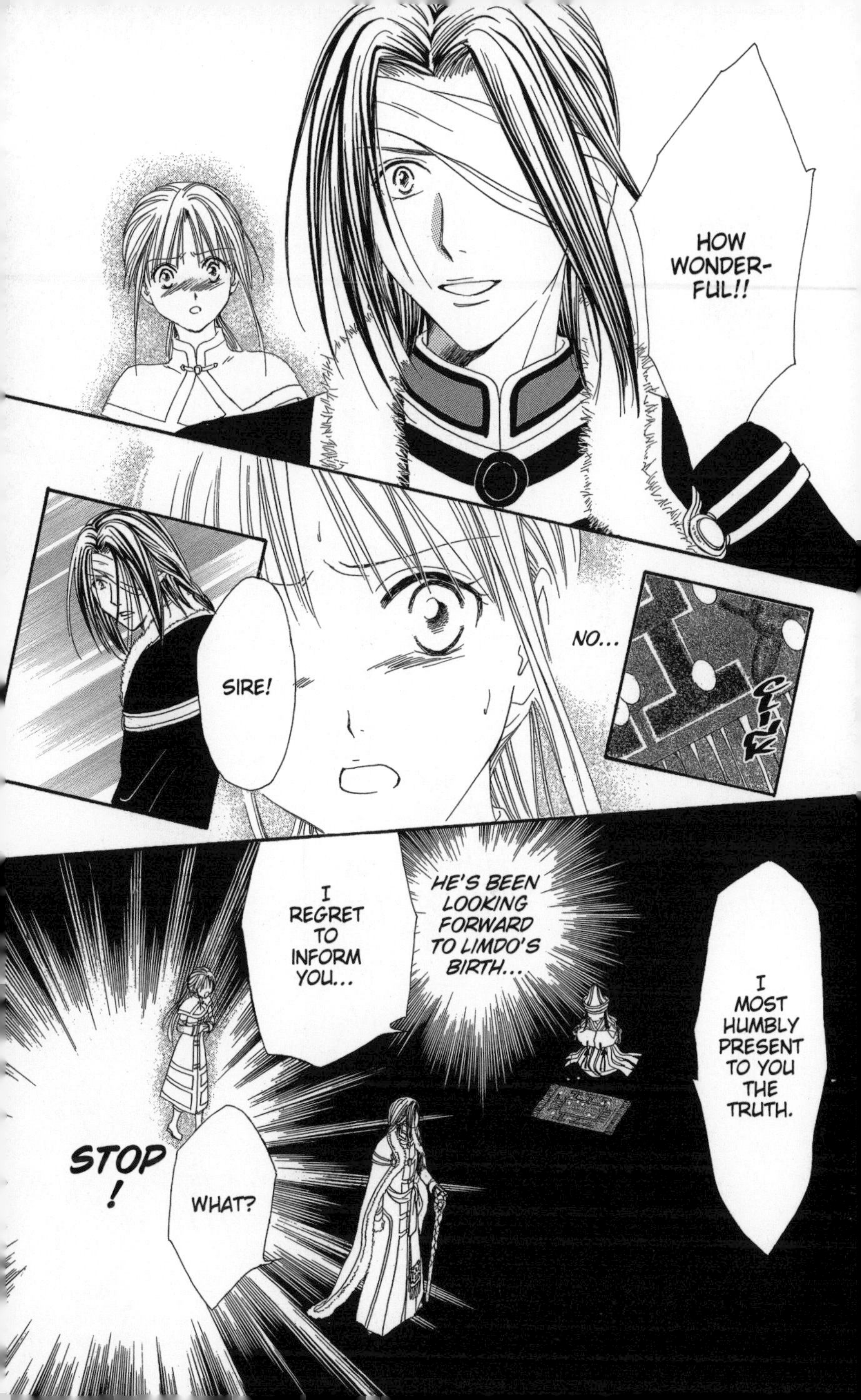
HOW WONDERFUL!!
NO...
CLINK
SIRE!
I MOST HUMBLY PRESENT TO YOU THE TRUTH.
HE'S BEEN LOOKING FORWARD TO LIMDO'S BIRTH...
I REGRET TO INFORM YOU...
WHAT?
STOP!

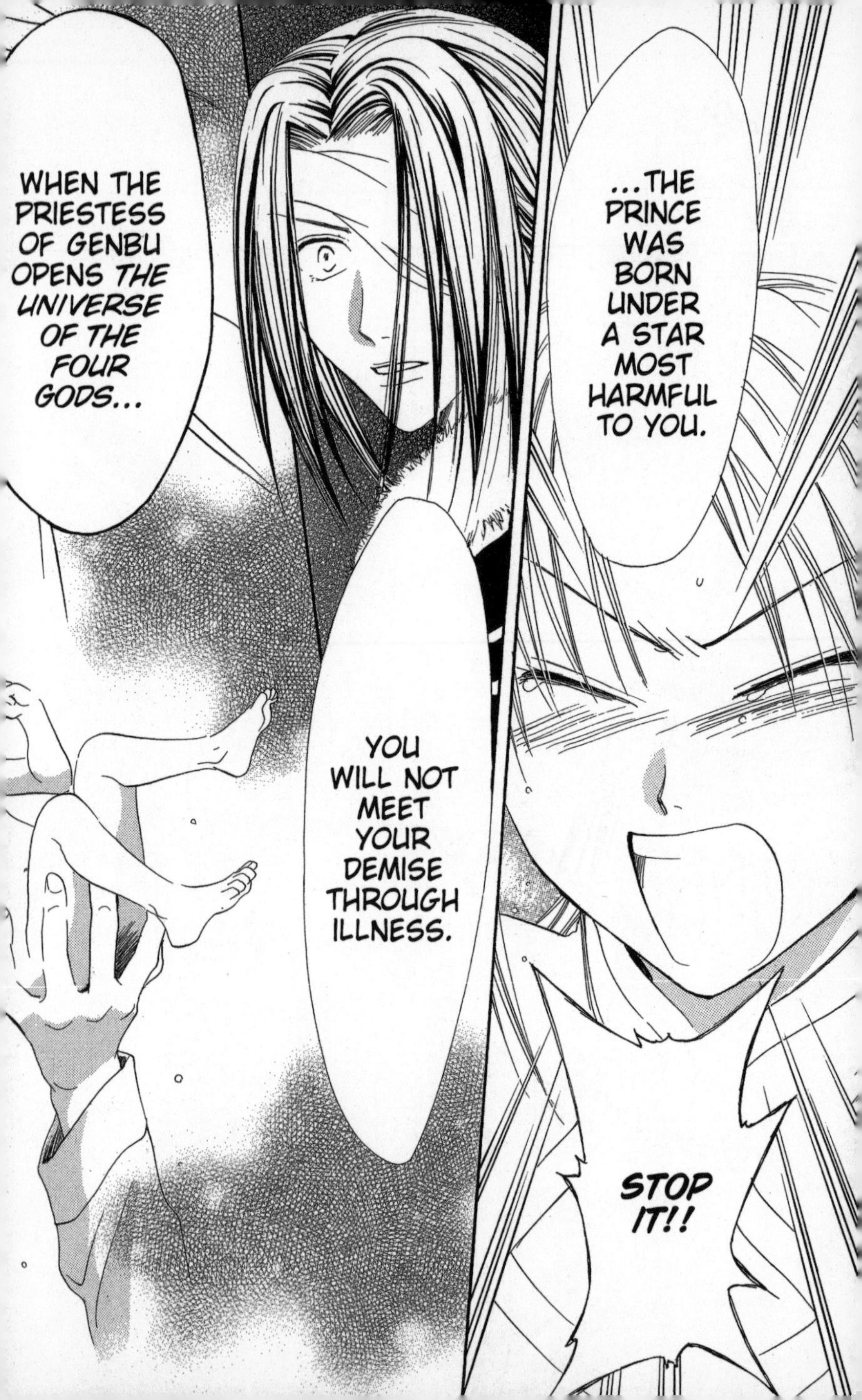
...THE PRINCE WAS BORN UNDER A STAR MOST HARMFUL TO YOU.
STOP IT!!
WHEN THE PRIESTESS OF GENBU OPENS THE UNIVERSE OF THE FOUR GODS...
YOU WILL NOT MEET YOUR DEMISE THROUGH ILLNESS.

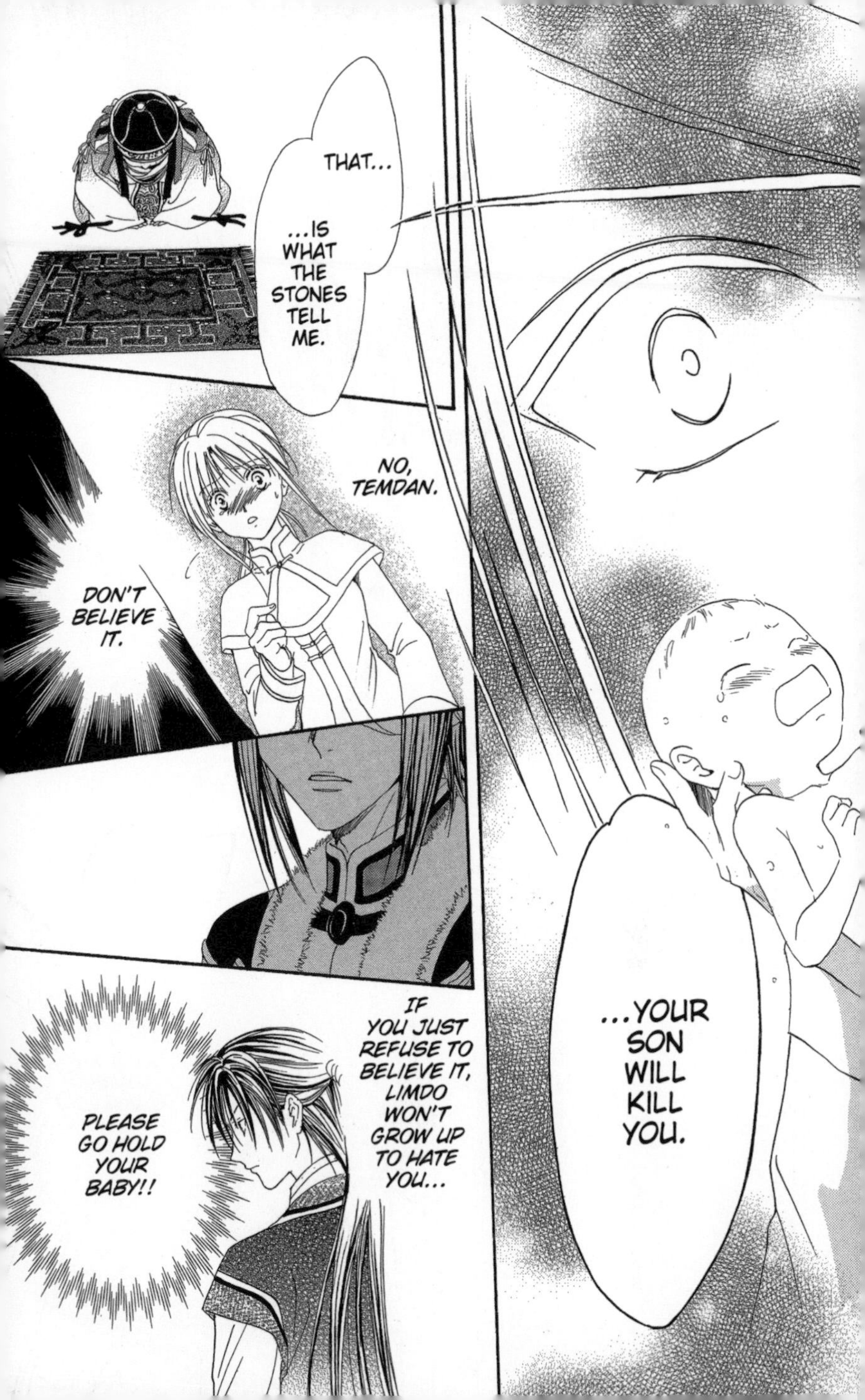
...YOUR SON WILL KILL YOU.
THAT...
...IS WHAT THE STONES TELL ME.
NO, TEMDAN.
DON'T BELIEVE IT.
IF YOU JUST REFUSE TO BELIEVE IT, LIMDO WON'T GROW UP TO HATE YOU...
PLEASE GO HOLD YOUR BABY!!

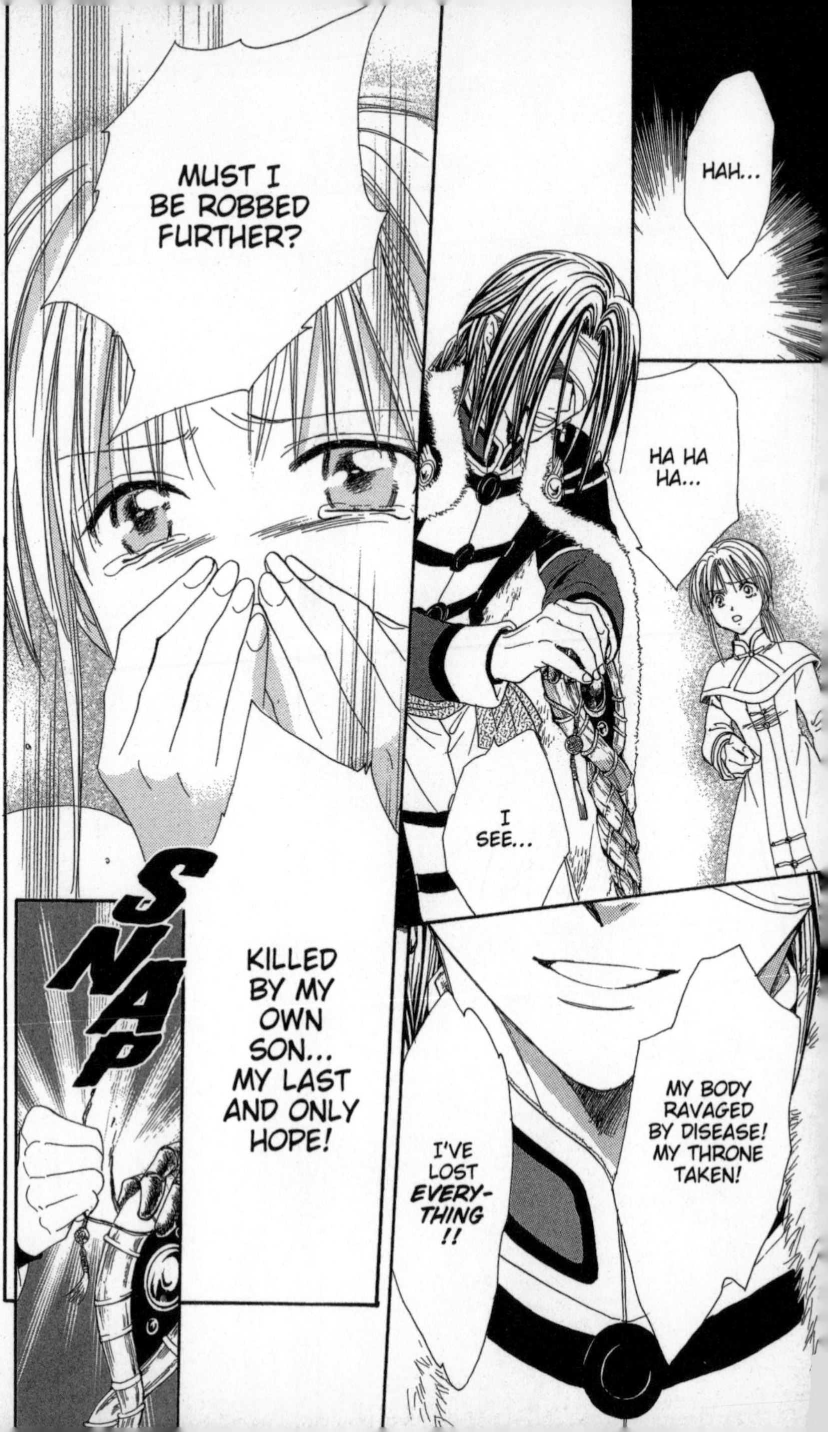
HAH...
HA HA HA...
I SEE...
MUST I BE ROBBED FURTHER?
MY BODY RAVAGED BY DISEASE! MY THRONE TAKEN!
I'VE LOST EVERYTHING!!
KILLED BY MY OWN SON... MY LAST AND ONLY HOPE!
SNAP

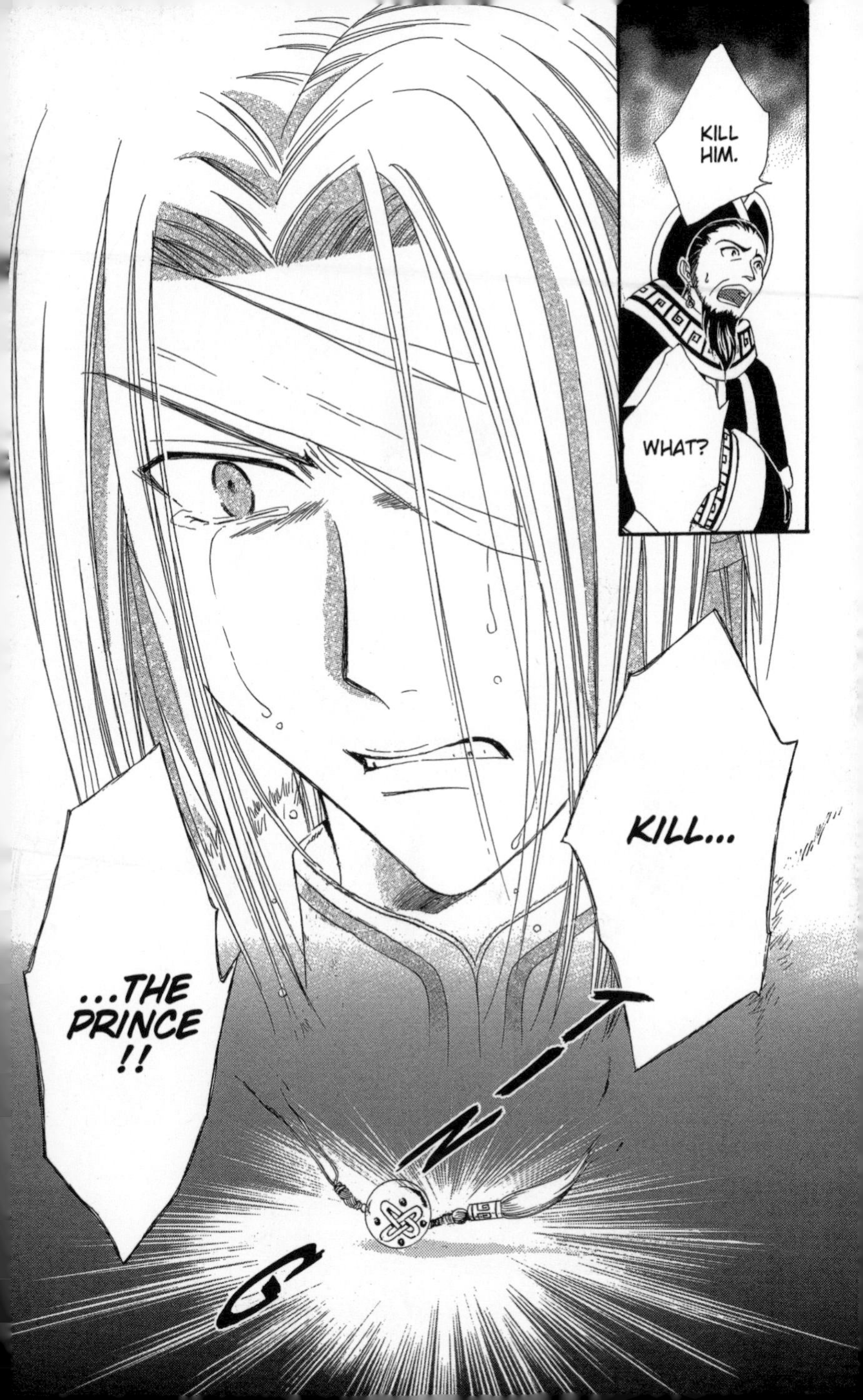
KILL HIM.
WHAT?
KILL...
...THE PRINCE!!
TING

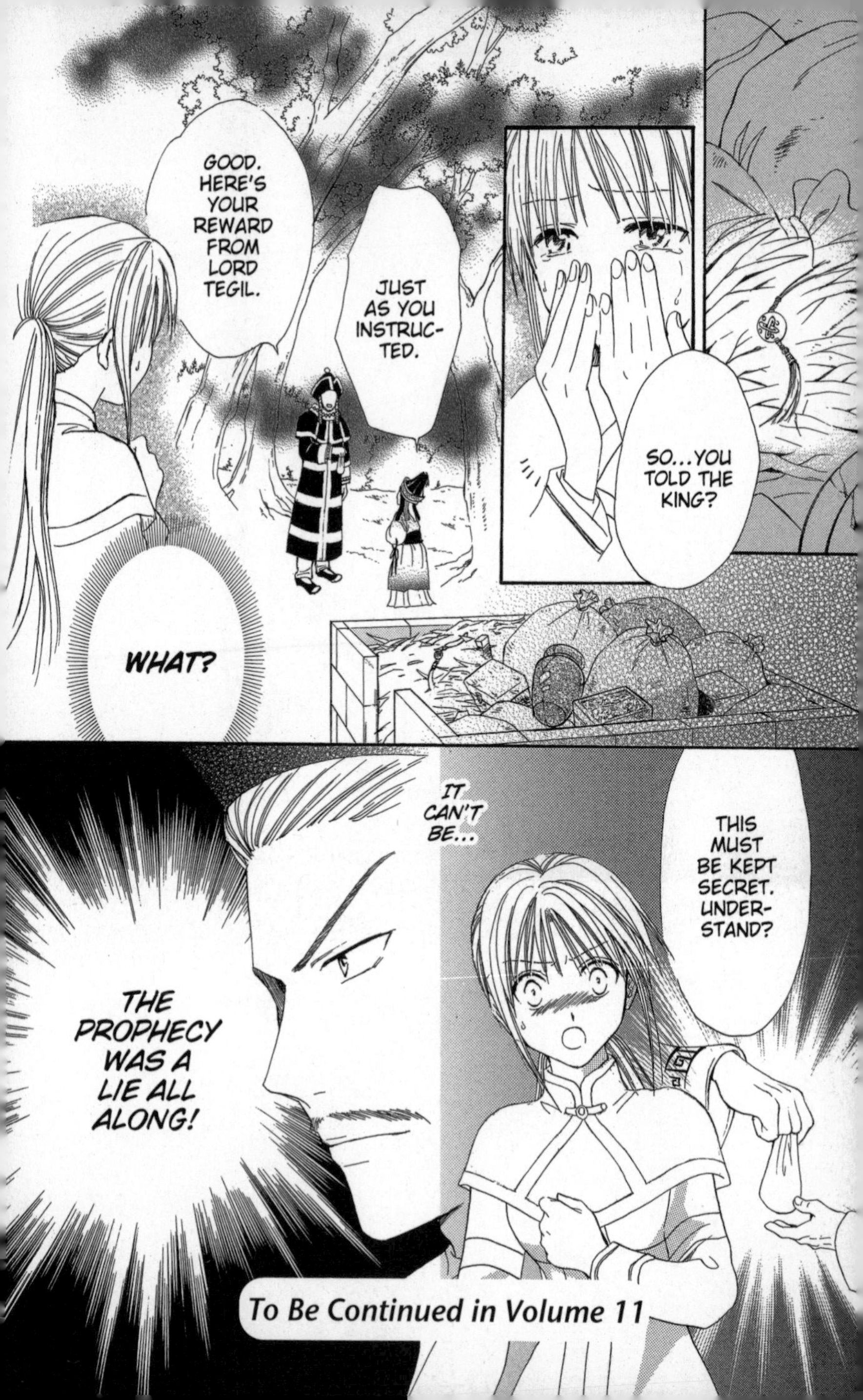
SO...YOU TOLD THE KING?
JUST AS YOU INSTRUCTED.
GOOD. HERE'S YOUR REWARD FROM LORD TEGIL.
WHAT?
THIS MUST BE KEPT SECRET. UNDERSTAND?
IT CAN'T BE...
THE PROPHECY WAS A LIE ALL ALONG!
To Be Continued in Volume 11

FUSHIGI YÛGI: GENBU KAIDEN

1

Sorry for the long silence!!

It's been a while since volume 9, huh? ...What's that? Two years? Seriously? Well, here's the next volume at last! I'm sorry to have kept you waiting for so long. The series went on hiatus for a while. I've received numerous letters asking, "When is it coming back?" ∩(--)∩

Well, the serialization of *Genbu Kaiden* continues in *Rinka*, a supplement to *Monthly Flowers* magazine (published three times a year)!! It goes on sale in February, June and October, so please keep your eyes out in your local bookstores. Before *Genbu*, the magazine ran my three-volume series *Sakura-gari*.

It's been so long since I drew *Genbu*, I was worried I'd have forgotten where the story was going. But when I met with my editor, it all came flooding back. We're close to the climax now... This volume is building up to it, I guess. *Genbu* has gone on hiatus several times now, so it's already been ten years since the series started! I really have to kick it into high gear for the grand finale!! As always, drawing it takes a huge effort; I'm barely keeping up. Each chapter is so long!

2

Meanwhile, my serial *Arata: the Legend* is currently running in *Weekly Shonen Sunday*. Yes, I'm killing myself. Since *Arata* runs weekly, it reached the ten-volume mark before *Genbu*!! That was fast!! It's a shonen manga, but with my unmistakable "Watase style," so please check it out if you can. (Man, I'm really shilling here.) For some reason, *Arata* has a whole lot of pretty boys.

I guess if you take the romance out of *Genbu*, it's not that different from a shonen manga... Heh. Nah, it's definitely shojo!! Takiko and Uruki are apart right now, but soon... Heh heh. Hearts will go pitter-patter! (Okay, I'm being silly.) It's been a long time since I lost my girlish innocence. I have to get giggly while I still can, before I turn into a crusty old man.

Oh, and *Fushigi Yûgi* was recently adapted into a live-action play! There were two performances, but if the reviews are good there might be more! It might even go on the road to a theater near you!! So please, everyone, show your support!! There's a DVD out now! It's really good!!

You can find all the information on my blog. Or check it out by smartphone at http://ameblo.jp/wataseyuu or http://ameblo.jp/wanohana-magazine. You can also get information on the official *Sakura-gari* artbooks, *Leaf* (a collection of sketches), *Sprout* (a collection of rough drafts), and the soon-to-be-released *Bud*.

This turned out to be a jumble of info! But please continue with your support!! I'm sorry my notes aren't very long in this volume, but I'll see you next time!

Volume 11 will be out before you know it!!

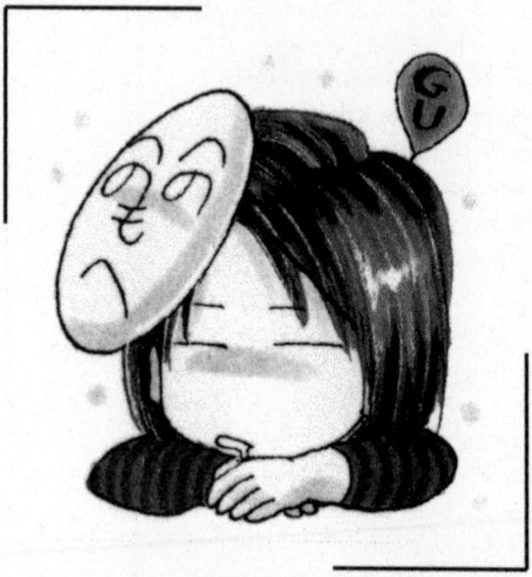
GU

Yuu Watase was born on March 5 in a town near Osaka, Japan. She was raised there before moving to Tokyo to follow her dream of creating manga. In the decade since her debut short story, *Pajama De Ojama* (An Intrusion in Pajamas), she has produced more than 50 volumes of short stories and continuing series. Her latest work, *Absolute Boyfriend*, appeared in Japan in the anthology magazine *Shôjo Comic*. Watase's other beloved series, *Alice 19th*, *Imadoki!*, and *Ceres: Celestial Legend*, are available in North America in English editions published by VIZ Media.

Fushigi Yûgi:
Genbu Kaiden Vol. 10
Shojo Beat Edition

STORY AND ART BY
YUU WATASE

©2003 Yuu WATASE/Shogakukan
All rights reserved.
Original Japanese edition "FUSHIGI YUGI GENBUKAIDEN"
published by SHOGAKUKAN Inc.

Translation/Lillian Olsen
Touch-up Art & Lettering/Rina Mapa
Design/Genki Harata, Florence Yuen
Editor/Shaenon K. Garrity

The rights of the author(s) of the work(s) in this publication to be so identified
have been asserted in accordance with the Copyright, Designs and Patents Act
1988. A CIP catalogue record for this book is available from the British Library.

Printed in the U.S.A.

Published by VIZ Media, LLC
P.O. Box 77010
San Francisco, CA 94107

10 9 8 7 6 5 4 3 2 1
First printing, September 2012

www.viz.com

www.shojobeat.com

SURPRISE!

You may be reading the wrong way!

It's true: In keeping with the original Japanese comic format, this book reads from right to left— so action, sound effects, and word balloons are completely reversed. This preserves the orientation of the original artwork—plus, it's fun! Check out the diagram shown here to get the hang of things, and then turn to the other side of the book to get started!

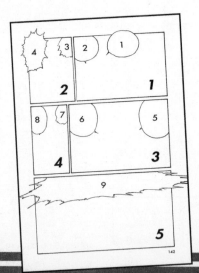